The Gun Digest®
SPORTING OPTICS

Premier Edition!

How to Use and Choose Riflescopes, Spotting Scopes, and Binoculars

Wayne van Zwoll

Published by

700 E. State Street • Iola, WI 54990-0001
Telephone: 715/445-2214
Web: www.krause.com

Please call or write for our free catalog of publications.
Our toll-free number to place an order or obtain a free catalog is 800-258-0929
or please use our regular business telephone, 715-445-2214.

Library of Congress Catalog Number: 2001097828
ISBN: 0-87349-322-2

Foreword

Optics For The Outdoors

Few people who use optics have the background – or interest – to explore how light has been harnessed by glass. Most of us are just delighted to see better. Sight is, after all, our primary sense. Unlike the deer we watch, we have only a rudimentary sense of smell. We can't detect subtle changes in temperature like a snake or echolocate like a bat. What we don't see goes largely unnoticed. Almost miraculously, optical glass gives us images that seem brighter, sharper and bigger than life. We who study wildlife and hunt game benefit most. Binoculars let us see details we'd otherwise miss – details that tell us volumes more about our surroundings than we'd otherwise know.

Scopes and red-dot sights help us hit targets that would be obscured by iron sights, indistinguishable or just plain invisible. With scopes, old eyes can compete with young eyes on the hunt and in shooting competition. Spotting scopes help us identify and assess the trophy quality of distant game animals and pick the best approach through difficult places. At the range, they show us our bullet holes, as well as the mirage that explains why they aren't all in the middle.

This book will tell you as much about the selection and use of outdoor optics as any that I'm aware of and more than most. After 35 years of hunting, competitive shooting and wildlife study, I'm still learning about optics. But because knowledgeable people have told me a lot about binoculars, riflescopes and spotting scopes, there's plenty of information here. Some of it has come from obscure scientific texts on light and optical glass. It's been my good fortune to use scores of new and old instruments afield. You should find in the many anecdotes some that remind you of your own hunting and shooting experiences.

Look here for practical help on evaluating optics – beginning with an explanation of industry lingo so you understand the terms used to describe the products. There's no-nonsense talk about price: How can a scope that costs five times as much as another scope be five times as good? And if it isn't, how can the expensive model sell? Do you *really* get better performance from binoculars with a blue-blood European pedigree? And what makes ED spotting scopes cost so much? You'll learn why it's hardly ever necessary to pay retail price for new optics and what to keep in mind when shopping for used glass.

The best instrument delivers its potential only when you learn to use it expertly. Here you'll find tips from optical engineers, big game guides and competitive marksmen – people whose business demands that they get the most from lenses. You'll learn how to test binoculars, scopes and spotting scopes before buying, how to adjust them in the field and how to ensure that they give you top service for many years.

There's a catalog section in this book too. Not a raw compilation of all products available, but a carefully sifted list of optics that excell or are especially good bargains. Who picked 'em? Me. The idea was to offer photos, descriptions and prices of items you might find useful and, by virtue of price and performance, particularly attractive. I did my best.

This book was several years in the making. I hope you find its text informative, the anecdotes entertaining and the illustrations helpful. And that your next trip afield is the best that good glass can make it!

— Wayne van Zwoll

Acknowledgments

You're about to read the handiwork of many people. Most are colleagues in an industry to which I've been loosely and intimately attached my entire working life. Since paying $30 for my first riflescope – a 2½x Bushnell in the 1960s, I've tried to understand how optics work and figure out which designs work best. Lots of help has always been available from people like Bill Cross at Bushnell, Garth Kendig at Leupold, and Pat Beckett at Burris. Visits to the offices, research facilities, production floors and quality-control rooms of these companies, and of Zeiss, Swarovski, Kahles and Schmidt & Bender, have shown me how superior optics are crafted, assembled and tested. When Weaver, originally a Texas company, went to new owners who contracted manufacture in Japan, I found the scopes as bright and the new staff as friendly as before. Now Weaver is part of Blount, which also owns Simmons and Redfield, the oldest American name in riflescopes. My friend Mike Larsen, who entered Blount with Federal Ammunition, keeps me up to date on three optics lines! Meanwhile, Bausch & Lomb scopes became Bushnells in a company move that Barbara Mellman and Laura Ollinger patiently explained so my readers would get it straight, too.

I appreciate the assistance of Mike Slack at Leupold and that of his late father Jack, with whom I once shared a moose camp. Lou Leonard, a gun enthusiast uncommonly well versed about vintage optics, introduced me to Noske and Fecker sights, the Unertl Hawk and Lyman Challenger. I've had direct help with this book from Pat Lytle and Rick Payne at Pentax, Leica's Terry Moore, Swarovski's Jim Morey, Jason Claybrook at Zeiss, Greg Jones at Kahles, and Chris Lalik at Bushnell. Shannon Jackson and Karen Lutto, whose firms represent Zeiss and Kahles to the press, were most gracious as well.

My thanks to Bob Bell, veteran journalist for the Pennsylvania Game News, who many years ago produced what I still think is an excellent book on optics for hunters and shooters. Impressive in its depth, it was arguably the first substantive time dedicated to glass for the outdoorsman. Another able writer, John Barsness, recently finished a readable book on optics. As would any serious scholar, I've scoured these texts and others that treat optics more obliquely, plus all the technical literature that seemed appropriate. My friend Bill McRae — who has written longer and more authoritatively on optics than anyone else in the industry — helped with information on testing. When I doubted my experience or a technical explanation, Bill was there to confirm or redirect.

Of course, my wife deserves more credit than anyone else. She put up with a cross, computer-bound troll for months, quietly making sure that other deadlines weren't missed, other commitments weren't neglected. Thank you, Alice.

— *Wayne van Zwoll, Bridgeport, Washington, August 2001*

About the Author

A full-time journalist for the outdoors press, Wayne van Zwoll lives in central Washington state with his wife Alice. His work has appeared in more than two dozen magazines, including *Sports Afield*, *Outdoor Life* and *Field & Stream*. He has published seven books and several hundred articles on firearms, optics and hunting. After serving for many years as technical editor for *Rifle* and *Handloader*, he is now on staff at *Rifle Shooter* and *Guns & Ammo*. He's been shooting editor for *Bugle* magazine for 12 years and edits the specifications section of *Shooter's Bible*. In 1996, he was named Shooting Sports Writer of the Year by the Outdoor Writers Association of America. He has taught both English and Forestry classes at Utah State University and earned his doctorate studying the effects of changes in hunting motive on wildlife policy.

About our covers:

Swarovski Optik produces sporting optics of the highest quality. It is a quality achieved by following the principle of its founder, Daniel Swarovski I: "To constantly improve what is good."

Intensive research, creative product ideas, modern and ergonomic design, unsurpassed precision and the strictest quality control are keys to the company's success.

Swarovski applies the same attention to detail in making its crystal-clear optics and world-renowned crystal.

The Austria-based company was launched in 1895 in the Tirolean town of Wattens. Three years earlier, Swarovski had applied for a patent on a precision grinding machine for precious stones. In 1935, his eldest son, Wilhelm, developed the prototype for a pair of binoculars, laying the foundation for the company's newly established optics department. The division moved in 1948 to Absam in Tyrol, where Swarovski Optik was founded in 1949.

The company rapidly developed a worldwide reputation for superlative quality optics, hence its slogan: "With the eyes of a hawk."

Today, Swarovski Optik has about 450 employees, is represented in 45 countries, and is ranked among the world's leading manufacturers of top-quality binoculars, spotting scopes, and riflescopes.

Pictured clockwise from lower left are: 6-24x50 L-Dot Target riflescope, 2.5-10x42 Pro riflescope, 20-60 Habicht AT 80 spotting scope, 15x56 ER SLC binoculars, 8.5x42 EL binoculars and the 8x20 B Pocket binoculars.

Table of Contents

*All photographs are by the author unless otherwise noted.

Introduction

This rifleman can hit small targets at long range using his Leupold variable scope, a sight marksmen could hardly have envisioned 100 years ago.

Light sends us pictures when we look for wildlife or into a rifle sight. Getting *sharp* pictures is important if we're to identify a warbler, distinguish an antler from a branch, or center a bullet.

Light coming in through your eye's protective cornea continues on through a lens. Images are formed at the rear of the eyeball, on the retina. The retina's light-sensitive cells send a message through the optic

nerve to your brain, which gives you the picture projected by the light.

Your eye's lens is controlled by muscles that change its shape. Flattening the lens or increasing its curvature, these muscles control its focal length, ensuring a sharp picture however far you're looking. But not all lenses are perfect. If you're farsighted, the lens fails to bend light steeply enough up close, so rays don't quite meet before they strike the ret-

ina. Near-sighted people have lenses that bend light from distant objects too steeply; rays meet (and form the image) before they reach the retina. Astigmatism occurs when the cornea's curvature is not the same on all axes. Lens flexibility diminishes with age, so eventually you will understand why people like me read menus at arm's length.

For more than 700 years, eyeglasses have brought sharp vision to imperfect eyes. The first were convex lenses, to help with far-sightedness. Concave lenses for the nearsighted followed. Then, in 1784, Benjamin Franklin came up with bifocals. A century later, contact lenses appeared. Outdoors enthusiasts look through other glass: binoculars, riflescopes and spotting scopes. This book is about them. But really it is a book about how smart people have figured out how to manipulate light.

Light is central.

Without light, the wall across the living room would still be there, but you'd not see it. Without light, there would still be horizons of high rock, but they'd never be photographed. Without light, most of what we think interesting would be suddenly without appeal. We need light to explore, find, recognize, understand. Even if plants could live without chlorophyll and we could navigate in the dark, life would be

Scanning a praire dog pasture with his Leica rangefinding binocular, the hunter here will also use powerful glass to aim.

The author takes aim with a Leupold 50mm variable on a Kimber rifle.

rack. Or it can provide a detailed look at the plumage of a house finch over your bird feeder. But the spotting scope would be worthless if you were trying to find a deer while still-hunting through a cedar swamp at dusk. The best glass is the glass that best helps you with a specific task; it is not always the most powerful or expensive or sophisticated instrument.

Reticles belong in riflescopes, where we need an aiming device. But reticle choice matters. The fine reticle useful for target shooting and varmint hunting is easy to lose in woodland shadows. You may find a lighted reticle helpful in one sight, a rangefinding grid helpful in another. An adjustable objective is useless on a shotgun scope but essential on a benchrest sight. The high magnification of a target scope becomes a liability when you're trying to aim quickly at a whitetail in overdrive. Best is as best does.

Choosing and using field optics would be easier if light were the same all the time. It is not. That is why we have rainbows and sunsets and moon-washed landscapes and all the other delights that make life a constant joy. No optics will give you the warm light of dawn and dusk at midday, or put shadows where shadows are not, or take them away. No field glass will give you clear vision if you look toward the sun or through a blizzard. No lens will give you a motionless picture if the wind is buffeting your arms, or wring the mirage from an image that swims.

So we are always reminded that the glass is but a window to light.

Outside there is light.

Light gives life. And light defines it.

different indeed without light. Small wonder that the Bible warns against an outer darkness and equates God and life with light.

It's easy to get caught up in the mechanisms that change the way we see. But a clever device is of no utility unless it helps us see *better*. Better vision may mean a higher degree of resolution, or a brighter image. Maybe a bigger image is all you need; then again, you might be better served with the widest field of view. You'll want true color rendition, a flat field and sharp focus. But how much depth of field are you willing to concede for higher magnification? What will you trade for less critical eye relief? How much weight

and bulk will you carry to get the optical qualities you want? Choosing glass is often an exercise in compromise. To get the best optics for the job, you need first to define the job, then to specify what's most important to your eye: What mix of image qualities is better than all others.

The best view isn't always through glass. Unaided vision is fast and gives you a panoramic view and good depth perception. John Colter would not have escaped the Indians if he'd run with a binocular to his brow. On the other hand, hunters using binoculars commonly find game that they'd miss with the naked eye. A spotting scope can help you tell if that distant bull elk has big antlers or just an average

This 6-24x50 Swarovski is typical of the big, high-quality scopes favored by long-range shooters now.

Chapter 1

Light

"…A day without sunshine is like night."

First light

WHOEVER BUILT THE first fire was underpaid. Not only did fire produce heat to keep people warm (and alive!), it enabled them to make tools for work and war. Fire could cook meat and heat water. Fire cleared trees and brush to make room for crops. And fire gave light. Light to make the night friendly and to signal other people at a distance. Light to follow a trail, to define a perimeter, to read, to brighten huts, then villages, then cities. Light to give people more time.

Legend has it that Zeus didn't trust humans with fire. Prometheus stole some from the mountain home of the gods and delivered it down to earth. We've since proven Zeus was right to have reservations. But on balance, fire has been a good thing. "Bringing the fire" to the Olympic games commemorates the Greek myth and reminds us of the central and elemental role of fire (and its light) in our lives.

Fire is chemical energy released as heat and light. Electrical and atomic action can also cause heat and light. We've harnessed both only recently. Oil lamps fueled by animal fat, on the other hand, date back more than 15,000 years. The first recorded lighthouse, the Pharos of Alexandria, was a 260-foot tower completed in 280 B.C. It was wood-fired. Gas lighting replaced oil in the 19th century. The lamps were brightened by use of a mantle, a chemically treated net placed over the gas flame.

The biggest fire, our strongest source of light, is the sun. An orb of flaming gases, it has burned non-stop for as long as anyone can remember and is likely to continue burning even after you finish reading this book. It is 93 million miles from earth. That's just far enough to keep the earth from browning like a marshmallow held too close to a campfire. But close enough to keep us from freezing when our planet's rotation, on its axis and around the sun, puts us on earth's cold side.

Compared to many bright spots in the heavens, the sun is bumper-to-bumper close to earth. Stars that twinkle on a clear night can be so far off that measurement in miles become ludicrous. Instead, we gauge their distance in light-years. Light travels about 186,000 miles per second, so a light-year – the miles light travels in one year – amounts to quite some distance. That's 186,000 miles x 60 seconds/minute x 60 minutes/hour x 24 hours/day x 365 days/year. That's one light-year.

Danish astronomer Ole Roemer was probably the first to calculate the speed of light. He recorded the time it took Jupiter's moons to circle the planet and noticed that sometimes the moons were behind or ahead of schedule. Over a year, he figured the lag was about 22 minutes and decided it was because of changes in the distance the light traveled from Jupiter to earth. Using simple math, he figured the speed of light to be 137,000 miles per second – a little low, as it turned out, but an impressive display of reasoning for the day. Roemer was born in 1644. Not until 1849 was a land-based measure taken of light-speed. Armand Fizeau's timer, a clever apparatus, had a toothed wheel that spun rapidly. Fizeau shot a light beam through the wheel at a mirror 5 1/2 miles away and registered the returning beam through another tooth. By knowing how fast the wheel turned, he was able to calculate the speed of the light. Leon Foucault, who worked with Fizeau, got roughly the same reading (185,000 miles per second) with a series of mirrors, one of which was spinning at a fixed rate.

Incidentally, 186,000 is the accepted figure for light in a vacuum, air refractive index of 1. Dense air slows light. So does water, which

Scopes don't gather light; they can only transmit it. Some is lost in the process. This 4x Redfield is very bright.

White light includes all the colors; each registers individually when reflected as a certain wavelength.

throttles it to 140,000 miles per second. In optical glass, light travels at about 124,000 miles per second, and in a diamond, 77,000.

Consider that many prominent stars are hundreds of light-years away – that tonight we see light reflected from them before we were born – and you get a healthy dose of perspective. We're tiny creatures on a speck of dirt so far from the hub of Creation that our ordinary use of words like "great," "awesome," "incredible," "blockbuster," and "world class" is shamefully self-serving at best.

On the other hand, we can't be blamed for a limited frame of reference if the perimeters of our pasture extend only as far as we can see. Indeed, for most of us, sight defines the boundaries and qualities of our world. We humans have a poor sense of smell and mediocre hearing. We take the measure of space in units we can visualize (a pace, a football field) or in arbitrary units that can be replicated by anyone who can read a map or odometer. Visual images matter more than auditory messages. Advertisers pay more for a color page in Time magazine than for a minute spot on the radio. We keep putting up billboards, and advertising on ball caps. Given their druthers, most people want an eyeful of entertainment, not an earful.

They'd rather watch television or a video than treat only their ears to a radio program or audio tape. They pay to see a movie, whether or not it is as good as the book whose words must be imagined into pictures.

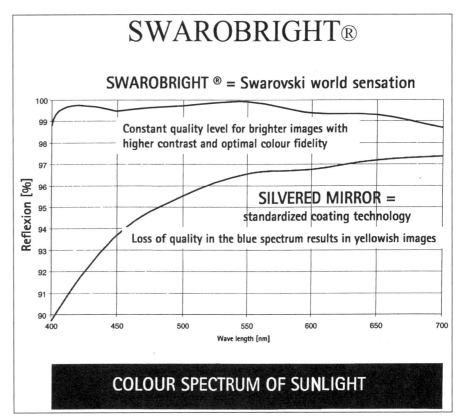

Swarovski's Swarobright is a superb lens coating that improves images over a wide spectral range.

We're now so accustomed to the electric light that we keep some bulbs burning until we have to change them. Actually, the bulb doesn't burn. The incandescent light owes its glow to electric current that passes through a filament, heating it. Electric lights dating to the early 1800s were called arc lamps. The current jumped a gap between two carbon rods, producing a very bright light. But the lamps were hard to install and proved a fire hazard. Thomas Edison tried many, many filaments in his search for a low-voltage lamp. When he first demonstrated a useful light in October 1879, he was actually a few months behind British inventor Joseph Swan, whose similar carbon-filament lamp also endured under partial vacuum.

After commercial production of electric lights began in the United States in 1880, hotel visitors had to be reminded by desk clerks that the new bulbs did not require a match for lighting. Modern incandescent lamps have a filament of coiled tungsten in argon and other inert gases. Though only about 8 percent of the electrical energy is converted to light. That light is very close in color to the sun's, so colors of objects seen under incandescent light are about the same as what you'd see in daylight.

Incandescent lighting actually followed the forerunner of fluorescent lighting. In the mid 1850s, Johann Heinrich Wilhelm Geissler fashioned tubes for low-pressure gases, then passed electricity through the gases, which glowed as a result. Today, fluorescent lamps illuminate workbenches, street corners and farmyards. Unlike the incandescent bulb, these gaslights do not mimic the sun; colors under illumination depend on the gas used. Mercury vapor lamps have no red component, so there's a blue look to its light. Low-pressure sodium street lights deliver a yellow hue. High-pressure sodium offers greater efficiency and truer colors, though its signature hue is bluish-pink.

Properties of natural light

Light seems to behave as if it were composed of gazillions of invisible particles. Isaac Newton had championed the particle theory, pointing out that "Light is never known to follow crooked Passages

nor to bend into the Shadow." Later studies would show, however, that light does indeed "bend" around corners. Newton also had trouble explaining refraction, the different speeds and angles of light traveling in distinct mediums. Particle acceleration and deceleration were easier to account for than were changes in light path.

In 1665, Francesco Grimaldi noticed that light behaved queerly when passed through a slit. It seemed to bend and spread. Grimaldi called this phenomenon diffraction. In 1690, the Dutch physicist Christian Huygens came to a thoughtful conclusion: Light was not a stream of particles, as nearly everyone thought. It traveled so

fast, it must be a series of waves. Huygens proposed that in his book, *Traite de la Lumiere*. The waves, he said, were carried in a weightless, invisible "ether" that permeated space. The light waves could be broken into wavelets, which could combine to form a wave front. He surmised, correctly, that a wave theory would account for the refractive properties of light. No mean scholar, Huygens also constructed the first pendulum clock and discovered the rings around the planet Saturn. But it would be many years before wave theory met with public acceptance.

In 1801, English physicist Thomas Young placed a screen with two slits behind a screen with one. The effect was to scatter the light

Shadow, backlighting and silhouettes are functions of light source position and the blockage of light rays.

between the screens, producing two secondary sources of light in the pair of slits. Young found that a solid screen behind the two-slit screen showed evidence of wave action. That is, there were convergence bands, where light waves emerged from the two slits in step with each other; and there were interference bands, where light waves were out of step and canceled each other. Young likened his results to the wave action set up by two objects dimpling the surface of water. He postulated that the colors he saw on the rear screen each had specific wave characteristics. Though his conclusions were sound, reinforcing Grimaldi's work, scientists of the day remained skeptical, convinced that light comprised particles.

Around the turn of the last century, William Crookes came up with a radiometer to measure the *pressure* of light on a surface. Light alone did turn the instrument's finely-balanced vanes. But when the radiometer's glass bulb was evacuated, the vanes stopped. Since then, both particle and wave theories have been established – and vigorously defended – to explain the behavior of light.

Some of the first recorded studies of light focused on shadow. The great Italian artist and scientist Leonardo da Vinci sketched light rays from two spaced candles casting shadows on both sides of an object between them. That was around the beginning of the 16th century. Roughly a hundred years later, German mathematician Johannes Kepler published *Astronomiae pars Optica*, a discourse that explained how light traveled in straight lines, cast shadows and bent when moving from one substrate to another. Perhaps best remembered for his discovery of the elliptical paths of our planets, Kepler also figured out why some people cannot see clearly up close, and why others see fuzzy images far away.

Shadow served Christopher Columbus when he landed on Jamaica in 1504. Short of supplies, he was unable to get help from natives – until he remembered that an eclipse of the moon was due. He called the Indians together at the appropriate time and "commanded" the moon to vanish. The awe-struck people gave him what he wanted. Incidentally, an eclipse of the moon occurs when the earth gets between the sun and the moon. An eclipse of the sun follows movement of the moon between earth and sun. If

you're in the relatively small middle of the shadow, called the umbra, you see a total eclipse. The penumbra, a much larger area of partial shadow, delivers a partial eclipse.

A small source of light blocked by an object close to an image-producing screen will form a sharp, clearly defined shadow. Move the screen or enlarge the light source, and a fuzzy image results. In the 18th century, a French government minister, Etienne de Silhouette, made "shadow portraits" as cheap substitutes for paintings. "Silhouette" has since come to mean any black shape seen against light.

Light can be reflected, as even cave dwellers must have realized when they looked into still water. In Greek mythology, the youth Narcissus grew too fond of his own reflection in a pool. He tried to touch it, fell in and drowned. In Egypt as early as 1300 B.C., polished bronze disks were used as mirrors – 1,000 years before the Greek mathematician Euclid figured out how light is reflected. About A.D. 1100, the Arab scientist Alhazen came up with a law that quite accurately described how light behaves when it bounces off a reflective surface. Clear glass backed by metal first appeared in Venice around A.D. 1300.

Reflection comprises two light rays: an incoming or incident ray and the outgoing or reflected ray. Looking in a mirror, you know you're getting a reflected image. But your brain perceives an object on or

behind the mirror, a virtual image that cannot be projected on a screen because it has no light source. Flat surfaces yield reflected images that are true to form but reversed right and left (police cruisers, fire trucks and ambulances sometimes have hood lettering reversed so that when seen in a rearview mirror it will be a quick read). Convex surfaces bounce light rays outward, so the virtual image, a miniature, forms *behind* the mirror. In contrast, concave surfaces form the image in *front* of the bowl, where reflected rays cross.

Refraction is the bending of light as it passes from one substance into another. In the second century A.D., Egyptian geographer Ptolemy devised the first law of refraction. It proved unreliable. Arab Alhazen had no better luck. In 1621, Willebrord Snell, a Dutch mathematician, determined that light bends in a precise and predictable manner, and that there was a specific ratio of the "angle of incidence" (light entering) to the "angle of refraction" (light path in the new substrate). He showed that every substance has a characteristic bending power or refractive index. Snell also pioneered the idea of triangulation to measure distance by using angles instead of point locations.

Bowfishing, or even reeling an underwater plug with a visible leader, you see refracted light. The image of an arrow entering the water breaks at an angle, though the arrow goes straight (that's why you must

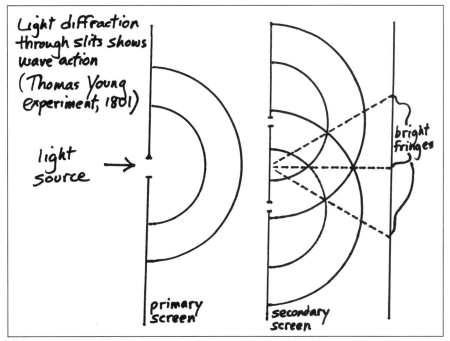

Early experiment showing light diffraction.

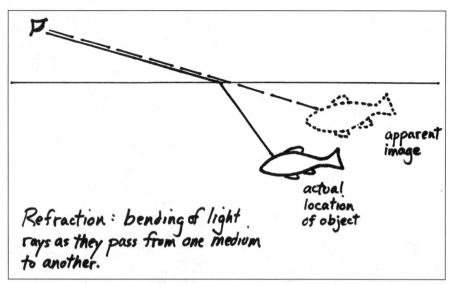

Refraction: bending of light rays as they pass from one medium to another.

apparent image

actual location of object

Refraction occurs when light passes from one medium to another that slows or accelerates its travel.

aim low; the image of the fish is higher than the fish!). The leader also bends at the water's surface. Air in different temperature layers conducts light along different paths, placing a distant image where it is not. A mirage occurs when a layer of warm air next to the ground is trapped by cooler air above. Light bent in an upside-down arc toward the horizontal line of vision eventually forms an upside-down virtual image on the ground. This is the mirage popularized in movies made in the desert. Mirage as a target-shooting or long-distance sighting problem is the flow of heat waves across the warm surface of the earth.

Here, too, lower air is warmer than upper air. You get the same effect if you look across the top of a hot charcoal grill in the back yard, or over a rifle or shotgun barrel after a few shots. Heat waves can make the target move. Refracted light tells you the target is where it isn't. This mirage can help you determine wind direction and speed, because the heat waves boil vertically in still conditions, and run ahead of a breeze. They flatten out and vanish when the wind becomes strong.

When a layer of cool air is trapped by warm air on top, a far-away object can appear to "loom" or hang above its real location. Light passes to you in an arc like a trajectory that bends toward the horizontal line of vision (an inverted version of the light path that delivers a mirage).

Refracted light was put to work by lacemakers in the early 19th century. Water-filled spheres bent the

incident light in such a way as to direct it onto a small part of the lace. The concentrated beam, focused on the fine embroidery, became a miniature spotlight.

Lenses use refracted light to correct and magnify images. The word "lens" comes from the Latin name for lentils. A lentil seed is small and round, with convex sides: a bulging disk. The earliest lenses were convex, making light bend inward. The bent rays exiting a convex lens meet at a place behind the lens called the principal focus. The distance from this point to the center of the lens is the focal distance. The shorter the

distance, the more powerful the lens. Concave lenses bend light rays away from each other. In either case, your eye traces the light rays back in a straight line, not along the actual path traveled by the ray. Result: A bigger or smaller image is formed beyond or in front of the actual image.

Roger Bacon, an English friar whose work with chemicals gave gunpowder a European home, used a glass lens to magnify printing in a book. German and Italian glassmakers soon found a market for lenses and began grinding them. In 1629, English King Charles I formed a spectacle-makers' guild.

Bifocal glasses typically have a convex lens (for distant viewing) atop a concave lens (for reading close up). Aspheric lenses are neither simply convex nor simply concave; their surfaces may feature more than one radius – for example, a convex periphery surrounding a concave center. Aspheric lenses in riflescopes and rangefinders can improve brightness and sharpness at field edges while making the entire field appear flat.

The effect of lens curvature stops at the surface – a fact used by Georges de Buffon in 1748 to trim the weight of ponderous lighthouse lenses. He cut out the inside glass, leaving the central lens and ribs of reflecting surfaces on the face. Emanating light traveled in a straight line from the light source to the face. Later, Augustin Fresnel modified these lenses.

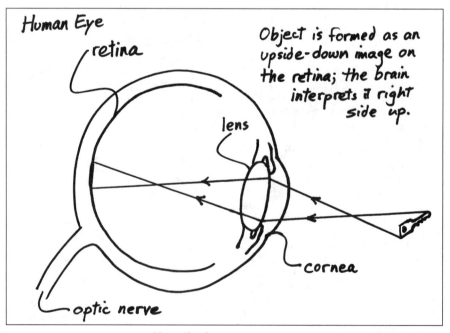

Human Eye
retina
lens
cornea
optic nerve

Object is formed as an upside-down image on the retina; the brain interprets it right side up.

How the human eye sees.

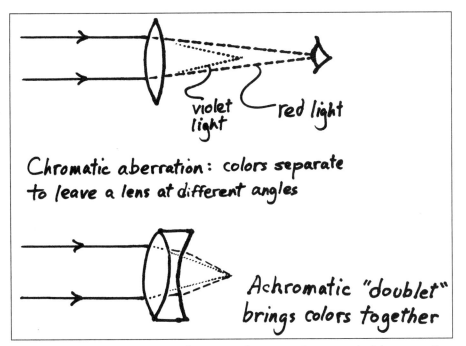

Color separation in a single convex lens can be corrected by use of a doublet.

Color

Sunlight comprises many colors, and they don't all behave the same in glass. The brilliant Isaac Newton used a prism to split white light into a spectrum of colors. A screen showed the spectrum. More importantly, Newton demonstrated that the spectrum was not contributed by the prism. A small slit in the screen caught only one color that passed through to another prism. The beam exiting that prism was just one color. Newton published his findings in his second major scientific book, *Opticks*, in 1704. Like the French philosopher Rene Descartes before him, Newton correctly concluded that rainbows result from the refraction of light in raindrops. He included an explanation in his book.

The various colors combined in sunlight represent an almost continuous spectrum of wavelengths, from 220 to 2300 nanometers (a nanometer, or nm, is a billionth of a meter). Ultraviolet light is at the low end of the spectrum, from 220 to 400nm. We can't see it. Infrared light, also invisible, extends from 700 to 2300 nm. Traveling through the atmosphere, "far" infrared waves are absorbed by carbon dioxide, water vapor and ozone. Ozone also filters out the "hard" ultraviolet light. Visible light, violet to red, occurs from 400 to 700 nm on the electromagnetic spectrum. In 1801, Thomas Young postulated that the human eye has color recep-

tors sensitive to specific wavelengths. He was right. Color-specific nerve endings, or cones, put a label on the incident light. Equal proportions of red, green and blue (the "additive primary colors") come through as white. Violet gives only one cone a signal, and the brain sees violet.

When light passes through a lens, colors separate by refracting at different angles. The result is chromatic aberration, or color fringing that detracts from the clarity of the image you're viewing through the lens. Chromatic aberration is most noticeable near the edge of the lens. In 1733, English mathematician Chester Moor Hall came up with an achromatic lens comprising two lenses of different types of glass. This "doublet" delivered a color-true image because the rear glass brought together colors that had separated in the front glass.

Color appears as a reflection or as endemic to the light source. An incandescent filament produces its own color; a leaf is green because it absorbs all the component colors of sunlight except green, which it reflects. The red tint on the lens of a red-dot sight reflects red to increase the contrast of the dot against the target. Spectroscopes are now used to determine if colors are pure or formed by "subtraction" – absorption of colors that don't appear. White cannot be made by subtraction, which is why

you can't add colored inks or paints to get white.

Photographers prefer the light of dawn and dusk to the white light of midday, because a red glow adds warmth and deepens the color of any landscape, and because the presence of shadows at day's edge adds contrast or "snap" to the photo. At dawn and dusk the sun is just as intense as at midday, but Earth's rotation has put the sun at an oblique angle to your position, and as the light must pass through more of the atmosphere, it loses more and more of its blue color component. By sunset, a clear sky may be very red.

Secondary colors result when the three primary colors are added in pairs. Red and green make yellow, green and blue make cyan, and red and blue make magenta. On their own, each secondary color is one primary color shy of white light. Overlap two secondary colors, and you get a primary color, because you've effectively subtracted two primary colors. Overlap three primary colors and you get black, because you've taken out all three primary colors.

Bringing things closer

Magnifying an object can be done with one convex lens, but bringing distant objects closer is a job for multiple lenses in series. Legend has it that Dutch spectacle-maker Hans Lippershay accidentally lined up two lenses on a far-away weathercock in 1608. The iron chicken suddenly looked as big as a cow! But in 1590, Zacharias Johnson claimed to have built a successful compound microscope. Whether it was Hans or Zack or, as some have suggested, Hans's assistant, the alignment of lenses in tandem added versatility to optics. Now they could be used at a great distance to view things that were hard to reach.

Like stars.

In 1609, the Italian astronomer Galileo Galilei built his first telescope. With this and subsequent instruments magnifying up to 30 times, he discovered four of the moons that orbit Jupiter. He also found that the Milky Way comprised countless stars invisible to the naked eye.

Galileo's first telescopes had a convex front (objective) lens and a concave rear (ocular) lens. Light rays bent by the front lens passed through

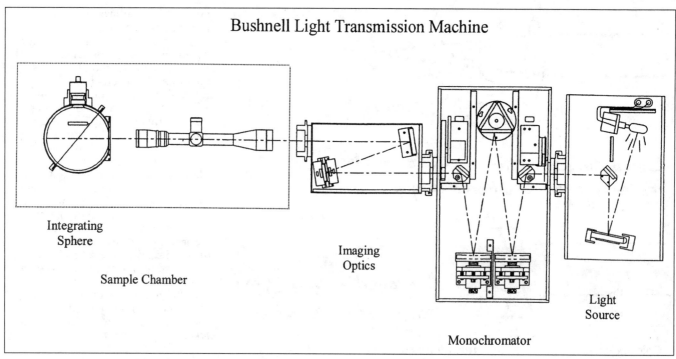

Bushnell Light Transmission Machine

Integrating
Sphere

Sample Chamber

Imaging
Optics

Light
Source

Monochromator

One of many optical test machines used in Bushnell's laboratory.

the rear lens before converging, so the focal point of the front lens lay behind the rear of the telescope. In modern scopes, the focal point lies within the scope, where an upside-down image is formed. The image is righted by an erector lens. Johannes Kepler changed Galileo's telescope to shift the image inside. He used a convex ocular lens, but didn't bother with an erector because distant stars

had no top or bottom. Like his colleagues, Kepler had to put up with spherical aberration: a fuzzy image caused by the failure of light rays to meet at a common convergence point on the scope's axis. The glass refracted each light ray a little differently than the next, and different parts of a lens would direct light to cross the lens axis at various distances behind it. Changing the lens

curvature might have helped if the engineers had had our technology. But they didn't. The solution: long focal length. In some of the first tubeless instruments, the lenses were several hundred feet apart! Spherical aberration would later be corrected by gluing together two lenses with different refractive properties to form a single lens. The doublet would also eliminate chromatic aberration.

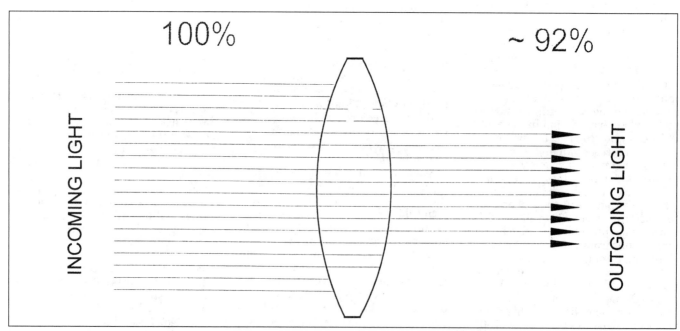

100%   ~ 92%

INCOMING LIGHT   OUTGOING LIGHT

About 4% of all light passing through an air-to-glass surface is lost, mainly to reflection and refraction. Total loss: 8% per lens or doublet. Lens coatings reduce that loss dramatically.

Big objective lenses give you a bigger bundle of light, a brighter picture at dawn and dusk.

Most of the first telescopes were refractors, with a big convex front lens that formed an image in front of the little concave rear lens, which bent the light rays again so they became parallel. But plate-size front glass caused unacceptable color dispersion; besides, these lenses were frightfully expensive and difficult to make. In 1668, Isaac Newton came up with a reflecting telescope that used mirrors instead of lenses to magnify. A large concave mirror at the rear of the scope collected light,

reflecting it into a small central mirror, which delivered the light and image through a rear ("Cassegrain") or side-mounted ("Newtonian") eyepiece. Mirrors proved so successful that they're still used in observatory telescopes.

As images in telescopes improved, four problems became apparent. Coma is a spherical aberration that looks like a teardrop-shaped blur. Lenses without coma are called aplanatic. Field curvature is another bugaboo, distinguished by a flat

image in the middle of the lens, but lines that wander at its edge. You can't eliminate this, but most good optics now have so little that you have to look for it to see it. Astigmatism, as in the human eye, occurs when lines at various angles can't be brought into focus together. Distortion is a term that can be used to describe the image skewed by various aberrations. But a singular form of distortion occurs when magnification varies from one part of the field of view to the other. High magnifica-

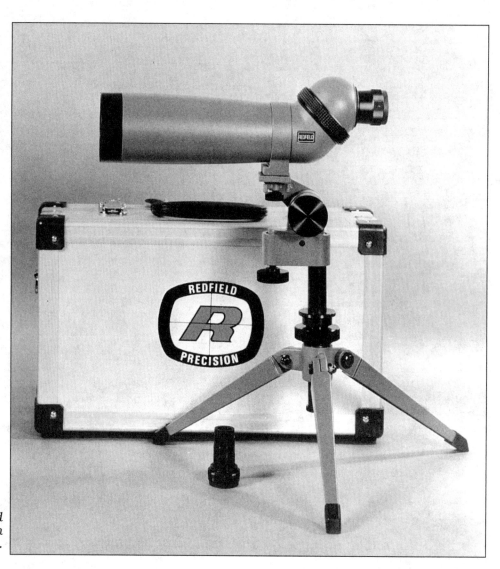

A spotting scope needs a tripod to make its high magnification useful.

tion in the middle of a lens will make a square object seem to bulge; low magnification will cause the sides to suck in. An orthoscopic lens is one that's been corrected for distortion.

Most of the instruments used to improve our vision in the outdoors are designed to bring things up close, to make them easier to iden-tify and study. The binoculars, riflescopes and spotting scopes available now give us remarkably bright, sharp, flat images. But the light they transmit has the same properties that Newton, Galileo and Kepler worked so hard to fathom. Computer-ground lenses and tolerances controlled to the third decimal place by CNC machines – plus several hundred years of improvements in engi-neering – have made modern field optics far more effective. For most outdoors enthusiasts, they're indispensable.

Still, you must have light.

Chapter 2

What is Good Glass?

"…There's no magic in good glass, only obedient light."

Glass types

IT'S EASY TO think that glass is glass. But that's like saying metal is metal or that blood is all the same. Actually, there are many kinds of glass, and optical glass is only one of several types used in optics. Field instruments may also contain laser glass, color filter glass and technical glass. To complicate things further, many optical materials aren't glass at all. These days they include ceramics and optical plastics, UV and IR crystals, fused quartz and even metals.

Optical glass is worth a word or two here because it is an important component of binoculars, riflescopes and spotting scopes.

In its most basic form, glass is a melt of silicon dioxide (quartz) with calcium and certain alkali. The melt is cooled so as to solidify without crystallizing. Optical glass is formulated to affect incident light in specific ways. It can be fashioned into lenses

and prisms that not only transmit light, but bend it and focus it.

The optical glass we know probably began life around 1884, in the Glastechnisches Lab in Jena, Austria. That facility later became the Schott Glaswerke. Now with salesmen and subsidiaries in more than 100 countries, Schott continues to supply much of the world's superior optical glass. Schott Glass Technologies in Duryea, Pa., is the U.S. branch. Though many prestigious optics firms use Schott glass, they also have backup suppliers. The glass technology used in Germany is available in Japan, and as long as the glass meets user specifications, its origin matters not. Besides, steps in the manufacture of lenses and prisms are as important to the product as the raw material from which they are made.

The two definitive properties of optical glass are its refractive index (n) and its index of dispersion (v). The refractive index shows how the

glass moves light relative to the unobstructed passage of light through air, which has an index of 1. The dispersion value, often called the Abbe number after optical pioneer Ernst Abbe, defines how the glass scatters light into its various wavelengths. Both measures vary with the wavelength of incident light, so for purposes of specification, a standard wavelength of 587.56nm applies. It is commonly noted by the subscript, d; Hence, nd, vd. A measure called principal dispersion shows how much greater the refractive effect is on short (blue) wavelengths than on long (red) ones.

Glass types with nd greater than 1.60 and vd greater than 50, plus those with nd less than 1.60 and vd greater than 55, are called crown glass. The letter designation K stands for Kron – German for Crown. A common crown glass in sports optics is BK 7, the B meaning borosilicate. Another popular crown glass is BaK 4, a barium-silicon compound. While BaK 4 is usually more costly than BK 7, you won't see much difference looking through binoculars.

"They're both prism glasses," said Bausch & Lomb optical engineer Bill Perkins. "You can tell prism type by looking into the objective end of a porro-prism binocular. If the exit pupil appears round, it's BaK 4; if it looks square, it's BK 7. The flat sides of the exit pupil are caused by shading, a function of the 90-degree turn of light between two 45-degree prisms."

Perkins said that although BaK 4 prisms are a recognized standard now, the most important attributes of a high-quality binocular are sound design, close tolerances, proper choice of glass for each component, coatings that boost light transmission, and mechanical lens settings that ensure ruggedness.

"You hear a lot about BaK 4 glass now, but it's not new," he said.

Optics help hunters find game and aim accurately.

A Swarovski binocular, rangefinder and scope teamed up with a Dakota rifle on this pronghorn buck.

"Anyone building binoculars can use it. It seems to me the hype is mainly a marketing ploy. Binoculars are lots better than they used to be – better coatings, smaller housings, tighter tolerances – but not much different in design. Spouting technical terms is one way to give products a fresh image."

The other main type of optical glass is flint. A common flint glass, SF 2, gets its moniker from "Schwerflint" – German for heavy or dense flint. The English name, FD 2. Glass designations include the index of refraction and the Abbe value in a 6-figure code. For example, BK 7 glass with a refractive index of 1.5172 and an Abbe of 64.19 is listed as BK 7 – 517642.

According to Dr. Walter Mergen of Zeiss, there should be several types of glass in a binocular or a scope. "Not to save cost," he said, "but to match each type of glass with a specific need."

The fact that some glass is more expensive than other glass is peripheral. In fact, you could *diminish* the performance of a scope or binocular if you chose only the most expensive glass for its optical system.

Mergen said that flint glass is typically heavier and more brittle than crown glass, and ill suited to placement on the exposed ends of a lens system. He also said that the differences in refractive index and Abbe number that distinguish crown from flint glass are necessary in an optical system.

"A collecting lens of crown glass manages light in such a way that flint glass – often as the second half of a doublet, or achromat – must correct for aberrations," he said. "But the flint glass won't serve in place of the crown glass. You need both."

For the most part, crown and flint glass share the same chemical constituents, but flint glass also contains lead oxide. Dense flint can have as much as 70 percent lead oxide. The composition of glass directly affects its weight, as well as its optical properties. Some other characteristics of glass that are important to optical engineers: elasticity, thermal expansion, thermal conductivity, stain resistance, moisture resistance, and resistance to acids and alkaline solutions.

Simple glass is not easily damaged by chemicals, except hydrofluoric acid. However, the polished surfaces of optical glass are quite vulnerable. Even water vapor can cause problems. Moisture condensing on a lens can draw alkali ions from the glass. These ions form an alkaline solution in the water droplets, which can erode the silica gel layer of the polished lens surface. The optical industry calls the result of water vapor attack "dimming." When the water evaporates, it leaves a film of silicon ions and alkali on the glass. You can't easily remove that film.

Laboratories test glass for resistance to water and to water vapor separately. Staining follows exposure to slightly acidic water – mainly, water that has absorbed carbon dioxide or sulfur dioxide. Deterioration of a glass surface changes the refractive index there, producing the visible colors in this thin layer of damage. In water tests, glass is graded according to the time in standard acetate solution (pH 4.6) required to produce visible discoloration. The higher the number, the more care must be taken to protect the glass during manufacture and use. Glass in stain class 3 will show staining after only one hour in the test solution. Glass in stain class 0 will show no color after 100 hours of exposure. Tests for acid and alkaline resistance are conducted in similar fashion.

Glassing in big country calls for a powerful binocular, but also a steady position.

The more time you spend looking through good glass, the more you'll see.

conditions for a specified time period. The amount of material removed determines abrasion rating. The higher the number, the less resistant the glass. BK 7 has been designated as a standard for the abrasion tests. It has a rating of 100. A soft FK glass (rating: 400) will lose the same amount of material to the grinder in a quarter of the time, or four times the amount over the designated period.

When you pay a lot of money for a scope or binocular, you almost always get good glass. You may also be getting *more* glass. Zeiss National Sales Manager Gary Reed said that his company's roof-prism binoculars feature bigger prisms than most, offering 6 percent more light transmission. Leupold emphasizes in its scope catalog that its lenses work for you all the way to the rim. You're paying for the glass coatings too. Fully multi-coated lenses (with several microscopically thin washes on every air-to-glass surface) transmit light more efficiently and offer a clearer view. Phase-corrected coatings, such as those on Zeiss roof-prism

Even mild chemicals can dissolve from the glass surface those components included to produce certain optical qualities. A permanent stain results, much in the manner that acidic water produces a stain. A good rule to remember: Gun oils and solvents can damage glass. Keep them off scope and binocular lenses! And don't touch that glass. There are acids on your hands and acids in your saliva.

Most of the physical properties of glass affect the manufacture of a scope or a binocular more than they do its use afield. Specific gravity tells you how many grams a cubic centimeter of glass will weigh. In optical glass, specific gravity varies from about 2.25 to 6.25 g/cm³. The popular BK 7 glass used in binoculars is quite light at 2.51 g/cm³. In high-quality optics, weight is a consequence of glass choice, but it does not determine which glass will be used. Optical performance matters far more than overall weight.

Glass hardness is measured by pushing a diamond point into the glass under a specified weight. Microscopic measurement of the indentation gives you the "Knoop hardness" expressed in kiloponds per square millimeter. (The kilopond is a measure of force.) Hardness values range from about 250 kp/mm² to 700 kp/mm². While this test tells how the glass resists penetration, it does not show response to abrasion. A hard glass may even abrade more

readily than a softer glass. Tests to measure abrasion put a grinder to the glass sample under controlled

Looking through glass is sometimes safer than getting a close look without magnification.

Optics bring us close to animals that are hard to approach, like this Montana pronghorn.

binoculars, and ED (extra-low dispersion) glass on Nikon spotting scopes, may or may not be noticeable at first glance. You'll have to make side-by-side comparisons *in natural light* to detect any differences between top-quality optics without special coatings, and those with them.

Buying a scope or binocular because the catalog lists BaK 4 glass as a component is like buying stock in a firm because it has an office in your hometown. The design of the instrument, like management of the company, will determine the value of your investment. Glass is a raw material. What it becomes after the grinding and polishing, and how it is coated and installed, matter as much as the melt.

Plastic lenses, optical voodoo

When I was a child, I thought glass was glass. Then I learned that the eyeglasses grownups wore each delivered a slightly different distorted view when I looked through them. Grownups couldn't trade glasses like we used to trade plastic

eyewear for different parts in vacation Bible school skits, which we performed at the behest of local church matrons who withheld graham crackers and Kool-Aid until Billy Grunnerveldt stopped running around long enough to recite one miserable line.

Had Billy not broken my plastic glasses by sitting on them at a Presbyterian potluck, I might still have them. Bill Cross of Bausch & Lomb assured me that I'm not missing anything.

"But new plastic lenses are not at all like what you had," he said.

Plastic is now serious lens material. "Plastic will do a lot of what glass can do," he said, "and it's lighter in weight." Of course, it isnt perfect. "Plastic is softer than glass so it is unfit for outside lens surfaces that might get scratched. Plastic also has a narrow refractive index range..."

"Wait a minute," I said. "Better remind me about that."

"Light changes speed when it goes from one medium to another," Cross said. "Think of the index of refraction as the ratio of those speeds, when light travels from air to glass or air to plastic. It is also the sine of the angle formed between the incident ray and the

refracted or bent ray that results from light passing through a lens."

Because of this narrow range, plastic cannot be used to make an achromatic or color-corrected lens. Normal achromatic lenses are doublets – two lenses cemented together. Flint glass and crown glass normally comprise this pairing.

"So if the plastic isn't as durable and scatters colors, what good is it?"

Cross explained that plastic is much less expensive than glass and can be molded into aspherical shapes. "Meaning that the lens surface needn't be spherical or a segment of a circle in cross-section. You see, a lens whose center radius differs from the radius at the edge can produce sharper resolution, a slightly wider field of view and flatter images at the fringe." He said that Simmons installs one in the erector tubes of some riflescopes and that it seems to work. "The image appears flat and bright, and the field is slightly bigger than normal."

Because the Simmons application is internal, the plastic lens surface is protected. Color correction is done by other elements.

"Plastic lenses appeared in cameras first," Cross noted. "Now they're not only in throw-away

High magnification and high resolution bring out details that you could not see with the naked eye.

models but in detachable lenses for very expensive SLRs. The unit can be made lighter and smaller, with no apparent sacrifice in optical quality – at least, none most people would notice. Incidentally, plastic can even be used as a coating on glass lenses."

While I had him on the phone, I decided Cross was just the man to ask about field of view. A wide field is what everybody wants, but what were the trade-offs?

"You can get more field by changing magnification and eye relief," Cross said. "Those three variables comprise what designers call the optical triangle. To get the most field or magnification or eye relief, you have to compromise at one of the other two legs of the triangle, maybe both. For example, we engineered our 2-6x B&L handgun scope so it offered a wide field of view at all power settings. But we found the eye relief shrank to only 12 inches at the high end. That was unacceptable – both from the standpoint of aiming comfort and safety. A .454 Casull could plant its hammer in your head from that distance. So we sacrificed a bit of field to increase eye relief to 20 inches at all the settings. That made sense to me, partly because I've never thought a wide field of view essential in an aiming device."

Neither have I. Field matters in binoculars, which are used mainly to find and examine wildlife at a distance. Shooting game requires concentration on the reticle, on the one spot you want to put the bullet. Save for short, quick shooting in brush, where extra field allows faster aim because it enables you to find the target sooner, wide-angle riflescopes don't seem worth compromises in eye relief or magnification. Besides, a scope suitable for fast action in the thickets will have low power anyway, and, naturally, a broad field of view.

Cross kindly offered to answer more questions, but there is no sense in exposing all your ignorance at once, so I hung up and then called Forrest Babcock.

Babcock, a lens designer at Leupold and Stevens, confirmed what Cross had told me about aspherical lenses. "Mostly they're used on eyepieces, to correct for field curvature," he added. "An

Everywhere you go, you'll see more with high-quality optics.

aspherical objective lens would be very costly."

Babcock said that the objective lens accounts for roughly a quarter of the cost of a scope and that most objectives are...

"Doublets," I said, as if I'd known that since the day Billy Grunnerveldt had shared his tuna sandwich with April Benson at the third-grade picnic. April.... "Oh, uh,

yes, I'm still here. What *is* ED glass, anyway?"

ED glass, explained Forrest, is extra-low-dispersion glass, a type that has been used for some time in expensive telescopes. It is normally added to a doublet to form a triplet. Its purpose is to give additional color correction in the secondary spectrum. It compensates for overlap in the angles of light rays

brought together by the second element in an achromatic lens.

"Is color correction substandard without ED glass?" I asked.

"Well, not to the average eye." Babcock meant that my eye was probably about as average as they come but was kind enough not to say so. "For people who need the sharpest true-color pictures – birdwatchers, for example – an ED

Even in tight cover, where shotguns and iron sights make sense, binoculars help you spot game.

element makes sense. It is, of course, expensive."

Of course. "How much does it add to the price of a scope?"

"That depends on where you put it," Babcock said. "The objective lens determines image quality, for the most part, so any ED glass really belongs up front. That means a big-

ger lens than if you could use it to good effect inside. A blank of ED glass costs between 170 and 200 times what normal crown or flint glass costs, so a really big objective bell will make the scope much more expensive when you install ED glass." He excused himself to page through an optics catalog. A few sec-

onds later he was back on. "This supplier lists a 6-inch blank of ED for five thousand bucks."

"So, what exactly does this glass do that's worth that kind of money?"

It was the wrong question to ask halfway through my last sheet of notepaper. Babcock reminded me that the white light coming into a scope's objective lens is actually a bunch of colors. The lens, in prism-like fashion, separates them. "In a lens that is not color corrected, the red and blue waves remain apart, giving your image fuzzy edges and perhaps a halo. Achromatic doublets gather the primary spectrum back into its white bundle. That's because the crown glass – say it's BK-7 – has a refractive index of 1.57. The flint glass backing it – let's use SF-6 – has a refractive index of 1.8. Dispersive powers also differ: 65 for the crown and 25 for the flint..."

"Wait," I said, now on the back of my second envelope and hunting for the church bulletin.

Babcock sighed. "The action of light as it passes through a lens depends on the type of glass plus its thickness, surface shape and index of refraction. IR is roughly 1.5 in optical glass and 1.3 in water. Anyway, color activity is also a function of a lens's dispersive power. The flint and crown glass in a doublet complement each other in this regard. ED glass merely helps them by sharpening the final picture."

He went on to explain that ED is not only expensive but hard to work with because it is soft. "You have to apply coatings right after grinding, and you don't want to use it on the outside of a scope where it might get banged up."

Kind of like plastic.

"Does Leupold use ED glass?"

"Not yet."

"Why not?"

"It doesn't do a heckuva lot of good. I mean, it adds a level of performance that most hunters won't even notice, at a price even the serious among them won't pay. At Leupold, we think mechanical integrity is a better place to put our money. Our optics get rave reviews without ED."

He'd mentioned F values, and I asked him if the F values in scopes were like those in cameras.

"Exactly. F is a ratio of focal length to lens diameter. It is a measure of the speed with which a lens bends light rays. Fast bending can result in spherical aberration. That's why when you look through a fisheye camera lens you see lines converging at the edges while the center appears to distend. An F value of 6 is fast for a telescope lens, but not for a riflescope..."

Babcock put me through the church bulletin and onto the wall calendar before he confessed that it was past quitting time there and he

This roof-prism Docter Optic binocular has both the main focus dial and diopter ring in the middle.

Very big binoculars can be too bulky and heavy. Very small ones rob you of light at dawn and dusk.

Stabilizing devices and compasses add substantially to a binocular's weight and bulk.

had a date with some trout. I told him that was OK and that I'd understood most of this very well before our chat and was just giving him some ink.

I rang off remembering the time I'd been fishing with April Benson and Billy Grunnerveldt had come along with an inner tube and before you could say aspherical plastic they were both in the water, leaving me to gut the bluegills....

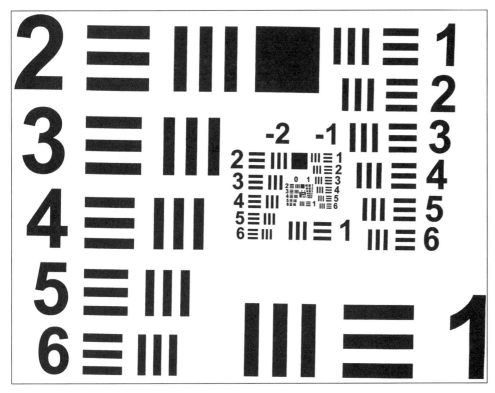

1951 Air Force optical resolution test images.

RESOLUTION CHART
For use with USAF 1951 Resolving Power Test Target with a 1524mm EFL Collimator
Resolution in seconds of angle (soa)

Elements	Groups							
	0	1	2	3	4	5	6	7
1	137.9	68.9	34.5	17.2	8.6	4.3	2.15	1.08
2	122.9	61.4	30.7	15.3	7.7	3.8	1.9	0.95
3	108.6	54.3	27.14	13.5	6.8	3.4	1.7	0.85
4	96.8	48.4	24.2	12.1	6.1	3.0	1.5	0.75
5	86.3	43.2	21.6	10.8	5.4	2.7	1.3	0.65
6	77.4	38.7	19.3	9.7	4.8	2.4	1.2	0.6

Resolution chart to pair with 1951 Air Force test images, yielding resolution in seconds of angle.

Chapter 3

What to Know About Binoculars

"…I found a better pair of binoculars in an officer's Jeep…. Word was they belonged to Gen. Matthew Ridgeway. A few years ago I met Gen. Ridgeway in Montana, fishing. I wanted to ask him if he lost his binoculars in Korea, but at the last moment, chickened out." – Jack Atcheson

Talking the talk

A HUNTING BINOCULAR can cost more than your rifle. It can also be worth more to you because the hardest part of shooting big game is still finding big game to shoot. A top-flight binocular helps you find more game. Here's what the optical jargon means, and how to use it to sift binoculars.

Big binoculars benefit from a tripod.

Center focus: A center focus binocular has a center wheel and one adjustment ring on an eyepiece (usually the right-hand eyepiece). The advantage of this design is speed of operation. Once you set the eyepiece, or diopter adjustment to produce a sharp image in concert with the other (left-hand) barrel, you don't have to adjust the eyepiece when changing viewing distance. The center wheel moves both barrels at once. Some modern center focus binoculars have the diopter adjustment in the middle – a companion wheel that can be moved independently of the main wheel but "locks" to it when you want to focus both barrels at once.

Exit pupil: The diameter of the "window" you see in a binocular barrel when you hold it at arm's length, exit pupil is derived by dividing magnification into objective lens diameter. A 7x35 binocular has an exit pupil of 5mm. That's a good number. Smaller exit pupils don't let enough light through at dawn and dusk. Because exit pupil shrinks if you boost power without increasing lens diameter, high-power binoculars exact a price: Either you give up brightness or put up with a bulky, heavy instrument. Exit pupils bigger than 6mm are unnecessary because your eye won't dilate any more in the dimmest of hunting light. Older hunters, with a more limited dilation range in their eyes, may find that 5mm is a practical maximum.

Eyepiece: Colloquially, the eyepiece is the part of a binocular that you hold near your eye – the rear of the instrument. Each eyepiece includes an ocular lens. Depending

Wind River™ Binocular and Spotting Scope

Leupold makes binoculars for finding game and spotting scopes for evaluating it.

on binocular design, it may also feature a focusing or diopter ring with registry marks on the ocular housing. Folding rubber cups or tubular sections that pull out or twist out on helical threads adjust eye relief (the distance of your eye from the ocular lens). If you don't wear eyeglasses, you'll want the cups extended. Angled eyecups block out peripheral light to give you a sharper, seemingly brighter picture.

Individual focus: An "IF" binocular has a focus adjustment on each eyepiece but no center wheel. Not as vulnerable to dust and water as is a center focus glass, it is inherently sturdy but slower to use. Whenever you want to change focus, you must do it twice, adjusting each barrel individually. Click detents and clear diopter markings on some modern binoculars speed the adjustment. With them, focusing becomes a bit like adjusting a riflescope for a more distant target.

Lens coatings: Around 1940, a Zeiss engineer discovered that a thin layer of magnesium fluoride reduced reflection and refraction at lens surfaces. Without coating, each air-to-glass surface can lose 4 percent of incidental light. "Fully coated" refers to all lenses, inside and out. "Multi-coated" indicates several coatings layered to enhance transmission of various wavelengths. Insist on fully multi-coated lenses. Don't go by the color you see in a lens. There's no "right" color of optical coating. Also, lenses can be tinted without being coated.

Objective lens: The biggest lens in a binocular, the objective is the front lens. It is not movable. Size of the objective has nothing to do with magnification or field of view. It does directly affect brightness and resolution. The bigger the glass, the bigger the exit pupil and the higher the values for relative brightness and twilight factor. Objective lens diameter in millimeters is the second set of numbers in a binocular designation (e.g., 7x35 signifies a glass of 7 power, with 35mm objective lenses).

Ocular lens: The ocular, or rearmost lens, in a binocular, is just one of many lenses assembled as a system. The placement, size and surface shape of the ocular lens affect field of view and eye relief. Brightness is not affected – unless, of course, the lens is not coated or is in some other way inferior to companion lenses. Eye relief (the proper distance of your eye behind the binocular) is measured from the rear surface of the ocular lens.

Porro prism:: This traditional binocular design features offset or "dogleg" barrels that offer a wider front lens spacing than roof prism models. There's an advantage to this spacing: better distance perception. Porro prism instruments are bulkier than those of roof prism design, but not necessarily heavier. Image quality is independent of light path; both types of binoculars can deliver superior performance. Most porro prism binoculars are offset horizontally; however, vertically offset barrels have recently

popped up in the market. Objective lenses bigger than 50mm are best used on porro prism glasses, because straight barrels won't allow the ocular lenses to swing close enough together for normal eye spacing.

Relative brightness: A measure of light transmission, relative brightness is calculated by squaring the exit pupil. Thus, while an exit pupil of 7mm is 40 percent bigger than a 5mm exit pupil, its relative brightness (49) is essentially twice what you get with the smaller "window" (25).

Resolution: Your optometrist's chart tests your eye's power of resolution. You want the highest resolution possible from a binocular, within practical confines of lens size and power. You'll need to see detail – the tip of an antler, the glint of an eye, the curve of an ear – in a jigsaw puzzle of autumn color. Test resolution outside, where you can target tiny objects in shadow and glass obliquely toward the sun. What you see is what you'll get afield. Twilight factor is a mathematical expression of resolution in dim light (square root of the product of magnification and objective diameter).

Roof prism: Roof prism binoculars lack the "dogleg" profile of porro prism glasses because the light path is cleverly manipulated by a prism that bends the light within a more compact space. Light leaves along the same axis that it enters. But the roof prism splits the light down the middle as it enters, cleaving incident light into color bands that must then

At dawn and dusk, a 5mm exit pupil is a practical minimum in binoculars as well as riflescopes.

22.3. Once more, high magnification results in a greater TF value. You need a 25-percent gain in objective diameter to equal a 20-percent boost in magnification. So, while brightness is an asset, reducing magnification to make the exit pupil bigger will not necessarily give you a higher twilight factor or better resolution in dim light.

Sifting out a good binocular

When I was a lad, famous big game hunters like Jack O'Connor carried binoculars of modest size and power. I remember finally saving enough money to buy a 7x35 Bausch & Lomb Zephyr, one of the lightest popular glasses of the day, and one of the most costly. It was also among O'Connor's favorites, and though it cost me a month's wages second-hand, I was thrilled to get it. I've spotted more game with that binocular than with any other, and I've since bought a couple more used Zephyrs. The optics are bright and sharp, even by today's standards. The frames are sturdy, and I haven't found a binocular of comparable performance that weighs less.

My B&L 7x35 stayed in my kit long after better glass appeared on the market. When I fell on the rocks with it and cracked the jacket, I wrapped thin buckskin around the barrels and bound it in place with

be brought back "into phase" to prevent color fringing. Zeiss was the first to come up with a lens coating that brings exiting light back into phase. Now, other companies offer phase-corrected roof prism glasses. Color or phase correction is necessary only in roof prism binoculars. Roof prism instruments weigh about the same as (sometimes more than) comparable porro prism models.

Twilight factor: A measure of resolution in marginal light, twilight factor is mathematically the square root of [magnification multiplied by objective diameter]. So if you have an 8x40 binocular, the TF value is the square root of 320, or 17.9. Increase magnification to 10x, and the TF becomes the square root of 400, or 20 – while the exit pupil shrinks from 5mm to 4mm. The extra magnification more than offsets the drop in brightness. If you make the objective lens 25 percent bigger (50mm), the TF for an 8x glass is 20. For a 10x it's

Varmint hunters use binoculars to find distant targets even if their rifles wear powerful scopes.

Birders insist on high resolution from their binoculars. Hunters should too!

electrician's tape. I bought for a friend a new porro prism binocular that was clearly superior. I carried the old 7x35 when the latest top-quality models were available on loan. I didn't want to give up that glass! It was like a comfortable pair of boots that had given me too much service. I'd grown to like the binocular not for how it performed but for how many miles it had been with me, and for hunts, long past, that came to mind when I picked it up. I justified my fidelity with the reminder that when it was discontinued in 1958, B&L's lovely Zephyr listed for $350. Only the best binocular could bring that sum when new automobiles left the lot for under $2,000!

But even the best gear reaches retirement age. I suspect that a few years from now, the best will be better than today's best. Still, the evolution will remain slow, because top-end glass now transmits more than 90 percent of available light and delivers images so sharp as to challenge the resolving power of our eyes. A high-quality binocular doesn't become obsolete in a decade. It makes no sense to wait for better binoculars to appear. As the fellow in the green trousers and pink tie on the car lot says, buy now!

But not before you shop. You have to know what's available before you can make a good buy. Here are a few things to keep in mind.

Catalogs don't always tell you all that you should know about a binocular. For instance, ad copy might specify "coated lenses." Assume, then, that not *all* lenses have been coated. Even inside the body, every uncoated air-to-glass surface can

still cost you brightness. Don't be misled by the straw, blue, green or purple hue on the outside lenses of models with no internal coatings. What you want are *fully multi-coated lenses.* Color tinting, available on some inexpensive binoculars, does not enhance brightness.

Steiner uses a UV lens coating on its Safari line of binoculars to cut glare and a green lens coating on its Predator series to filter the transmission of green color to your eye. The UV film protects your eyes in bright sunlight; the green coating

enhances browns and reds so big game more readily pops out of green background. I don't like tinted lenses because they reduce the amount of light my eye receives. At dawn and dusk, I want *all* the light to come through! Steiner Nighthunters have no such "block" coating.

You shouldn't detect any difference between the images of porro prism and roof prism glasses of similar quality. But you might find one more comfortable than the other. I choose center focus binoculars over models with individual focus simply because they're faster to adjust while I have the binocular to my brow. Avoid binoculars with no focus adjustment ("permanent" focus is a myth).

An increasingly popular feature is rubber armor. It's a good idea, not only protecting the binocular but muffling the sound of it banging against rifle or rocks as it swings during a climb. Rubber gives you a sure grip with cold hands. You don't need a *thick* rubber jacket, or one with a camouflage print. Rubber armor helps keep water out of your glass too, though it is not by itself evidence of waterproofing. I don't insist that a binocular be waterproof. A few are, but many models of the very best optical quality are not. I've yet to catch my binocular leaking, though I've often hunted in the rain. A binocular that doesn't pass mili-

This Docter Optic 30x80 is like two spotting scopes on one tripod. It's great for prolonged glassing!

Mid-size binoculars are the best choice for hunters in mountainous country like Montana.

tary submersion tests may never leak. As with boots, if waterproofing is important to you be sure you know the terms. Not every salesman who says "waterproof" is guaranteeing to the same standard. Waterproofing, by the way, is not fog proofing. Nitrogen, introduced under vacuum, prevents interior fogging.

When you compare binoculars, consider their feel and ease of operation. The focus dials should turn smoothly, but not so easily that they'll turn accidentally if you brush them lightly. Detents or the click adjustments on some binoculars appealed to me at first, but after using them I've come to prefer binoculars without those stops. Invariably, perfect focus comes between the clicks. At least it seems to. A smooth turn of the wheel gives me a sharp image quicker. Remember that on a center-focus binocular, you won't have to adjust the individual barrel often, if at all, in the field. You set that barrel, or the diopter, and the center wheel adjusts it in concert with the other barrel when you focus.

Traditional fold-down rubber eyecups have given way to firm eyecups that pull out. Those that pull out with a twist are best because you can press them against your brow when glassing without having them collapse. Eyecups angled to block out sidelight help concentrate your vision in some light conditions.

Optical qualities are the most important feature of any binocular, but they're seldom evaluated by the buyer. Partly that's because a rigorous evaluation requires equipment and a knowledge of optics that few buyers have. But you can get a pretty good idea of how any binocular will perform in the field just by stepping out the door of the shop in the evening.

Outside is a must. Artificial light differs from natural light. Besides, you want to see how each product performs when you're looking into shadows and at an angle toward the sun. If you can't test it in rain and thick mirage, you at least want to look at far-away targets. Check resolution by picking apart the detail you can't resolve with your naked eye. It's useful to bring a cardboard box with a resolution chart like the 1951 Air Force grid on page 27. You'll then have a repeatable test that lets you assign numbers to each trial, and separate product by fineness of resolution. Check peripheral distortion by looking to the edge of the field. Look at billboards or fences with straight lines, and move the glass so they ease out of your field of view. Do lines stay straight? Corral a square object in the middle of the field. Do the sides stay straight? Move your eye slowly off-axis so a clamshell of darkness bites into the field. Are the colors welded in place, or do you see color? When you swing the binocular toward the sun (don't target it directly!), what happens to the image?

Bear in mind that no binocular can deliver as much light as the amount that strikes its objective lens. If you get 95 percent, you're getting a very bright picture. Why

The best multi-coated lenses deliver a great advantage when you're glassing into light.

do some binoculars seem to gather light? They don't, of course. An aperture or tunnel can make images seem brighter and sharper by blocking out peripheral light. My friend Bill McRae demonstrates this phenomenon with a pair of cardboard toilet paper spools fastened together and painted black, inside and out. A block in the middle maintains proper interpupillary distance. Looking through these spools, you'd think you were looking through optics. Everything appears brighter, with crisper detail. No wonder that unwary shoppers snap up cheap binoculars, thinking they're a great buy! But next time you're tempted, remember that toilet paper rolls are cheaper still.

At first, you'll work hard to see differences between inexpensive binoculars and those that cost hundreds of dollars more. But eventually they will pop out. And then you won't be able to ignore them.

It's easy to be misled in binocular comparisons. You'd think that all 7x35s would have the same field of view, for instance, and if one had a wider field than another, you should choose it. But wide-angle binoculars are not always the best choice. A 400-foot field is more than you can study at a glance. Land sakes, you're looking at the breadth of a high school football stadium! Even at distances under 1,000 yards, where field shrinks proportionately, it's much bigger than you need. Commonly, binoculars with big fields show more edge aberration – image bending and "fuzzing."

Incidentally, "wide-angle" binoculars are by definition those with an apparent field of view of 65 degrees or greater. Apparent field is determined by multiplying degrees times the power. A 7x binocular with a 9-degree field thus has an apparent field of 63 degrees and would not be classified as a wide-angle binocular. One degree equals 52.36 feet at 1,000 yards, so that glass would give you a field of 9x52.36, or 471 feet. It's *almost* a wide-angle binocular, and may indeed give you a broader field than its competition.

(Riflescopes, because of their long eye relief requirements, become "wide angle" with narrower fields of view. A fixed-power scope is a wide-angle model if its apparent field is 26 degrees; variable scopes meet the standard at 23 degrees.)

Looking close

It's late in the season. Hunters and worsening weather have driven animals to timber. You've watched enough meadows. Time to shed clothes and binoculars and prowl the thickets – right?

Yes and no. Certainly, to shoot game you must go where the game is! Layer off the longhandles so you can move. But leave the binoculars? You might as well hunt with a cardboard box over your head.

Binoculars aren't just to magnify distant game in open country. Good glass sharpens detail. And though a binocular cannot manufacture light, the best can seem to brighten the dark places where big animals lurk. A binocular makes you look deliberately, methodically. With it, you'll find game.

Of course, using a binocular won't guarantee that you'll *shoot* game. I'm sometimes better at the finding than the shooting…

We slipped off the rim and sneaked along an elk trail threading into the shadows. The urine-stale duff beneath the Douglas firs had been churned to muck by elk traffic. We moved quietly despite our brisk pace. The bull had been vocal, but this late in the morning he might quit braying any time.

Everything around us got dark and cool, and elk smell came feedlot-strong. I slowed. Ken kept tight behind me. The muzzle of his .300 bobbed ghostlike alongside my ear.

Elk don't always do what you think they should, and when this bull doubled back he nearly caught us moving. But I saw the antler tips slide against the blackness, like a

Cabela's Alaskan Guide binocular delivers a crisp image at a modest price.

squadron of white wasps dipping in unison. I stopped abruptly, and Ken braked so close I could almost hear his heartbeat. In a second, the legs came into an opening, then the glint of an eye and a great neck the color of a burnt steak. My binocular was suddenly at my brow. The bull came on, filling the field.

If you haven't been really close to a really big bull elk, you can no more imagine it than you can imagine rocketing along a racetrack if you haven't driven a very quick automobile. There's a presence that only old bulls have, a sense of urgency other elk can't evoke. This stud moved like a Hereford bull as he approached, almost slouching between the rhythmic bunching of those great hams and shoulders. He had the easy rolling, arrogant gait of an athlete with more muscle than he needs to walk but supremely aware he can use it explosively whenever he chooses. The head sagged and weaved almost drunkenly but in a deft, practiced effort to pilot those eye-popping antlers through the brush. Then he stopped. I reckoned he stood about 18 steps away.

What followed was, I concluded later, a prime example of what not to do on an elk hunt. Oh, I didn't make any of the really stupid mistakes, like move. Or yell, "Shoot, Knothead!" In fact, I made no mistakes at all because I didn't do anything except try to corral that truck-width bone in the field of my glasses so I could score it accurately and whisper calmly to the hunter beside me that yes, this was indeed a fine bull and that he should consider giving him a Nosler.

But no decision is always a decision. And doing nothing can damn you as effectively as inactive bungling. I found, after a couple of milliseconds, that I couldn't possibly score that bull. There was too much antler too close, and much of it hidden by the enormous front tines. The elk was staring our way, waiting for our scent to pool. I wanted desperately to hear the .300 but couldn't bring myself to give the signal. Six-point elk in thickets all look bigger than they are. Most shrink several sizes as they drop.

I watched as the tide crawled to his nostrils and he swung that huge rack around. Too late I saw fifth points as long as rolling pins and thick beams that hooked down along the last ribs.

"We'll find another," I whispered when he was gone. Ken said nothing. "He probably wasn't as big as he looked." I grinned weakly. Ken

said nothing again. "It's always best to pass 'em up when you can't get all the antler in the binocular," I added, feigning logic. "Besides, you don't want to quit now."

Ken was still staring saucer-eyed after the bull when I turned to walk briskly back up the trail. At this point, I just hoped he would not shoot me.

You can't buy a binocular that will stand in for good judgment. I decided as we climbed, though, that I could easily have handicapped myself with a binocular designed for long-distance hunting. Most binoculars are made for looking long because that's what lots of hunters think they should be doing with binoculars. High-magnification glass is becoming more popular as riflemen look primarily for game in the open where they can shoot it deliberately and from a solid position with their flat-flying bullets.

I'd been using my old Bausch & Lomb 7x35 Zephyr, a lightweight glass with a field big enough to find game quickly and frame any elk rack (almost). A glass like this is still an ideal pick if you hunt where most animals live and not where most hunters think they should live to accommodate benchrest shooting styles. Except for pronghorns and caribou, most North American big game is shot in or near woody cover where high magnification can get you in trouble.

Though 8x and 10x binoculars have become popular of late, the 7x is still a fine all-around choice. And 6x glass is adequate for most

hunting. In the timber, it's hard to beat a 6x30, a compact instrument with a 5mm exit pupil. My friend Bill McRae has an old Zephyr 6x30. Old is what you'll have to look for these days if you want *any* 6x30. Like low-power, fixed-power riflescopes, they're victims of a public so enamored with high power and big glass that utility often drops out of the equation.

It's important when glassing to know what you're seeing. Up close in thickets, you need a wide field of view to get the whole picture rather than an undecipherable dollop of brush. You want great depth of field to keep everything in perspective and so you don't have to refocus your binocular often. You can also use a big exit pupil to keep images bright under shadow. These are the attributes of low-power glass.

All that became clear to me years ago when I was inching through dense riverine alders in Oregon. I knew two deer had entered this patch, and I moved very slowly. Midway through I stopped, convinced that if the deer had not sneaked out, they were close enough to see. My world became the drab latticework of branches inside my binocular field. I held the glass still and mentally picked the branches apart. Then I moved the barrels slightly to the right and began again to disassemble. I'd come to doubt the wisdom of this tedium when suddenly a white spot appeared in the field of my 7x35 Bausch & Lomb. I let my eyes

High resolution only matters if you can hold a binocular still.

Kahles 8x42 and 10x42 roof prism binoculars are marketed in the U. S. by Swarovski.

Weaver's Grand Slam binocular is reportedly a reincarnation of the excellent Simmons Presidential.

work inside the glass. The spot became the throat patch of a doe. A branch behind her became an antler. My bullet hit the buck below the eye, my only aiming point.

If you're hunting without a binocular, you're hunting handicapped. So, too, if you move it when you're looking (notice how deer stand statue-still when looking for *you*?). When you take glass into the places where big game lives, *use it often and deliberately*. Remember that at ranges measured in feet, any animal you see will be close enough to detect you. Indeed, odds are that any game you see will already be

Minox, a Leica brand, has expanded its line of mid-priced roof prism binoculars.

aware of you and ready to catapult away. Your job is not to see a buck before he sees, hears or smells you. That's a great line but so difficult as to be impractical. No, your real job is to spot the animal *before it thinks you can see it*. In a thicket, game will commonly stay put until discovered. Spot a piece of the animal while you're still so well-screened that you're not an immediate threat, and

you may get a shot. Naturally, when you do see antlers, you pretend that you don't, moving casually and slowly and keeping your gaze averted until you're looking through the sight at the vitals.

But that's the finale. First you must *find* the beast. Here are some tips:

Power down. Stay with 7x glass – 8x at the most. More powerful optics are harder to hold steady without a rest. Also, the lower the power, the bigger the field of view and greater the depth of field. Field is especially important up close because, while its angular measure is the same as when you're looking far, the *actual* window is much smaller. A wide field helps you quickly find something you spotted with your naked eye, and to see more without moving the glass.

Consider convenience. Glassing helps most when you glass often. Choose a binocular that's easy and comfortable to use. Center-focus models are my pick because pressure from one finger can sharpen the image instantly. Sliding, twist-out and collapsible rubber eyecups all work, but I like twist-outs. They're quick, and they stay put. Waterproof models make sense in rainy places. Thin rubber "armor" is also an asset. It provides a sure grip and won't make noise when slapped by brush or bumped

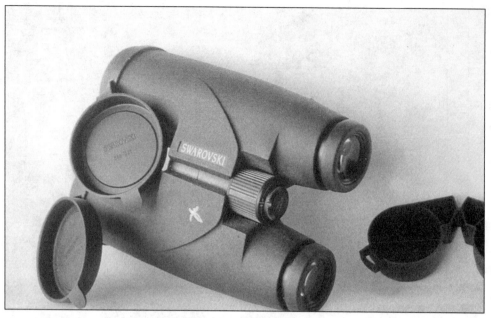

Swarovski's 7x50 SLC delivers more light than your eye can use under normal field conditions.

by your rifle. Make sure the binocular focuses as close as you'll want to look.

Get small, but not too small. You'll want a binocular that stows inside your jacket front, a glass light enough to carry easily. But tiny lenses won't deliver the brightest images. Remember that exit pupil, the diameter of each shaft of light visible in the lenses with a binocular at arm's length, is a good measure of brightness.

Buy quality. Looking close doesn't mean you can make do with substandard optics. If you miss the glint on a buck's nose, you may have missed the deer of a lifetime. Superior glass is costly, but you can get the fully multi-coated optics responsible for bright, sharp images without selling your first-born into slavery. Shopping the used markets, you'll keep a lid on prices and perhaps turn up a discontinued glass that's just right for your woods hunting – like B&L's 6x30 Zephyr.

Here are a few binoculars that make sense for tight places, where game is alert and short shots are the rule. These models are also excellent all-around birding and hunting binoculars, contrary to what you might hear from people enthralled by bigger glass. A bright 8x binocular gives you all the magnification you can hand-hold easily, and enough to sort out wing primaries at reasonable yardage, or pick an antler tip from a tangle of deadfall. (rp = roof prism, pp = porro prism.)

Make/Model/Description	Field (ft. @ 1000 yds.)	Weight (oz.)	Retail Price
Bausch & Lomb Elite, rp 8x42	365	19.5	$1,585
Bausch & Lomb Discoverer, rp 7x42	420	28.0	650
Bausch & Lomb Custom, pp 8x36	330	25.0	547
Brunton, rp 8x32	393	20.6	239
Burris Signature, rp 8x42	328	24.0	684
Burris Fullfield, pp 8x40	430	31.0	396
Bushnell Legend, rp 8x42	330	30.1	502
Cabela's Alaskan Guide, rp 8x42	368	25.0	510
Cabela's Waterproof, rp 8x42	328	29.0	280
Kahles, rp 8x32	399	21.5	610
Kahles, rp 8x42	330	26.5	721
Leica Ultra Trinovid, rp 8x32	360	23.3	995
Leica Ultra Trinovid, rp 7x42	420	31.4	995
Leica Ultra Trinovid, rp 8x42	390	31.4	1,045
Leupold Wind River WM, rp 8x32	325	19.9	563
Leupold Wind River W2, rp 8x42	280	22.0	384
Leupold Wind River, pp 8x42	330	25.4	304
Minox BD, rp 8x32 BR	394	21.7	439
Minox BD, rp 8.5x42 BR	315	30.0	529
Nikon Venturer LX, rp 8x42	366	34.6	1,695
Nikon Superior E, pp 8x32	393	22.2	957
Nikon E2, pp 8x30	461	20.3	731
Optolyth Alpin, pp 8x30 BGA	405	16.8	449
Optolyth Alpin, pp 8x40 BGA	330	20.5	459
Optolyth Royal, rp 8x45 BGA/WW	360	32.0	799
Pentax DCF WP, rp 8x32	393	21.2	655

Make/Model/Description	Field (ft. @ 1000 yds.)	Weight (oz.)	Retail Price
Pentax PCF V, pp 8x40	360	26.5	250
Sightron SII, rp 8x42	340	23.0	520
Steiner Nighthunter, pp (indiv. focus) 8x30	390	18.0	600
Swarovski EL, rp 8.5x42	390	28.9	1,499
Swarovski SLC, rp 8x30 WB	408	19.0	866
Swarovski Classic Habicht, pp 7x42 MGA	336	26.8	767
Swift Audubon, pp 8.5x44 BWCF	430	24.6	570 (790 w/ED)
Swift Ultra-Lite, pp 7x42 ZCF	367	21.0	430
Swift Ultra-Lite, pp 8x32 ZWCF	436	19.6	425
Weaver Grand Slam, rp 8.5x45	314	29.0	529
Weaver Classic, rp 8x42	332	23.6	404
Zeiss Classic, rp 8x30 B/GA	405	20.5	1,000
Zeiss Classic, rp 7x42 B/GA	450	28.2	1,150
Zeiss Victory, rp 8x40	405	25.1	979

Chapter 4

More Choices in Binoculars

"... any color at all, so long as it's black."

Compact – but not too compact

HOW BIG IS big enough for a binocular objective lens? That depends on what magnification you want, and what you want to look at. Brightness is a function of exit pupil diameter, which you determine by dividing objective lens diameter by the magnification. The bigger the exit pupil, the more light you'll get through the glass. But your eye can dilate to only about 7mm in total darkness (that's why binoculars built for use on naval vessels and other applications where portability matters not, have 7mm exit pupils: 7x50, 8x56, 10x70). To see game in dim light or watch songbirds in the shadows, you'll want a 5mm exit pupil, maybe 6. So for a 7x binocular, a 35mm objective is about minimum. Want 10x magnification? To get that 5mm exit pupil, you'll need 50mm front glass.

When I'm not toting a rifle, I'll strap on a harness to carry 10x50 Swarovski or Leica binoculars. The higher magnification gives me more

detail, and bigger front glass ensures plenty of light transmission in the shadows. When packing a rifle myself, however, I'll leave these 42-ounce glasses at home. The hills aren't getting any easier to climb. A 50mm binocular all but mandates a harness to transfer the weight from your neck to your shoulders. Harnesses make that weight bearable, but they're annoying when you want to shed or put on a jacket. You must extricate yourself from the straps and set the binocular down. Then, when you're

finished adjusting your outerwear, the harness must go back on. Even if the weight and inconvenience don't nettle you, the bulk of a 50mm binocular may. It's not a glass to slip easily into your shirt, and most models are long enough that you'll notice them banging against your rifle.

To be honest, I'm getting perilously close to liking *little* binoculars. They fit in a big jacket pocket and ride under a jacket front with hardly a bulge. They don't require a harness.

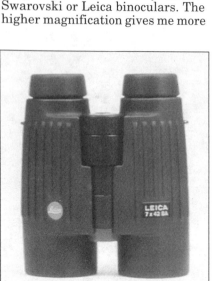

The Leica 7x42: superb all-around binocular.

Glassing for bears in British Columbia, this guide holds the binocular still and "reads" the field.

The Zeiss Victory binocular is a phase-corrected, roof-prism, center-focus glass.

For all their advantages – and a proliferation of the type during the last two decades – pocket-size binoculars have become something of a counter-culture in the hunting community. Binocular companies these days hawk image brightness as if all game were shot in the dark. Bigger front glass is promoted as if it could somehow suck animals out of the shadows. The fact is that game can be spotted only when game is there, and you'll glass up a lot of antlers when light is adequate for iron-sight shooting. Toting enough binocular glass to probe the darkest thickets at dusk is like packing a bipod, tactical scope and target-weight barrel on your hunting rifle in the expectation of cross-canyon shots. Where weight and bulk don't matter, performance comes cheap. But if your mobility is compromised by a heavy binocular, it can keep you from looking where the animals hide.

Still, the true compact binoculars aren't bright enough for all-around big game hunting or birding. A 9x28 binocular has an exit pupil of 3mm, useful only in very good light. Binoculars with exit pupils this small are like glove compartments too cramped for maps, and jacket pockets too tight to get your fingers in. Like an undersize spare tire, they're better than nothing, but not much. Optics firms have worked hard to design better compact binoculars. Some of these have very good lenses. Some are even easy to hold. But in my view, they are not bright enough

or comfortable enough in use for people who glass a lot. Hunters and birders who are serious about what they do glass *a lot*.

With that in mind, there's much to like in binoculars that are almost but not quite compacts: those that weigh 16 to 24 ounces and feature objective lenses of 30 to 35mm. They're available in both porro and roof prism configuration. Largely overlooked in the rush to higher magnification and bigger objective lenses, they may now be gaining slightly in popularity. Properly so.

My last hunt in Alaska turned up a lot of open landscapes. So did a recent deer hunt in Oregon and a pronghorn hunt in New Mexico. On these trips, I carried an 8x30 Zeiss Diafun binocular that looked more appropriate for a football stadium. I took it along because it was lightweight and compact. Despite an exit pupil just shy of 4mm, it was very bright. I was reminded again that a large exit pupil becomes an advantage only in light conditions *that seldom occur*.

Here are five almost-compact binoculars (as shown on the next page) that offer top-rung performance in a package not much bigger than a good ham sandwich.

The Victory's diopter adjustment is in front of the hinge, not on the right-hand barrel.

Maker	Power x Objective (mm), design	Weight (oz.)	Field (ft. @ 1000 yds.)
Leica	Ultra Trinovid 8x32 BN, roof	22	405
Nikon	Superior E 8x32, porro	22	393
Pentax	DCF 8x32 WP, roof	21	393
Swarovski	SLC 8x30 WB, roof	19	408
Zeiss	Dialyt MT 8x30B/GA T*, roof	21	405

For comparison:

Leica	Trinovid 8x42 BA, roof	31	390
Leica	Trinovid 8x20 BC/BCA, roof	8	345
Swarovski	SLC 10x42 WB, roof	31	330
Zeiss	Dialyt MT 8x56 B/GA T*, roof	36	330

Note that the field of view for an 8x32 Leica is slightly greater than that for an 8x42 Leica. The 8x32 is more compact and weighs 9 ounces less. It also costs less. The tangible advantage of the larger glass is 1mm in exit pupil diameter. The 8x20 Leica carries like a feather, but its field of view is 60 feet smaller than that of the 8x32, and with an exit pupil of 2.5mm, it is hardly what you want for the shadows.

Swarvoski's excellent 10x42 SLC offers about the same size exit pupil as its 8x30 SLC. Boosting the magnification increases definition. But you also get a smaller field: 330 feet compared to 408. And the weight jumps from 19 ounces to 31.

The Zeiss Dialyt 8x56 has a giant 7mm exit pupil, but the field of view is a bit smaller than that afforded by the Dialyt 8x30. Also, the 8x56

Zeiss Diafun: A small but very tough binocular with superior optics.

The Cabela's 10x42 Alaskan Guide binocular has an easy-to-reach focusing wheel.

weighs nearly a pound more. Its overall length of 9.4 inches amounts to nearly double that of the 8x30 (5.6 inches).

Nikon's porro prism Superior E and the Pentax DCF also fall near the 20-ounce mark and deliver smashingly bright images. Though they feature slightly smaller fields of view than the other 8x32s, you still see more than through the 42mm and 56mm binoculars on the comparison list.

Life is fraught with trade-offs.

The best 8x30s? Well, you can't beat a Swarovski, Leica or Zeiss roof-prism hunting glass. Not long ago, I carried a Zeiss to Alaska. A hunting partner couldn't understand how I saw distant game when he didn't – until he looked through my binocular. With it I spotted a grizzly he later killed.

You don't have to spend a lot of money to get a serviceable 8x30, which is why a lot of hunters carry one. Choose a 10x50 or even a binocular with 42mm objectives, and you'll pay lots more for any given level of quality. Big front glass really boosts the price. I'd rather have a top-rung 8x30 than a mid-quality binocular with bigger objectives. Better lenses and lens coatings can boost brightness as effectively as larger front glass.

If you hunt from a stump or a rock, or are simply finding game for someone else to shoot, a full-size binocular makes sense. As it does if you're watching birds from your living room or automobile. If you carry a rifle on solo treks in the mountains or must cover lots of tough terrain to find new bird species for your list, an 8x30 or 8x32 binocular can be a better choice. It gives you greater mobility and almost as much brightness – perhaps as much brightness as you'll need all season.

Mid-size hunting binoculars

It's as easy to buy a binocular as it is to buy a mutual fund. You just ask people for their opinions until someone says what you want to hear. Recently, good binoculars have been better investments than most mutual funds, so you might consider spending more than you wanted to for your next glass. Beware, though, of people who point you toward the biggest or most powerful binocular, or toward models small enough to fit in James Bond's wallet.

In my opinion, the most useful all-around hunting binoculars are those of 8 to 10x, with lenses of 30 to 42mm. You'll carry 18 ounces to about 2 pounds, depending on lens size, frame material, glass type and optical design. The 7x35 Bausch & Lomb Zephyr I used for years was at that time ideal, but I've since come to appreciate more magnification. Climbing that ladder, you'll find as I did that 30mm front glass is a bit small. Boost power and you need more glass to keep the dark out.

The 8x42 roof prism seems to be replacing the 7x35 porro prism as a standard all-around hunting glass – at least, where I travel. And a lot of hunters are using 10x42 binoculars. The popular Zeiss 10x40 showed a lot of big game guides and hunters that high magnification in a high-quality instrument could

deliver a bright picture without the bulk of a huge objective lens. Using twilight factor as a measure of what you can discern in poor light, it's clear that extra magnification is worth some reduction in exit pupil diameter. The smaller field of view and an increase in apparent wobble are liabilities, but apparently not serious ones to most buyers. To my mind, an 8x42 is probably the best choice for general use, the 10x42 a specialist's glass for open country.

The list of close-cover hunting binoculars that appears a few pages back is full of 8x glass. As I pointed out there, you may not want more magnification, even for open-country hunting or for picking itty-bitty warblers out of a latticework of tree-top limbs. If 10x is more to your liking, that list is still useful, because many of the best binoculars with

The Pentax 10x50 DCF is a top choice if you need high magnification at dawn and dusk.

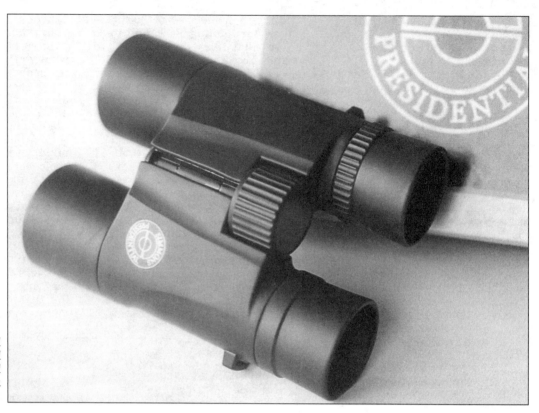

The modestly priced Simmons Presidential has been re-engineered and boxed up as a Weaver.

42mm objectives – the Bushnell Elites, Leica Trinovids, Nikon Venturers, Zeiss Victorys (40mm) to name just a few – are available in 10x magnification, too. The weight and physical dimensions are normally identical or very close. Price may be slightly higher.

A binocular with a 42mm objective is just about as heavy a glass as you can hang from your neck without a harness, and for some models a harness is a pious idea. Weight ranges from 25 to 35 ounces among the top ships in this fleet (Zeiss 7x45 BT*MT binoculars weigh 42). Nikon's 10x42 Superior E porro prism glass is among the lightest. So

Steiner's 8x32 Predator features a 4mm exit pupil in a very small package.

A good glass does you no good unless you're looking through it.

too the new Kahles 8x42 and 10x42. The Zeiss 10x40 Dialyt B/GA T* and Pentax's 8x42 and 10x42 DCF binoculars weigh in at about 27 ounces. Swarovski's new premier-class EL 8.5x and 10x binoculars register either side of 28 ounces, while Leupold Golden Ring 10x40s and Bausch & Lomb's 10x42 and 8x42 Elites are 29. The Swarovski 10x42 SLCs and Leica 8x42 and 10x42 Ultra Trinovids weigh 31 ounces, as does the Fullfield 8x40 by Burris. Nikon's Venturer tips the scale at 35 ounces, in 8x or 10x.

How much should you pay for a mid-size binocular? Well, as little as you can. If you can find a used glass without much wear, you might get a great bargain. My 10x42 Swarovski was once owned by a fellow who appreciated its quality but thought it too heavy for sheep hunting. I got it for less than half the cost of a new binocular. List prices for 10x42 binoculars range to more than $1,800. You don't have to buy at the top to get a serviceable glass. On the other hand,

you won't be doing yourself any favors by looking below $500 retail, and $900 is more realistic. But don't pay list! In optics, retail prices are great for your comparisons, but when

you start toting a loaded billfold, focus on street prices, which can be hundreds of dollars less. On a tight budget? Burris offers good value with its 8x40 porro prism Fullfield, and

Leica's 10x32 Ultra Trinovid delivers high magnification in a compact glass. Great for sheep hunts!

The Burris Landmark is one of only a few vertically offset porro prism binoculars.

Weaver recently adopted the affordable Simmons Presidential (it's in Weaver's line as the 8x42 and 10x42 roof prism Classic).

Whatever your price bracket, remember that a binocular is an investment. It should last as long as you do – and then some. Amortize the price over the years you expect to use it, and you'll come up with a ridiculously low annual figure. How much would you pay to see a big buck's eye in the shadows? Or the black belly line of a six-point bull elk? You burn dollar-and-a-half gasoline by the tankful to reach hunting country, driving a pickup that's likely worth what I paid for my first house. If you hunt out of state, you'll fork over several hundred dollars for a *one-time* permit to shoot. An outfitter will charge you hundreds, or thousands, more. If you spend as much on your binocular as on a rifle and scope, you're in the minority. But the binocular will likely help you find game. If you don't find it, the rifle is useless. The binocular is your primary tool for hours; aiming and shooting are over in seconds. You can make do with an ordinary rifle, and even a cheap sight. If you play Scrooge shopping for binoculars, you're handicapping yourself!

Where big glass makes sense

"It's all wrong," he said, shaking his head. "We have mini-binoculars and scopes the size of tractor axles." He leaned on the counter and shifted the toothpick. "That's like havin' donut tires all around, and a full-size spare. Give me a big binocular any day."

The gunshop proprietor had always been free with his opinions, and usually they were just about worth their price. But this time, I concluded, he had something. We hunt with binoculars; we shoot with scopes. We spend a lot of time each day looking through the binoculars to get a few seconds in the scope. Most days we don't use the scope at all.

So why carry a big scope and shirt-pocket binoculars?

"I'll tell you why," said a fellow at the range the other day. "Binoculars are dead weight. So is the rifle, but you gotta have the rifle anyway. A few more ounces in the scope doesn't seem like much. A heavy binocular hangs like an anchor. Besides, little binoculars are so good these days, you don't need big glass to get a bright, sharp picture. And you can sprint if you have to, and slip

Steiner's 12x50 Night-hunter has a very high twilight factor. Angled eye-cups reduce side glare.

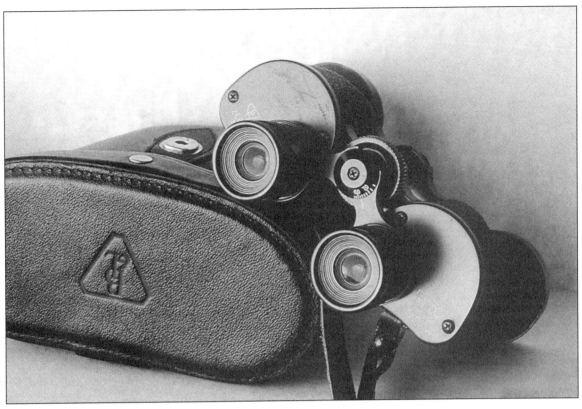

The 7x35 B&L Zephyr was a premier glass in the 1950s. It came in 6x, 7x and 9x, IF and CF.

through thickets without hangin' up. At the end of the day, your neck won't feel like you've been yoked to a plow." He pulled the 7mm Magnum off the sandbags and handed it to me. It wore a big scope. "Aimin' may not take long, but it's mighty important," he said. "You can put *my* glass in a scope."

Who's right?

Well, there's a time and place for just about everything short of charred hotcakes and a pickup that won't start. If you're climbing where even the goats get dizzy, and you feel each ounce by the end of the day, you may want a light-weight binocular *and* a little scope. But if you're hunting on the prairie, or where you'll spend lots of time sitting and looking, and if you expect to spot game at a distance and only when the sun is half-immersed in the horizon, you're smart to choose a bigger binocular, no matter what scope you use.

Remember that a scope is a sight. You don't use it to find game or to judge antlers. Because you aim with one eye, you wouldn't spend much time looking in the scope even if you left your binocular home (good gravy, you might as well leave without your pants!). A few minutes peering through optics with one eye will make you tired of looking. So the scope's role on a

hunt is a lot smaller than most shooters (and scope makers) would have you think. Certainly you'll want a sharp, flat, bright sight picture. But you can get that with a small scope. Just keep the magnification at a reasonable level, and you won't need an objective bell the size of a coffee can to funnel light to your eye. If your scope is a 6x – or a variable set at 6x – a 36mm front lens will give you all the light your eye can use. At 4x, you'll get almost that much light if your scope has no objective bell at all! A straight tube is surely big enough to give you all the light your eye can use at 2.5x and 3x magnification – which, incidentally, is adequate for most big game shooting.

You're also wise to keep scope bulk to a minimum and scope weight to 10 or 12 ounces – at least where I hunt in the mountains of the West.

A binocular for open-country hunting is another story. You spend a lot of time looking through it, and you look farther than you would aim. You judge antlers with a binocular, sometimes at great distance. A binocular should be of higher magnification than your scope, and as you jack up the power, you must increase objective diameter or lose brightness. Though many hunters get along nicely with an exit pupil of

5mm, you may want to give your eye all the light it can use, especially if you won't be toting the binocular for miles or negotiating steep hills. An 8x glass with a 50mm objective should suffice. A 10x60 binocular gives you the same 6mm exit pupil but is too heavy and awkward to carry on a strap. That's why you don't see many. Binocular makers market instead the 10x50, a handier size that trims exit pupil to a still-respectable 5mm.

Want more power? Start shopping for tripods. Manufacturers rightly divine that binocs of 12x and up magnify your wobble enough that hand-holding is impractical – even if you aren't concerned about exit pupil. If you're going to reduce wobble with a tripod, you might as well make the binocular bigger for a brighter picture. Tripod adapters come standard on 12x60 and 15x60 binoculars, but not on 12x or 15x binoculars with smaller front lenses. Nikon's 12x50 Superior E and the Leica 12x50 Trinovid are notable exceptions. Both these first-cabin binoculars and the 12x50 Bushnell Elite have adapters. One high-power binocular that's in a class by itself is the Zeiss 20x60, whose internal mechanical stabilizer takes the jitters out of the glass and enables you to hand-hold it under most conditions.

The phase-corrected Signature is Burris's best binocular. Choose an 8x42, a 10x50 or 12x50.

The Nobilem 15x60 accommodates a tripod adapter, as do the Optolyth "Royal Series" roof prism binoculars imported by Deutsche Optik: a 9x63 and a 12x63. The "Alpin Series" porro prism line includes a 12x50. With an exit pupil of 7mm, the 9x63 would be a fine choice where low light is a concern.

Any binocular with 60mm glass is best carried in a rucksack, with the tripod.

A common response to that suggestion: "If it's going in a pack, you might as well take a spotting scope!" Well, if you need the extreme power of a spotting scope, yes, you might as well. But a binocular is much easier on your eyes than a spotting scope because it allows you to use both eyes at once. You can glass longer in comfort when both eyes are working and one pupil isn't trying to dilate while the other is all but shut down. The longer you can look in comfort, the longer you'll look — and the greater your chances of spotting antlers. Time looking is time hunting. Binocular vision also gives you better depth perception.

My friend David Miller, the Tucson gunmaker, is a master at using big binoculars. He can sit long hours picking apart the ocotillo growth to find a piece of a Coues deer hundreds of yards below a Sonoran rim. He needs the comfort of a binocular but the power of a spotting scope. Solution: a Docter Optic "Aspectem" 30x80 binocular on a sturdy tripod. This instrument measures 20 inches long and weighs just shy of 10 pounds, so it's not for neck carry. In fact, it will use up enough of a day pack that you may have to tote your sandwich in a lunch bucket. But it's incredibly effective at sifting deer country from afar. The huge objectives keep exit pupil diameter near 3mm, and the twilight factor is a whopping 49. (Twilight factor of a 10x40 glass figures out to be 20, that of an 8x32, 16).

There aren't many binoculars like the Aspectems, which also come with 40x and variable 20-50x eyepieces. Both have 80mm objectives. I like the 30x model. Mirage and the jarring effects of wind can cause problems at 40x, and you'll have to deal with a very small field. The 20-50x eyepieces are so bulky they contact the bridge of my nose before my eye is close enough to see a full field of view.

Kowa makes an excellent 30x80 binocular. Steiner manufactures a glass with 80mm objectives, but it is a 15x. I've not used one. A military model is available too, with compass and rangefinder. Like all instruments of this size, it is designed for tripod mounting. You won't need a studio-quality Gitzo; but a tripod that wobbles in the breeze or that won't allow you to pan a hillside, isn't worth buying. You should find a serviceable medium-weight tripod for $50 or so.

There's an alternative, if you need high magnification some of the time but don't want to carry a spotting scope or a binocular the size of an Indy car's exhaust manifold. Swarovski offers a doubler for its SLC and EL binoculars. A lightweight, 6-inch tube with high-quality optics, it doubles the magnification of your binocular. You install it in seconds without tools. It can't give you Technicolor brightness when clouds come in at dusk. And you won't use it for extended glassing. But in a pinch, it gives you a close look at game far away. You might not even miss your spotting scope! Zeiss boosts magnification another notch with a similar tripler that fits Zeiss binoculars.

Seldom, though, will you need more than 10x magnification in a binocular, or an exit pupil bigger than 5mm. The various 10x50 binoculars comprise a practical ceiling in magnification, size, and weight. My two favorites are the Swarovski SLC and Leica Ultra Trinovid. Optically, they're hard to tell apart. They even feel the same. I like the SLC's helical eyepieces; Leica eyepieces pull straight out. At just over 40 ounces, the Ultra Trinovid is an ounce lighter than the SLC, whose polymer frame is renowned for its sturdiness.

If weight doesn't matter, the 52-ounce Zeiss 10x56 BT*MT deserves a look. You get almost 6mm of exit pupil, and quality on par with the Swarovski and Leica binoculars. The 10x50 Pentax PIF Marine binocular is in this regalia. It features individual-focus eyepieces, weighs 56 ounces. None of these models is cheap. But in my view, if you glass enough to need a 10x50 glass, you need a *good* one. Looking for a big binocular at a bargain-barn price is like shopping for a competition-class speedboat at yard sales.

Where brightness matters more than magnification, an 8x50 is a better pick than a 10x50. Leica and Swarovski offer 8x versions of their 10x50 glasses. Bausch & Lomb sells an 8x50 Elite. Zeiss lists two 8x56 binoculars. (The Dialyt B/GA T* weighs only 36 ounces, while the BT*MT registers 52.) For the brighter picture and wider field, you get a bit less resolving power than a 10x. For any given model, size and weight of 8x and 10x glasses are the same

or nearly so. Some manufacturers offer 7x50 binoculars. With their 7mm exit pupil, they're popular for marine use in the dark. But on a hunt or watching birds, you won't be looking in the dark. A 7x42 offers all the brightness you can use in a handier package. **Top picks**: the Zeiss BT*MT and B/GA T*, Swarovski SLC, and Lieca Ultra Trinovid.

To carry a binocular with 50mm objectives, you'll need a harness. Three pounds is a lot to dangle from your neck all day. An elastic harness transfers that weight to your shoulder, and it keeps the binocular from swinging out away from your chest. It's even a good idea for lighter glass. The only drawback: you have to take it off to shed or put on a shirt or jacket.

The edge you get with a big binocular is the combination of high power and a big exit pupil. You can't get this duo with small or mid-size front glass! It's what you need to see all your eyes are able to see in dim light. Taking hunters after elk, I've spotted bulls they did not see simply because I had a powerful binocular with a 50mm front end.

On one afternoon hunt, John and I were climbing a steep north face, keeping to the sunny side of a shale spine so we'd be hidden from the stringer of aspens to the east. I suspected it held elk, but this was early in the season, and the foliage hung heavy in the shadows where the animals would bed. I stopped for a breather and glassed anyway.

A tiny spot of color caught my eye. It was 150 yards away, in the dappled half-shade where aspen leaves fluttered. Hard to see. I looked at it a long while, and fixed some markers so I could return to it. Motioning for John to join me, I gave the russet spot another look. It seemed to be an elk's ear. I slid over a few feet and looked again. Sure enough. And there was an antler base.

I tried to point out the bull to my companion. He couldn't see it at all in his glass, so I set up my spotting scope sideways as a rifle rest and talked John onto the bull. Still we had no shot. In fact, John could see only color in his scope, not an elk. When minutes later we maneuvered into position for a shot, I had to tell John to shoot at the uphill side of what he could see. Dutifully, he held where my binocular had shown me a forward rib. The concussion of the .375 took our eyes off the bull, and when I looked again, he was gone. We made our way forward and found the elk dead, hit through the lungs as perfectly as you could wish. Terrific, disciplined shooting. But we really owed that kill to my Swarovski 10x50 SLC. Its extraordinary resolving power had drawn my attention to one spot of color and had allowed me to identify key details at long range in a riot of color and movement.

I still carry that heavy binocular. It's become a habit. Kind of like driving on full-size tires.

Chapter 5

Buying Binoculars

"…You'll remember quality; you'll forget cheap."

Die Eurospendy-butgoot optiks

"I'd git me a good binoc'lar t'morrow if this outfit'd pay me what I'm worth." The cowboy picked yellow horse-teeth with a pine sliver from the debris on the flatbed. His old pickup smelled of sunburned steel and last year's hay. A veteran blue heeler eyed me as he might a trespassing cat. In this noon-white heat, he'd keep to the shade under the tack rack, I thought. Still, his one blue iris had the look of glass with crosswires.

"What would you buy?" I asked.

He leaned out the window and rubbed a cracked side mirror with his bandanna. "German."

"A German?"

"German glass, Greenhorn." The cowboy pawed his stubbled chin. It sounded like leather on a steel brush. "I took a German mule deer huntin' once – special favor to the

boss. Anyway, we got on a dandy buck and this feller couldn't see it. Big as a beef and plain as fresh paint on a barn. Finally ambled off. I offered to plug it fer 'im, but he wouldn't have that…."

I scuffed my toe in the road dust and started to say something vapid about hunters and deer in general, but the cowboy broke in.

"You German?"

I allowed that I wasn't.

"You got any German glass?" He didn't wait for a reply. "Not many folks do. Pity. They're good. *Goot!*" He cackled. "Been that way since '25."

The blue heeler had gone to sleep by the time I'd learned all the wizened man cared to tell me about Leica optics. The legend began, he said, in 1911, when one Oskar Barnack joined the company as director of research. An amateur photographer, Barnack balked at having to carry, set up and manipulate the heavy plate cameras of the day.

"Smart cookie, that Mr. Barnack. Figured the movie film he was workin' with could double for still cameras. He even convinced ol' Ernie Leitz hisself to build a camera for 35mm film. That was the Ur-Leica. Came out about the time Ferdinand stopped a bullet in Sarajevo. Anyway, the big war put a hold on things, but Leica had a commercial camera ready for the Leipzig Spring Fair in '25."

The blue heeler seemed to have lost interest. The cowboy unloaded on me an abbreviated history of a German company now known as much for its carriage-class sports optics as for expensive cameras.

"Ain't very many hunters with Leica cameras," he conceded. "A few o' the smart ones have Trinovid binoc'lars, though. Great glass. A few years ago, Leica went high-tech with the Geovid binoc'lar. It has an electronic compass and built-in rangefinder. They work, too! But you can give me the Televid spotting scope. The APO model. It's brilliant. Sharp as snake teeth. Best tube in the world for lookin' far away."

The cowboy was about done with his story. He picked a couple of '06 cases from the dusty dash and tossed them into the ashtray. "I ain't got much glass, but I figure I know what good glass is. Say, what're you packin', friend?" He eyed the rifle on my shoulder, the binocular bulge under my jacket.

I didn't want to show him. In that rusty oven of a pickup was a connoisseur of fine glass. I bade him good day and took my leave across the forest road into the aspens. The blue heeler stayed still in the shadow of the rack, his parting look a sneer.

You can buy a binocular for $29.95, and you can spend $2,000. Some of the differences in pricing are obvious. Big lenses, fully multicoated and culled to meet rigid dimensional specs, cost a lot to make and to install. Engineering that yields lighter, sturdier binocular

A big glass, this modestly priced Nikon 10x50 has a 5mm exit pupil and a high twilight factor.

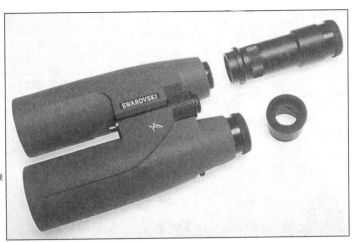

The Swarovski doubler can be installed on most Swarovski full-size binoculars in seconds, in the field.

frames, smoother, more precise focusing and coatings that give you a brighter, sharper image must be paid for.

On the other hand, some high prices are hard to figure out. Long acknowledged for fine optics, Zeiss and Leica of Germany, and Swarovski of Austria, seem able to command huge premiums for their binoculars, riflescopes and spotting scopes. Are they worth their price, or are gullible outdoorsmen just paying for a name? I asked Gary Reed, then U.S. national sales manager for Zeiss.

"Yes, they're worth it," he said without hesitation. "Our research shows that a 40-year-old hunter who has avoided high-priced glass is on his third binocular. If he had bought one Zeiss binocular to begin with, he would not only have enjoyed superior vision during his hunts; he would have an instrument that's still worth about as much as when he bought it. Some Zeiss optics have actually *gained* value over time. Cheap glass depreciates like a new car, starting when you buy it."

Reed pointed out that the Zeiss firm is more than 150 years old, worth about $2.5 billion and does nothing but make and market optics. Zeiss products have been sold in the U.S. since 1911. "But even if you don't care about history or reputation, you ought to appreciate our lifetime warranty. It's the only one in the industry that's transferable. If you hand a Zeiss binocular or riflescope to your son, that instrument is still fully covered."

According to Reed, the single biggest cause for binocular returns – across brands – is collimation failure. That is, the barrels get knocked out of alignment. "For most companies, that's evidence of normal wear and tear. It's not the result of defective workmanship or poor materials. So they charge you to fix it. Not many hunters will want to spend $100 to repair a $200 binocular. With Zeiss, you needn't worry about collimation problems. First, the new barrels are painstakingly aligned when the binocular is manufactured. Secondly, Zeiss hinges are very rugged. And third, if you *do* manage to bang the instrument so hard as to skew the hinge, we'll fix it at no charge."

A personal note: Some years ago, hunting above the timberline, I lost my footing on steep rock and fell, twisting to clutch the mountain. Unable to get a hand- or toe-hold, I slid 50 feet down a granite face, stopping just shy of a precipice when my fingers caught a crack in the rock. Many breathless minutes later, I managed to inch sideways to better footing. My Zeiss binocular had ridden down the rock face under my weight, and its housing was badly scratched. But there was no internal damage, and the collimation was still perfect. I suspect that cheaper glass would have been trashed. I used that Zeiss the rest of the hunting season.

Lightweight binoculars are a must if you log lots of miles in broken country like the Missouri breaks.

The author got close enough to kill this bull with an iron-sighted rifle – but spotted him with a binocular.

"Optically, Zeiss optics are superior, not only to bargain brands, but to the best-selling American makes," said Reed, somewhat predictably. "Our most recent tests show that a Zeiss 3-9x36 riflescope is brighter than the most popular 3.5-10x40 American model. All Zeiss optics are fully multi-coated. Period. All objective lenses are achromatic (color-corrected). We build extra contrast into our lens coatings." He pointed out that the best cameras in the world – Contax and Hasselblad – incorporate Zeiss lenses.

Reed noted that Zeiss spends 10 percent of its annual sales revenue on research and development, not only for sports optics, but for the space industry as well. Zeiss introduced the first variable riflescope (1904), and a Zeiss engineer came up with the notion of coating lenses with magnesium fluoride to enhance light transmission (1939). In 1988 Zeiss was the first optics company to use phase-corrected lens coatings, and it has aggressively courted the U.S. hunting market with 1-inch scopes and rear-plane scope reticles.

"Most of what you pay extra for won't be obvious at first glance," Reed said. "For example, Zeiss uses bigger binocular prisms than does most of its competition. Our Abbe prisms admit 6 percent more light than the common Pechan prisms. We grind our glass to very tight tolerances too. The right-angle surfaces of prisms are held to 12 millionths of an inch. Not all manufacturers can even measure to that

degree of precision." He explained that binoculars and riflescopes are assembled in the company's "clean

Binoculars bring you face to face with animals most people only see as specks in the distance.

rooms," where temperature and humidity are controlled and dust all but eliminated.

Other advantages of Zeiss optics: constant eye relief throughout the power range of riflescopes, the "B" feature in binoculars that ensures precise focus of light rays for people wearing eyeglasses, and etched reticles that are manufactured by Zeiss. Few scope-makers supply their own reticles. "You won't see erector assembly lube showing up as specs on our reticles either," said Reed, who went on to claim that the rail-mounted erectors on V-Series Zeiss scopes reduce stray light from 4 to 2 percent.

"Some manufacturers add gimmicks to inflate the price of their optics," Reed observed. "Not Zeiss. For example, we don't install adjustable objectives on every hunting scope. There's a place for this device, mainly on target scopes that are used on super-accurate rifles at precise distances. But any high-quality scope with parallax set for 200 yards will give you a parallax error at 400 yards of only about half an inch.

Photo by J. R. Hunter

Goat hunting without a binocular is like orienteering without a compass.

How many shooters or rifles can keep bullets inside half an inch at 400 yards?"

Zeiss scopes in my rack are among my favorites, so it was hard to play devil's advocate against Gary Reed's salesmanship. But his tongue-in-cheek dismissal of all things Austrian was an easier mark. The Swarovski label has made huge inroads stateside. In fact, more Swarovski sports optics are now sold in the U.S. than the products of all other European sports optics makers combined. The Austrians work hard to figure out what Americans want; the products are peerless in quality, cosmetically attractive and cleverly advertised. As this is written, Swarovski has logged record sales in 31 of the past 35 months. And most of the growth has been on the high-priced end of the line: the EL binocular, the 6-24x50 riflescope. Swarovski's 10x50 binocular is my choice for big game hunting in open country. Use it once, and you may not bother with any other glass. I have a Swarovski variable scope on my favorite elk rifle, simply because it is an unbeatable sight.

No one can tell you if you should pay the premium charged for Zeiss, Leica or Swarovski optics. Remember that a binocular, riflescope or spotting scope is a long-term investment. Amortize the cost of an expensive glass over 20 years of hunting and you'll find you spend more each year for camp groceries. When someone tells me he can't afford the best optics, I advise him to buy the best he can't afford.

Bargain glass

"You get what you pay for." We've all heard that, and mostly it's true. But sometimes you may not want to pay for the best, either because you can't afford it or because you decide the best isn't twice as good as something that costs half as much. Near the top of a price scale, little

improvements come at very high cost; and just the label can add enough dollars to a sticker to claim most of your tax refund.

For example, at $1,818, the Nikon Venturer LX 10x42 is a frightfully expensive binocular. In my view, it's also among the best. But Nikon's Superior E 10x42 costs nearly $600 less, and it is

Even in thick cover, a binocular is an asset. This one is the author's beloved 7x35 B&L Zephyr.

Not all elk are this easy to spot. A binocular gives your eyes more reach and helps you in heavy cover.

top-deck. If you insist on a water-proof glass, or if you prefer a roof-prism design with phase correction, Venturer might be worth the price. Or not. You'll pay handsomely for Swarovski's new EL, and the best Zeiss binoculars, too. Good glass is a good long-term investment; it is not always a bargain, or affordable.

Whatever your budget, look for binoculars with fully multi-coated optics. Nothing else matters as much. Choose roof prism or porro, center focus or individual, high power or low – all options are available at low and high prices. Pick features you want, then limit your comparisons to binoculars that have them. For all-around hunting or birding, I prefer 7x to 10x binoculars, roof prism or porro prism, with 30 to 42mm objectives, center focus adjustment and twist-out eyecups. Light weight is important, but not at the expense of optical quality. For extended glassing, I'll bear the extra weight of 50mm glass on a harness.

Mostly, price depends on what you see through the lenses. Compare binoculars in natural light by looking into shadows and back-lighting to find tiny detail. You can't test for ruggedness, so you'll have to rely on a warranty. The best optics have lifetime warranties; Zeiss's is even transferable.

Below are some good binoculars priced below $900. Optics are often heavily discounted, so "street" price may be substantially less than the retail numbers shown (i.f. = individual focus).

Make and Model	Description	List Price
Bushnell Legend	8x42 roof	$455
	10x42 roof	479
Fujinon BFL	8x42 porro	470
	10x42 porro	480
Kahles 2000	8x42 roof	721
	10x42 roof	772
Minox	8x32 roof	439
	10x42 roof	549
Nikon E2	8x30 porro i.f.	731
	10x35 porro i.f.	801
Optolyth	8x45 roof	799
	10x45 roof	899
Pentax DCF WP	8x32 roof	655
	8x42 roof	780
	10x42 roof	900
Simmons Hydrosport	8x42 roof i.f.	220
	10x42 roof i.f.	236
Weaver Classic	8x42 roof	446
	10x42 roof	469
Zeiss Diafun	8x30 roof	480
	10x30 roof	549

This tripod attachment grips any standard binocular. It makes glassing more comfortable, effective.

A long time ago, a friend offered me a used binocular. I bought it. For many seasons thereafter, that binocular went with me to the mountains. It was a very good binocular, lightweight and sturdy. The optics were as bright and sharp as any available when it was made.

I've bought a couple more B&L Zephyrs. One went to a good friend, the late Jack Slack, icon at Leupold for many years. I still have the other. I don't use it because I would like to keep it in its as-new condition. The old Zephyr with the scratched lenses and chipped jacket and deerskin taped on the objective bells has been replaced in my hunting kit with newer glass. But it is still my best binocular buy.

Used optics can be great bargains for three reasons. First, high-quality binoculars, riflescopes and spotting scopes are built to last a long time, and the moving mechanisms are not high-speed or subject to rapid wear. Secondly, pre-owned glass sells at a much bigger discount than, say, used rifles. Finally, most optics get little use in the field. Only hunting guides and a few dedicated sportsmen and birders carry their binoculars enough to cause even cosmetic wear. Except for abuse (crushing optics under duffle, dropping them on rocks and garage floors, staining lenses with oil or drying them with gritty clothing), outdoor glass is more durable that it needs to be.

There was a time not long ago that more than half the scopes on my rifles had come to me second-hand.

Save for the technological improvements evident in the newest scopes, those old models are as good as any in the rack. I've had no malfunctions from used riflescopes, or from my used binoculars.

Here are a few things to keep in mind when shopping the second-hand market.

1. Look in local newspapers, and visit gun shops to find second-hand optics. Used guns are often over-priced because the common belief is that age equals "collector value." Not so with optics. Some fine glass may be owned by people who have no idea what it cost to begin with, or how it ranks in quality or scarcity with other optics. My Bausch & Lomb 7x35 Zephyr was a gun show buy. I bought it for $100; it was 20 years old. Optics dating that far back now won't be as bright as new models, because lens coatings have been much improved. But sometimes the price of an old scope or binocular will be so attractive that performance comparisons with the latest models become meaningless. I'll buy all the Zephyrs you'll sell me for $100!

2. Get the instruments in your hands. Use the same routine as when you examine new products. Look into the shadows at dusk, steadying the instrument against a support so you can check the resolution. Look to the edge of the glass for color aberrations or field curvature. You'll find the image deteriorates a little as you move it out of center. But it shouldn't fall apart. Look toward (not at!) the sun, noting how the wash of backlight begins to erode detail. Check eye relief by easing your eye closer to and farther from the ocular lens. You want generous eye relief in a scope, and as much latitude as you can get – recognizing that scope engineers must

Seeing animals up close is reward enough for toting a binocular.

Individual focus is going out of vogue because it's slow. But mechanically it's a strong design.

balance eye relief with field of view. Next, move your eye side to side, then up and down behind a scope to see if there's excessive reticle shift (parallax). Be aware that no scope is parallax-free at all ranges. Typically, a riflescope without an adjustable objective is set for zero parallax at 150 yards or so (closer for rimfire and shotgun scopes).

3. Finish wear doesn't mean a scope or binocular has been abused, but it degrades the appearance. While scope tubes can be re-anodized, you probably won't want to have that done. On a well-worn rifle, a scarred scope may look right at home, but on a new rifle, it will have all the appeal of a broken windshield on a new car. Even like-new scopes can look out of place. Matching scope finish to the rifle was never a problem when all rifle steel was polished and blued and scopes had a shiny dark anodizing. But with the growing popularity of matte blue and stainless steel, and with scope and ring finishes in matte and silver as well as black gloss, you may look hard to find a scope that seems to fit the rifle.

4. Consider not only what you want, but what you'll accept. If you want a Swarovski, will you take another brand? Knowing in advance about comparable scopes might net you a great bargain. If you don't know retail prices for the type of scope you want, or haven't examined a competitor's scopes, you can't appraise what you'll find. Limiting yourself to one brand can extend your search unnecessarily. On the other hand, there may be a difference in bell and turret spacings that limits your options for mounting a scope. You should know the ring spacing you want, as well as maximum allowable diameters for ocular and objective bells. Big bells can force you to use higher rings. I'm less concerned with instrument design than some people are. Even magnification is negotiable. If I'm looking for an 8x42 roof prism binocular, I'll consider a 7x35 porro prism. Shopping for a 4x scope, I'll look at 2-7x variables. I'm not so flexible on size, because in my experience, a glass that's a little too big or too small constantly reminds me that it's too big or too small. Likewise, my standards for lens quality and exit pupil diameter are pretty rigid. Your areas of compromise will likely differ. Think about them before you shop. If you're after a used scope, for example, how firm will you be on reticle choice? I'm easy to please because I prefer the popular plex. If you'd rather have a dot, the used market won't give you much choice. A few makers still offer a dot reticle at extra charge on new scopes, but you won't find as many dots – or the variety of reticles in used scopes – that I did in the 1970s. Changing a reticle is an option, but with some brands, the procedure is very costly. If you're looking for a scope of certain manufacture, contact the maker before you shop so you know how much a reticle change will cost when you find an otherwise-perfect sight with 13 stadia wires, a retractable post and a rangefinding grid from a field cannon.

5. Don't fall for a more expensive scope or binocular than you want just because it's available at a good price. A 30mm scope with a 50mm objective from one of the great European optics firms may seem a steal at half its retail price, but if it's not what you're looking for, you're doing yourself no favor buying it. Remember that you'll need 30mm rings, which cost more and are harder to

Pull-out or twist-out eyecups are replacing folding rubber. The rubber offers intermediate positions.

Traditional porro prism glasses aren't as trim as roof-prism binoculars. Weight is about the same.

find than 1-inch rings. Also, a scope must complement the rifle underneath it. A beautiful optical instrument that doesn't mate well with the rifle's purpose or design is best passed over.

6. When shopping, take a small bottle of lens solution and a soft cloth, to clean the outside lenses for close examination. Use a couple of drops and wipe each lens dry with gentle circular strokes. In good light, look closely for scratches. Those you find may not show up when you're looking through the scope or binocular, but they should affect how much you pay – if indeed you want a sight

with a scratched lens. I don't. Check lens color. Coated lenses generally reflect straw, blue or green light. Colors vary by maker. Inside lenses do not show you their coatings, so you'll have to know the specs of a scope or binocular to determine if every lens is coated, even if you see color from the outside. Except on red-dot sights, avoid *tinted* lenses. Tinting is done to enhance contrast between certain colors but also to add shelf appeal to the discount-store optics that carry it. You'll know tinting when you see it; it's like a coat of paint. You won't find tinting on the best scopes or binoculars.

7. Use your fingers. Adjust the focus and diopter rings on binoculars. Change parallax settings on riflescopes. Turn windage and elevation dials, reticle illumination knobs and scope eyepieces. If the scope is on a rifle, mark the initial settings so the owner doesn't have to recalibrate. Check the adjustment dials on riflescopes for evidence of abuse. Slots that are roughed up by an improper tool show that the owner was probably impatient as well as ham-handed. They may also indicate that at one time, the dial did not turn easily. I'm squeamish about jimmied dials, and I want the caps to spin on without fuss. Binocular and spotting scope focus adjustments should yield smoothly when you turn them. A gritty feel to a binocular wheel or diopter ring means the mechanism is dirty, loose or both. Some scopes (Leupold's Vari-X IIs, for instance) lack click detents. Neither they nor click-stop dials should show any take-up or slack. Make sure variable-power mechanisms move smoothly, and that variable scopes do not "track out" between power settings. To test tracking, clamp the rifle or scope in a vise and turn the power ring from high to low and back up again while watching the position of the crosswire on a distant spot. It should stay put.

8. Insist on seeing scope tubes under the rings. You'll almost surely have to move the scope in the rings to accommodate your shooting style, even if you intend to use the same rings. You'll want to know those ring screws are not seized or the ring holes stripped! Scratches and small dents from rings will show up as you change ring position. They rarely affect scope performance but should merit a discounted price. A crease under the front ring of a dovetail-type mount can mean the scope was used as a lever to turn the ring into place. That operation can put a lot of pressure on the scope tube and jeopardize the lens mountings inside. Deep dents from accidents on the mountain warn of possible internal damage. Check front and rear bell ends. A fellow I know dropped a nearly new scope on flagstone. The impact left only a small scuff on the rim of the ocular housing – but shattered the lens.

9. Flex a binocular around the pivot. It should seem tight but not rough or sticky, and should *not* loosen up as you flex it. Scrutinize

The normal place for a diopter adjustment is on the right barrel of a center focus binocular.

Fully multi-coated lenses earn their keep when you're glassing into the shadows at dawn.

binoculars for evidence of rough handling. You can't always see barrel misalignment when you look briefly through a binocular, but extended glassing will point it up. You'll get headaches as one eye tries to look one way and the other eye in a slightly different direction. Look away, and you'll find yourself refo-

cusing. Binoculars can be recollimated, but there's no telling at a glance how much correction will be needed or if the frame has been damaged.

How much should you pay for used optics? That depends on original retail price, whether or not the model is still manufactured, the age

and condition of the instrument, and the motivation level of the seller. It also depends on where you look. Pawn and gun shops are good places to start (ask about scopes on used rifles for sale). The periodicals Gun List and Shotgun News are other sources. While soaring prices of the best new optics have raised second-

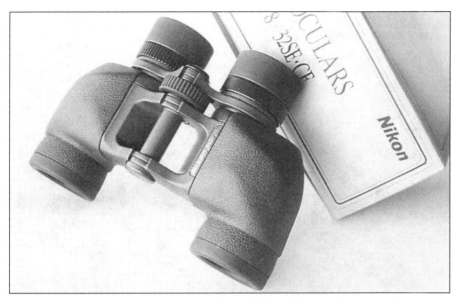
Nikon's 8x32 Superior E is one of the author's favorite hunting glasses.

Learning to look

Most of what we read about hunting optics is about hunting optics, not about using them. But the best instruments give you no edge if you don't use them well. Like an accurate match rifle in the hands of a tyro, or a fast race car operated by someone who's just learning to drive, top-quality glass can do nothing by itself.

A couple of years ago, hunting elk in central Washington, I climbed from dense cover to the brow of a thinly wooded hill. The opposite ridge was open, a logged area I wanted to glass. Eager to begin, I neglected to look into the draw below me. My focus was on a distant ridge when I heard an elk move close by. I dropped the binocular and flung the rifle to my shoulder just in time to see a bull trot into the timber only 80 yards away. He'd been standing in front of me for perhaps half a minute, watching me glass.

Rule No. 1: Glass close first. Game at a distance tolerates you longer than does game up close. Many animals far away won't even know you're glassing them. So you have more time to look, or ready yourself for a shot, when the range is long. A deer or elk you've startled at hip-shooting range may not bolt immediately. But if it holds tight, you'll have limited time to spot it and make the shot. Concentrate on the cover around you as you move toward a place from which you'll glass. Remember that high places that help you see far appeal to animals like mule deer for the same reason.

Another time, I'd crested a ridge that snaked up to a bare peak. Below me, dawn's light brightened clumps of whitebark pine, scattered on a hillside that had produced many bucks. After methodically working my binoculars from one patch of cover to the next, I stopped to rest my eyes and glanced casually uphill. On the face of the peak, climbing silently to safety, was the deer I thought would be near cover. I wrapped my arm into the sling and, from the sit, found the buck in my scope. One shot from the .270 dropped him.

Rule No. 2: Use your unaided eye to update yourself often on the "big picture." Powerful optics help you see into brush that hides game, to spot the glint of an eye, nose or antler. But focusing on detail blinds you to peripheral things. You can't

hand prices in the last decade, you can still get pre-owned glass in nearly-new condition for less than wholesale. What you may or may not get with the used product is a manufacturer's warranty.

Not long ago, I went bargain hunting for optics, specifically for a high-quality binocular. I started at the top, with one manufacturer. I asked about "blems," those slightly imperfect units that can't really go on the dealer's shelf but to the untrained eye have no defect. I was told that, sorry, there were no blems of that model available – meaning I should have called before Uncle Sam mailed tax refunds to the company employees.

The longer you look, the more likely you are to find what you want. Bargains will come quicker too, if you're looking for something that's common and not of blue-blood lineage. When I was growing up, you could buy used Weaver K-4 scopes for next to nothing. It wasn't that K-4s were inferior or that they wore out. Indeed, some hunters preferred them to all others, and no one questioned their iron durability. But Weavers were affordable and thus widely owned. When improved lens coatings, sealed tubes and constantly centered reticles appeared, Weaver was one of many optics firms adopting the new technology. The competition – Leupold and Redfield and Bausch & Lomb in those days – established itself as solidly as Weaver had decades earlier. A market hierarchy evolved, with Weaver remaining the scope of the working-class deer

hunter, while other makers played to other customers. The prestige associated with a brand name affected second-hand prices. The cost of used optics still reflects not only utility but perceived value.

Because high-end optics have become so expensive, many firms have tried to increase sales by adding entry-level and mid-priced lines. The new Zeiss Conquest riflescopes are an example. Meanwhile, firms that used to sell only mediocre optics have tried to upgrade their products and image. You thus have more choices but are no longer just "buying a name." It's important to look at features and prices. Insist on clear, complete explanations. If you don't understand the details, find someone in the company who can make them explicit.

The premium you pay for a respected name remains with the scope or binocular when it is resold. In fact, the less expensive optics seem to get cheaper relative to the blue-bloods when they change hands a second time. Inexpensive riflescopes on the used market commonly get treated like fourth-owner Yugos with 200,000 miles, charred valves and a bad clutch. I've found some of these scopes to be extraordinary bargains. So if you're looking for optics that will retain their value while giving you top-end performance, stay with the recognized leaders. If, on the other hand, you want a serviceable scope or binocular at a price so low it should be illegal, look at glass produced for the masses. And use that tax refund on ammunition.

Glassing in Washington's Blue Mountains, the author looks to timber's edge for elk.

see outside your field of view; even obvious movements escape notice. I spend about 70 percent of my time "in the glass" and 30 percent studying country around me with my naked eye. Dropping my binocular every minute or so gives my eyes a rest and enables me to spot game sneaking away.

A friend of mine carries small glasses and holds them with one hand, panning his surroundings each time he stops walking. Another fellow hauls a ponderous 8x56 binocular in his daypack, and takes it out only when he sets up for a lengthy glassing session. You're smart to compromise. A binocular should be light and compact, so you can hang it from your neck. That way, you'll use it often.

Rule No. 3: Carry a binocular that gives you a useful image but that leaves you fresh after a hard day in rugged country (my own weight limit: 30 ounces). Equip it with a durable, supple strap

A binocular is more important than a rifle-scope, though you're smart to buy high quality in both.

These Simmons porro prism glasses are offset vertically, not horizontally.

adjusted (or knotted) so the ocular housings just clear your chin when you lift the instrument. Magnification of 7 or 8x will allow you to glass comfortably without a rest, an advantage when you're on hillsides or in brush. Still, a rest helps; high magnification makes it mandatory. Glassing on the move, while better than not glassing at all, gives you just a cursory look at your surroundings. Serious hunters don't glance at promising cover; they examine it. Stopping to look hard can save you walking and show you game you'd not see if you hunted close to it.

Last fall, I was poking along a trail in lowland brush, hoping to spot a whitetail. I did – but not before it saw me and crashed away. I caught a glimpse of antlers, but there was no shot. This deer had seen me before I saw it partly because it had been still. How many times have you seen a deer or elk scan cover by moving its head? But few hunters take the hint. They swivel their heads like the ship captains in World War II movies whose binocular fields, in some miraculous way, move without the slightest quiver across your TV screen – despite pitching seas and booming 16-inch guns.

Rule No. 4: When you look, move only your eyes, not your head or the binocular. Steady the glasses by holding them firmly with both hands. The patch of hillside in your field of view shouldn't be abandoned

until it's wrung out. I do this by reading each field as I would a book, from left to right, top to bottom. Then I move the binocular to another "page." Page sequence is from top left to bottom right, unless there's a particularly promising piece of cover I want to investigate. This grid-pattern looking gets boring, but it's the most thorough way to examine a sector. If you become weary or inattentive, rest. But don't give up until you're satisfied that there's no game to be seen!

Some years ago I bought a binocular for a good friend. He was delighted with the gift. One day that fall, we were atop a mountain and he asked to see my binocular, which was older but of the same make. He peered through it, then shook his head. "You need what you gave me. This glass is as clear as wax paper." I compared the two. My friend was right. Then I noticed my lenses were dusty. Using lens tissue and cleaning solution, I wiped them free of dust and stains. The picture suddenly got bright again.

Rule No. 5: Keep your lenses clean! It's foolish to pay hundreds of dollars for premium-grade optics, then let field debris make the image as dim as one you'd expect in a discount-store binocular. A lens-cleaning kit, with air bulb and brush, tissue and a small vial of solution, is cheap and lightweight. A damp soft cotton sleeve, or a facial or bathroom tissue, will do. Blow the loose dust

off first, and don't rub vigorously; dirt abrades. Clean only as often as you must. Protect the lenses from dirt and rain in the field by using lens covers or by buttoning your jacket over your binocular

One fellow I met on a hunt groused that his binocular wasn't as sharp as it once was, then shrugged and mumbled something about getting what he paid for. I took a peek. The lenses were almost clean, but they were not focused for my eyes. The focusing dials stuck; finally they yielded. The picture got better. "What did you do?" asked the man. Without a word, I handed him the binocular. "Wow!" he yelped. "They're like new!"

Rule No. 6: Check your focusing often. Dials can get bumped and spun during a hunt. Someone might fool with your glasses when you aren't around. And you'll use different focal settings as distance varies. If yours are individual-focus (IF) glasses, simply adjust each barrel while leaving both eyes open but holding your hand over the opposite objective lens. If your binocular has center focusing (CF), it will have one adjustable ocular ring, plus the center wheel. Adjust the center wheel first, again with both eyes open. Hold your hand over the barrel with the ocular dial. Then switch hands and focus the barrel wearing the dial. To adjust focus for distance, you must turn both rings on an IF binocular but only the center ring on a CF binocular. Use those adjustments! Don't make your eyes do all the work.

Like any device, a binocular benefits you only if you know what you're looking for. When a pickup stopped at one game check station a few years ago, it drew stares from everyone not used to seeing a dead mule with a tag on its leg. After an awkward silence, one agent strode over. "I'm guessing," he told the driver, "but I'll bet that's your first cow elk."

Rule No. 7: Know what you seek. While few hunters tag mules, many hunters don't have clear ideas of what they expect to see. Any preconception of what an animal should look like programs your eye to ignore images that don't conform. The "whole animal" mirage causes you to reject the conspicuous curve of a deer antler or the black belly-line of an elk as unimportant. To see more game, you must program your eye to register less of it. Search not only for pieces you'd recognize, but for colors, shapes and textures that don't fit into the background. Be alert to anything unusual, just as animals are attuned to discordant notes in the rhythm of the woods.

Knowing where to look is as important as knowing what to look for. "A deer's back comes up to your belly button," an old hunter told me once. "Look low." Deer backs and our belly buttons vary in elevation, but the advice is sound. Even experienced hunters miss deer because they look too high. An amigo who'd shot lots of deer once bet me that big mule deer measured 5 feet tall at the shoulder. I should have wagered.

Rule No. 8: Look first where game is likely to be, second where it might be, and don't look where it can't be. Time in the field will show you what bedding sites a deer prefers, where it eats and what paths it travels. Pay attention to slope and aspect. Not only may these determine soil type and vegetation; they can make a hillside either attractive or unfit for game. Deer and elk avoid steep slopes except when pushed. East-facing slopes warm up first each day; south slopes are more open than north ones. Type of cover is important: High canopies offer no food and block sunlight so brush and grass can't grow. But mature forests provide shelter from snowstorms, and shade at midday in autumn.

"Take a photograph of anything without light," said the fellow at the lecturn. "And you'll get a photo of darkness." That simple observation also applies to hunters: Without light, there's no game to hunt. Like cameras, hunting optics can only manipulate images. What we see is what light shows us. To make the most of the light available, it's best to put it in your back pocket – that is, look with the sun behind you. Then the sun is a spotlight, shining into the eye of your quarry while giving you the clearest, sharpest picture possible. Wind direction and terrain can force you to look into the sun or across its rays. To spot animals in their beds, you may have to glass mostly into the shadows where sunlight is locked out. But planning your hunt to better use light can help you see.

Rule No. 9: Make the sun work for you by keeping it behind you or looking from shadows where your eyes are protected from glare. Remember that game is also looking for you, so glass from a place that hides your outline. If you must peer into shadows from front-lit places, rest your eyes frequently. Your spotting scope should have a sunshade; if it does not, tape a piece of black cardboard on the objective housing. Look down when you can, because it's easier on your eyes than looking up. That means hunting high – and being alert, because game is more alarmed by a threat from above than by one from below. Engineer your hunt so you'll be at good glassing places at dawn and dusk, when you'll want to look for long periods.

Chapter 6

These People
Help You See

"…quality is our most important product."

Leupold:
America's
best-loved scope

AMERICAN SHOOTERS LUST after Leupold scopes. At least, they buy a lot of them. Would they switch to European models if the prices were lower? Some would. But many would not. You can ogle a Lamborghini from behind the wheel of your Ford pickup without wanting to make the trade. Leupold is the name many stateside shooters equate with both high quality and practicality. The Beaverton, Ore., firm covets that reputation.

Leupold's late vice president, Jack Slack, admitted to me in an interview a few years ago that the firm actually targets a narrow market: "We don't try to make scopes everyone can afford; we just make the best scopes affordable." How does that philosophy sell? A recent survey reported in *The Sporting Goods Dealer* requested dealers nationwide to list the brand names they felt "best help with their overall performance" in the marketplace. There were many categories, from fishing gear to arrows to shotguns. In riflescopes, Leupold was No. 1.

The reasons for Leupold's popularity are on file at the firm's 90,000-square-foot facility just west of Portland. Dozens of letters from satisfied users and dealers confirm the com-

pany claim that Leupold scopes are among the most fog-proof.

A Pennsylvania dealer wrote: "I have been selling your scopes exclusively for the past 10 years, for the simple reason that I have never had a Leupold scope returned …. [Since the disastrous Johnstown flood,] 260 guns have been brought into my shop [with] 90 to l00 scopes. Not one of the Leupolds was filled with water or fogged up in any way. In fact, I took the Leupold scopes off the rifles and washed them off with the water hose and they were all in as good a shape as the day they came out of the box … Yesterday a customer brought into my shop [a Leupold] that had been buried under tons of mud … it was still in perfect condition."

Another Johnstown dealer with an analytical bent and 1,585 scopes in stock found that "of these, 828 (52 percent) fogged; Brand A — 168 of 455 (37 percent); Brand B — 344 of 515 (67 percent); Brand C — 3ll of 311 (100 percent); Leupold — 5 of 304 (2 percent)."

Legendary dependability combined with stylish exteriors, bright optics and clever marketing aimed at sophisticated shooters have helped Leupold scopes establish and maintain its lead in a competitive industry. A handful of manufacturers, here and abroad, have challenged Leupold for its piece of the upper U.S. scope market, but with limited success.

Frederick Leupold hailed from Germany, where around the turn of the last century he was trained in an instrument manufacturing plant. After immigrating to the United States, he went to work for C. L. Berger & Sons, a Boston firm

This thick-walled aluminum stock at Leupold's plant is scope-tube material.

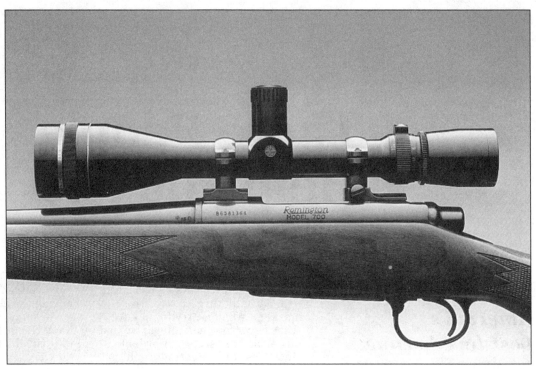

This 3.5-10x AO Varmint scope has target knobs. Sleek lines are a Leupold trademark.

that built surveying instruments. Searching for a new place to establish his own enterprise, Leupold landed in Portland, Ore. There, with financial help from brother-in-law Adam Volpel, the 27-year-old machinist opened a one-man shop in 1907. Specializing in the repair of surveying and drafting equipment, Leupold built a business that soon outgrew the fourth-floor room of the old Phoenix building on the corner of 5th and Oak.

In 1911, the young man received from Germany a new dividing machine, one that would make precise graduated circles on surveying instruments. Unfortunately, street vibrations compromised its accuracy. About that time, a fire elsewhere in the building caused smoke damage to the Leupold shop. Fred Leupold moved his operation to a residence near his home at Northeast 70th Avenue. Continuing to work long hours at the new shop, he pursued a wide range of avocations. He read prodigiously, learned to play the flute, studied Spanish, cultivated a stunning flower garden. But for the appearance of one other man, Fred Leupold might have remained simply a mechanic with a successful survey-instrument business.

John Cyprian "Jack" Stevens, born in 1876 near Moline, Kan., earned a degree in civil engineering at the University of Nebraska. In 1902, he began work for the U.S.

Geological Survey in Nebraska, then moved to the Pacific Northwest, where he became a district engineer for the USGS. In 1910, he turned his inventive mind to hydrologic instruments, leaving government employment to start his own civil engineering practice.

Stevens saw the need for a water-level recorder that could operate unattended much longer than the eight-day interval covered by recorders then in use. He invented a recorder that needed checking only a few times a year – a blessing to hydrologists using the recorders in remote places. To get his Type A Recorder into production, Stevens concluded a royalty agreement with Leupold & Volpel. A year later, in 1912, he went to Spain to help with the construction of hydroelectric dams and plants. Stevens returned to Portland in 1914, when he became a partner in the company that had marketed his invention and would now be known as Leupold, Volpel & Co. The Type A Recorder would remain in active service throughout the world for the next 50 years.

As America's electric utility industry grew during the 1920s, so did Leupold, Volpel & Co. A steady, if unremarkable, rate of growth sustained the instrument firm through the depressed '30s. During the leanest times, working hours were reduced, but none of the 40 employees were laid off. Jack

Stevens continued to invent new hydrologic devices, one of which, the Telemark, was years ahead of its time. Developed in 1937, the Telemark was a water-measuring instrument operated by a float and connected to a telephone in such a way that when the phone was activated, it produced an audio signal revealing the water level.

In 1940, Adam Volpel died. Two years later, the company name was changed to Leupold & Stevens Instruments, and operations moved to a bigger building at Northeast 45th and Glisan Streets. Rapid growth prompted the addition there of a second story – just in time for the Second World War. Leupold & Stevens Instruments became a subcontractor for bomb fuses and a prime contractor to the Maritime Commission for sextants and peloruses. When Fred Leupold died in 1944, company management fell to Fred's sons Marcus and Norbert, and Jack Stevens' son Robert. The three men were already part of the firm; all three were destined for active roles in its future.

Norbert Leupold had earned a civil engineering degree from Oregon State University in 1929. After working for two electric utilities and the engineering firm of Stevens and Koon, he joined the U.S. Army Corps of Engineers in 1934. Nine years later, he became part of Leupold & Stevens, and in 1972 was appointed board chairman.

Leupold & Stevens grew into this facility in 1942; shortly thereafter it was making bomb fuses.

Robert Stevens did a stint for publisher P.F. Collier & Son after graduating from the University of Oregon in 1935. He joined Leupold & Stevens in 1939, then managed its advertising business. A Navy man during the war, he became president of Leupold & Stevens in 1972.

Though both these young men were drawn to the out-of-doors, it was Marcus Leupold who steered the company into the scope business. Having

joined Leupold & Stevens in 1914, Marcus pursued a music career in his spare time. He played piano for the Portland Junior Symphony during the 1920s and there met his future wife. When he was 22, Marcus turned down a music-teaching job at the University of Oregon to commit his working life to Leupold & Stevens. In 1949, he became company president, and 20 years later chairman of the board. Marcus died in 1975.

The telescopic rifle sight was still a new thing in dustbowl days – new and unsophisticated. Legend has it that Marcus missed an easy shot at a deer one autumn and was so disgusted with his scope that he vowed to build a better one. Whether the scope was to blame is moot: Leupold & Stevens had struck another course.

During World War II, Marcus and company engineers developed that

Marcus Leupold, Fred's son, started development of the company's first scope, the Plainsman, just after World War II. He became Leupold's president in 1949 and died in 1975.

The late Jack Slack, here with a pronghorn, took an active role in scope development at Leupold.

better scope, announcing it as the Plainsman in 1947. A worthy product, its adjustment mechanism was still not airtight, and damp weather caused fogging. The crew redesigned the scope without internal adjustments, reducing but not eliminating its tendency to fog.

War technology provided the real answer. To keep sighting optics clear on Merchant Marine vessels, engineers had evacuated the air from each scope, replacing it with nitrogen. The nitrogen prevented fogging. In 1949, Leupold & Stevens became the first American manufacturer to market riflescopes with nitrogen-filled tubes. At the same time, they were the first to manufacture scope tubes and bell housings that were leakproof. That year, Leupold & Stevens Instruments became Leupold & Stevens Instruments Inc., adding financial strength and flexibility to the firm. On assuming the company presidency, Marcus told his peers: "Quality is our most important product."

By the early 1950s, Jack Stevens had patented 17 hydrologic devices. In 1953, he suffered a stroke. Though he subsequently recovered, his productivity at the firm was impaired.

In 1960, Leupold & Stevens sold its line of forestry surveying instruments (including compasses and hand levels) to devote more energy to its riflescopes. Eight years later, it moved headquarters to Northwest Meadow Drive in Beaverton. The workforce then exceeded 150 – and was growing fast. In 1977, a 38,000-square-foot addition gave the company more than half again as much space at the new facility; still, in four years another 5,500 square feet were necessary. By 1982, Leupold & Stevens had expanded its scope line to 30 models. It was also selling several types of binoculars and (beginning in 1969) John Nosler's Partition bullets. Annual receipts topped $25 million; employees numbered more than 500.

These years of rapid growth brought many new products. In 1962, Leupold & Stevens announced its Duplex reticle, with coarse outer wires for quick sighting, and finer wires at the center for precise aiming at small targets. It has been widely copied and is by far the most popular scope reticle now available. Two years later, the company installed a punishing test machine to ensure that every Leupold scope is watertight. It is still in use. No test in the industry is more demanding.

To make competition rifles more manageable, Leupold & Stevens designed, in 1974, the first lightweight, high-power target scope. Four years later, it announced a line of compact hunting scopes – another first. Since then, the company has engineered a strong and sleek "Dual Dovetail" scope mount, an improvement on John Redfield's 1916 design. Later a quick-detachable mount came along. Leupold & Stevens also developed the industry's first turret-mounted focusing (parallax-correction) system, as well as a 12-40x spotting scope that uses a mirror to reduce overall length and is as waterproof as any Leupold product.

Throughout the 1960s, the company's hydrologic instrument business flourished. Sewage flow meters, introduced in 1961, proved especially profitable. In 1970, the last vestige of Leupold & Volpel's original firm disappeared with the closure of the survey instrument repair and rental shop. But one year later, the company captured a share of another market with its digital traffic counter. In 1975, its sophisticated Print-Punch Traffic Recorder generated so much demand before its debut that formal introduction was delayed six months to allow for accelerated production.

Leupold's assembly room, a busy place, and very, very clean.

In March 1978, Leupold & Stevens acquired Transportation Data Corp. of Arlington, Texas. Assets were moved to Beaverton and helped Leupold expand its line of traffic counters. In 1983, Werner Wildauer, a German immigrant and graduate of the Gauss Institute of Technology, was named president and chairman of the board at Leupold & Stevens. Having been with the company since 1958, he used his leadership post to spur the development of new products, like porro-prism binoculars and spotting scopes. At his direction in 1984, the company bought Fabmark, a maker of sheet metal products. It bought Biamp, an audio systems firm, in 1985 – but quickly sold it when profits dipped.

In 1988, Leupold sold its Nosler bullet division back to the Nosler family. Bullet production had never moved from the Bend, Ore., plant (though Nosler advertising was done from Beaverton). In 1989, Leupold & Stevens moved Fabmark to a 40,000-square-foot factory in nearby Hillsboro.

Most shooters just say "Leupold" when speaking of the scopes with the distinctive gold ring. It's like saying Mercedes instead of Mercedes-Benz. Everybody knows what you mean. The "Stevens" part of the firm is very much alive – its hydrologic instruments have been installed in 92 countries worldwide – but the scope reputation is all Leupold.

Jack Slack came to Leupold & Stevens in 1953. An avid rifleman, Slack hunted with people like Jack O'Connor, who once told him that external scope adjustments would become obsolete. O'Connor also urged the standardization of a one-

Photo courtesy Leupold

This sextant was produced by Leupold & Stevens during World War II.

Leupold engineer Forrest Babcock adjusts a test fixture in the laboratory.

There's plenty of sophisticated electronic gear in the Leupold laboratory. Some of it is mounted on a table with pneumatic legs that damp the least bit of floor vibration.

Down in the machine shop, there's less optical voodoo and more noise, as 25 automatic lathes make scope parts, and a 10-ton hydraulic broach spits out precisely-shaped scope mounts. "We don't have to match ring halves," Slack told me at my first visit. "Every one is so perfect, it will mate exactly with any other."

While Leupold scope tubes were once made from pieces of light-weight alloy threaded together, a new process with state-of-the-art CNC (computer, numerically controlled) machines allows for the machining of a one-piece scope tube. Slack showed me the thick-walled stock to prove it. At the CNCs, I watched as a perfectly formed scope shell emerged, the turret cut with the detail you'd expect from an engraver in a London gun shop. The innards are added in bright, surgically clean rooms, where each finished scope gets a trip to the pressure tank. Submerged in 120-degree water, the scope is purged of air. Bubbles mean leakage and instant rejection. Then it's on to the "guillotine," a bruising device that jerks the scope with more Gs than an elephant rifle. A sampling of scopes goes to the basement range and loading room, so company

inch scope tube. (Before the war, scopes ranged from 7/8 inch to nearly 1 1/4 inches in diameter.)

Slack, a careful listener, took O'Connor's wisdom to Leupold's board room. Subsequent "Pioneer," "Mountaineer" and "Westerner" scopes became prototypes for the famous "M8" fixed power and "Vari-X" variable scopes that American shooters now covet.

Jack Slack later married Marcus Leupold's daughter, Georgia, and spent many fruitful years with the company. He helped design several flagship products. While Slack admitted that the reintroduction of Lyman's famous "Alaskan" scope did not get the reception he'd hoped, the company's Vari-X IIs and Vari-X IIIs have become by far the most popular big game hunting scopes in the mountains of the western U.S. In surveys I've run for the Rocky Mountain Elk Foundation, 3-9x Leupolds showed up on more elk guns than all other 3-9x variables combined! Slack also scored a bullseye with Leupold's compact scope line.

Leupold's research is carried out in-house by an able team of engineers. I interviewed one of them, an unassuming fellow with an inventive mind and an uncompromising eye. Forrest Babcock is also a scrounger. One machine in his lab looks like a big hollow ball. It's for measuring the incident light reflected inside the riflescope – a great detriment to bright, sharp

images. The ball is white inside to reflect the glow of a high-intensity light all around the scope, whose objective bell fits into a window in the ball. Opposite the scope is a black spot the size of the scope field, so any light coming to a viewer's eye through the scope is unwanted. Impressive!

"That ball came cheap," Babcock said. "It was one of those big orange balls you see on high utility wires to warn off airplanes."

One-hole groups, and photos of Jack Slack with John Jobson, grace a Leupold bulletin board.

shooters can put them through more practical paces.

Leupolds get plenty of field tests, too. One Canadian hunter lost his rifle in 9 feet of water when his canoe swamped. Weeks later he dug it out of the gravel. The action was welded shut by sand and rust, but the Leupold scope had not fogged or leaked!

Another Leupold, lost by a hunter in a lake, was recovered five years later by a fisherman. The rifle was "in poor condition," but the scope was still usable!

Not all testimonials involve water. An Alaska hunter watched his horse fall 400 yards down a rock slide, his rifle wrenching free of the scabbard. The horse rolled on it several times, but at the bottom, while horse and gun were badly bruised, the Leupold scope had not even shifted zero!

Another loyal fan testified: "One [of my Leupolds] was buried under 12 feet of mud from the 1980 Mt. St. Helens eruption. I dug it out of my destroyed home, cleaned it up, and it works very well."

Most riflemen concede that Leupolds are good scopes. But the devotion of some to this brand borders on fanaticism. An unusually comprehensive warranty no doubt contributes: "If any Golden Ring product is found to have defects in materials or workmanship, we will, at our option, repair or replace it. Free. Even if you're not the original owner. No warranty card is required. No time limit applies."

This Leupold scope has a stainless finish, which is increasingly popu-

That warranty has been tested:
"Two weeks later I got the scope back [at] no charge."

"You repaired and returned the scope in like-new condition. I fully expected an invoice...."

"We were shocked ... to see there would be no charge."

"In both cases, payment for the service was declined [and repair] was completed in 15 days or less."

As careful as I am with my rifles, I thought I'd never have to test Leupold's warranty. But in Alberta, as I climbed a hill on foot with a horse in tow, the animal fell and rolled down the steep slope. My rifle was still in its scabbard at the bottom, but the 3x scope's ocular housing was so badly bent that I couldn't open the bolt.

Leupold's repair was quick. On the blank invoice: "A good story. Next time choose another horse."

Sharp optics, reliability, good looks and a warranty that can be taken at its word. These are reasons Leupold can claim a customer satisfaction rate of 99.8 percent, why more benchrest shooters use Leupolds than all other brands combined, and why custom rifles and outfitters' rifles and the rifles used by published outdoor writers often wear Leupolds.

Preferences can calcify if not exercised. "I own 18 Leupold scopes," wrote one customer. "If it isn't a Leupold it isn't a scope." While some shooters no doubt disagree, the Beaverton company that started life as a repair shop for survey instruments is working hard to keep that view alive.

Like many of Leupold's test devices, this one was built largely in-house.

Leica: From the men in lab coats

The chance that you'll run into someone with Leica optics in the woods is probably not much greater than the odds that you'll see a bigger buck than you've ever seen before. Leica doesn't make riflescopes, and its binoculars cost more than most hunters are willing to pay. Its cameras, also very expensive, are at once an industry standard and far less popular here than Japanese models.

The first people to use Leica optics weren't hunters at all. Leica got its start building microscopes. It still manufactures them, in an impressive facility in Wetzlar, central Germany. When a few years ago I visited the Zeiss plant, also in Wetzlar, I had no time for a Leica tour, or to see the new Leica factory in Solms, 10 miles to the west, where the firm now assembles its binoculars, cameras and spotting scopes. Leica's 1988 move to Solms gave the company about 100,000 square feet of floor space, putting design, manufacture and warehousing operations under one roof.

Leica's rise to prominence in the optics industry paralleled the development of cameras. As early as the Middle Ages, the idea of recording imagery with instruments challenged inventors. Cameras preceded by centuries the chemical fixing of photosensitive paper. In 1826, a Frenchman, Nicephore Niepce, hit upon a way to preserve photographic images. Nine years later, Englishman William Henry Fox Talbot duplicated the feat. Both men kept their findings secret, as did the Frenchman Daguerre, who developed his process in 1837.

In August 1839, Daguerre went public with his work. It earned him a fine pension from the French government, which offered the method to the world. But not everyone could take advantage of it. Making daguerreotypes required a bundle of heavy equipment, plus a dark place to process plates. Talbot's calotype process, and "wet collodium" photography were equally taxing. A complete outfit, with camera, tripod, plates, trays and chemicals could weigh 130 pounds. During the mid 19th century, photographers were specialists, lugging their equipment to county fairs to generate business, and in the U.S. recording the settlement of the West from wagons on military expeditions.

The idea of more portable cameras came close on the heels of Daguerre's work. In December 1839, August von Steinheil invented a camera with a format or frame size of 11 x 8mm – roughly, 1/2 inch by 1/3 inch. Neither this nor the many similar attempts that followed made much headway at market until after the turn of the century.

In 1871, English physician Richard Maddox invented the dry plate. Unlike earlier plates, this silver-bromide-coated glass did not

Minox is Leica's mid-priced brand. This 8x32 is a fine glass for the deer woods.

Leica had some scopes assembled at the Leupold plant, but the relationship didn't last.

have to be developed immediately after a photo was taken. Any number of plates could be stored for several days and developed at once when the photographer returned to a darkroom. Even more significant was the announcement, in 1881, of a $25 camera. Designed by American George Eastman, it held 100 frames. To take a photograph, you pulled a string, pressed a button and cranked a winder. After you'd exposed all the film, you sent the camera, or "Kodak" to Eastman's company. A few days later you got prints, plus the camera loaded with a new roll of film – all for $10! But Eastman's camera was quite bulky. Because negatives of that day could only be used to make contact copies, the film had to be as big as the finished photo.

Not long before the Great War, Oskar Barnack, director of the research department at the Ernst Leitz microscope plant in Wetzlar, began work on a small-format camera. An asthmatic, Barnack knew that other photographers also objected to the size and weight of contemporary cameras. He wanted one that needed no tripod, could be held in one hand and had plenty of film capacity.

After experimenting with 35mm movie film, Barnack designed a camera that featured a retractable lens of 42mm focal length, a focal-plane shutter with 40mm opening, a winder for single-frame advance and a 40-frame counter. In 1914, the new

camera recorded troop mobilization in Europe; in 1920 a catastrophic flood that swept through Wetzlar. In 1924, Ernst Leitz placed Barnack's camera in the company product line. A year later, at the Leipzig fair, the new camera with its 35mm film and strikingly sharp prints amazed people who had the notion that good photos came only from big film.

Still, many photographers thought the new 35mm too small a format. The pocket-size camera didn't look serious. But people at the Lietz facility had other ideas. They improved on Barnack's camera, announcing in 1930 the Leica I, with its threaded mount for interchangeable lenses. Two years later, the Leica II appeared, with a built-in rangefinder. The Leica III that came along in 1933 had shutter speeds as low as one second. By 1940, a die-cast body and one-piece top cover had been added.

You might say that during the 1930s, the snapshot was born. Leica's new interchangeable lenses, with focal lengths ranging from 28 to 600mm, gave photographers unprecedented flexibility. The Carl Zeiss firm proved stiff competition when it introduced the Contax camera in 1932. Kodak followed two years later with its budget-priced Retina.

At Leitz, war halted development of a bayonet mount, something the firm had been working on since 1936. But in 1954, the M3 camera appeared, with the bayonet feature

that was to become an industry standard. The M3 had a hinged back, a "brightline" viewfinder that showed the image area, a more precise rangefinder, shutter speeds from one to 1/1000 second and a film counter with an automatic reset. It was not only a costly camera to build but represented a huge investment in research. Still, its stiff price did not deter photographers. The new camera proved as popular as beer and bratwurst.

Leica hedged its bets with a new screw-in camera in 1957, but the M3 obviously had a future. During the 1950s the MP, M2 and M1 appeared as variants. In 1967 Leica brought out the M4, featuring a fast-loading takeup spool and foldout crank. The M4-P, which came 10 years later, accommodated a motor drive. In 1971, Leica unveiled the M5, the first rangefinder camera in the world with selective through-the-lens light metering. Two years later, Leica and the Japanese firm Minolta cooperated to build the Leica CL, similar to the M5. As war memories dimmed in the 1960s, Japanese 35mm cameras captured a huge chunk of the 35mm market. Nikon, Canon, Pentax, Olympus and other makers offered serviceable cameras and lenses at attractive prices, prompting Ernst Leitz Wetzlar GmbH to transfer portions of its operations to Canada and Portugal, to reduce manufacturing costs. In 1971, Leica entered into a cooperative agreement with Minolta.

As this is written, Leica's flagship camera is the M6, a model startlingly similar to the one designed by Oskar Barnack before our Great Depression. More than 30 variations of this camera have been produced since Barnack's original. An M6 can seem frightfully expensive to young amateurs brought up on Kodak Instamatics and efficient Japanese SLRs. But Leicas are still costly to manufacture. The M6 rangefinder system has 104 components, including a beam-splitting prism and an achromat. The M6 offers the cachet many photographers covet, a precision that all can admire, the flexibility that accomplished hands and eyes can use to good advantage. The M6 accepts lenses of 21 to 135mm. Leica also manufactures single-lens-reflex cameras: the R6.2 and the R7, which accommodate lenses of 15 to 800mm focal length. A Leica mini II and mini zoom are available for people who want an automatic pocket-size camera that thinks for them.

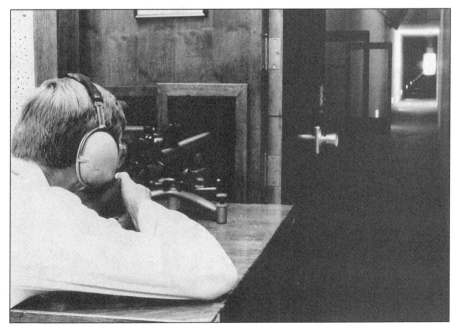

A shooting tunnel helps optics firms check scope adjustments under real-life conditions.

In 1986, Ernst Leitz Wetzlar GmbH was reorganized, and in 1988, Leica Camera GmbH appeared in Solms. On January 1, 1989, the Leica Camera Group assumed production and distribution of Leica cameras, lenses, binoculars, spotting scopes and projectors. Manufacturing facilities now include Leica Camera GmbH in Solms, Feinwerktechnik Wetzlar GmbH in Wetzlar, Leica Projektion GmbH in Braunschweig and Leica Aparelhos Opticos de Precisao S.A. in Vila Nova de Famalico, Portugal. Leica sales offices in Germany and France, Great Britain, Canada, Switzerland and the United States handle the distribution, along with more than 100 ad agencies. Of the firm's 1,400 employees, roughly 900 are based in Germany.

If you're a hunter, Leica catalogs have all the raw material for wish lists. Leica optics aren't budget optics. But then, there's not much to be said for budget optics. Saving money at the counter once can cost you in the field repeatedly.

One of the most impressive binoculars I've used is the Leica 10x50 Trinovid. Before I handled this glass, the Leica 8x42 had seemed to me a top choice for open-country hunting. The 8x has a slightly larger exit pupil (5.25mm, compared to 5mm), and it is less bulky. But the weight difference seems hardly noticeable, and the 10x50 brings out detail I can't see with its smaller brother. This is no criticism of the 8x. If you want a glass to probe the shadows as the sun sinks, you can't do better than the Leica 8x50, with a 6.25mm exit pupil. The newest Leica, a 12x50, is a top choice for glassing long distances in open country, or from deer stands across farmland. Its 328-foot field of view is nearly as great as that of the 10x (345 feet), and the 12x actually focuses closer – to only 10.7 feet. Birders should appreciate that flexibility.

Leica Trinovid and newer Ultra Trinovid binoculars aren't lightweight. The 7x, 8x and 10x models with 42mm objectives weigh 31.4 ounces apiece; the 8x50 and 10x50 scale 40.5 ounces. Even the compact 8x32 and 10x32 models exceed 23 ounces. To get a featherweight Leica, you have to accept the tiny exit pupils of the 8x20 and 10x25 glasses (they register a mere 8 ounces!). These binoculars work fine in good light, but to my notion no "mini-binocular" can match a full-size instrument for extended glassing or looking into shadows.

A lot of hunters would use Leica optics if someone else paid for them. Binoculars with the little red Leica emblem come dear. The 8x32 and 7x42 are the only hunting glasses priced shy of $1,000. The 8x and 10x binoculars with 42mm objectives cost $1,045 and $1,095; the 8x50 is $1,145, the 10x50 $1,195, the 12x50 $1,345. But binoculars aren't like hunting licenses that must be bought every year. Top-quality glasses will last as long as you do. If you amortize the cost of an expensive binocular over several years, per-season cost might not even match what you pay for gasoline to get to camp. Keep in mind that a race horse that wins commands a much higher price than one with a consistent record of second-place finishes, though the disparity in lap times might be small.

Should the IRS find you have overpaid for a couple of decades and are due civil damages as well as interest and principal, you'll find the Leica Geovid binoculars worth a look. The 7x42 Geovid BDA appeared in 1993. It featured both a compass and a rangefinder. The BD model, announced late in 1994,

Binocular magnification has increased of late, a benefit in mountainous country like this.

Scopes help beginning shooters aim easily – and give old eyes a chance to keep bullets in the bullseye.

In 1994, Leica introduced two spotting scopes: the Televid 77 and the Apo-Televid 77. They look the same on the outside, but the Apo-Televid has an extra lens element that enhances resolution and corrects for color aberration at high magnification. Leica's Televid retails for $895, while the Apo-Televid costs $1,395. Both models are available with straight and angled eyepiece assemblies. Eyepieces attach via bayonet mount without focus change. Dual focusing lets you focus quickly or precisely, and as close as 13 feet! The "T2" adapter turns either scope into a telephoto lens. The adjustable tripod base allows for vertical photo frames, too.

As an optics firm, Leica is solid, with deep roots. Recent sales have been steady, despite the strong Japanese competition and high costs of German production. As long as there are hunters and birders who want the very best optics and photographers who value tradition as well as quality, Leica glass will have a market.

Nikon: From photography to field optics

If you're old enough to remember bias-ply pickup tires and black and white televisions with dials, you may remember when Nikon didn't make riflescopes, binoculars and spotting scopes. In my youth, a Nikon was a camera. A good one.

is minus the compass – and 48 ounces lighter! It's also $1,000 less expensive than the BDA. To make the laser rangefinder work, you press a button, then place the red aiming device that appears in your field of view on any object as distant as 1,000 meters. Press the button again, and a laser beam shoots out to the object, bounces back and gives you an LED readout of the range in meters.

About as heavy as a standard 8x56 binocular, even the new 7x42 Geovid needs a harness. Your neck would soon look like a camel's if you hung this glass over your collar for a day in the mountains. It is hardly a necessary instrument, but if weight is not a concern and accurate range assessment is, you might find the $3,300 tab reasonable.

Then again, you might opt for a standard binocular and the lightweight LRF rangefinder that recently joined the Leica stable. At only 11 ounces with its 9-volt battery, it is easy to carry in a coat pocket. You get an accurate read (+ or – 1

yard) from 10 to 800 yards, with 7x magnification. The LRF 800 is affordable, too: just $449 at retail. To my mind, it is one of the best buys out there in rangefinders for hunters.

Nikon scopes are well known for their brightness.

News reporters used 'em. But nothing Japanese belonged in a hunting camp. I recall hearing of Dave Bushnell importing Japanese scopes to serve hunters who couldn't afford a Redfield. We laughed then.

You'll forgive our ignorance. That was before Sony and Toyota. Before Redfield collapsed and Bushnell earned its credentials with Bausch & Lomb. Now if you question Japanese optics, you'll still get laughs, but a different kind. Almost every (if not every!) optics firm in the world, including German and Austrian companies, has used Japanese lenses. And during the last few decades, binoculars and riflescopes assembled in Japan have made big headway in the American market.

Nikon is perhaps the most prestigious name in Japanese sports optics. Nikon F-series cameras were the workhorses of serious news paper journalists before American hunters had abandoned iron sights. In 1984, a fellow named Jim D'Elia cranked up the sports optics division of Nikon Inc. (formerly Nippon Kogaku) to pioneer new products for outdoorsmen. Now that division generates 10 percent of the huge company's income. More than half of sports-optics revenues comes from hunters. Jim D'Elia is still vice president in charge of the operation, and you'll never find him apologizing for Nikon optics!

Not that he has to. In all its 16 years, Nikon Sports Optics has hewed to high standards of quality. Its riflescopes carry a no-questions-asked guarantee: If you find a manufacturing defect in a Nikon scope, the company will repair or replace it free, even if you aren't the original owner. For binoculars, spotting scopes and field scopes (the premium-grade spotting scopes), Nikon charges a nominal $10 plus shipping for any repair not covered by its 25-year limited warranty – even if the damage is your fault!

Manufacturing takes place in Japan, Thailand and the Philippines. A few binoculars are produced in China. The most recent facility, a tremendous plant in Bangkok, was built specifically to manufacture Nikon cameras and lenses and the Monarch UCC riflescopes. The scopes are built from scratch there, with components made there. Jim is quick to point out that "all American-made scopes utilize lenses and other components sourced from various suppliers." He is proud of the flagship riflescopes that come from the Bangkok plant. "Every scope is impact-tested and leak-proofed before being boxed and shipped." It goes without saying that the lenses are fully multi-coated, the tubes turned from aircraft-grade aluminum.

Nikon's first riflescopes appeared in 1985. The Monarch UCC didn't come along for another 11 years, but even those first scopes were very good. I own a 4x Nikon from the mid-80s, and it is still one of my brightest scopes. The Monarchs are better because lens coatings have improved since that day, so you can expect better light transmission. Still, you may be hard-pressed to *notice* the advantage of Ultra Clear Coat except in very dim conditions. "That's one mistake a lot of hunters make when shopping for optics," said D'Elia. "They look through several scopes in good

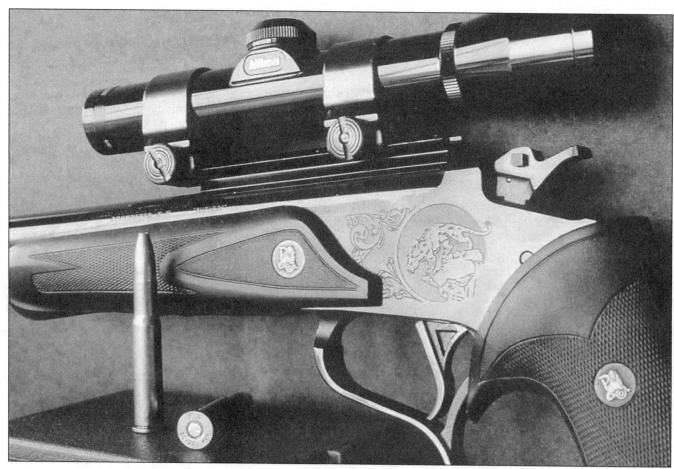

Nikon builds scopes with long eye relief, for use on pistols.

One of Nikon's latest scopes features a lightweight titanium tube.

of matte or gloss finish. The standard plex reticle (or fine crosswire in the big scopes) works fine. However, a dot reticle might also sell, and a mil dot almost surely would.

Like other optics firms, Nikon offers price alternatives, though it unabashedly steers clear of the "something for everyone" philosophy. "We aren't interested in competing at the lowest price points," D'Elia says. "But we do want to give hunters on a budget a good value. You can't get something for nothing, and you can't make a serviceable instrument for pennies. Our aim is to earn business in the medium- and higher-price arenas by giving customers the best product they can get for their money. Anywhere." For instance, the Buckmasters scopes, introduced in 1997, came along as modestly priced alternatives to the Monarchs. They have most of the Monarch features and are available in 4x40, 3-9x40, 3-9x50 and 4.5-14x40 versions. There's also an 800-yard Buckmasters laser rangefinder.

Sky and Earth spotting scopes appeared in 1995 to woo buyers who couldn't afford the top-rung Fieldscope (introduced in 1981, just before the Sports Optics Division got its charter). The Fieldscope gets plaudits from some pretty critical hombres. It's available with 60 or 78mm objectives, and a plethora of eyepieces. You can spend more to get ED (extra-low-dispersion) glass for images so perfect you'll think you got a new pair of eyes. The Sky and Earth scopes, incidentally, are not far behind; they've been given

light, see no difference, then buy either the cheapest or the one with the best-known name. In the field, they can be short-changed because they didn't test the scope under dim light."

D'Elia said that Nikon's biggest challenge in earning market share with American hunters is getting them to look beyond American brands and European reputations. "Nikon optics have set the standard in cameras for decades," he said. "We're committed to the same high level of quality in riflescopes, spotting scopes and binoculars. We work hard to give hunters the best value at every price point."

Nikon's Monarch UCC scope line includes about all the configurations you could want, except for a fixed 2½x or 6x. Praise be, the firm still offers a fixed 4x! The 2-7x32 is another of my favorites, a slim, bright, sturdy sight that has all the versatility you'll need for big game hunting. There's a 1.5-4.5x variable with a heavy plex reticle that Nikon calls a Sabot/Slug scope; it would also complement big game rifles. The 3-9x40 remains a top seller. The 3.5-10x50 is in my view less useful. High-power variables include a 4-12x40, 5.5-16.5x44 and 6.5-20x44, all with adjustable objectives. With most Nikon scopes you have a choice

Chief of Nikon's Sports Optics Division since its inception is New York executive Jim D'Elia.

high marks for optical quality and for my money rank among the best bargains out there. The Spotter XL is a 60mm 16-47x variable spotting scope that's waterproof and fog-proof and mid-range in price. Unique to Nikon is the Field Image System MX, combining a miniature CCD camera with a field scope and a color monitor. Align the scope with a target at the range, or with a big game animal or warblers in a nest, and back off. The monitor, connected to the CCD camera by cables, shows you on-screen what the spotting scope "sees." You can get up to 80x magnification with the 60mm scope, 100x with the 78mm. Cables can be connected to a video camcorder or VCR.

Nikon fields a broad selection of binoculars, including roof-prism and porro-prism models, big, little and mid-size. Some are downright inexpensive, some very costly. The company introduced its first mini-binocular in 1921 and hasn't abandoned that line. For hunters, however, there are better choices.

"Nobody does glass like Nikon," said D'Elia. Even if you think highly of other products, there's no denying that Nikon's Venturer LX 8x42 and 10x42 roof-prism binoculars are among the best field glasses ever made by anyone. They're expensive, but if you must have the best, you don't need to look elsewhere. The flat, sharp, bright image is instant proof. The less costly porro-prism Superior E (8x32 or 8x42) is one of the best values in binoculars – at least in my opinion. Friend Bill McRae, who also looks at lots of good binoculars, agrees. The SE is a light-weight glass with an image eerily like that of the Venturer.

D'Elia likes to explore new product possibilities. This past year, Nikon introduced a titanium scope. It weighs about the same as alloy but is much stronger. It is also much more expensive, and since I've not yet had a scope tube collapse, I'm unwilling to pay the extra tariff. Maybe some shooters will. Another recent Nikon product was a rangefinding scope that looked a lot like the Swarovski: substantial enough to mount on a half-track. I'm told that patent squabbles led to its quick demise. More promising is a laser rangefinder still in development as I write this. The lithium-powered instrument will be no bigger than a cigarette pack. It will apparently be made by Nikon in Japan, not contracted as is the case with so many rangefinders.

Nikon still makes some of the best 35mm SLR cameras available. Hunters and birders have come to appreciate that quality in binoculars and spotting scopes, and riflemen are having a tough time finding a brighter scope than a Nikon. Even among makers that use Japanese glass.

Redfield: An American icon

John Hill Redfield was no optics engineer. Born in a log cabin on the western frontier, he left school after grade 4 about the time a transcontinental rail trip first became possible. By the end of the buffalo-hunting era, he was shooting deer to supply workers on the Northern Pacific Railroad. He got 10 cents a pound plus the hides. As inventor and entrepreneur, Redfield bloomed late. His first accomplishment of historical note was the invention of

the Redfield Rock Drill, which he sold to miners in Washington State. He also took a turn as a Deputy U.S. Marshal in Washington's Yakima County, where his skill with guns became useful. He carried four bullet scars from that experience.

Redfield followed gold-seekers to Colorado in 1906, when he was 47. There he hawked his drill and continued his hobby of designing firearms. He fashioned a rifle with a delayed-blowback, autoloading mechanism in .25 Remington, a straight blowback pistol in .22 Short and a single-shot .38-55 rifle that shared features of the dropping- and rolling-block designs popular at that time. He also built a 12-gauge shotgun and began tinkering with rifle sights.

Soon Redfield was building improved rifle sights in his garage, mostly for friends. His wife helped him assemble the parts at night on the kitchen table. By 1909, the future of mining in the Rockies

Redfield built its business by giving big game hunters bright, rugged scopes.

Photo by J. R. Hunter

began to look grim. Redfield decided there was enough of a demand for his rifle sights to justify a commercial venture. To that end, he invested in more equipment and established the Western Gunsight Co. in his garage.

John Redfield quickly proved he could produce superior products – not just open rear sights, but fully adjustable receiver sights and front sights that gave marksmen a sharp aiming point. The Redfield Sourdough, with its flat, square, gold face angled up to catch skylight, is still among the most popular front sights ever made. It is my personal favorite – and that of many hunters who likewise find it superior to the rounded beads that reflect light off-center. The Sourdough is quick to pick up because it is big and bright, but it allows for precise aim because its edges appear as sharp to the eye as a blackened post.

During World War I, special U.S. Army units were issued scopes. John Redfield designed bases and rings to endure the rigors of battle, with a rotary dovetail arrangement that is still one of the strongest and simplest of attachments. Several other companies have copied the Redfield "JR" mount. I suspect that, in its various forms, it is now the most popular scope mount design with American hunters.

John's son, Watt, learned the business from his father and began building sights himself. An avid competitive shooter, he was largely responsible for development of the Redfield Olympic and International sights. I've used both and, like many target shooters, consider them among the most precise commercial sights ever built. For years they were arguably the best value available to serious target shooters. Some of the tightest groups I've shot in smallbore prone competition, including five-shot, 50-yard groups no bigger in diameter than a .338 bullet, were made with Redfield's International.

Watt fashioned many of the special tools, jigs and fixtures needed to expand what later became the Redfield Gunsight Co. When John Redfield died in 1944, Watt took the helm. Under his leadership, business continued to grow. In 1958, Redfield bought the designs and tooling to manufacture the Bear Cub scopes made popular by the Kollmorgen Optical Co. Two years later, Redfield was purchased by Ed Hilliard, who owned the firm until his death in a climbing accident in 1970.

During the 1970s, Redfield and other scope companies began focusing on variables. The potential was obvious, but sportsmen would not buy scopes whose reticles changed size or drifted off-center with a change in magnification. There was no use for a scope with a wandering zero, either. Redfield engineers solved these problems by moving the reticle from the first, or forward focal plane in the scope to the rear, or second plane. There the reticle did not move during changes in magnification; nor did it grow or shrink. This improvement helped ensure the market success of all variable scopes. Most American hunters still insist on a fixed-size reticle, though European shooters prefer reticles in the first focal plane.

In 1971, Redfield sold to Outdoor Sports Industries. In 1980, it changed hands again, to the Brown Group of St. Louis. The 1980s brought great technological improvements to the task of manufacturing riflescopes – which by then had relegated iron sights to only a token place in Redfield's business. Computer-controlled (CNC) machines turned out scopes faster and to closer tolerances than had earlier equipment. In 1983, a special lathe enabled the firm to produce a one-piece alloy tube, eliminating the possibility of leaks and weak joints that could plague multiple-piece bodies. According to Redfield engineers I've interviewed, the one-piece tube is up to 400 percent stronger than traditional tubes. News of this

Redfield played to the needs of woods hunters with its "Widefield" scope.

manufacturing coup at Redfield all but overshadowed the debut, also in 1983, of the firm's Tracker scopes, a modestly priced series. In 1985, Franklyn Schadrack bought Redfield from the Brown Group. His passion was high quality. He replaced the traditional line of Redfield scopes with the Golden Five Star family, the first Redfields to feature multi-coated optics.

During this time of rapid change in manufacturing technique, Redfield designers fashioned their own tools and machines for specific jobs. One was a "purge and fill" station that drained and "baked out" moisture from a scope tube while filling it with nitrogen to prevent fogging. But some of the old methods of manufacture, and the old components, remained. Redfield refused to use stamped internal parts in its scopes, insisting that only carefully machined components could guarantee the close tolerances needed for accurate adjustments and long scope life. Not only were such parts checked routinely; the tools were as well, to prevent dimensional changes before they showed up in finished products. A machine known as an optical comparator subjected parts

and tooling to 50x magnification so operators could find any flaws that weren't visible to the naked eye.

As in competitive shops, Redfield scopes were assembled under carefully controlled conditions. During assembly, each scope endured 115 checks. Then it had to pass final inspections and ride a recoil simulator that subjected the scope to 60 jolts a minute at forces approaching 1,300 Gs. After chilling out in a freezer at 0 degrees Fahrenheit, the scope was immediately dunked in 130-degree water. The sudden heat expanded the nitrogen inside, applying more pressure to the seals than they'd ever encounter during normal hunting use. If a leak showed up, the scope was immediately sent back for remanufacture.

Among Redfield's best-known scopes of that era were the Widefields, with the television-screen ocular lens. The Widefield offered the same field and eye relief possible with a round ocular lens whose diameter equaled the width of the Widefield's ocular. But the "squashed" profile may have allowed lower mounting on some rifles. And the perception of an extra-broad field surely sold scopes! Another sig-

nature product at Redfield during the 1980s was the Accu-Trac, a device to help shooters determine target distance and help them hit at long range. Accu-Trac evolved from the company's Accu-Range mechanism, which came along in 1965 as the first built-in range-finder for sporting riflescopes. Though Accu-Range lacked the trajectory-compensating feature that made Accu-Trac so popular with hunters, the U.S. Marine Corps considered it worthy of issue to snipers in the final months of the Vietnam War.

By the mid-1980s, Redfield was in the spotting scope trade, with six models. Franklyn Schadrack's desire to build a European-type riflescope resulted, in 1988, in the Ultimate Illuminator. Its 30mm tube and 56mm objective were formed from one piece of alloy. Redfield binoculars came along in 1990. The firm expanded its mounts to include Weaver-style bases and rings and see-through rings. Like other makers, it offered matte and nickel (silver or stainless) matte finishes on riflescopes and expanded the scope lines to accommodate pistoleers, shotgunners and riflemen who needed short-range parallax set-

"Buck" Buckner prefers classic rifles and traditional scopes like this Redfield variable.

tings for .22 rimfire shooting. Red-field also built a collimator.

In June 1995, Lester Jones became Redfield's president and CEO. Jones had worked 17 years at Federal Cartridge Co., leaving as vice president of sales and marketing. He also managed that firm's Champion Target division. Franklyn Shadrack, Redfield's outgoing president, sold his interest in Redfield to his partner, TCW Capital of New York.

Redfield's biggest riflescope of that time was a 6-24x Varmint Scope with an adjustable objective, target knobs and either a fine crosshair or 1/8-minute dot reticle. Its 50mm lens ensured bright images even at high power settings. These days, big game hunters are warming to such sights, despite their weight and bulk. Expectations of long shooting and a pre-occupation with small groups shot from a rest make a 6-24x salable, if not practical. On the other hand, 6x provides enough field and brightness for most hunting, and the high end lets you test the limits of your rifle

and load. I'll admit to shooting one buck at 410 yards with a scope set on 20x. The bullet hit exactly where I planned.

When I was busy competing on the smallbore prone circuit, my Red-field 20x Model 3200 scope helped clinch two state championships. This long, barrel-mounted sight was the first target scope from any commer-cial firm to feature internal adjust-ments. It was introduced in 1968, but I was just starting college then and had no extra money. I bought my scope a couple of years later, used, for $100. The 3200 stayed in production for a relatively short time; it was replaced by the receiver-mounted 6400. The number 3200, incidentally, corresponds to the possible score over a two-day prone match: 1600 points each for scope and iron-sight events. For the iron-sight stages, I relied on Redfield's International rear sight with an Olympic globe front and orange disk insert.

Other Redfield scopes I recall with some warmth had much lower magnification than that lovely 3200.

One was a 4x Bear Cub I mounted on an early Model 70 .30-06. It had a post, as I recall (posts were popular reticles during the '40s and '50s). That .30-06 became a favorite. It was one of those rifles that shot where you looked no matter how long you left it in the rack or what load you chose. Probably it wasn't exceptionally accurate. But the bul-lets seemed to have a nose for the forward ribs of deer.

Among its trophies was a buck I really didn't deserve. The opener had dawned warm, and by noon, the high rocks in Oregon's Wallowa Mountains were baking. The few mule deer I'd seen at first light had melted into conifer tangles on the steep slopes of Translator Ridge. Six hours of hard climbing had drained even my young legs. Wearily, I pulled myself up to a deer trail that snaked along a narrow bench into the wreckage of a few fat Douglas firs that had fared poorly against a rockslide. I was looking for a shady spot to eat some cheese and the last of my raisins.

Companies that help us see help us get the most from our time afield.

Just as I entered this tattered copse, deer hooves drummed their way out of the shadows. A couple of does and a little buck raced straight at me, and I stepped aside as they flew by on the trail. Memorable. But not the object of the hunt. I stopped a few steps farther on, in the middle of the patch, then decided to push through to the other side, just to see upslope along its edge. As soon as I emerged, I spotted him. He was a couple of hundred yards above me, just standing there. He may have been with the other deer and decided to use another exit; he may have been roused from his bed as they took flight. He seemed unsure of where he was and what was going on.

I sat down, snugged the sling and fired as soon as the post looked right. He crashed to the rocks, legs flailing, and bounced down the steep slide almost to me. There were seven points on one side, eight on the other – a better mule deer than I'd hoped to find. The old Bear Cub and the Winchester seemed to have a knack for making good fortune better.

The other Redfield I wish I still owned was a Golden Five Star 1-4x variable. It graced a Mark V Weatherby in .340 Magnum. The day I paired these two, I drilled minute-of-angle groups while clocking 250-grain Noslers at an even 3,000 fps. Elk would have to watch out.

Soft snow had fallen all night in the Wise River drainage of south-western Montana, giving hunters the first good tracking of the season. I was one of them, slipping the Weatherby out of its case in the dark while my breath smoked in the cold.

Before the eastern sky showed even a hint of color, I was trudging up the mountain in dry powder. When rose light showed detail in the timber, I had put myself well above the pickup headlamps winking from forest roads.

I soon found tracks: a small group of elk, knee-deep in snow, meandering. I followed. Shortly, I saw the plow marks of one animal skirting a thicket that the others had gone through. The trails merged on the off side. This was encouraging.

Now the gouges in the snow separated more often, like a rope unraveling, the strands all snaking in different directions, weaving among the lodgepoles. I slowed. In this bowl they could bed, and the sign indicated they wanted to. They were probably bedded now, separated, watching their backtrail for Filson jackets and the black sticks that spat fire.

Piles of fluffy snow lay on the branches, reducing visibility. But the snow helped, too. All but a few random patches of bark and bough were white. In these cottony billows of snow, a sliver of elk would catch my eye as it never would in the dun-and-gray of a snowless wood. The trick was to spot that color before the elk saw, smelled or heard me.

Luck was with me on my side. Stopping once more to glass, I glimpsed a patch of tawny hair peeking from the branches of a deadfall. Slowly I moved to the side. Antler! The Redfield showed me just enough shoulder; the report was muffled to a pop by the snow. The bull dropped

where he stood, the bullet having severed his spine where it dipped between the shoulders.

I also remember the only Redfield seminar for journalists that I attended. It was held at the White Oak Plantation near Tuskeegee, Ala., in 1998. I shot a whitetail buck a little too low with a .270 and had a tough time finding the animal. But with a single exception, the proto-type sights and binoculars that Redfield trotted out worked well. They showed a commitment to better optics and aggressive marketing. It was a big surprise, then, when news came not long afterward that Redfield had folded.

The oldest optics company in the country gone? Surely not.

But it was indeed true. Decades of manufacturing had apparently left the Redfield plant site out of compliance with new environmental ordinances – rules that could not have been imagined when John slid his first dovetail scope rings into place many decades ago. More threatening to Redfield, it seemed, were the fine riflescopes and brilliant ad campaigns by Leupold. Bushnell and Nikon were competing too, with well-built Japanese scopes. Still, Redfield was more than a brand name. It was an institution, dating to the days of Hensoldt scopes and Noskes. It had outlived Lyman and Unertl as a maker of big game scopes for the masses, and unlike Weaver, had retained an American manufacturing base. Losing a company of Redfield's stature was like losing an old hunting partner.

One shooter, one spotter. Good glass gives distant prairie dogs plenty to worry about!

But the name did not fade away. Blount bought it. Blount is the conglomerate that owns Speer and CCI, Federal, Outers and RCBS – as well as the optics firms of Weaver and Simmons. Why add one more scope company to the tribe? Mike Larsen, who's long been in charge of marketing for Federal and now also represents other subsidiaries for Blount, thought that was a fair question.

"We're having the new Redfield scopes built to high standards of optical quality and ruggedness," he told me. "We intend to market them as Redfield once did, emphasizing their brightness and durability. They'll sell mostly to serious hunters who demand a lot of a scope and are willing to pay a little more than once-a-year hunters are for high quality."

That was in 2000, when the new Redfield lines were announced by Blount. They included some Redfield names familiar to riflemen like me: Illuminator, Widefield, Golden Five Star, Tracker. These had defined the four families of scopes in the Redfield line in the company's last years. New Illuminator sights, 3-9x42 and 3-10x50, are top-of-the-line. They feature the wide eyepiece that the firm pioneered – as do the 3-9x27, 2-7x22 and 4x22 Widefields. The Golden Five Star series includes 3-9x40, 3-9x50, 4-12x40 and 6-18x40 scopes. Economy-level Trackers, like the Golden Five Stars, have round eyepieces. They come in 3-9x40, 3-9x50, 3-12x44 and 4-16x44 configurations. The new Redfields are available in silver, matte and gloss finishes, depending on model. Redfield dovetail rings and bases complement the optics.

It's too early at this writing to say how the Redfield name will fare these days. Leupold's market share is virtually unassailable. There's heightened competition from Japan and aggressive marketing by Swarovski and Zeiss, plus an expanding line of sights under the Bushnell name. Even dismissing Tasco and Simmons as price-point optics (some models like the Simmons Aetec deserve a better label), Redfield will be challenged. Weaver, now a sibling company, has models that compete directly with new Redfields.

Whatever its corporate fortunes, I hope the name stays on scopes a long time. Because it's been there a long time already.

Swarovski Optik: Clear as crystal

You cross the river in the shadow of the Alps, then wind among tall trees and Tyrolean houses. The road straightens. You're headed into the hills, past neat rows of small, modest homes on quiet streets.

The factory comes as a surprise. Swarovski Optik is one of the biggest industries in Hall, an old mining town on the western tip of Austria. From the Autobahn, you can glimpse an observatory dome peeking above Hall's northern sector, Absam. Wilhelm Swarovski, eldest son of company founder Daniel Swarovski, learned about optics by building telescopes to view the stars. The observatory, still functional, is surrounded by buildings at one time used to warehouse supplies for the German Army. Now those structures serve the modern Swarovski Optik, KG, parent company of Swarovski Optik North America Ltd.

The Austrian firm of Swarovski started doing business before the turn of the last century. In 1883, Daniel Swarovski, who lived in the Czech Republic, attended an industrial exposition in Vienna. From that visit, he developed a crystal-cutting machine. In 1895, he established the Swarovski company for making crystal, an enterprise that still generates most of the firm's $2 billion annual revenue. Daniel chose the Tyrolean village of Watten for his new plant because of its abundant water, used then to power machinery. The Absam plant was established in 1948 to manufacture eyeglasses. It grew quickly; within six months, 150 people were on the payroll. The next year, Swarovski developed its legendary "Habicht" (ha-beesh, meaning "hawk") 7x42 binocular. An 8x30 wide-angle Habicht came along in 1952; a 10x40 wide-angle in 1954. These binoculars were marketed only in Europe. Two years later, the firm changed from a limited-liability company to a limited partnership. It remains so today. Swarovski is still managed by Swarovskis. Helmut, in charge of the crystal division, and Gerhardt, president of Swarovski World Wide, are fourth-generation managers. Six family members are on the board of directors.

The first Swarovski riflescope, a 4x32, appeared in 1959. A second factory was added in 1962, near Matzleinsdorferplatz in Vienna, to meet the growing demand for Swarovski optics. In 1965, Swarovski bought 51 percent of the Miller Brothers, Ltd. Workshop for Precision Mechanics, later moving it from Innsbruck to Absam. Innovative company engineers gave Swarovski a boost in 1979, with the introduction of Habicht SL 7x42 binoculars built "from the inside out." Instead of fitting optical components into housings, technicians with sophisticated machinery molded shells around the optics. This process earned the company the Austrian National Award for Outstanding Industrial Design. To date, no other optics firm makes its binoculars this way.

Guiding elk hunters, the author has often used a 10x50 Swarovski SLC.

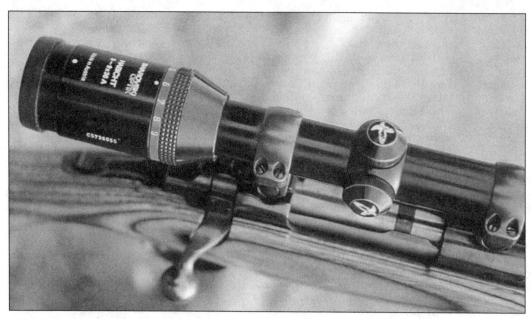

The Swarovski Hawk has become a symbol of quality worldwide.

By the end of 1979, Swarovski had acquired full ownership of the Miller factory and was employing more than 700 people, many of whom lived in company-supplied housing. Swarovski went abroad to court foreign markets. The Habicht binocular line came to the United States in 1983, and seven years later, Swarovski Optik North America Ltd. was born. "SONA" is not just a sales arm; it has a repair facility and customer service and support branch.

SONA president M. James Morey has been with Swarovski for many years. He's a good salesman, as you'd expect; but there's genuine enthusiasm in his voice when he tells you about his products. "The best way to choose a scope or binoculars is by comparison," he says with conviction. "Put Swarovski up against cheaper glass, and you'll see the difference. Compare our glass with the most expensive optics, and you'll wonder why the others cost more."

Swarovski unabashedly hawks the quality of its glass; it makes no apology for the prices, which some American hunters still think is too high. The firm has worked hard to bring American shooters what they want in riflescopes. One-inch alloy tubes and quarter-minute adjustments are concessions to U.S. riflemen. So is the reticle placement. In Swarovski scopes built for the American market, the reticle is in the second focal plane (toward the rear of the scope) so as you change magnification, it stays the same apparent size. In traditional European scopes, including Swarovski's Nova series, the reticle gets bigger when you increase power.

That's because it's installed in the first focal plane, up front. Europeans like this arrangement because the relationship of reticle and target remains the same throughout the magnification range, so the reticle can act as a range-finding device regardless of the power setting. Also, there's no reticle shift during power changes. American shooters have long balked at a reticle that grows and shrinks in variable scopes.

"To expand its sports optics business, Swarovski convenes a team of industry consultants twice a year," said Jim Morey. "They come from France, Germany, Italy and the U.S. as well as from Austria. The family wants to grow the firm." And grow it has, especially in North America. "Our 1-inch AV variable scope, made just for the American market, drove scopes sales up 48 percent in just a year," said Morey. The AV, he

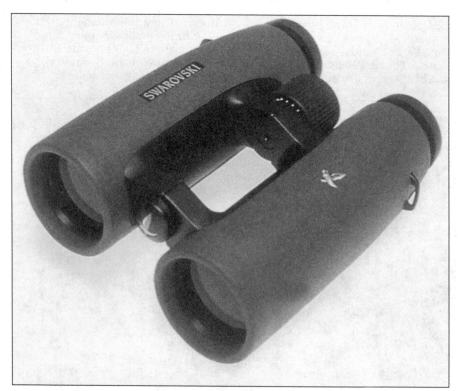

Swarovski's EL binoculars are considered among the best, if not the best, available.

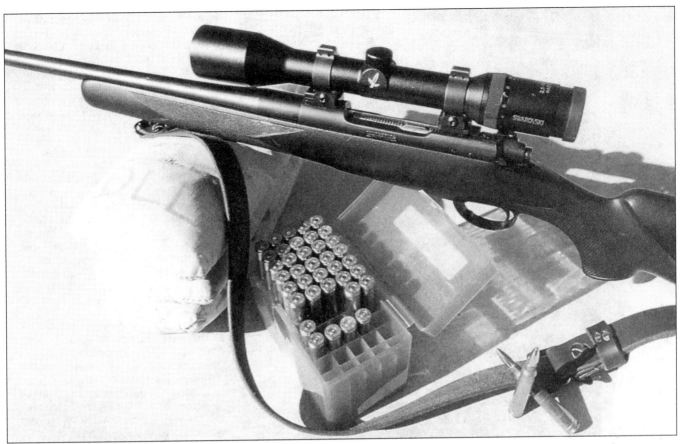

This Swarovski is its owner's favorite scope and has helped take several fine big game animals.

said, resulted from meetings with U.S. hunters and members of the shooting press. Jim says the 3-10x42 and 4-12x50 AVs were so popular the first year that Swarovski couldn't meet the demand. "We probably lost another 20 percent in growth by not being able to deliver." Orders for the EL binocular, widely acclaimed as the best that money can buy, have exceeded expectations – and production capacity – for two years running. "Our 6-24x50 scope is another hot seller," Morey said. "In fact, sales are strongest at the upper end of our price spectrum. Hunters are willing to pay for the best."

A Swarovski scope and binocular help this marksman find deer and hit them at long range.

A Swarovski binocular is expensive but can make any hunter more effective.

of a red-dot sight and is as quick on target, but it doesn't *obscure* the target, and it can be turned off to get a traditional black reticle. I've not used it on game, and frankly could do without that inner circle. But if you do a lot of hunting at the edge of day, a little illumination in the center section of a crosswire can add precision to your shooting.

All scope tubes are machined in one piece from solid bar stock. The Swarovski P scopes measure 30mm in diameter and feature a powerful coil spring inside the shoulder of the ocular bell. This spring pushes forward on the internal tube holding the reticle and erector lenses to ensure constant pressure against adjustment posts. As in other high-quality scopes, reticles are etched from steel wafers. Recoil is less apt to wreck these than it is wire reticles.

Of course, Swarovski optics are fully coated and multi-coated. Each scope is filled with dry nitrogen to prevent fogging, then is submersed to check for water-tightness. Click adjustments move point of impact 1 centimeter at l00 meters. P scopes share with all Swarovskis a spring-loaded ocular housing that collapses if it bangs your brow on recoil. The padded ocular ring helps cushion the blow, too.

Like other European scope-makers, Swarovski sticks to reticles that are essentially variations of the plex and post. There's no dot, and in the P series you can't even order a crosswire! Most of us can tolerate this limited selection, because the plex is so versatile. And of the eight P reticles listed, four derive from the plex.

Completing its selection of riflescopes is the ponderous but optically excellent LRS, the only hunting scope I know of that incorporates a laser rangefinder. It is too heavy and bulky for use with lightweight rifles, either in the whitetail woods, or on trails at timberline. Beanfield snipers have fun with it. Portability may have had something to do with the less-than-spectacular sales of Swarovski's RF-1 laser rangefinder, one of the first of its type but heftier and more expensive than many that followed. It and Leica's Geovid are still among the best instruments of their kind, with almost instant recovery between readings, 1-yard accuracy to extreme range and first-class lenses for bright images in dim light. Still, the most promising products for Swarovski stateside seem to be riflescopes and binoculars.

Model designations of Swarovski scopes have changed enough over the last few years to confuse even the company's faithful. A-series Swarovski scopes used to wear green rings on the forward edge of the ocular housing. Also known as the Nova series, they feature 1-inch tubes and rear-plane reticles that don't change size when you change magnification. Besides cosmetic updates in the line, the 4x and 6x have been discontinued. My pouting was to no avail. "The 4x and 6x models generated only about 1 percent of our total sales in 1997," Morey said. "When the 6-24x50 PV came out, we sold five times as many of those scopes as both of the small fixed-powers

put together. And the 6-24x is a very costly sight."

There's still a 3-9x36 and a 1.5-4x20, plus a 3-10x42. The PF scopes include a 6x42, 8x50 and 8x56. Only the 6x has a 1-inch tube. The others are 30mm, just like the tubes in the PV (variable) line, which spans a broad range of magnifications: 1.25-4x24 to 6-24x50. "N" versions of the PF and PV lines have illuminated reticles. One of Jim Morey's favorites is the illuminated "dangerous game" reticle, available in Swarovski's 1.25-4x PV. The reticle, whose center brightness is controlled by a rheostat, is a crosswire within a circle that spans about 40 inches at 40 yards. It has the eye-catching appeal

Swarovski builds several styles of binoculars. Porro-prism 7x42 and 10x40 glasses that look just like their WWII ancestors are now available in green rubber armor. So is the more compact 8x30. The 6x30 has, alas, been dropped. The SL 8x56 porro-prism binocular is a marvelous glass for dim light conditions. As do most binoculars these days, the SL has center focus adjustments. But the wheel is in front of the hinge.

Swarovski's 8x30 WB, smallest of the SLC roof prism series, are trim and light enough to carry on strenuous climbs. Clarity and brightness are tops in their class. You focus with a dial forward of the hinge. Diopter adjustment is set with a rear dial you must depress to rotate, so accidentally brushing it against your jacket won't change the setting. The bridge of the binocular housing shields both dials; they don't hang up in clothing.

Among the features that makes these glasses so bright is their P-coated, or phase-corrected, prisms. According to Jim Morey, the phase correction is necessary in roof-prism systems to counteract the splitting of light into bands of colors. "This technology has been available for about five years, but P-glass is expensive, and rejection rate in grinding is about four times the rejection rate for standard optical glass. So only a few of the best instruments have it." The best include Swawrovski's other SLCs: 7x42, 10x42, 7x50, 8x50 and 10x50.

The premier Swarovski binocular, the EL, has a magnesium frame that brings it under the polymer-frame SLCs in weight. Its prism coating is a proprietary product that Swarovski claims delivers an image unparalleled as regards sharpness and color integrity.

The biggest binocular in the Swarovski line is a 15x56. Morey said he proposed it – and was so confident it would sell that he asked for 90 percent of the first year's production. "Turns out I was far too conservative," he said. This instrument is expensive. Why would hunters pay dearly for a binocular twice as powerful as traditional binoculars and so heavy it begs a tripod? "Part of the reason," said Morey, "is that hunter demographics are changing. Eighty percent of the U.S. population lives within 100 miles of the seacoasts. That means many people must travel far to find popular big game. The U.S. economy has been

good, and baby-boomers are emptying the nests. Hunters pay several thousand dollars for elk hunts, and several hundred a day for guided deer hunts in Alabama. High-quality optics make sense. So does glass that's more powerful than hunters used to use in the back 40."

To give hunters more power in a portable package, Swarovski came out with a "doubler." It replaces the eyepiece of an SLC or EL binocular and doubles the power. You can make the switch in seconds without tools. "It's like having a spotting scope in your pocket," says Morey.

Bulk is easier to reduce to an acceptable level in binoculars and riflescopes than in spotting scopes. Given the size of objective lenses needed to yield even a 3mm exit pupil in spotting scopes, plus the requisite tripod, many hunters who'd benefit from a spotting scope don't even own one.

Swarovski hasn't yet come up with a tripod that fits in fanny packs while offering the sturdiness and adjustment range to satisfy a studio cinematographer. But it *has* developed extendable scopes that slip easily into most daypacks. The 30x75 S and 25-40x75 S were the first; they've been replaced by the CT-75 and CT-85, which lack ocular designations because they accommodate interchangeable lenses: a 15x, 22x, 30xWA, 32xWA and 20-60x. The 30x is a "double-wide-angle" lens, with a field of 120 feet at 1,000 yards. The 32x has a 99-foot field. Wide-angle lenses give you lots to look at, but they also impose more critical eye relief.

The CT-75 has one draw tube; the CT-85 has two. Collapsed, each is as short as or shorter than most compact scopes. The 75mm and 85mm objectives give you much brighter images than do the 50mm objectives common to compacts. Like Swarovski's 7x30B and 8x30B roof-prism binoculars, the CT spotting scopes have phase-corrected prisms. So do the firm's AT-80 and ST-80 non-extendable spotting scopes. The AT and ST indicate angled and straight eyepieces. The CT lenses also work on the 80-series scope bodies. You can get "HD" (ED or extra-low-dispersion) lenses for the AT-80 and ST-80. As this is written, Swarovski has told of a new 65mm spotting scope with a full complement of lenses, to be unveiled in 2002.

Swarovski has made substantial progress targeting its ad campaigns to U.S. hunters and birders. But the

high-profile company with the high-priced optics isn't out to unseat companies that sell to discount stores.

Morey smiled. "A lot of people think that because we've become so competitive in the optics field that we're a major player. Nope. Even though Swarovski sells more scopes and binoculars in the states than all other European firms combined, it has less than 1 percent of the U.S. market in sports optics. That means we have lots of room to grow. We're not after the huge volume realized by firms selling low-quality glass to casual users. But there's plenty of demand for high-end scopes and binoculars, and we'll continue to pursue that slice of the market."

The penchant of U.S. hunters for bigger and more powerful riflescopes will no doubt influence Swarovski's development work. This company has proven that it is serious about staying on the leading edge of trends in hunting optics. And its North American operations have expanded considerably since 1990, when the staff totaled four people. The Rhode Island headquarters then was a small office suite, which eventually proved too small for the growing firm. Now, Swarovski of North America employs 40 staffers. There's a modern assembly facility that allows the company to import parts instead of complete optics on which it would be subject to duty. Swarovski optics sold in the United States are mostly assembled in the United States. Warranty work is taken care of in Rhode Island as well – though the people in charge of that office say there's not much call for their services.

Despite the prominence of its name in the optics industry, and its stunning success in penetrating the North American market for riflescopes and binoculars, Swarovski's optical division accounts for just 4 percent of the company's income. Crystal makes up 68 percent of the business, and the Tyrolit division, which manufactures tooling for the crystal industry, earns 28 percent of the revenues. Swarovski jewelry is renowned worldwide, and a Swarovski Collectors Society boasts 450,000 members, 115,000 in the U.S. A production run of 10,000 special "Eagle" crystals for the Collectors Society was among the first of its kind. One week after the announcement, Swarovski had received 10,500 checks for the purchase price of $1,700.

A couple of years ago, part of the Swarovski family and a traditional Austrian band traveled to the United States to celebrate the company's success. I thought briefly of reminding them that a decade ago, while visiting a Swarovski crystal store in Austria, I caught a couple of street pigeons that had flown in the door and were strafing, under low ceilings, many thousands of dollars worth of glass.

I didn't say anything. Swarovski probably would have survived the damage.

Zeiss: The last word

German optics, like French wines and Italian sports cars, have a loyal following of people who value tradition. There's no reason to think top-grade optics must come from Germany – not now. Other countries have the same level of technology, the same access to the best materials. Other companies could challenge Zeiss for a share of the carriage trade.

Zeiss gives hunters a broad choice of top-quality sights.

But of firms aspiring to the Zeiss reputation, none have shown equal strength in the marketplace. Of the handful that have earned reputable names among discriminating buyers, Leica and Schmidt & Bender share with Zeiss the countryside of northern Germany. Leica and Zeiss have factories in Wetzlar, a city of 50,000; Schmidt & Bender assembles its scopes in nearby Fellingshausen, a small town only a few blocks long with a single, narrow, twisting main street and the clean stucco houses with thick-beamed roofs that you'd expect in a traditional German village.

Getting the Zeiss story straight is harder than getting a true accounting of entertainment expenses in Congress, but for different reasons. The history of Zeiss is the most convoluted of any that I've heard in the optics industry. Perhaps, though, it became more complicated in the hearing: I got most of it a decade ago, listening to a high-placed Zeiss executive, Volker Claudi, through interpreter Ilona Simshauser at the Hensoldt plant in Wetzlar, where Zeiss products are fashioned.

I still have some of the notes from that visit.

Ilona's English was impeccable – no doubt partly because this German-born woman spent 10 years in New York. Now, after 18 years with Zeiss, she's an executive secretary in sales. She knows her company. And she wants me to get the history right.

"No, no; it wasn't quite like that." She fires something in German to Volker, who smiles patiently, nods and waits for Ilona to explain to this slow-witted American that Zeiss, Jena and Zeiss, Wetzlar are of the same origins but that Zeiss, Jena has now become state-owned Jenoptics and independent Docter Optic, that the Zeiss Foundation, which includes 17,000 employees worldwide, is not the same as the venerable Wetzlar firm in the Hensoldt factory that makes Zeiss optics under the supervision of Zeiss, Oberkochen.

"You understand now?" she probes, hopefully.

I look up from my smoking pencil and manage a weak smile. "Uh, sort of."

She knows better, and sighs. Volker lights another cigarette.

We go through it again, how Zeiss dates to the turn of the century, where it pioneered the use of short scopes on rifles with a "prism" scope in 1904. This looked some-

A 5-15x Zeiss and a Winchester rifle netted this pronghorn at over 300 yards for Patrick Meitin.

what like one barrel of a porro-prism binocular stuck on a rifle receiver. But it worked.

In the 1920s, Zeiss owned stock in Hensoldt, the optics firm that made high-quality binoculars and riflescopes between the two world wars. Zeiss would eventually acquire the Hensoldt company and facility. A 1926 Zeiss catalog in my file carries the logo of Carl Zeiss, Jena. It lists 1x Zeileins and 2.5x Zeilklein scopes for $25 each, the 4x Zeilvier at $45, the 6x Zeilsechs for $52. An 8x Zeilacht cost $60. Variable l-4x Zeilmulti and 1-6x Zeilmultar scopes retailed for $66. The standard No. 1 reticle ("graticle" in the text) had one vertical and two horizontal posts that don't quite touch in the middle. The gap between the horizontal bars subtended 25.2 inches at 100 yards. It was bisected by the pointed tip of the bottom post. Four special-order reticles, variations of the three-post design, were available at nominal extra charge.

Zeiss literature of that day stressed that "the outer tube, together with the lens socket of our sighting telescopes, is drawn in one piece." Now, nearly 70 years later, scope firms that use one-piece tubes still make quite a fuss about it.

One feature of those early Zeiss scopes that has *not* survived is their focusing adjustment. It and the reticle adjustments were both on a top turret, so that "the adjustment of the graticule and that of the focus are made at one and the same place on the scope."

The 1926 catalog lists Zeiss factories at Jena, Wien (Vienna) and Gyor, with more facilities in Berlin, Hamburg, Wein, Buenos Aires and Tokyo. Distribution agencies had then been established in London, New York, Paris and Milan.

In the 1930s, A. Smakula, a Zeiss engineer, found that coating a lens surface with magnesium fluoride changed its refractive index to better transmit light through an air/glass boundary. Uncoated lenses lost up to 4 percent of incident light at each air/glass juncture, primarily because of the light-bending change in refractive indices between the air and glass. Smakula's discovery was immediately seized and classified by the German government, which was then arming for war. When the war ended, lens coating became common practice the world over. Later, multiple coatings of rare-earth substances made images even brighter. Now, light transmission through fully coated optical systems exceeds 95 percent.

Post-war Germany was a shambles. The Zeiss offices were moved by U.S. mandate to Oberkochen, near the Black Forest in southwestern Germany. The Jena plant continued to operate but manufactured only binoculars. During the 1950s, companies in eastern Germany became independent. After the Berlin Wall went up, Carl Zeiss, Jena, built binoculars for the Warsaw-Pact countries; and Zeiss, Oberkochen looked for other opportunities. In 1964, it started making binoculars and riflescopes at the Hensoldt plant in Wetzlar, marking them "Zeiss, West Germany." When the Wall came down in 1989, "West" was deleted.

About 3000 employees worked at the Carl Zeiss, Jena factory when I visited there in the early 1990s. Like Zeiss, Wetzlar, it is managed by Zeiss, Oberkochen. In Wetzlar, 850 people work for Zeiss at the Hensoldt plant, down from about l,000 a few years ago.

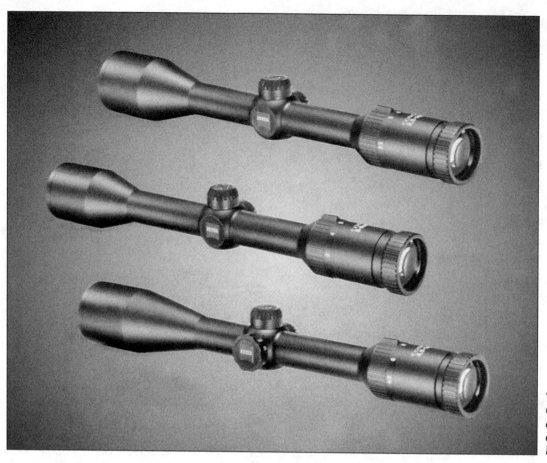

The three Zeiss Conquest scopes are all variables, all designed for American hunters.

"Broad, long-lasting recessions like this one affect demand," Ilona confirms. "We're in good shape financially but have had to tighten things up a bit. We've reduced the payroll through natural attrition, and we'll likely keep it at conservative levels, using workers overtime during heavy periods of demand."

Mostly, those come from military contracts, which then comprised 20 percent of Zeiss orders. Like other optics manufacturers, Zeiss is pleased to get these profitable contracts; but the cost of tooling up for each project can absorb a lot of the gravy – "especially if you can't shift the tooling or workers elsewhere after the job, or if you must let a new part of the factory lie idle." Ilona notes that additions to the Hensoldt plant have been made prudently; the last major work was completed in 1984. Still, some sections of the modern-looking, four-story building, with its central courtyard for materials handling, show little activity.

My tour of the factory is well organized and as complete as a half-day tour can be. Volker tells me through Ilona that Zeiss buys much of its optical glass from Schott, a German company long respected for its top-quality lenses and prisms. Schott is a Zeiss Foundation subsidiary. "But depending on just one supplier is bad business in our business, so we also buy lenses locally." As long as the glass meets Zeiss specifications, I'm assured that it can be fashioned at the Zeiss plant into a superior lens.

Lens grinding and polishing require many fixtures and tools, and lots of water. "We recycle water," says Ilona, adding that Zeiss has its own wells plus a line to the city supply. Any water discharged must meet very stringent environmental standards.

Prisms are glued to rail-like fixtures, then ground to establish flat, smooth surfaces. "Fine milling" is the term Volker uses to describe the process that has replaced traditional grinding at Zeiss. "It's faster," Ilona says. "We can mill a lens in two minutes." I look surprised. "Of course, polishing can take up to eight hours." Diamond abrasive paste is the common cutting agent. Zeiss holds tolerances to .0001 mm, producing a lens or prism that can't be gauged mechanically. The inspectors use light. When cleaned, prisms pressed together will stick by vacuum.

"We then check each batch with an interferometer, to ensure that the optical and mechanical axes of each lens coincide." Ilona repeats in English what Volker is saying. Having worked in many parts of the Zeiss factory, he knows the answers to my technical questions. I wish I'd studied German.

Assembly rooms are clean, bright, quiet. Here people put the lenses in the tubes, mainly with cement. Retaining rings still work best for some applications. Shock testing comes next, then temperature testing. Zeiss scopes must function at extremes of -25° and 50° Centigrade and survive the quick temperature changes induced in the lab. Each must also work perfectly after exposure to storage extremes of -35° and 70° Centigrade.

Nitrogen gas is injected to prevent fogging after the scope is purged of air in a heated vacuum cell.

I ask about scope sales and am told that big objective lenses get plenty of attention in Germany, where hunting is often done at night. Volker concedes that most American hunters don't need and probably seldom use the extra diameter and would be better served with less bulky scopes. "But we'll happily sell them our big scopes." Worldwide, about 65 percent of Zeiss sales come from variables. Stateside, the percentage is higher.

Ilona adds that in Germany, Zeiss 8x56 binoculars have become quite popular with hunters. "Many choose the 8x56 scope to match." The company's 7x42 binoculars sell almost as well.

Volker says that 90 percent of the parts used by Zeiss are manufactured by Zeiss. "We contract some small parts. Binocular housings are cast elsewhere but machined here."

Zeiss offers two lines of riflescopes: the "Z" models, which feature 26 and 30mm tubes with or without mounting rail, and the "C" types, built with 1-inch tubes for American shooters. Other differences: Elevation and windage markings on Z-scopes are marked in centimeters (a click moves point of impact 1 centimeter at 100 meters), while C-scopes feature 1/4-minute clicks. A Z-scope reticle is in the first image plane, meaning that when you crank up the power on a Diavari-Z variable, you increase reticle thickness. C-scopes have reticles in the second image plane; they don't change in apparent size as you change magnification.

Germans like the first-image-plane arrangement because it lets you use the reticle as a rangefinder no matter what power you've chosen on your scope. The relationship of reticle and target stays the same as you turn the dial. American shooters for the most part favor a reticle that does not grow and shrink, so it remains fine enough for precise shooting at long range when you turn the power up, and stays bold enough for quick sighting in dark timber when dialed to low magnification.

Zeiss scopes feature a rubber ocular ring to protect stock-crawlers. That ring and the rubber sleeve on the objective bell of my 4x32C are the kind of practical things Zeiss designers consider. Positive adjustments are another Zeiss coup; those on my scope are both repeatable and as crisp as first frost. Still, the best part of a Zeiss is the sharp, flat, brilliant image it transmits.

To help those of us who loathe military-length labels and can't decipher German names, Zeiss has come up with monikers that are at least pronouncible: Diatal for fixed-power scopes and Diavari for variables. An "M" means that the scope has mounting rails. The integral rail is quite popular in Europe, according to

Volker. "We developed this mount; then we made it part of the scope tube. It's a solid system. And it won't jeopardize the lens mountings or mar the tube like a set of rings will if they're not properly machined, or if you cinch them down too firmly in the wrong place."

A "C" suffix means the scope has an American flavor – most notably a reticle that, in variables, does not change size when you change power. The Diavari C 3-9x36 MC that Zeiss introduced a few years ago has been supplanted this year (2001) by the Conquest, a variable that like the Diavari C is assembled in the United States. The Conquest is available as a 3-9x40, a 3.5-10x44 and a 4.5-14x44. The 3-9 can also be had with a 50-yard parallax correction, for short-range shooting.

But the workhorses of the Zeiss line are still the ZM/Zs introduced in 1990. They include two fixed-power scopes with one-inch tubes (a 6x42 and an 8x56), plus four variables with 30mm tubes. In 1998, a new optical system, designed to reduce weight while increasing field of view and eye relief, was installed in a series called the VM/V. These more costly scopes are all variables. Two of the six have 1-inch tubes; the others are 30mm.

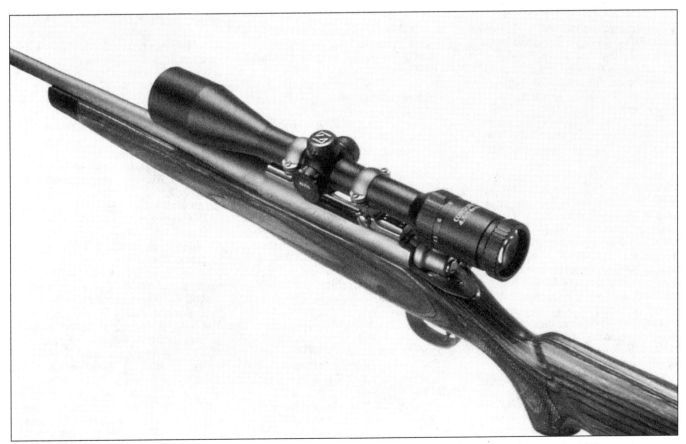

The Conquest line is the latest from Zeiss, which has been making rifle scopes for nearly 100 years.

Zeiss Victory binoculars are recent additions to a selection that offers everything but low quality.

lar, that incorporates a stabilizing system to dampen movement.

Zeiss optics cost too much, say people who don't think beyond the price sheet. Prices *are* relatively high, all right, but the instruments are also superior. Besides, it's useful to recall that in 1926, when a 4x Zeiss scope cost $45, you could buy a new Chevrolet for under $1,000. You can also amortize the price of any new scope or binocular over the number of years you expect to use them. Spending $600 to $1,200 for a Zeiss glass that will give you, say, 18 years of service, you're in hock only $35 to $65 annually for the best optics around. Compare that with the cost of one non-resident deer tag – or even a month's gasoline tab during hunting season!

Other companies, at a glance...

Bushnell/Bausch & Lomb

In 1853, John Jacob Bausch, a German immigrant, set up an optics shop in Rochester, N.Y. To keep the business afloat, he borrowed $60 from friend Henry Lomb. In the bargain, Bausch promised that if the business grew, Lomb would be offered a full partnership. Bausch & Lomb eventually became the premier optics firm in the United States. In 1971, it bought Bushnell, an upstart company established by Dave Bushnell in 1947. Bushnell didn't make optics; it imported them from Japan and sold them directly to consumers, partly through newspaper ads. Bushnell pricing had posed a threat to B&L. After the merger, B&L shut down its sports optics division in Rochester.

Bausch & Lomb sold Bushnell to Worldwide Sports and Recreation in 1995. That year, WSR also bought Jason Inc., a supplier of binoculars and spotting scopes. WSR moved Bushnell to Jason's Overland Park, Kansas, headquarters and bought licensing privileges for the B&L name. A couple of years ago, a Detroit investment firm called Wind Point Partners bought Bushnell/Bausch & Lomb. Since then, it has also acquired Moonlight Night Vision (now under the Bushnell name), Serengeti Eyewear and Bolle. While the Bushnell name continues to appear on rifle-

Ten traditional reticles are available – one more than for the ZM/Z line. Also, there's a "Varipoint" illuminated dot that comes on the 1.1-4x24 T*. The T* symbol on VM/V designations, incidentally, refers to the lens coating, Zeiss's best.

The click adjustments on modern Zeiss scopes are finger-friendly. I've found them to be repeatable as well as accurate.

It's easy to treat Zeiss scopes as the main event. That is, it's easy to forget that they are sights, and that their primary purpose is to help you aim. It's easy to buy too big. For example, Zeiss claims its 3-12x56 is "the answer to every hunter's dream." Obviously not all hunters share my dreams. While an alloy tube keeps its weight (26 ounces) within reason, this scope is too bulky for many applications. Its giant objective means you won't be using the saddle scabbard Uncle Roy made for his Model 721 with the K3 Weaver. Nor will you be able to use low rings. If its optical system matches the one on my Zeiss Diatal-C 4x, this husky variable has superior glass. But it may not serve the hunter who carries a rifle over moun-

tains or shoulders it quickly for a shot in timber, looking low over the bore with his cheek tight to the stock.

Unlike some optical firms that specialize either in riflescopes or binoculars, Zeiss has stayed strong in both product areas. Its Classic binoculars include 7x50, 15x60 and 20x60 porro prism models, plus six roof-prism glasses ranging in size from 8x20 to 8x56. There's also a roof-prism Diafun, lightweight but so sturdy that when I fell on one and rode it 40 feet down a rock face in the mountains recently, it needed only a dusting off to get back in service. In 1993, Zeiss introduced its Night Owl line: 7x45, 8x56 and 10x56. That has been replaced this past year by the Victory 8x40, 8x56, 10x40 and 10x56 models, with the advanced optical system that Zeiss put into the VM/V riflescopes. Apparently the Zeiss 10x40 roof prism glass that has been used so widely by hunting guides is no longer necessary in the line, because the latest catalog does not list it.

Zeiss also offers seven types of monoculars, including one with night-vision technology and another, like the 20x60 porro prism binocu-

scopes, binoculars and spotting scopes, the Bausch & Lomb name has been taken off of riflescopes.

In 1996, the big news at Bushnell was the Holosight. I'd be oversimplifying to say it resembled one of the "red-dot" sights (from Aim-point, Leupold, others) without a tube. Most red-dot sights derived from 1950s-era military "Nydar" technology. Until recently they offered no magnification. The Holosight was also a 1x sight but employed a removable screen atop the rear end of its flat housing. The housing contained two lithium 3-volt batteries, a microprocessor and a brightness adjustment for the reticle that it produces. You looked into the screen, over this unit. The screen frame included

The author thinks the lightweight (but obsolete) B&L 7x35 Zephyr an ideal glass for big game hunting.

windage and elevation screws with 1/4-minute clicks.

The Holosight has since been improved. But the principle of its operation is still that of the hologram, a three-dimensional image captured on film by a split laser beam and "played back" to the viewer. It is what F-14 fighter pilots see when they find a target in their "heads-up" displays. When the Holosight is switched on, the red reticle is superimposed on your target, which is as easy to see as if you were looking through a picture window instead of the holographic window. You put the reticle where you want it, then shoot. Head position doesn't matter; as long as you can see the reticle, it shows you where the shot will go. Parallax is no problem. Your window of eye relief is huge: half an inch to 10 feet. There are 20 levels of brightness.

The Holosight has a couple of advantages over a tube-type red dot sight. Its frame is compact (only about an inch high and 4 inches long) and fits tight to a standard scope base, so it won't impair handling. The screen protrudes like a big receiver sight but is contoured so as not to hang up in brush. While there's nothing wrong with a dot reticle, the Holosight offers you a choice of four reticles, which can be changed in the field in 30 seconds by switching screens. Current Holosights weigh only 6 1/2 ounces and batteries last a long time. To prolong battery life, there's an automatic shutoff that kills the image after 8 hours.

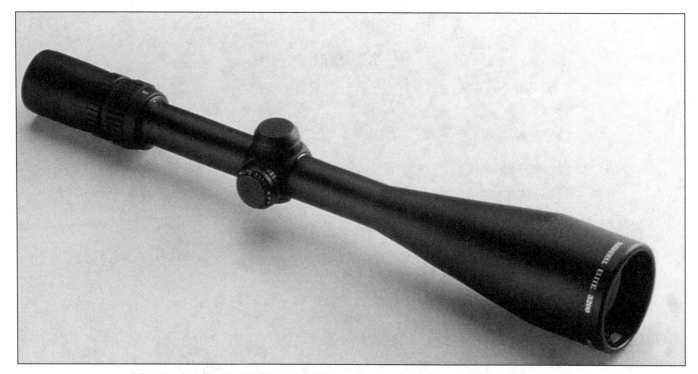

The Bushnell Elite 3200 and 4200 series used to be under the B&L banner.

The Bushnell Holosight, here on an Ithaca shotgun, is a fine choice for deer hunting in thickets.

Bushnell's 2.5-10x Elite on a 7mm Dakota rifle delivered these groups for the author, from the sit.

Bausch & Lomb's binocular and spotting scope lines are among the most extensive in the world.

This is a short-range sight. The reticle appears a little grainy to me, and of course the 1x image won't help you see details. But it is remarkably fast – and foolproof. The acid test is with it mounted on a shotgun. It is high enough that you can't look down the barrel; you must use the Holosight. Shoot the shotgun left-handed, and you shed the crutch of conditioned reflexes. I can't say I felt comfortable shooting this way, but I shattered enough clay targets to convince myself that the Holosight has merit. On a handgun, it may be the best choice of all. From unsupported positions, I've shot better pistol groups with the Holosight than with any other sight.

Another, more recent Bushnell innovation is Rainguard, a coating applied to the outside lenses of Elite series binoculars, riflescopes and spotting scopes. Its purpose is to disperse water droplets or smears into fine pellets that enable you to see more clearly through the wet glass. The Rainguard surface is so hard and slick as to keep water from "gripping." Bushnell's Chris Lalik, who had a part in developing the coating, demonstrates its unique properties by writing on a coated lens with a permanent felt marker. Then he applies a piece of tape – ordinary Scotch tape – to the mark. And lifts it off. Don't try that on scope lenses without Rainguard unless you want to spend some time scrubbing with solvent (which may affect lens coatings applied to enhance light transmission). No, Rainguard does not block light. According to the people at Bushnell, it may even crank up the brightness slightly. It's surely useful for hunters and birders who go afield where rain and snow are often in the forecast.

Kahles

"K-ZF84-l0-V2 instructions / note: do not be confused!"

OK. But there's something disconcerting about a scope whose name

Karen Mehall dropped this black bear with a Kahles scope and a Remington rifle.

revisits organic chemistry. This scope is a Kahles. It is a tactical scope, which means the rangefinding reticles are for bracketing people. But the firm also makes scopes for sporting guns. Deciphering the specs has become easier since Swarovski took control of Kahles marketing stateside in 2000. Still, the company's historical sketch in its brochure takes you into the 1800s without telling you how to pronounce Kahles (it's Kah-less, not Kay-leez).

Some years ago, I interviewed the Kahles executive manager at that time, Johann Peternel. "We do not believe in rigidly sticking to tradition, but it is our intention to cultivate traditional knowledge and develop a specific know-how. This should not imply, however, that we are ignoring new technologies."

Translation is fraught with perils. Public relations have traditionally taken a back seat to design and production at Kahles, whose roots wind back to 1898 when Karl Robert Kahles assumed control of a small Austrian optics shop founded 75 years earlier by Simon Plossl. Kahles died suddenly in 1908, but his widow carried on until sons Karl and Ernest took charge. Kahles scopes were used extensively by snipers during World War I. Later, Kahles developed binoculars and scopes for the sporting trade. World War II drove the firm to manufacture military glass. In the last days of the conflict, the factory was bombed and young Karl was killed. His widow, then Karl's son Friedrich, rebuilt the company.

In 1974, the Kahles family sold its optics enterprise to Daniel Swarovski, who then made it a branch of Swarovski Optik. In 1989, Kahles Ltd. became an independent company. In the summer of 1992, Kahles pulled its marketing arm from the Swarovski group and established a dealer network under Kahles USA. Eight years later, Swarovski Optik of North America began marketing efforts for Kahles. "It's a great marriage," said Greg Jones, whose job it is to carve a niche for Kahles optics in the United States. "Kahles is owned by Swarovski, but its products are developed as a separate line. We like to think they complement Swarovski scopes and binoculars, perhaps enabling people to buy a high-quality Austrian glass when they couldn't quite afford a Swarovski." Kahles optics are not cheap, but they're a deep notch below Swarovski on the retail price lists.

Though many U.S. hunters have yet to use Kahles scopes, they've benefited from Kahles' engineering. In 1959, Kahles was the first company to use multi-coated lenses. In 1972, it was the first to employ an 0-ring to seal the turret. Kahles has pioneered lightweight 30mm scopes that are also relatively short. They feature one-piece tubes, popular now on top-quality scopes. The company's commitment to growth has prompted the development of new scope models and binoculars. Their success is evident in sales figures: in 1999, Kahles revenues jumped 300 percent, and American distribution has increased steadily since.

Kahles scopes are bright. A decade ago, the firm claimed that its K-ZF84 military scope delivered the highest light transmission in the industry: 99.8 percent. Available in 6x or 10x with a 1-inch matte-black tube, it had a ballistic cam shaped to compensate for bullet drop at extreme range with Federal 168-grain .308 ammo. You could buy six other cams for various loads. Kahles recommended a 300-meter zero to give the cam its full range of operation. The company's traditional scope line then included a 2.5x20, 4x32, 6x42, 7x56, 8x56, 1.1-4.5x20, 1.5-6x42, 2.2-9x42 and 3-12x56. All but the 7x in this "Helia" family offered a choice of eight reticles and a steel or alloy tube with or without mounting rail. Variables all had 30mm tubes. List prices compared with those of other good European scopes.

Times change; so has Kahles. No longer does it claim 99.8 percent light transmission, because that's significantly higher than what's practical to achieve even with current technology. The company has dispensed with its unpronounceable catalog designations to lump scope models into two groups. Those with 1-inch tubes, fashioned mainly for the American market, give big game hunters five practical choices. There's a 2-7x36, a 3-9x42, a 4x36, a 6x42 and an 8x50 that's also available with an illuminated reticle. I lobbied for the 2-7x36 and am pleased with the result. Like many European variables, it has a long ocular housing, which can keep you from sliding the scope as far forward as you might like in some mounts. But overall it's a fine scope, and at a list price of $532, the least expensive of the Kahles sight selection.

The 30mm stable includes a 1.4-4x24, a 1.5-6x42 and a 2.5-10x50.

There's also a 12x56. The 1.5-6x and 12x can be had with a lighted reticle. Traditional reticle choices apply to both Kahles lines. I like the tough matte finish, the finger-adjustable knobs. Kahles still makes tactical riflescopes: a 6x42 and a 10x42. Reticles feature mil dots or stadia wires.

Binoculars in Kahles boxes also reflect attention to the hunter's needs. The 8x32 is newest, a compact companion to the 8x42 and 10x42. Prices: $610, $721 and $722, respectively.

Pentax

When I started shooting with scopes, five companies dominated the U.S. market: Lyman, Leupold, Redfield, Weaver and Bausch & Lomb. A fellow named Bushnell had begun importing Japanese scopes, but everybody knew they were second-rate, like the new Japanese automobiles and electronics. Eventually we would learn differently, after using optics from Bushnell, Nikon and Pentax.

Pentax, now 75 years old, manufactures high-quality binoculars, riflescopes and spotting scopes. Its Lightseeker line of riflescopes includes nine variables and two fixed-power models. The 1.75-6x39, 2-8x39, 3-9x43 and 3.5-10x50 cover most big game hunting needs. The 3-11, 4-16, 6-24 and 8.5-32 models with 44mm front glass and adjustable objective bells are available for long-range shooting. Woods hunters can choose from three shotgun scopes: a 2.5x25, a 0x27 EER and a 0-4x27 variable. Lightseekers feature one-piece aircraft-alloy tubes and fully multi-coated lenses, each with seven layers of image-enhancing film. The Lightseeker II series includes three variables: 3-9x43, 4-16x44 and 6-24x44. They have all the features of original Lightseekers plus finger-adjustable windage and elevation knobs and a reticle-snugging device called Perm-Align. It's a turret screw that works like the Burris Posi-Lock. I don't care much for it. Pentax also catalogs three pistol scopes (two variables and a 2x) outside the Lightseeker line.

Windage and elevation adjustments on Pentax scopes move point of impact from 1/8 to 1/2 minute, depending on the scope model. Reticle choices: a standard "Penta-Plex," plus finer and heavier versions, and a "Deepwoods Plex" with a circle in the middle that subtends 30 inches at 40 yards. Turkey hunters will

Pentax, a latecomer to the scope business, builds fine sights under the Lightseeker label.

understand. There's a dot for the 6-24 AO and a mil-dot for the 8.5-32 AO. Pentax's Tony Tekansik told me some months ago that dots can be installed in most Pentax scopes for a $50 charge.

What makes Pentax special? Besides radiused objective and ocular bells, the scopes have internal lenses that are 40 percent bigger than most – this according to Tekansik, who adds: "They make for a brighter image by offering a bigger funnel for incoming light." He points out that oversize erector lenses can limit windage and elevation adjustment range, but that shooters will never notice if their rifle and scope mounts are properly drilled and matched. Slimmer erector assemblies are best fitted to tactical scopes, which must be adjustable for ranges to 1,000 yards. That's why tactical scopes commonly have 30mm tubes and erector assemblies no bigger than those in standard 1-inch scopes.

Tekansik explained that the forward placement of turrets on Pentax scopes results from their bigger internal glass. "The larger the lens,

the longer the focal length," he says. Still, there's ring space aplenty.

Pentax scopes come in either gloss or matte finish. Tekansik tells me that about 70 percent of the scopes shipped are matte. And, as with Nikon, the most popular model is the 3-9x.

Like any progressive firm, Pentax is committed to improving its products. Little things matter. "For instance, we've replaced the O-ring seal standard on the turret stems of many scopes with a threaded collar. O-rings can drag when you back off on the adjustment – that is, the spring tension doesn't always move the erector tube assertively if you're turning the screw out. That's why some shooters tap turrets with screwdriver handles after adjusting, and why some scopes don't register a change in point of impact until after a shot and the attendant recoil. We've eliminated this worry. Besides, we use two leaf return springs in the Lightseeker II. Each is a quarter inch wide, or twice the width of a standard spring."

Tekansik noted that Pentax pays a lot of attention to internal dimen-

sions, including those of the solid brass zoom tube. The combination of tight fit and self-lubricating brass guarantees that zero won't shift as you change magnification. "If you allow a thousandth — just one *thousandth* — of an inch of slop in the guts of a scope," he said, "you'll see an inch of shot displacement at 100 yards."

Pentax claims its tube walls are thicker than those on competitive scopes, and that its reticles are three times stronger than industry standards. The company is definitely courting the hunter, whose need for precision is often less than for durability. Such market savvy dates back to 1957, when the "Asahi Pentax" camera was introduced. (Asahi was the parent company, formed in 1919; Pentax was a trade name showcasing the camera's pentaprism.) Few firms in the photo business can claim as many industry awards.

Pentax dropped its fixed-power 4x and 6x scopes when it started selling Lightseekers. That must have made good economic sense, but it irritates a few of us curmudgeons

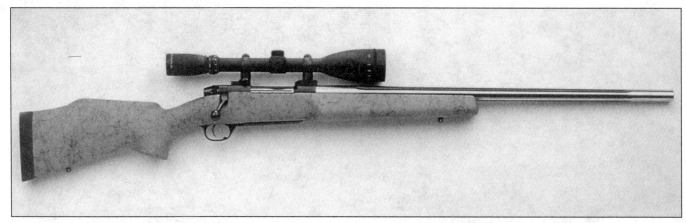

The Pentax on this Weatherby shows the rounded objective bell of the Lightseeker series.

who think a 4x scope is, like one hole in the right place on a belt, all a hunter should ever need.

On the other hand, the expanded line of Pentax binoculars includes traditional as well as new and sporty models. At the top of the heap is the DCF, center focus, roof prism series. The "HR" suffix on the 8x42, 10x42 and 12x42 models means high resolution. They're phase-corrected and unusually bright. You don't have many choices in 12x binoculars small enough to carry on a hunt or birding expedition. This one should be a first pick. Pentax makes 13 compact binoculars (with objective lenses smaller than 30mm); but for prolonged glassing, I'll pass them by. The PCF porro prism series is more useful. Less expensive than DCF binoculars, they still feature seven-layer multi-coating. Choose a 7x35 or 8x40 for all-around use, or a 10x50 or 12x50 for long-distance looking. There's a 7x50, and, to use with a tripod, plus a 16x50 and a 20x50. Pentax also lists marine bin-oculars, and an 80mm spotting scope so new that it's not yet cata-loged. I've put one to use on the Montana prairie. The zoom lens brought pronghorns (swimming in the mirage a mile away) right up to my face. I could have photographed them with the camera adapter. I've yet to run a resolution test, but the images in this spotting scope seems sharp, the colors true.

Japanese camera companies have come up with some mighty fine field glass.

Binoculars

*T*he most useful binoculars for hunters are compact enough to carry under a coat, light enough that you don't need a harness, with enough power for long-distance glassing and enough field and brightness for up-close looking in dark timber. Many years ago, I thought I had the ideal binocular in my Bausch & Lomb 7x35 Zephyr. And it *was* ideal. But since then, better lens coatings and advanced roof-prism designs have put other binoculars on the podium. Here are the most noteworthy models introduced recently.

This hunter relies on his 10x50 Swarovski binocular to find game.

BSA:

Following up its aggressive entry into the riflescope market, BSA has just unveiled a binocular line. It comprises six Silver Star porro prism models: 7x35, 8x40, 10x50, 12x50, 7-21x40, and 10-30x50. I'd leave variables alone, but with prices starting under $80, the others are worth a look. Compact Silver Stars include an 8x22, a 10x26, and a 12x26, from $60 to $70. Armored 8x21, 10x25, and 12x25 models are also available: $30 to $50. The Classic line, with 9x22, 12x26, and 8-18x25 binoculars, is also under $100. Budget-priced pocket glasses have a place; however, their proliferation makes you wonder if we shouldn't keep them in their boxes during rut. **954-581-2144**.

Bausch & Lomb/ Bushnell:

Bausch & Lomb's top-end binoculars, the 8x42, 10x42 and 12x50 Elites, are unchanged for 2001 – save for the addition of RainGuard lens coatings that enable you to see clearly even when there's water on the glass. RainGuard, proven on B&L (now Bushnell) 4200-series riflescopes, also appears on Elite spotting scopes. A close focus limit distinguishes Elite binoculars: 5 feet for 8x ($1,585) and 10x ($1,664) models.

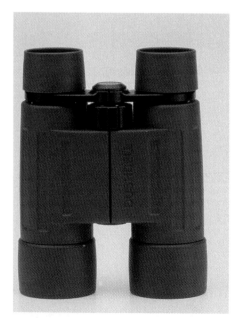

Bushnell's 10x42 Trophy is a mid-size, mid-price binocular of sound design and good quality.

Bushnell's Legend binoculars all feature Rain Guard® coating for a clearer view in wet weather. New models are a 9x25 compact and this 8x32 mid-size.

B&L roof prism Discoverer (7x42, 10x42) and porro prism Custom (8x36) binoculars are less costly alternatives. The 8x36 ($547) reminds me of my Zephyr 7x35. It's a great buy! The budget-priced Legacy binoculars, from 8x24 to 8-24x50, now feature twist-out eyecups and larger center-focus rings. If you're waiting for NASDAQ to recover, you'll like the prices of Bushnell's "H20" binoculars. The 8x42, 10x42, and 12x42 porro prism glasses, plus a new 8x24, retail for under $100. They have fully coated optics and rubber armor with no-slip ribbing. **913-752-3400**.

Burris:

The roof prism 8x42, 10x50 and 12x50 Burris Signature binoculars have been improved this year, with an enhanced phase-correction coating for better resolution. The long eye relief should please hunters who wear eyeglasses. I'm fond of the 8x42 ($684). These center-focus glasses feature click-stop diopter wheels and a tripod adapter. Burris also makes a Landmark binocular series, both roof prism and vertically offset porro prism models, at lower prices. The 8x40 and 10x50 porro prism Fullfield binoculars offer the wider objective spacing some hunters prefer. **970-356-1670**.

Fujinon:

Waterproof at Fujinon is waterproof indeed. The firm's roof prism HB, CD and HS binoculars, and the porro prism FMTR-SX, meet military specs: 14 days submersion in 6 feet of water, with no leaks. The CDs (7x42, 8x42, 10x42) have a center diopter adjustment. The HSs (8x32, 10x42) are of traditional design. The big HB series includes a 10x60, 12x60 and now a 15x60. Of course, they're tripod-adaptable. And can get a 2x doubler for extra resolution. Fujinon roof prism hunting glasses all have phase-corrected coatings. **973-633-5600**.

Kahles:

The excellent 8x42 and 10x42 Kahles roof prism binoculars earned a makeover this year, with the option of Advantage camouflage. Archers and turkey hunters, especially, should appreciate the new finish. These all-around binoculars retail for $777 and $832. Another development at Kahles: an 8x32 roof prism glass that, at 21 ounces, weighs 5 ounces less than the 8x42 and 10x42. It shares high quality optics, twist-out ocular lenses, and a waterproof housing. It also has a rubber armor jacket and a wider field of view than the 8x42 (399 feet at 100 yards, compared to 330). List price is $610. **800-426-3089**.

Leupold:

The Wind River line of binoculars has a bundle of new entries this year: six roof prism models and two compact porro prism glasses. The 8x42 and 10x42 WM and W2 binoculars are waterproof and rubber armored. These four binoculars feature an internal center focus mechanism and Multicoat 4 lens coatings. The WM versions ($563 and $621) have extra-long eye relief; the W2 ($384 and $438) feature retractable eyecups of soft rubber. Other roof prism models, the 8x25 and 10x25 compacts, weigh 14 ounces. New porro prism binoculars, 8x23 and 10x23, feature aspherical lenses and inverted design; that is, the ocular lenses are farther apart than the objectives. All four of these small center-focus binoculars are waterproof. **503-526-1421**.

Leica:

Minox, a Leica company, now offers useful mid-size binoculars.

Leica's 12x50 Trinovid ranks among the best of the few high-quality binoculars more powerful than 10x.

Nikon:

Nikon's best binoculars, the Venturer LX 8x42 and 10x42, are unchanged at present, though at $1695 and $1819 they cost less than they did two years ago. You bet they're still expensive! But you won't find a better binocular anywhere. Nikon has another good buy for less money: the Superior E 8x32. It's a very sharp porro prism glass that doesn't get much fanfare. At $957 retail, it's on the high end of mid-price, but you'll find it discounted. There's also a 10x42 and 12x50 in the line, at $1231 and $1337. Nikon's new binoculars are much more affordable. Porro-prism Action models, from 7x35 to 10-22x50, list from $151 to $273. They feature aspherical lenses, BaK4 prisms, center focus. New 8x36 and 10x36 "Sporter I" rubber-armored, roof prism binoculars cost $251 and $271. **631-547-8632**.

Optolyth:

Marketed in the United States by Deutsche Optik, German-made Optolyth binoculars come in popular sizes and configurations from 8x30 to 12x60. Traditional models feature individual-focus, porro-prism design and light rubber armor. Multi-coated glass brings bright images from the shadows. New this year are 8x45 and 10x45 roof-prism models with phase-corrected Ceralin-coated lenses. They boast an extra-wide field of view (63 degrees for the 10x) and long eye relief. At $799 and $899 retail, they're not the most costly binoculars, but the optics seem very sharp. Exit pupils are 5.6mm and 4.5mm – adequate for almost all the looking you'll do, even if your eyes are young. Optolyth's Royal 15x63 BGA roof-prism binocular has more power than you'll need – unless you need a spotting scope. Put this glass on a tripod, and your eyes won't burn out so quickly as with a scope. At 45 ounces, it is relatively light. Still, it has

phase-corrected glass and nitrogen-filled, center-focus barrels. The housing: rubber-armored magnesium alloy.

Pentax:

The waterproof roof prism DCF WP series now includes a 10x50. Phase-corrected optics, slide-in eye-cups and a lightweight magnesium frame distinguish this glass and the other DCF WPs: 8x32, 8x42, and 10x42. Priced at $655, $780, $900, and $1,058, respectively, these binoculars cost a little more than the DCF glasses that aren't waterproof or phase corrected. But they're a fine value. My 8x32 yields very sharp images. Pentax also makes a PCF V porro prism line. The 8x40 and 10x40 may be the most practical for hunters; at $370 and $394, the 16x60 and 20x60 offer a lot of power for the money. **800-761-4422**.

Steiner:

Steiner, founded in 1947, has only recently throttled up its marketing in North America. Predator binoculars have been its core product; this year there are three new models. The 10x30 and 12x30 weigh less than 11 ounces each, though their objective glass is bigger than that of most compacts. Shockproof to 11 Gs, they're waterproof and rubber armored, with fields of 261 and 216 feet at 1,000 yards. Retail price: $399. The other new Predator is a roof prism 8x32, a useful center-focus hunting glass with a close-focus range of 5 feet. Field: 328 feet.

Nikon's Travelites, and other very small binoculars, have limited utility for birding and hunting but can be great companions on a backpack trip or in the car

Steiner's 8x32
is one of a growing
number of small roof
prism binoculars with
an exit pupil of 4mm.

Swarovski's EL binocular is the latest
and best of the line.

Waterproof to military specs, it lists for $599. Steiner's Nighthunter line, new last year, did not make the G&G roundup then. It comprises five porro prism models: 8x30, 7x50, 10x50, 8x56, and 12x56. They range in price from $600 to $950 and feature bright, sharp optics with HD high-contrast coatings. All Steiner binoculars have a shock-resistant rubber jacket. **800-257-7742**.

Swarovski:

New 8x20 and 10x25 compact binoculars from Swarovski are waterproof and phase corrected. Clip-on polarizing filters make these glasses a good choice for fishermen who want to see trout through the glare of sun on water. Prices: $520 and $575. Swarovski's SLCs have been favorites of hunters for years, but the line has just been updated. The 7x, 8x and 10x SLCs have "Swarotop" multicoatings on all lens surfaces, one-piece rubber jackets, twist-out eyecups, locking diopter wheels, phase-corrected prisms. A 2x Swarovski doubler fits 42, 50 and 56mm models There's also an 8x30 and 15x56 SLC. Swarovski's EL 8x42 and 10x42 binoculars, introduced last year, continue to impress hunters who can afford them. No cost was spared to make these the best you can buy. **800-426-3089**.

Weaver:

A year after their debut, Grand Slam scopes are selling so well, supply can't keep up with demand. The logical encore: Grand Slam binoculars. The 8.5x45 and 10x45 roof prism glasses have phase-corrected prisms, twist-out eyecups, and ribbed rubber armor. Of course, they're fully multi-coated. Weight: 28 and 29 ounces. Weaver also offers a more affordable Classic line, its 8x42 and 10x42 models looking suspiciously like the old Simmons Presidential. I'm told that Blount SEG, which owned both Simmons and Weaver until very recently, was not above fattening one line at the other's expense. (The new owner is Alliant Tech Systems.) The Presidential was, to my eye, one of the great bargains in binoculars – a very good image at a modest price. These binoculars weigh 24 ounces. **800-285-0689**.

A Sightron scope complements this elk hunter's binocular. Even in the woods, you get help from optics.

Zeiss:

In 1894, Zeiss started producing binoculars. Nobody else was. These days, the competition is a lot stiffer. But Zeiss maintains a reputation for the best glass in the business. It also probes market niches with new models like the Victory series. These roof prism binoculars feature twist-lock eyecups, rubber armor, T* lens coatings. The 8x40 and 10x40 weigh 25 and 26 ounces; the 8x56 and 10x56 scale 41 and 42 ounces. Weight savings are due partly to glass that is lead- and arsenic-free. The Abbe-Koenig prisms have phase-correction coatings. **804-530-8300**.

World War I ads from the government asking citizens to loan their Zeiss 6x30 binoculars to the U.S. Navy.

Early 1900 ad for Zeiss "field binoculars."

Roald Amundsen was the first explorer to reach the South Pole in 1911 using Zeiss binoculars.

Ernest Hemingway was photographed using Zeiss binoculars while covering the war.

Riflescopes

Not even the best optics can take the place of practice from hunting positions.

I've concluded that we don't need any more riflescopes. We have enough. It's not that there's a scope for every need; rather, we can choose from myriad scopes for every need. The scopes that enable us to aim quickly and precisely at targets from whitetail deer to rockchucks have been available for some time. Substantive improvements – better lens coatings, sturdier reticles, tighter seals, more precise adjustments – distinguish the better scopes. Conveniences like finger-friendly windage and elevation dials and quick-adjust ocular sleeves are minor but sensible improvements. So, too, developments like a turret-mounted objective dial, mil-dot reticle and matte finish. Sifting refinements from the gimmicks is part of your job when shopping for scopes.

Excepting cosmetic makeovers of existing models, there aren't a lot of new scopes. This list includes most of them. I've paid some tribute to new and old models I think particularly worthwhile.

BSA:

It's a young company, as optics firms go, but BSA scopes are proliferating. This year there's a Big Cat line to complement the flagship Cats Eye variables. There's a 2-7x42, a 3.5-10x42, and a 4.5-14x52 AO, all with 1-inch tubes. Three with 30mm tubes and 42mm objectives complete the line: 1.5-4.5x, 3-9x, and 3.5-10x.

They're all waterproof, with finger-friendly adjustment dials. No Big Cat is over 13 inches long or priced higher than $270 retail. BSA has introduced an oversize turret-mounted parallax adjustment to its Platinum Target scopes. The "Big Wheel" is available on 6.5-26x42, 6.5-26x52, 8.5-34x42, and 8.5-34x52 scopes, all with AO. Prices: $300 to $400. A new Mil Dot scope series priced even lower ($150 to $200) includes a 4-16x40, 6-24x40, 8-32x40 with standard mil dot reticle, and the 4-16x and 6-24x with a lighted mil dot.

Electronics have come to the budget-priced Deer Hunter line, too, with a 3-9x40 illuminated-reticle scope at $130. Its rheostat has 11 brightness settings.

This 6x50 Burris is a heavy but optically excellent scope. It has a Posi-Lock erector-locking device.

The daylight/twilight ring of this Burris scope moves an adjustable field stop.

Expensive titanium tubes on Burris and Nikon scopes may be more a novelty than a useful option. The lightweight aluminum tubes commonly used have proven strong enough and light enough.

Bushnell's Elite 3200 Series now includes this 10x40 with a Mil-Dot reticle and target turrets.

The Burris scope on this custom Springfield is ready for zeroing.

Burris:

Burris offers one of the largest scope selections of any manufacturer, worldwide. Every year it grows. For 2001, Burris added a new 4-16x50 Black Diamond, the top-end model that includes a titanium variation, the 2.5-10x Mr. T. You may not need the extra strength of a Mr. T, but you'll appreciate lenses that are too tough to scratch with a knife. Sorry, they're not available on other Burris scopes. The Fullfield II line,

revamped recently to offer better ring spacing, now includes a 6.5-20x50 that weighs only 19 ounces. Like many of Burris' high-power variables, it's available with a mil-dot reticle. The 3-9x40 Fullfield II now comes with a lighted "Electro-Dot" ($506). Burris still manufactures 4x and 6x scopes ($330 and $360) in its Fullfield and Compact lines, for those of us who see no need to change magnification. The firm offers nine popular reticles, though availability for

many models is through the custom shop. I like the Ballistic Plex, a simple rangefinding reticle that helped me shoot a pronghorn at nearly 400 yards last fall.

Bushnell:

Since all Bausch & Lomb riflescopes became Bushnells a couple of years ago, the lines have continued to evolve. Now the budget-priced Sportview scopes have been replaced by the Sportsman series, with fully multi-coated optics, finger-adjustable quarter-minute dials, and fast-focus eyepieces. The line includes mostly mid-power variables but also 1x and 4x scopes. The 3-9x40 Sportsman is available with a three-step plex called the "3-2-1 Low Light" reticle. This reticle is also offered in Elite 3200 3-9x40 and 3-9x50 scopes, Bushnell's higher-grade models that list for $351 and $429. The company's *best* sights, the 4200 series, as well as the 3200 series, boast RainGuard, the Bushnell coating that disperses raindrops so you can aim even through wet lenses. Now the 6-24x40 in that line is available with a mil dot reticle. Calibrated at 12x instead of the highest power, this AO scope weighs only 20 ounces. Retail price: $469. There are six other 4200s, from 1.5-6x36 (my favorite for big game) to 8-32x40.

Docter Optic:

After drifting out of the U.S. marketplace, Docter Optic returned in 2000 with several European riflescopes, all variables with one-inch tubes: 3-9x40, 3-10x40, 4.5-14x40, and 8-25x50. Bigger 30mm tubes (also alloy) define another Docter line of variables, from 1.5-6x56 to 3-12x56. Fully multi-coated lenses complement quarter-minute adjustments that offer 50 inches of movement. A rubber eye ring and quick-focus European-style eyepiece come standard; aespherical lenses are optional. A 30mm Docter 1-4x sits low on a .35 Whelen in my rack. Though this scope is no longer offered (a pity), you'll find the same sharp, bright images in the current line.

A red dot sight has been added at Docter Optic. Less than 2 inches long, an inch high and an inch wide, the Doctersight weighs a mere ounce. The frame is stainless steel, brass and aluminum, not plastic, and has been recoil tested to 500 Gs. Optical glass, multi-coated between elements, yields a sharp image. Batteries last up to five years, though the sight is never turned off.

Kahles:

Long affiliated with Swarovski, Kahles is an old Vienna firm that just became part of Swarovski's North American operation. Its scopes are a little more affordable than Swarovski's P series, offering high quality at mid-range price. This year, Kahles added a 2-7x36 scope to its K line. At $532, it lists for about $90 less than the companion 3-9x42, and several hundred less than the Kahles C1.5-6x42, 2.5-10x50 and 3-12x56. The new 2-7x has fully multi-coated lenses and a second-plane reticle. Though the 1-inch tube is machined from a solid alloy billet, the scope weighs only 12 ounces. I'm particularly pleased to see this 2-7x cataloged, because I've lobbied for its introduction. In my view, there's no more useful all-purpose big game scope than a 2-7x. The 36mm objec-

tive allows for low mounting but gives you a 5mm exit pupil at the highest magnification. Kahles also lists 4x36, 6x42 and 8x50 fixed-power 1-inch scopes, from $555 to $749. The "C" variables, including a 1.1-4.5x24 ($722), have 30mm tubes.

Leica:

Word from Leica this year is that the three variable scopes marketed by this firm have been discontinued. Reason: contract problems having to do with scope manufacture. Leica's high quality standards may have had something to do with the decision – so too the high scope prices in a competitive market. Leica is not going away, though. Its binoculars remain at the top of the performance charts, with the Televid spotting scopes and Leica's latest hit (and a personal favorite), the LRF 800 RangeMaster laser rangefinder.

Leupold:

LPS is short for Leupold Premier Scopes, built on 30mm tubes in a not-so-subtle response to the aggressive marketing of European scopes to American shooters. The 1.5-6x42 LPS didn't come off the line as quickly as anticipated, and the 4.5-14x could have sold better. Now there

The 50mm objective lens of this Leupold variable may not be necessary, but it still sells well, and more hunting scopes with big objectives are no doubt on the way.

Scopes like this Leupold variable help you shoot military-style rifles (here an AR-15) more accurately.

Stainless steel rifles have boosted sales of scopes finished to match: like this Leupold on a Model 70.

Dr. Van Zwoll examines a rifle in .358 Hawk. It's equipped with a Leupold Vari-X III.

Here are some Leupold scopes for the 2002 model year.

are three LPS scopes: the original 1.5-6x, plus a new 2.5-10x45 and 3.5-14x50. They feature scratch-resistant lens coatings, resettable dials, and 4 inches of eye relief behind a quick-adjust eyepiece. The 3.5-14x50 has a turret-mounted parallax knob and weighs just 19 ounces. Leupold says each lens surface in the LPS scopes transmits 99.65 percent of incident light. The other Leupold lines are essentially unchanged. They include some of my favorite scopes: for big game hunting, the Vari-X III 2.5-8x36 and Vari-X II 2-7x33 – also the fixed 4x33 and 6x36; for varminting or sil-houette matches, the 12x40 or Tactical Mark 4 M3 with one-minute elevation clicks; for carbines or slug guns, the 2.5x20 Compact. The 4x28 Compact especially for rimfires is my top pick for a .22 sporter.

Nikon:

For whatever reason, Nikon chose not to couple high power with objective lenses the size of ashtrays. I'm impressed. You can still mount a Nikon 3.3-10x or 5.5-16x Nikon Titanium scope close to the rifle, where it belongs. A better long-range big game scope is hard to imagine. These 44mm AO models complement an equally sensible Monarch UCC line, which includes a 4-12x40, 5.5-16.5x44 and 6.5-20x44, all with AO. There's a 3-9x40 ($431) and, my favorite for lightweight rifles, a 2-7x32 ($427). For shotguns and woods rifles, Nikon offers a 1.5-4.5x20 ($371). The Monarch UCC series has one 50mm scope, a 3-9x. I'm told the other Nikon line, Buckmasters, has done well since its introduction a few years ago. The 3-9x40 and 3-9x50

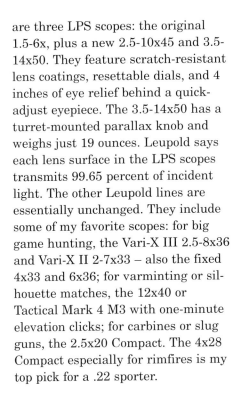

Target games like BR-22 will influence scope design. The Nikon on this Cooper .22 is outfitted with target knobs and adjustable objective.

Light Force imports huge scopes with illuminated reticles for varmint shooting.

A European-style eyepiece is quicker to adjust than the traditional fine-thread oculars with lock rings.

remain most popular ($303 and $453), but at $245, the 4x40 is an overlooked bargain, $85 less than the excellent 4x40 Monarch. Those Buckmasters scopes are tough, too. I know of two hunters who drove over theirs. Neither scope broke, and one didn't even lose zero. Better, though, that you drive elsewhere.

Pentax:

The Lightseeker series of Pentax variable scopes gave way a couple of years ago to the Lightseeker II line, with Perm-Align locking screw (per Burris Posi-Lock; I don't care for it), finger-adjust dials, and a

Pentax lightseeker scopes have been aggressively promoted. The consensus is that they are fine scopes.

Yardage Estimating System. There's nothing new in Lightseeker IIs recently, but its parent line now has a 3-9x50 and a 2.5-10x50 to complement the 1.75-6x35, 2-8x39, and 3-9x43. List prices for these two carriage-class scopes: $844 and $946. Pentax has also unveiled a new Lightseeker 30 line, with 4-16x, 6-24x, and 8.5-32x models – all with 30mm tubes and 50mm front lenses. If you want a more compact, less costly scope, look at the new Whitetails Unlimited stable: 2-5x20, 3-9x40, 3.7-11x42, and 4.5-14x50, from $398 to $698. I've found Pentax scopes to be extraordinarily bright, with resolution comparable to that of the most expensive scopes available. The 2-8x39 is probably the most versatile big game scope. I also like the 2.5x25 Shotgun scope, available with "Deep Woods" circle-in-plex reticle. Pentax offers six useful hunting reticles.

Redfield:

John Redfield's scope company served shooters for decades before environmental strictures put the Denver facility out of business. Now ATK (Alliant Tech Systems), which also owns Weaver and Simmons, is reintroducing the Redfield line. Quickly: The Illuminator 3-9x42 and 3-10x50 are the flagship models, followed by the Widefield (2-7x, 3-9x and fixed 4x). The television-screen lens shape gives you a field 30 percent wider than that of most conventional

scopes, says Redfield. The Golden Five Star variables are of conventional design. If they're like the old model of that name, they're worth a look. Pick the 3-9x, 4-12x or 6-18x. All have 40mm front glass. Prices: $300 to $470. Redfield's economy Tracker series comprises a 3-9x40, 3-9x50, 3-12x44, and 4-16x44, starting at $210. The new Redfield scopes feature 1-inch tubes of lightweight alloy. Black gloss and matte finishes are available, with a silver finish also on some models. "Rugged and reliable" fit descriptions of the original Redfield scopes. Redfield emphasizes that the new scopes are every bit as tough.

Schmidt & Bender:

"If you had to hunt big game with only one scope, which would it be?" Cornered, I weaseled out by saying there were plenty of scopes that would do – "But give me a Schmidt & Bender 4x36." There's not much if anything new at S&B these days. The boys in the white lab suits just keep making the best scopes they can. They're among the most costly scopes you'll find, and worth the money. Fixed-power scopes include that 4x, plus a 6x42, 10x42 and 8x56, all with 1-inch tubes. Variables have 30mm tubes. A 1.5-6x42, 3-12x50 and 2.5-10x56 can be had with illuminated reticles. There's a "Flash Dot" reticle option in the 1.25-4x20.

Long-range scopes include a 3-12x50 and 4-16x50 AO with bullet-

The rifleman as woods hunter gets less attention in the sporting press than does the rifleman as sniper. The evolution of optics reflects that view.

drop compensator and 1/5-minute clicks – and the Police/Marksman variable scopes with *34mm* tubes. Like the 4-16 Long Range scope, these have turret-mounted parallax adjustments. There's also a 10x42 P/M. With each, you can choose among three rangefinding reticles, including a mil dot with illuminated center.

Sightron:

Recently, Sightron acknowledged the trend to bigger scope lenses with three new models, all wearing 50mm objectives: 1.5-6x, 3-9x and 3-12x. They augment an already-comprehensive line of scopes, which now features "Zact-7 Revcoat" lens coating, a 7-layer broadband multi-coat that Sightron claims enhances light transmission and contrast. Another selling point is the "ExacTrac" ring around the erector tube inside the scope. ExacTrac ensures constant contact between the windage and elevation dials and the erector tube. Sightron's new offerings include (*hooray!*) the return of a 6x42 scope. Also, there's a 2.5-7x32 Compact. It's 11 inches long, weighs 12 ounces and would be on my short list for an all-around big game scope. At $243, it's affordable, too. I've used Sightron 3-9x and 2.5-7x Shotgun scopes and just mounted a 2.5x fixed power on a .338-06 Weatherby. They're good scopes! Most of the models have 1-inch tubes, but the SIII series features 30mm tubes. The 10x42 and

3.5-10x44 wear turret-mounted parallax wheels. The new 1.5-6x50 has no parallax adjustment.

Simmons:

For 2001, Simmons is emphasizing aspherical lenses. Used for years in cameras, aspherical lenses weren't available in riflescopes until Simmons introduced them a few years ago. An aspherical lens sharpens and flattens the image because at least one surface of the lens is not spherical; rather, it is shaped to better focus light rays bent by the other spherical surface(s) in the system. The Simmons Aetec scopes (2.8-10x44, 3.8-12x44 AO) both have this feature. New in 2001: illuminated reticles in these models. Aspherical lenses appear in the Whitetail Expedition series too: 1.5-6x32, 3-9x42, 4-12x42 AO, 6-18x42 AO. Prices range from $210 to $320. My Aetec does indeed deliver a bright, flat

image. On a tighter budget? The Simmons 44 Mag line has 3-10x44 and 4-12x44 AO scopes at $160 and $190 – and a 6.5-20x44 AO at $200. Blackpowder shooters and turkey hunters should like the compact shotgun scopes: 1.5x20, 2.5x20, 2x32, 4x32, priced as low as $56. They have a "ProDiamond" reticle that speeds your aim. I've used it on turkeys.

Swarovski:

Swarovski Optik has gone out of its way to find out what American hunters want in their scopes. The latest result: a 6-18x50 AV with adjustable objective. The AV line also includes a 3-9x36, 3-10x42 and 4-12x50. They feature 1-inch, one-piece tubes, with reticles in the second focal plane. Prices are under $800. The 6-18x50 follows the trend to high-power scopes with big objective lenses. The firm has also announced

New optics by Swarovski and other major manufacturers are getting better lens coatings for brighter images.

PV 4-16x50 and 6-24x50 scopes for shooters who can spend more and want 30mm tubes. These sights (with the PV 3-12x50) offer a new rangefinding reticle that's beautiful in its simplicity. The PV-1 1.25-4x24 has a 30mm tube and a five-intensity lighted reticle. Now the tube for this "dangerous game" scope is almost an inch longer, for flexibility in mounting. Like all Swarovski scopes, it is waterproof. Swarovski typically announces few new items each year; but those items consistently rank among the best anywhere as regards resolution, brightness, contrast, click repeatability and ruggedness – the things that matter in riflescopes.

Swift:

Swift scopes are affordable, and the line is impressively complete. Variables range from the 1.5-4.5x21 to an 8-32x50. There are a 4x40 and a 6x40 for curmudgeons like me; even a 1x20 Shotgun model. The nine Premier scopes have a helical, quick-adjust ocular lens. All models are advertised as waterproof and multi-coated. The 2.5-10x50 features a 30mm tube; the others have 1-inch tubes. For long-range shooting at big game, and for dual-purpose rifles, the Swift 4-12x40 Premier makes a lot of sense. It's only half an inch longer than the 3-9x40. Mainly because of the adjustable objective, it's 2 ounces heavier – but still under a pound. It lists for $250. For a bargain sight on that deer and elk rifle, look to the standard line. The 4x40 sells for $125, the 2-7x40 for $160. I'll be

hunting varmints with a 6-18x44 Swift this summer. Its target-style knobs make field corrections for wind and range easy. They're lower knobs than some, a feature that I'll appreciate when sliding that .22-250 in and out of its case.

Tasco:

Oval is the news at Tasco this year. The 1.5-5x and 3-9x EXP scopes have 42x54 oval objective lenses that are said to transmit more light than round 40mm objectives. I'm not sure they do. Looking from the front of an EXP, you can see internal mechanics impinge on the light path as you change power. Besides, light transmission also depends on lens quality and coating (these *are* fully multi-coated). The Tasco folks have a good idea in boosting lens size while keeping scope profile low for low mounting. Windage and elevation dials can be turned with gloved hands. Prices: $200 and $240. The World Class series has a new 4x40, a value-priced, fully multi-coated scope. There's a new illuminated 3-9x40 World Class, too. Tasco added a 4x32 illuminated-reticle scope to its Compact line, and developed a Black Powder series with four scopes: 1x32, 1.75-5x20, 2-7x32, and 3-9x32. There are two WC scopes for rimfire rifles: 2-8x32 and 3-12x40, plus a new 3-9x40 Bantam Shotgun scope. Tasco also lists new varmint scopes: a 2.5-10x42 and a 6-24x42.

Weaver:

Last year, Weaver introduced its Grand Slam series. Hunting models

include the 1.5-5x32, 3-10x40, 3.5-10x50, 4.5-14x40, and 6-20x40, along with a 4.75x40 fixed-power. All models are fully multi-coated, have finger-adjust windage and elevation dials and helical quick-focus ocular glass. Now the 6-20x is available with a dot and fine crosshair. Both it and the 4.5x40 come standard with adjustable objectives. Weaver's T-series 6x and 36x AO scopes have target knobs and 1/8-minute adjustments. I'd like to see other choices in magnification – say 10, 16 and 20x. This is a dandy varmint scope with either fine crosshair or dot. If you want a variable version and a mil dot reticle, check out the new Weaver Tactical scopes. The 3-9x40 and 4.5-14x40 AO both feature 1/8-minute clicks. My list of underappreciated scopes includes Weaver's K2.5.

Like the K4 and K6, this is a fine no-nonsense sight. It's less than 10 inches long, weighs only 7 ounces!

Zeiss:

Mention Zeiss, and you think "expensive." But the legendary German optics firm has tried hard lately to bring its products in line with the common man's budget – especially in the United States. To do this without letting quality slip, Zeiss got tough with its engineers. Result: the Conquest line, 1-inch scopes with fully multi-coated glass, non-magnifying etched reticles, and a 64-inch range of elevation adjustment. Pick a 3-9x40, a 3.5-10x44 or a 4.5-14x44. Choose from six reticles, including mil dot and center-circle "turkey." Prices for these waterproof Conquest

Swift offers a wide selection of modestly priced scopes. Most of the scopes sold are quite inexpensive, albeit the most widely known scopes cost a great deal more.

scopes range from $499 to $799. Also new from Zeiss is the VariPoint 1.5-6x42T* illuminated scope. The electronic dot in this scope remains a constant size, while the first-plane reticle changes size with magnification. At $1,350, the VariPoint scope isn't for everyone, but it does boast the best Zeiss optics – which some would say are the best scope optics in the world.

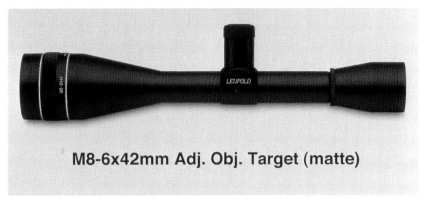

M8-6x42mm Adj. Obj. Target (matte)

Target knobs and adjustable objectives are becoming more popular; not so fixed-power scopes.

The Zeiss scope on this Sauer rifle features a 30mm tube, something that many scope buyers now seek.

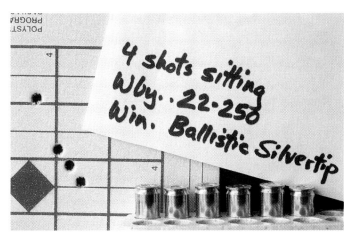

Some stringing, but a fine group from the sit. Light recoil helps keep you from jerking the trigger. No need for a high-power scope to shoot this well.

Expectation of long shooting with hot-rod cartridges will continue to draw many hunters to bigger and more powerful rifle scopes.

Spotting Scopes

Dr. Van Zwoll gives the Leica Televid high marks for optical performance, though it's a heavy instrument.

Y ou'll need a spotting scope for competitive shooting. You'll use one if you're sniping at prairie dogs far away, as your partner takes his turn. Hunting big game, a spotting scope can be an asset too — or an unnecessary burden. Depends on your hunting style. A 60mm scope suitable for big game hunting should have a straight eyepiece for quick pickup of animals you've already spotted. Variable power is an asset, the 15-45x range perhaps the most useful. You can find game easily at 15x. Above 30x or 40x, depending on objective size, you get bigger images, but no better resolution. Mirage can make high power a liability. On the shooting range, you don't need portability. So consider a 30x or a 20-60x scope with a 77 to 85mm objective lens – and an angled eyepiece so you didn't have to get out of shooting position to see the target.

These spotting scopes all have fully multicoated lenses unless otherwise specified:

Alpen:

Alpen is an imported line of outdoors optics. Among its products are two spotting scopes, with 60mm and 80mm objectives. Standard eyepieces are 20-60x variables. Listing at less than $400, even the 80mm is affordable; and users report excellent images! **www.alpenoutdoor.com**.

BSA:

BSA has recently added five new spotting scopes to its line. The best retail for under $200. They're a 10-30x50 and a 20-60x60. If you're a backpack hunter, you'll appreciate their light weight: 22 and 25 ounces. Focus and power rings encircle the tube. **www.bsaoptics.com**.

Bausch & Lomb/ Bushnell:

Bausch & Lomb and Bushnell, trade names under one roof, catalog the most extensive line of spotting scopes anywhere. The 20-60x80mm Elite is the best. Its brilliant, phase-corrected lenses make it a smart buy even at retail (just over $1,200). Field of view ranges from 98 to 50 feet at 1,000 yards. At 53 ounces, it's no lightweight. To save weight and money, look to the 20-60x70. At 40 ounces, it's not burdensome, and the objective diameter is still sufficient for low-light glassing. Or choose the 15-45x60 (26.5 ounces). A 60mm Discoverer, with straight tube and 15-60x60mm eyepiece, rounds out the B&L list. Focus and power rings encircle the main tube and aren't as easy to find under gloved fingers as traditional focus knobs and power rings. The myriad of Bushnell spotting scopes fall under Nature View, Spacemaster, Xtra-Wide, Trophy, Sentry and Sportview labels. The Spacemaster series offers the highest quality – plus a sighting tube atop the housing to help you find game in a hurry. Standard eyepiece is a 15-45x. For years, I used a Spacemaster 25x spotting scope on both the target range and in the field. It proved a durable scope, with a level of clarity that belied its modest price. I'd not hesitate to buy another! **www.bushnell.com**.

Burris:

Burris offers two spotting scopes. An 18-45x60 Signature is camera-adaptable. It weighs 29 ounces – not much more than some binoculars. It focuses down to 36 feet and has a field of 112 to 63 feet at 1000 yards. The Signature costs $819 with variable eyepiece, $644 with a 30x. The less costly 60mm Landmark ($277) has a 15-45x ocular lens and focuses to 13 feet. **www.burrisoptics.com**.

Fujinon:

Fujinon Super 80 (and 80 ED) spotting scopes have earned a place among the world's best. Available with 25x, 30x, 50x, 80x and 20-60x eyepieces, these scopes also accept camera adapters. They weigh 46 ounces and feature what Fujinon claims is the longest eye relief of any spotting scope: 31mm. A sighting tunnel gets you on target quickly. Now there's a compact version of this superior scope. The 60mm Fujinons are just 12 inches long and weigh about 28 ounces. They accept the "flat-field" eyepieces of 80mm Fujinons. **973-633-5600.**

Leica:

The Televid and Televid APO still rank among the best, with 77mm objectives and a choice of eyepieces: 20x wide-angle, 32x wide-angle, 40x and 20-60x. (Like the Nikon and B&L ED models, the APO has fluorite lenses that virtually eliminate distortion.) They're heavy scopes (53 and 60 ounces) but as bright and sharp as you'll find anywhere. They'll break your piggybank. They're worth it. **www.leica-camera.com**.

Leupold:

Leupold offers a compact spotting scope in its 12-40x60mm model with a mirror system that keeps length to under 12 inches. Weight: 36 ounces. At $1,271, it's not the cheapest scope, but it's a rugged instrument with great resolution. I've used one for years guiding elk hunters.

Now there's a padded jacket for this "Golden Ring" scope. Leave it on for use; just unzip the ends. It has a detachable shoulder strap. A new "Wind River" 15-45x60 spotting scope retails for just $355. It's waterproof and delivers a brighter, sharper image than you might expect. **www.leupold.com**.

Nikon:

Nikon has new eyepieces for its outstanding Fieldscope spotting scopes. The eyepieces range in price from $151 to $441 and include 24x wide-angle, 30x wide-angle, 40x, 40x wide-angle, 60x wide-angle, 20-45x zoom and 20-60x zoom (magnifications run a bit higher if you install the eyepieces on 78mm Fieldscopes instead of on the 60mm models). The 78mm ED Fieldscope is to my mind one of the very best spotting scopes on the market. The 60mm version is available in the Nikon Field Image System, which incorporates a tiny CCD camera that you install on the ocular housing. A cord transfers the image to a screen that you can set up anywhere to view what the scope "sees." You can thus videotape a range session or even a hunt!

For shooters on a budget, Nikon offers value in its 60mm and 80mm Sky & Earth spotting scopes, and in the 16-47x60mm Spotter. **www.nikonusa.com**.

Optolyth:

The best spotting scopes in Optolyth's line have 80- and 100mm fluorite front lenses. And they're good scopes indeed! Nitrogen filled and advertised as waterproof, they can be ordered with either straight or angled eyepieces (the straight one is best for hunting because you can find game more quickly). Optolyth sells fixed- and variable-power eyepieces from 20x to 70x in the 80mm scope and 30x to 60x in the 100mm model. Incidentally, fluorite is from a crystal that is grown, not manufactured. It enhances resolution and makes for truer colors. **www.deutscheoptik.com**.

Birders can well use the additional resolution from big front glass like that on this Pentax 80mm scope.

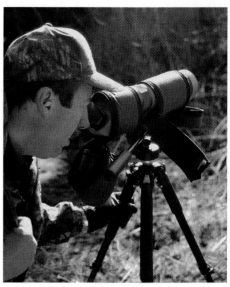

Swarovski builds fine 80mm spotting scopes. They're a bit heavy for the hill.

Pentax:

Pentax, now well known for its binoculars and riflescopes, offers a carriage-class spotting scope called the PF-80 ED. With a 36x eyepiece, it weighs a hefty 61 ounces and is nearly 18 inches long. But the image is sharp enough to justify the $1,720 price. You won't find better. **www.pentaxlightseeker.com**.

Simmons:

Simmons optics have evolved over the past couple of years. The Presidential spotting scope is no longer. The waterproof HydroSport 15-45x50mm and 20-60x60mm offer good service for $240 and $260. Optics are multi coated but not advertised as fully coated. There's a sighting tunnel. **www.simmonsoptics.com**.

Sightron:

Sightron has two spotting scopes in its line, one with a 63mm objective, one with an 80mm. The eyepiece selection is limited: a 20-50x for both. These scopes measure 14 and 15 inches, weigh 31 and 34 ounces. They're reasonably priced. Choose the 80mm model. **www.sightron.com**.

Swarovski:

Swarovski offers three spotting scopes: the ST-80 (and angled AT-80) conventional and CT-75 and CT-85 collapsible models. The ST-80 is available with HD (color-corrected, high resolution) lenses. Eyepieces include a 15x, 22x, 30x wide-angle and 20-60x. Weight is 52 ounces. These are expensive scopes, but like the others in their price range, a worthwhile investment if you spend much time looking through them. The CT-75 and CT-85 (41 and 49 ounces) differ from each other only in objective diameter. Their four-piece tubes slide into one compact unit for easy backpacking. At $1,132, the CT-85 body is the same price as the ST-80. Eyepieces range from $240 to $354. One other item worth considering is the 2x doubler Swarovski has added to its binocular line. It costs $288 and replaces the ocular assembly on one side of an EL or SLC binocular, doubling the magnification. Use it in a 10x glass, and you get 20x magnification. It won't yield the exit pupil of a large spotting scope, but it's a compact, fieldworthy attachment. On the 15x56 SLC, it gives you 30x and an exit pupil approaching that of a 60mm spotting scope! **www.swarovskioptik.com**.

Swift:

Swift has a spotting scope for every budget, from the $1,800 Nighthawk ED (eyepieces extra!) to the $580 Searcher (with 20x, 30x, 40x or 50x eyepiece) to the $435 Panther (15x, 20x or 40x) and $160 Leopard (a 25x eyepiece). The 80mm Nighthawk ranks among the best of spotting scopes. All six versions feature a 1.8x optical sight for quick target acquisition. At 31 ounces, it's extraordinarily lightweight – much lighter than most scopes of its caliber. It focuses to 24 feet. Even closer focus (15 feet) is possible with the front lens attachment of Swift's Searcher. This high-quality 60mm scope has a rotating ocular housing, to give you instant access to a straight or angled eyepiece. **www.swift-optics.com**.

Weaver:

Weaver lists two spotting scopes – or one with two objective sizes. The 50mm version comes with a 20x eyepiece, the 60mm with a 15-40x. The 50mm is especially compact (10 inches) and lightweight (just 21 ounces). They're both affordable. **www.weaveroptics.com**.

Chapter 7

Scopes, So You Can Shoot Far

"...Aim comes before hit."

Beginnings

SCOPES ARE SIGHTS for shooters who want to hit farther than they can aim without help. They can also help you aim farther than you can shoot without help. No matter how far we reach with rifle bullets, our reach is only useful if at its limit we can still direct the bullets accurately. When you paint a house, the ladder's top rung gets little use. It will extend your reach but compromise your control. A missile can be crammed full of explosives and given tremendous acceleration, but without an adequate guidance system, it is worthless.

Flat-shooting bullets from accurate rifles extend a rifleman's reach beyond the limits of his vision. A .243 Winchester bullet is still moving at nearly 2,000 fps 400 yards downrange. Most of us have trouble seeing small targets that far away; aiming without the help of optics makes any hit mostly luck. A scope won't stretch a rifle's reach; it just adds control so we can use that reach.

Primitive hunters used lenses before anybody thought of making lenses. That's because their eyes had them: curved corneas that bent (refracted) incoming light rays into tight cones or bundles. Early telescopes by Lippershay and Galileo were designed for looking at stars, not targets. But a couple of centuries later, riflemen were using optical sights. In America, riflescopes date to about 1840. The famous New England gunsmith Morgan James equipped his match rifles with scopes shortly thereafter, and snipers used them during our Civil War. But scopes got poor reviews on the frontier. Up to 34 inches long, they added a lot of weight to any rifle. They offered only dim, fuzzy, distorted images in good light, and hardly any image at all when the sun didn't shine. Delicate mounts and reticles, and adjustments prone to failure, made them unreliable. Repair shops were hard to reach from remote homesteads.

After the plains had been swept clean of game and hostile red men, rifles no longer had an everyday use. Suddenly they became a sportsman's tool. Sportsmen were more apt than market hunters or settlers to buy things yet to be proven. So by the turn of the last century, German and American inventors were experimenting with short riflescopes.

Around 1901, the J. Stevens Tool Co. began manufacturing scopes. Among its customers was barrelmaker H.M. Pope, who favored a 16-inch 5x that retailed for $24. Winchester's A-5 followed, becoming in 1929 the Lyman 5-A. Oddly enough, riflescope companies proliferated during the Depression. Litschert, Souther, Wollensak and others competed with firms whose main business was guns: Mossberg, Marlin, Savage and the like. One of the most successful of scopes from this era was the Lyman Alaskan, similar in form and function to the rival Noske, but longer-lived.

Bill Weaver built the prototype for his first scope by hand when he was 24. Introduced in 1930, the 3x Weaver Model 330 sold for $19, complete with a "grasshopper" mount that resembled an oversize paperclip. The 3/4-inch tube had internal adjustments: 1-inch increments for windage, 2-inch for elevation. A flat-topped post was the standard reticle, but you could special-order a crosswire for $1.50. Lighter than the contemporary German scopes, which had already built a reputation for high quality, Weaver's was much less expensive. Its price and reliability also gave it an edge on its domestic competition.

The 1930s proved a banner decade in the evolution of scopes. While Bill Weaver made them popular, Professor A. Smakula of the Carl Zeiss company made them better.

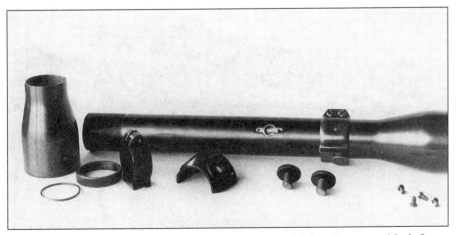

Early scopes were not sealed, so they could be disassembled for cleaning and mounting in one-piece rings.

The Redfield 3200, here on Vic Fogle's Winchester 52, is ideal for competitive smallbore shooting.

Smakula discovered that by coating lens surfaces with a thin layer of magnesium flouride, he could dramatically boost light transmission. The Nazi war machine prevented publication of Smakula's findings until 1940; after that, coated lenses became commonplace on top-quality optics. Germany's Schott Glassworks was the first company to use multiple lens coatings; it had a three-layer process in place before the end of World War II.

That war finished off many American scope companies. But Weaver and Lyman survived. They met stiff competition from Redfield, Leupold and Bausch & Lomb. By the mid-1950s, American scope firms had adopted a 1-inch tube as standard, while European makers stuck with 26mm tubes (slightly larger than an inch). The 7/8-inch tube had become obsolete. At the same time,

Early scopes like this Lyman Alaskan had plenty of eye relief – and latitude in eye relief.

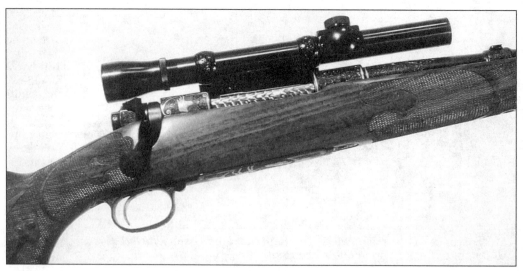

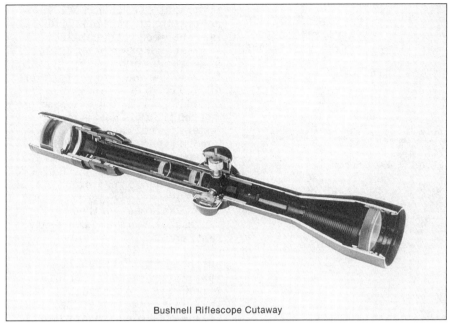

Bushnell Riflescope Cutaway

Scopes comprise many parts, which must be mounted to withstand the sudden shock of recoil.

The picture you see through a modern riflescope is so bright and sharp that it's almost magical. You get fine adjustments, durability that stands up to recalcitrant pack mules and recoil from cartridges the size of anti-tank rounds. But even modern scopes have limits. Rather, they impose limits on shooters. Parallax is one example. It's the apparent movement of the target in the scope field as you move your eye up and down or from side to side. To see how parallax works, sandbag your rifle with the crosswire on a target far away. With the full scope field in view, move your head in a circle as if tracing the rim of the ocular lens with your eye. You'll see the crosswire move, though the rifle stays still. Because the rest holds the rifle on target, the bullet will hit center, no matter where the crosswire appears. But if *you* were holding the rifle and didn't consider parallax, you'd correct your hold to plant the crosswire in the middle. If your eye was off center in the scope, you'd miss.

A function of target distance, parallax can't be corrected with compound lenses. The images formed by targets at various distances fall at different points between objective and erector lenses, and so are at different points between the erector and ocular lenses. Because the scope's reticle does not move along the tube's axis to compensate, it meets a focused image only when the target is a certain distance from the rifle. That distance can be programmed into the scope. Most hunting scopes are set to be parallax-free at 100 or 150 yards. Scopes designed for rimfire rifles or shotguns are commonly corrected for parallax at 50 or 75 yards. Some target and varmint scopes, and big-game variables of high magnification, have parallax adjustments so you can program the scope for zero parallax at the range you want to shoot.

If your eye is centered on the axis of the scope, you needn't worry about parallax, no matter what the range. If your eye is off center when you're shooting over a zero-parallax distance, you don't have to fret either. Parallax becomes a problem only when you're peeking into the scope from an angle, at a very close or a very distant target.

aluminum alloys replaced steel in scope tubes. More important than tube diameter or material were internal problems: reticles that moved off-center as you moved the adjustments, reticles that grew as you turned up magnification on a variable scope, reticles that broke, seals that leaked moisture, fogging induced by temperature change.

The reticle problems were soon solved by clever engineers. Now reticles in American scopes remain centered in your field of view, and in variable scopes most are located in the second (rear) focal plane so they stay one apparent size. Advocates of first-plane reticles, still popular in Europe, point out that they subtend the same measure on the target no matter what the power, so you can more easily use them as rangefinding devices. Front-plane reticles also eliminate point-of-impact shift when you change power on variable scopes.

After the Second World War, scope makers started offering more kinds of reticles. The flat-top post and medium crosswire remained popular, but dots, tapered crosswires and, later, dual-thickness crosswires stole increasing market shares. T.K. Lee retrofitted target and hunting scopes with dots suspended by web strands from black widow spiders. Though a 4-minute dot looks big through the scope, it measures only .008 inch in diameter. "Tackhole" Lee, an accomplished target

shooter, had the patience and the delicate touch to build this hobby into a business. By this time, reticle breakage had been all but eliminated. The "plex" reticle appeared, eventually replacing the crosswire as the most popular choice among U.S. hunters.

Leakage around scope seals diminished as better seals came along. The number of joints in scopes declined as manufacturing techniques permitted use of one-piece tubes. Now even scopes with big objective bells can be machined from one piece of tubing. But the fogging continued until, in the 1950s, nitrogen gas was injected into scopes that were then sealed at the factory. This gas prevented any condensation from temperature changes within the scope; it has become a standard feature. At the same time, scope rings were split to allow installation without removing turret or ocular housing. Disassembling a scope to mount it had been a common practice before the advent of sealed tubes.

Since the1960s, few fundamental changes have been made in riflescope design – certainly none that compare with the advent of lens coatings or nitrogen-filled tubes. But we have a much greater choice of scope styles, sizes, magnification ranges, options and finishes than did our forebears. There's no excuse for you not to have the perfect scope for your kind of hunting or target shooting.

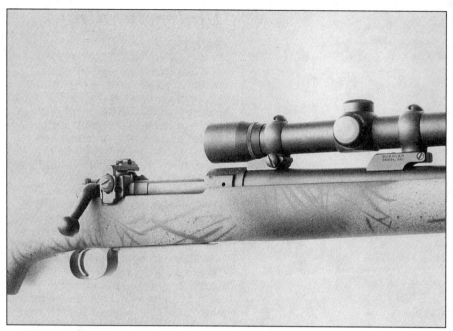

This scope has intermediate eye relief (and a small field of view) so it can be mounted on the barrel.

Eye relief, like parallax, is an optical feature of any scope. Since nobody's come up with adjustable eye relief, you must live with the eye relief built into the scope you buy. It's the distance in inches from the ocular lens to your eye when you see the scope's full field of view. If the field "blacks out" on its periphery, giving you only a fuzzy-edged peephole in the middle, your eye is either too close to or too far from the lens. A crescent of black in any quadrant of the scope's field means your eye is off-axis. Most riflescopes have an eye relief of 3 to 3 1/2 inches. Pistol scopes and those intended for barrel mounting on rifles have much longer eye relief so you can see the full field in normal firing position. Keep in mind that eye relief is measured from your cornea to the glass, not to the rim of the eyepiece. An ocular lens deeply recessed can mean a bloodied brow if the eye relief is short enough to bring the rim to your face during recoil. Rubber eyepiece rings make sense.

Eye relief is called "critical" when you don't have much back-and-forth leeway before the field gets smaller and blacks out. Big game scopes should have non-critical eye relief because sometimes you must aim quickly from unorthodox positions that put your eye closer or farther from the scope than you'd like. Rifles of heavy recoil are best equipped with scopes of relatively long eye relief so you don't get whacked when you're shooting uphill or from prone.

Scope makers can build in less critical eye relief, but at a cost in magnification. Increasing the focal length of the ocular lens or decreasing that of the objective lens gives your eye more room to move but a smaller image. Decreasing the focal length of the erectors makes eye relief less critical too, but also reduces your field of view.

The eye relief for variable scopes typically diminishes from low to high power. Scope specs may list only eye relief at the low end of the power dial. Check before you buy – not only that there's enough distance between your eye and the scope at high power, but that there's an acceptable difference in eye relief between low and high power. After all, you can only mount a scope in one place, and that should be where you can get a full field of view instantly when cheeking the stock. You'll do yourself no favor with a scope that requires you to cheek it at different places when you change magnification. Some variable scopes are designed to give you constant eye relief throughout the power range. This, to my mind, is a significant benefit.

The size of the field depends not only on eye relief, but on the size of your ocular lens and the scope's magnification. When you look through a scope, your eye becomes the apex of a cone of light whose base is the perimeter of the ocular lens. From the side, that cone is an angle. Say that angle is 30 degrees, and your scope is an 8x. A 30-degree angle subtends about 150 feet at 100 yards. Dividing 150 by 8, you get a field of not quite 19 feet. The size of the objective lens has nothing to do with field of view.

Big objective lenses are in style now. According to the people who market them, hunting scopes with 50mm objectives sell faster than lemonade at July farm auctions. An oversize lens transmits more light because it provides the scope with a larger exit pupil. The exit pupil of a

Big scopes are fine for varminting or shooting from the bench; they're cumbersome in the hills.

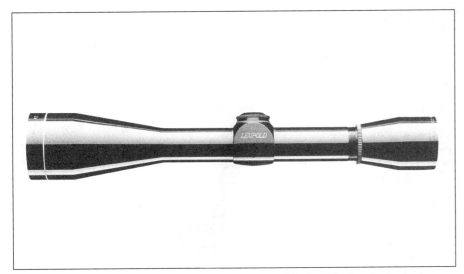

Leupold's 6x42 gives you a 7mm exit pupil but still fits nicely in low rings on most rifles.

scope, like that of a binocular, is simply a ratio of objective lens diameter, in millimeters, to the scope's magnification. That is, a 4x scope with a 32mm front lens would have an exit pupil of 8mm.

Your eyes (actually, young and perfect eyes) have pupils that vary in size from about 2.5mm in bright daylight to 7.1mm in the dark. At dawn or dusk, those pupils adjust to 6mm or so. No matter how big the front lens of a scope, eyes dilated to 6mm can only take advantage of an exit pupil that wide. As your eyes age, your range of pupil dilation shrinks, so you may be looking through 5mm holes (or even smaller), when the sun goes down. Any 4x32 scope is transmitting more light than even a young shooter can use, even if he were to shoot in total darkness! Oversize objectives earn their keep only when you're using high magnification in dim light. If you've set your 3.5-10x variable at 10 power, your exit pupil with a 50mm objective would be 5 – roughly 20 percent greater than with standard objectives. It will brighten the target image in dim light.

Why then do 4x scopes have an objective bell at all, when a straight 1-inch tube would yield an exit pupil of 5? Because a big exit pupil gives you more latitude in head placement when you aim. If the exit pupil is bigger than the pupil in your eye, the alignment of your eye in the scope is less critical. A scope with a big objective enables you to pick up your target more quickly. It's also true that bigger glass increases resolution, or the ability of the instrument to show you detail. However, there's no benefit to using a scope

that brings you more resolution than your eye can use, and the low power of most riflescopes prevents you from seeing all the resolution possible with objective lenses of common size.

There are other terms having to do with light transmission in scopes. Relative brightness is one. It's the same as in binoculars – simply the exit pupil measurement squared: 25 for an exit pupil of 5mm. Relative

light efficiency is 50 percent added to the relative brightness (to show differences in lens coatings). Twilight factor is the square root of the product of objective lens diameter and magnification. Provided you buy a high-quality scope, exit pupil and twilight factor are all you need to know about light transmission.

Experienced shooters know that a scope's main advantage over iron sights is not its magnification. It is instead a clearer, single-plane image – that perfectly focused reticle superimposed on a target sharply defined and, in dim light. Barrel-mounted iron sights pull your eyes toward three focal points – at different distances. You can't focus on the rear sight, front sight and target at the same time, so two of them will remain fuzzy. A receiver sight eliminates one fuzzy image (actually, it enables you to aim without a sharp view of the aperture), but the front sight and target are still fighting for your attention. In a scope, you get superior definition of the target and reticle, allowing you to control each shot.

Many shooters don't take full advantage of this sharp sight picture because they don't bother to adjust the ocular lens to get the reticle in perfect focus. All you have to do is loosen the lock ring in front of the ocu-

You don't need high magnification on big game scopes, even for long shooting at delicate antelopes.

lar housing, then screw the housing out several turns. Throw your rifle to your shoulder, aiming it at a clear patch of sky. The reticle should be fuzzy. Screw the housing in a turn and repeat until the reticle appears tack-sharp against the sky. You can't hold the gun to your shoulder and watch the reticle become sharp because your eye will automatically try to bring the reticle into focus. It must appear sharp immediately, so when you throw the rifle up to test focus, it's a good idea to close your eyes, opening them only when the reticle is against the sky. European-style eyepieces have a sleeved adjustment on helical threads that's a lot easier to use. However, once the crosswire is clean and sharp to your eye, you shouldn't need to adjust it unless high magnification combined with changing target distance forces your eye to shorten its focus from infinity.

How much magnification is best in a hunting scope? You might as well ask how much should a bird dog weigh, how many is too many children, and what's a good interest rate. A lot of hunters buy more power than they can use, because with a 4x scope and normal eye-sight you can see clearly enough to shoot deer-size game to 400 yards. Most hunters can't shoot well enough to keep nine of 10 shots in the vitals of a deer at that range under hunting conditions, no matter what scope they're using, or how accurate their rifle. Oddly enough, most scopes bought by deer hunters now are variables with a high end of at least 7x.

Elk-hunter surveys I've done show 3-9x and 3.5-10x variables to far out-number alternative scopes. To my mind a 4x is just as useful. It's also lighter, less expensive and sturdier because it's less complex. A bright 4x enables you to distinguish quarter-inch black-and-white grids at 100 yards. That means it can resolve 1-inch grids at 400 yards. You don't need more definition than that for chest cavities as big as grocery bags.

Varmint hunters understandably choose higher magnification, because most varminting is done from a steady position at small targets, and few shots are urgent. Varmint hunters usually shoot in good light, where a tiny exit pupil is no handicap. They have time to figure the effects of wind and range for a shot before they take it and can make use of high magnification to help them "shade" their hold. Varmint hunters prefer scopes with enough magnification to help them milk the potential from long-range cartridges and accurate barrels.

My favorite varmint scope isn't very big or powerful. It's Leupold's 8x36, a lightweight scope that looks as good on a trim sporting rifle as it does on a thick-barreled varmint gun. The 36mm objective gives me an exit pupil of 4.5, which is as much as I need for most shooting, even on early-morning coyote hunts. I can't quarter the eye of a crow at 300 yards, but if the rifle I'm shooting can hold a half-minute group at that distance and the wind doesn't kick up, the crow is still in trouble. An 8x scope can define targets I'm not

skilled enough to hit, and it is much easier to use than, say, my 20x Redfield 3200. Running jackrabbits and coyotes are hard to find with scopes of more than 10x magnification. If you're an avid prairie dog shooter, high magnification makes the shooting easier and more graphic.

Scope tube diameter has increased since the likes of Rudolph Noske settled on a 7/8-inch tube nearly a century ago. European shooters got accustomed to 26mm tubes, which appeared stateside in scopes like the Lyman Challenger. The 1-inch (25.4mm) diameter established itself as the American standard, while in Europe the 26mm pipe was supplanted by the 30mm. Now you see lots of scopes with 30mm tubes on the U.S. market. And a handful of commercial sights have even featured 34mm tubes. What's the advantage? Well, there isn't much of one, unless you're shooting at extreme ranges. Contrary to popular myth, 30mm tubes do not guarantee either a bigger field of view or brighter images. In fact, many have the same erector lenses as in 1-inch scopes! The bigger tube allows these erector assemblies more room to move, for when you need lots of elevation adjustment to reach distant targets. Expect the same picture as you get from a 1-inch scope. In 30mm scopes with super-size innards, like Swarovski's PH scopes, you'll have a little more glass, and an optical advantage. Still, you'll be hard-pressed to see it. I prefer 1-inch scope tubes for most applications, with a satin finish that's both attractive and non-reflective in the field.

The 4x Redfield on this Winchester is an old favorite of the author's.

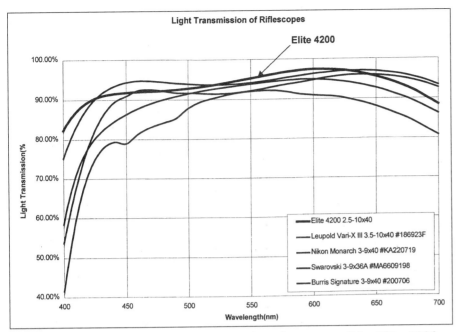

Light Transmission of Riflescopes

Elite 4200

Light Transmission(%

Wavelength(nm)

- Elite 4200 2.5-10x40
- Leupold Vari-X III 3.5-10x40 #186923F
- Nikon Monarch 3-9x40 #KA220719
- Swarovski 3-9x36A #MA6609198
- Burris Signature 3-9x40 #200706

Bushnell is proud to show the optical performance of its Elite 4200 scopes.

Leupold and some other makers now use one-piece tubes, machining them from stock like this.

Manufacturers who offer one-piece scope tubes point out that they are sturdier and more perfectly sealed than two-piece tubes. True enough. However, two-piece scopes have served hunters well for more than half a century. There are more important things to consider when shopping – like how much tube you have available for the rings and whether the turret location allows you to mount the scope as you wish. A lot of variable scopes are short on tube sections, or wear the turret in a bad spot, or have such a long ocular housing as to make any standard ring location problematic.

It's essential that the adjustments be repeatable. That is, if you turn a 1/4-minute windage dial four clicks, you should get an inch of movement at the 100-yard target every time. To test a scope, I "shoot around the square," firing a three-shot group, then moving right 12 clicks, firing again and moving up 12, firing again, moving left 12, firing again and moving down 12. The final group should be double the first.

Some scopes designed for tactical or long-range shooting have special adjustment knobs. Leupold offers two types. Its Mark 4 and Long Range series include scopes with the "M3" turret, whose elevation knob is a bullet-drop compensator. The dial is calibrated to compensate for bullet drop out to 700 meters (1,000 on some models) with specific loads. One turn of the dial gives you enough elevation to bring you from 100 to 1,000 yards, in 1-minute increments. The coarse clicks are necessary for quick elevation change. The "M1" target knobs on other Leupold Long Range scopes are taller and calibrated in 1/4-minute clicks. If you hunt prairie dogs or shoot big game at extreme range from a stand, you might use the target knobs to "dial in" corrections for wind and bullet drop. Most hunters are better served with the compact, covered adjustment knobs standard on fixed-power scopes up to 8x and variables as powerful as the 4.5-14.

I like a soft eyepiece rim on a scope, because I've been clobbered by scopes without one. Properly mounted, the sight should not bite you during recoil. But because shots at game are sometimes taken from positions that put your eye closer to the lens, the soft eye ring is still a good idea. You may want to shoot uphill from prone, kneeling,

Keep the scope well forward for fast sighting and to prevent a scarred brow.

The Leupold variable on this Winchester Featherweight is typical of hunting scopes these days.

sitting – all positions that tip your brow forward and the scope back. To give yourself ample clearance and speed aiming, mount the scope far enough forward that you see a full field of view only when your face is thrust ahead as far as is comfortable on the comb. You don't want to throw the rifle to your shoulder and have to back away from the scope. Not only does this waste time; you'll always be fearful of a drubbing by that eyepiece. A natural stock-crawler, I position scopes well forward. On most bolt-action rifles, the eyepiece barely extends beyond the rear guard screw. You might find when you experiment that your scopes would give you more eye clearance and quicker aim if you moved them a bit farther forward.

In my view, scopes should be mounted low. Most stock combs designed for scopes (just about all stock combs since the 1950s) put your eye into the scope axis if the scope is mounted in low rings. Stocks designed for iron sight shooting may have too much drop, but I've yet to see a factory-built stock that had a comb too straight for low

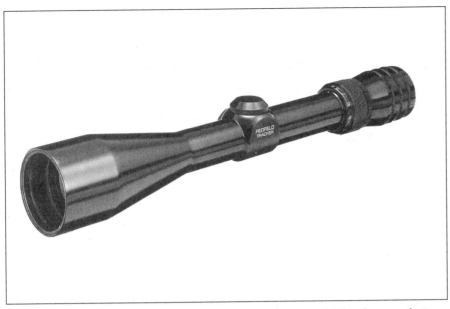

Redfield's scope line is now owned by Blount, which also markets Simmons and Weaver scopes.

for iron sights. As costly as they seem, high-quality scopes make sense as investments for big game hunters. And, compared to other hunting items, they're still affordable. When Bill Weaver was selling primitive scopes for under $30, you could buy a Winchester Model 70 Super Grade for $96. A comparable gun now costs more than $1,500; but you can buy a scope that's far superior to the first Weavers for well under $500.

Hunting optics are heavily discounted, even at retail outlets. For the best deal, shop even after you decide on what you want. And consider second-hand scopes. If they look new outside, they're probably like new inside. Use the criteria outlined here in Chapter 5. Beyond the bargain hunting, consider a scope an investment. With care, it should last many years. Buying quality in a scope is smart; but

rings. If you are forced by a large objective bell to mount a scope in medium or high rings, you'll lose some face contact with the stock when you aim, and that's bad business. You'll also find the rifle does not handle as well because the center of gravity has been pulled high. Such a mount will not endear you to outfitters, either, whose job it is to fasten your rifle on saddles. Slim scabbards have too little room for 50mm objectives and high rings.

It's important to remember that a scope is a sight, not an instrument to be used alone. It must be compatible with your rifle and suited to the hunt. A lot of big game hunters over-scope themselves. I can only assume that they are not thinking about what their riflescope is to *do*. It is neither a binocular nor a spotting scope. If you buy a riflescope for any purpose besides aiming, you'll make aiming more difficult.

How much should you pay for a scope? Probably more than you want to. When I was growing up, a lot of hunters were still using iron sights, and scopes were yard-sale cheap. You could buy new B&L or Redfield 4x scopes for less than $60, a Weaver K4 for under $50. Now equivalent scopes list for more than $300. Actually, early post-war scopes were bargains. They had features we think important – yet were priced like scopes from the 1930s, which had none of those features. Scope tags now reflect a higher demand from hunters, many of whom own rifles with no provision

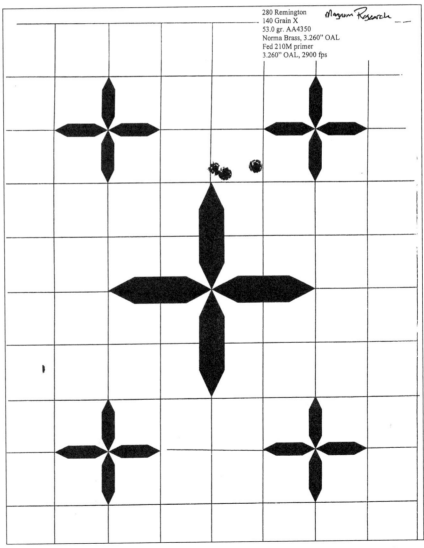

280 Remington
140 Grain X
53.0 gr. AA4350
Norma Brass, 3.260" OAL
Fed 210M primer
3.260" OAL, 2900 fps

Magnum Research

This tight group was made with a Burris variable scope and a Magnum Research rifle.

don't confuse quality with sophistication. Oversize lenses and high magnification, electronic reticles, 30mm tubes, exotic materials and range-finding devices will run the ticket up without adding much to the utility of the scope. Optical performance – brightness, resolution and flatness of field – plus durability are what matter most.

If I were in the market for a new scope for a big game rifle, I'd look at the best 4x and 6x scopes, and variables of 1.5-6x, 2-7x and 2.5-8x. The 1-inch tube would have an objective lens no bigger than 42mm – preferably 32, 36 or 38mm, depending on magnification. I'd spend enough money to feel a pinch, because the best of these ordinary-looking scopes are still quite expensive.

Your tastes may differ, but I suspect you'll find the shopping as much fun. Keep in mind as you thumb through catalogs and squint through the glass that a riflescope is not a telescope; it is a *sight*! "A real marksman can hit with any rifle," an old hunter once told me, swabbing the lens of a well-used Weaver K4. "And any sight." A self-styled expert on rifles, I laughed him off at the time, confident that better gear would make for tighter groups and more center shots. It did. On paper. But in the field, my mentor rarely missed, while I embarrassed myself often. "If you spent as much time shootin' as you spend shoppin', you might do better," he observed. He was right.

Scope weight

Most of what matters in a scope has to do with magnification and light transmission. Reticles and adjustments come next, and of course we want scopes to be sturdy. Nobody talks much about the weight of riflescopes, however – an odd omission, given the race to make rifles lighter than empty ice cube trays.

Browsing scope catalogs not long ago, I made note of the heaviest of each brand. Here they are:

Bausch & Lomb: 5-15x50	24 ounces	
Burris: 6-24x50	25	
Leica: 4.5-14x42	18	
Leupold: 3.5-14x52	22	
Nikon: 6.5-20x44	20	
Pentax: 8.5-32x44	24	
Sightron: 6-24x42	19	
Simmons: 6-20x44	20	
Swarovski: 2.5-10x56	25	
Tasco: 10-40x50	25	
Weaver: 6-24x42	18	
Zeiss: 3-12x56	18	

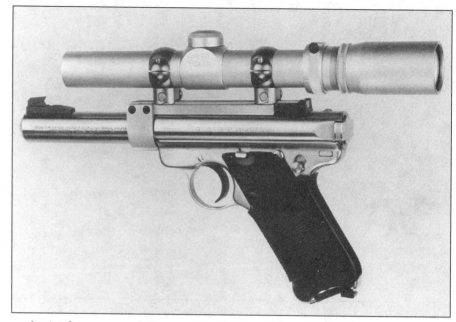

A pistol scope can help you aim, but small pistols like this Ruger are certainly handier without them.

Weight can be an asset. I remember as a lad on the farm piling cast-iron weights on the nose of a tractor. While moving that extra weight soaked up some horsepower, it was an effective way to keep the front tires on the ground under a heavy load. Without weights, you couldn't steer! We also filled rear tires with a chloride solution to give them more traction.

Ballast goes into a boat to keep it upright.

Heavy rifle barrels deliver more consistent accuracy under sustained fire.

Wrecking balls and bowling balls and Sumo wrestlers need great mass to perform well.

Weight in bullets helps them penetrate, in shotguns keeps us from stopping our swing, in pistols deadens the gyrations of the front sight.

In a scope, the less weight the better. Beyond the weight of good glass, you want parts as light as possible. Weight may add strength, but there's benefit only as it contributes to *necessary* strength. A scope tube need not be as strong as a rifle barrel, so it need not be as heavy. Unnecessary weight in a scope does three things, none of them good:

1. It adds to the overall weight of the rifle, increasing your burden afield.

2. It raises the rifle's center of gravity, so it points like a bazooka instead of an English shotgun.

3. It adds to the inertia of the scope on recoil, so that hard-kicking rifles are more apt to tear a giant scope free of the rings, or the rings or bases from their moorings.

Scope weight doesn't matter if you shoot a rail gun. On every other rifle, it matters a great deal. A heavy scope drags you down after a long day on the trail, just as surely as a heavy barrel or receiver or stock. Each is part of your rifle. Add ounces to any one of these components, and you either boost overall rifle weight or must trim ounces from another component. Heavy scopes can also impair rifle balance and handling speed – especially if they are mounted high. Add weight to a scope and you add inertia, which can cause a scope to slip in its rings under severe recoil.

The most useful place for weight is in the rifle barrel, where it boosts stiffness, thus accuracy. Fluting can delete ounces from a barrel without compromising stiffness, but it's nonsense to flute a barrel so you can carry a heavy scope. Magnum cartridges call for relatively long barrels, which limit the amount of steel you can remove without losing velocity or stiffness. Actions on big game rifles must have plenty of beef to handle large, powerful cartridges. But there's little to recommend heavy optics.

Scopes offer many advantages over iron sights, so we accept their greater weight and bulk. But heft beyond what's necessary for function is bad business. What makes modern scopes so heavy are oversize

Big country calls for powerful – but lightweight – scopes.

front lenses, fatter tubes and in some cases batteries that light up the reticles. Hunters have flocked to these scopes faster than mayflies plaster a windshield.

Climbing a ridge not long ago, I met a fellow deer hunter with a slender rifle that wore a big scope. "Go ahead, handle it," he urged. I found it weighed about the same as my rifle, but the feel was different. It was top-heavy, and while quick to mount, did not calm itself as readily as Old Death, whose longer, heavier barrel ran the center of balance forward and stilled the tremblings of my left hand. The scope weighed a lot because it had lots of glass up front and a 30mm steel tube. I got the impression this rifle would turn belly up in your hands as soon as you weren't looking.

But I didn't say that. "Thank you," I smiled, handing the gun back. "Your scope certainly is bright." He beamed; we separated. My 3x scope with its straight front looked a bit small over lunch, but by the end of the day I was used to it again.

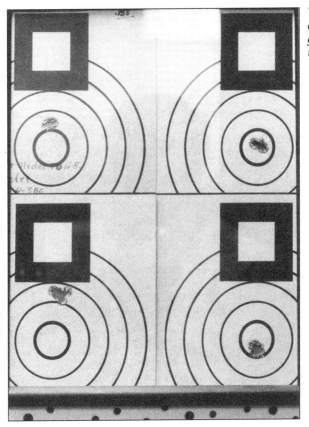

You can't hit what you can't see. One-hole groups are tough to get with iron sights.

Eye relief in variable scopes can change with the power. You're better off if it doesn't.

This fellow probably thought my petite optics inadequate for the cross-canyon shots he'd anticipated when buying that pie-faced variable. While low magnification didn't give me the precision at long range that he enjoyed, it gave me enough to keep my bullets in a 6-inch circle at 300 yards. That's as far as I like to shoot, and considerably farther than most killing shots on mule deer. My Leupold's 22mm objective lens was less than half the diameter of his scope's, but with only 3x magnification, I had an exit pupil of 7mm, which is all the human eye can use. Though we shouldered approximately the same weight that day, the other hunter had 10 ounces more in his scope, 10 ounces less in his rifle. He might not have noticed its top-heavy feel; perhaps he considered the shift in balance a fair price to pay for variable magnification and a bright picture at the high end. Perhaps his rifle was so accurate that additional barrel weight would have accomplished nothing. Maybe he was indifferent to the bullet speed he could have realized from a longer barrel, or was unwilling to carry a long rifle into thickets.

At any rate, he was pleased with his choice, I with mine.

Choosing a scope, a spouse or an automobile by weight is bound to give you second thoughts. The scope must have the appropriate magnification, adequate brightness and field, the proper reticle and positive adjustments. These days, you can assume any scope offered by a reputable maker will be stout enough to stand up under heavy recoil and normal bruising afield. It will also be nitrogen-filled to prevent fogging. But weight varies a great deal.

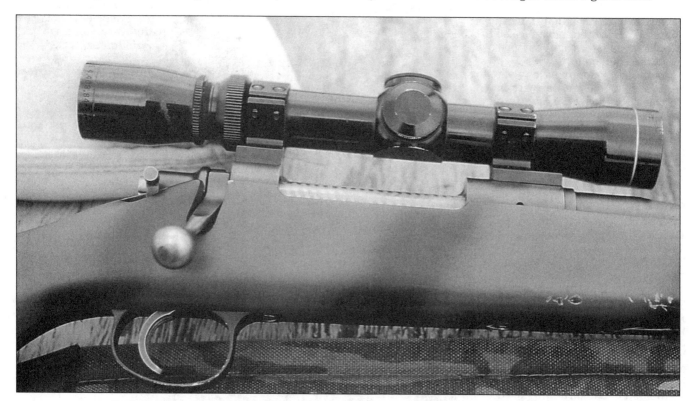

Leupold's Compact line includes this variable, a perfect fit for an Ultra Light rifle.

Light weight is an advantage, especially in hunting scopes.

The lightest scope I've found listed for big game hunting is Leupold's 2.5x compact. It weighs 6.5 ounces. At the other end of the spectrum is the Kahles 3-12x Helia S, with its 30mm steel tube and a 56mm objective lens. It scales almost 25 ounces. Depending on tube dimensions, a steel housing adds roughly 30 percent to the weight of an alloy scope. An increase in objective lens diameter from 40mm to 50mm adds a couple of ounces in a 3.5-10 variable – as does rubber armor or the use of a 30mm tube instead of the 1-inch. Increasing magnification piles on ounces, but in small increments. There's only a .1-ounce difference between Tasco 4x and 6x scopes, .7 ounces between Leupold's 4x and 6x. The Leupold 6x42 weighs 1.3 ounces more than the standard 6x36.

Below are weights in ounces for the selected 4x and hunting-class variable scopes cataloged by major manufacturers. Tubes are alloy, an inch in diameter unless otherwise noted.

Some of the variation here is easy to track down. The Tasco's 44mm objectives naturally weigh more than the 38mm glass in Weaver scopes; the power-change apparatus in variables makes them about 11 percent heavier than fixed-power scopes with the same lens diameters and similar outside dimensions. But not all 3-9s outweigh 4x scopes. Weaver, Leupold and Nikon offer 3-9x models that weigh *less* than the 4x scopes offered by four of the other makers listed. There's apparently no correlation between price and weight, either. For the carriage trade, Zeiss builds a middle-weight 4x scope, and a heavy variable. The budget-priced Simmons 4x is comparable in weight to the fixed-power

Zeiss, yet its 3-9x is 2 ounces lighter – roughly the same weight as the Swarovski 3-9.

A scope of, say, 12 ounces is half the weight of a big variable, but even on most trim sporters will contribute less than 10 percent of the weight of the scope and rifle combined.

It's good to think about scope weight not only as tacked-on ounces, but as a percentage of the rifle's total weight. There's no magic formula, but to my mind a scope shouldn't account for more than 10 percent of rifle weight plus scope weight. So if your rifle tips the scales at 7.5 pounds with mounts, and you want to equip it with a 4x Kahles, you add 11.2 ounces to 120 ounces to get 131.2 ounces combined weight. Divide 11.2 by 131.2 to get the percentage weight of the scope: 8.5. Fine. Now try a steel-tubed 4x Schmidt & Bender at 14 ounces: 14/144 = 9.7. The S&B puts you near the upper limit if you adhere to this rule.

Fudging makes all rules bearable, and there are times when a relatively heavy scope makes sense. I have a 2.5-10x Bausch & Lomb on a 6mm Remington 700 Classic. The scope accounts for 14 percent of the combined weight; but it is such a marvelous instrument, and so well suited to the application of the rifle and cartridge, that it will stay where it is. The reason for thinking in percentages is to keep the scope from making the rifle top-heavy. Low mounts help in this regard. A rifle with a relatively heavy, low-mounted scope can feel less tippy than one wearing a featherweight scope perched on see-through mounts.

In choosing between riflescopes of similar price and quality, you're smart to buy the scope with the smallest objective that will work for your kind of hunting. We shooters

get little benefit from an objective lens larger than 28mm in a 4x scope. It transmits the same amount of usable light as a 44mm lens of the identical glass quality and coating; its usable field is just as broad (field is mainly a function of ocular diameter). The advantages of an oversize objective: It permits greater deviation of your eye from the scope axis before your sight picture blacks out, and it provides greater resolution (that you probably can't detect). Stack that against the extra weight and bulk and you'll probably choose the smaller bell.

One caveat when comparing scopes: Objective lens diameter has a lot to do with weight as well as brightness, so it's important to distinguish the "effective" or "unobstructed" lens diameter from the outside diameter of the objective bell, which is commonly 5 to 8mm larger. Many catalogs include both dimensions. A field stop that's sometimes inserted in a scope to make the field flatter and the detail sharper (as does a small aperture in a camera lens) reduces the diameter of the bundle of light reaching your eye. You can see a field stop if you look into the front of the scope.

The 3.5-10x and 2.5-10x scopes seem to be replacing the flagship 3-9x in many lines. They average about an ounce heavier. By the same measure, 2-7x variables average an ounce lighter than 3-9s. While the useful 2-7x is fading (replaced in some catalogs by 2.5-8x models), there's been a rash of low-power variables to match the recent stampede to safari-style rifles and rifled-barrel shotguns. These scopes for short- to mid-range shooting offer a low-end magnification of 1x or 1.5x, a high end of 4x, 5x or 6x. Save for a handful of excellent 1.5-6x42 variables from

Bausch & Lomb	*4x32 (compact) - 10.0*	*3-9x40 - 16.5*
Bushnell	4x32 - 9.3	3-9x40 - 13.5
Burris	4x42 - 14.0	3-9x42 - 15.5
Kahles	4x38 - 11.2	3-9x42 - 15.4 (30mm)
Leupold	4x33 - 9.3	3-9x40 - 12.0
Nikon	4x40 - 11.3	3-9x40 - 12.5
Pentax	4x36 - 12.2	3-9x40 - 15.0
Redfield	4x33 - 10.6	3-9x40 - 13.8
Schmidt & Bender	4x36 - 14.0 (steel)	1.5-6x42 - 17.0
Simmons	4x32 - 12.0	3-9x40 - 13.4
Steiner	6x42 - 14.0	1.5-6x42 - 14.0 (30mm)
Swarovski	4x32 - 10.8	3-9x36 - 13.0
Tasco	4x44 - 13.5	3-9x44 - 15.8
Weaver	4x38 - 10.0	3-9x38 - 11.1
Zeiss	4x32 - 11.3	3-9x36 - 15.2
Averages	*11.6*	*14.2*

The inexpensive Tasco 6x, left, withstands heavy recoil as surely as the costly Zeiss.

Germany and Austria, they have no objective bell – which means an effective objective lens diameter of about 22mm. That's plenty big for late-dusk shooting in the middle of the scope's power range.

Leupold has long been a pioneer in scope development, and was one of the first companies to offer a compact scope line – scopes with 1-inch tubes and centerfire-class brilliance and sturdiness, but with shorter overall length and smaller objective and ocular bells. Shooters have warmed to the idea slowly, but fast enough to prompt other makers to design compact scopes. Leupold's 4x Compact weighs only 7.5 ounces, features a 28mm objective lens and a field of view that's essentially the same (marginally wider!) than that of the standard 4x Leupold. The firm also offers 2.5x, 2-7x and 3-9x Compacts. Variables have 28mm objectives, the same field widths as standard variables; they weigh 8.5 ounces.

Pentax catalogs 3-9x and 4-12x Compacts that weigh 13 and 15 ounces, almost as much as scopes of regular dimensions. Their advantage: better fit on short-action rifles with low rings. Extension rings and bases may be needed to mount compact scopes on standard-length actions.

For most big game hunting, a 2.5x or 3x scope is sufficiently powerful and needs only a tube-diameter objective. These scopes are inherently lightweight. Alas, few 2.5x scopes remain. Bushnell still offers a 7.8-ounce Banner, and Tasco a 7.1-ounce Pronghorn. Neither of them are top-line scopes. Weaver has kept the K2.5 alive. At 7.3 ounces, it's lighter than Burris' 2.5x shotgun scope (9 ounces), and *much* lighter than the Kahles steel-tube Helia S 2.5 (12.6 ounces). Leupold's fine M8 3x, I fear, is forever dead.

The main purpose of any scope is to give you a bright, clear, flat sight picture so you can aim quickly and precisely. But the physical properties of a scope can affect the handling qualities of your rifle, and your own effectiveness as a marksman. Rifles that feel lively in the hand and jump to the cheek like a fine bird gun are ill-equipped with scopes too bulky for the scabbard, too heavy for the hike, and as esthetically pleasing as a lumber rack on a Ferrari.

A lightweight scope can keep you fresh on the trail and perhaps give you one more covert to explore at the end of the day. It can also make the rifle livelier, should that last copse of aspens spew a bull elk with antlers like truck axles.

Reticles

Between the Depression and the Vietnam War, the most popular scope reticles among hunters were the crosshair and the post-and-crosshair. Some riflemen paid extra for a dot installed on fine spider webs by T.K. "Tackhole" Lee. In 1962, Leupold & Stevens introduced what has since become the overwhelming reticle of choice among hunters. The Duplex, a crosswire

Pick a scope of modest power, and practice with it. The results will please you!

with heavy outer sections and slim lines in the center, makes a lot of sense. The thick shanks grab your eye, directing it to the middle of the scope, where the thin intersection allows you to aim precisely. In very poor light, you can aim with the heavy wire alone. Knowing the sub-tention of the center wire at a set magnification and yardage, you can use the Duplex as a rangefinder. Lots of scope makers have copied this reticle, but of course they can't call it the Duplex.

Leupold's Duplex is a mechanical reticle, meaning it is suspended on a mount. Leupold employs .0012 plati-num wire that's flattened to .0004 to make the outer sections of the wire wider ("thicker") than the middle sections. Burris points out that its plex reticle is .0035 to start and is flattened in the middle but at 90 degrees to make that section of the wire very narrow. Critics object to the edge contact in the middle, claiming recoil can deform the edges to produce a thickening that appears as a dot. Premier Reticle Ltd., a Virginia firm that has sup-plied reticles to every major scope company except Zeiss, uses ribbon wire, twisted in the middle, to make a plex.

The other way to fashion a plex reticle is to use a photo-etching pro-

This 100-yard group shows what the rifle will do. A scope sight is assumed.

The author killed this caribou with a Winchester M70 and a 4x Red-field scope.

cess on metal foil, in which chemicals strip away all material around the etched pattern. The foil is only about .0007 thick and must be cemented to the mount, whereas wire reticles can be soldered. Proper tension of foil reticles is critical. Too little, and the foil will whip under recoil; too much and it won't withstand extremes in temperature. Allowing a scope with such a reticle to point at the sun can result in a reticle burned apart. Still, many fine riflescopes have foil reticles. All come from offshore companies, I'm told, because the etching process involves nasty chemicals.

The various plex reticles now include fine plex and heavy plex versions. Burris offers a fine plex in its 8-32x target/varmint scope. So does Pentax in a 6-24x. For its 1.75-6x variable and fixed-power shotgun scopes, Pentax installs a heavy plex reticle, and offers it as an option in scopes as powerful as its 3.5-10x Lightseeker. Steiner's "Ultimate Z" series of hunting scopes (made here in the United States) features a heavy plex option. Leupold's M8 4x and Vari-X II 1-4x and 2-7x shotgun scopes also wear an extra-heavy plex reticle.

There's not much you can say against the Duplex. I can't think of anything.

But there are other reticles available. The crosshair is simple and still useful. I have a slender one in my 20x Redfield 3200. With it I can quarter the X-ring of a 50-meter smallbore target or, if wind and mirage warrant, "shade" a bit by holding it tangent to the ring. If time's running low and the breeze picks up, I can target a spot in the 10-ring, or hang the reticle on a bullet hole. Actually, a fine crosshair

To adjust reticle focus, loosen the eyepiece lock ring and turn the eyepiece until the reticle comes clear.

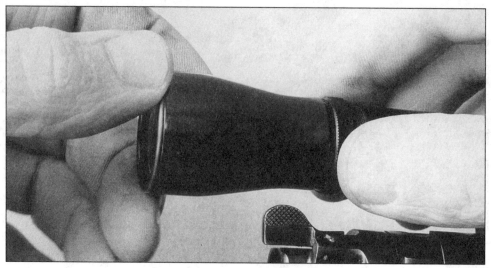

Learn to use ordinary plex reticles to help you estimate range.

works well with any high-power scope. The thick shanks of a plex reticle serve no purpose if you're shooting in good light, deliberately, at small targets far away.

On the other hand, crosshairs can be *too* fine, even for bench shooting at paper. A 36x scope on an XP-100 pistol I shot recently had such a fine reticle that I could barely make it out on white paper at midday. "It *is* a bit hard to see," admitted Phil Johnston, who let me fire a group with the pistol. It was chambered in .17 Remington. By focusing on the vertical wire, then trying to hold the gun motionless in the Bull Bag rest as I looked for the horizontal wire, I was at last able to squeeze off three shots. My eyes ached, but the 100-yard group measured .6 inch. No

way could my eyes pick up that reticle against color!

Fine crosshairs used to be fashioned of spider web because stronger material couldn't be made thin enough. Dick Thomas of Premier Reticle Ltd. said his father Bob — who christened his optical career working on the Norden bomb sight during World War II — later kept a brown spider in a Dixie cup to make crosshairs. "He'd pinch the spider gently with tweezers to get a defensive reaction. The spider would start releasing web, and my father would pull it to keep it coming. After he started making reticles for Lyman in the 1950s, and later for Redfield, milking spiders just couldn't give him enough material. By the late 1970s we had tungsten

wire. We can draw that down to .0001, or about a thirtieth the diameter of a human hair."

A heavy crosswire in a low-power scope is hard to beat for whitetail shooting in close places. You won't need a rangefinder. A thick intersection won't hide anything important. Sadly, most crosshairs now are too fine for use on big game in thickets or when the light is poor.

Before the Duplex, hunters who wanted a prominent reticle chose a post. Some posts had parallel sides, others were tapered. A post properly pokes above the horizontal wire just a little bit. You zero with the tip of the post, not the intersection of post and wire. Posts have fallen on hard times because the plex is as easy to see and can help with range estimation. Very heavy posts obscure the target if you have to hold over. In failing light, there's no guide to center from any direction except 6 o'clock. Posts were popular in early scopes because shooters were accustomed to using blade or post front sights, and the transition was easy. Posts are essentially unavailable from U.S. scope makers now, though Burris and perhaps others can be bribed to install one. Some European firms like Swarovski still list a tapered post and crosswire (called a No. 2 reticle). Post reticles can be made from stiff wire soldered to the mount ring.

I used to like dot reticles until I lost one on the shoulder of a bull elk in the timber at dusk. With nothing to point your eye to the dot in poor light, it's a poor woods reticle. Useful in open country under bright light, dots also work for target shooting. In my view, a dot for hunting should be larger than most riflemen think, and a dot for target shooting should be smaller. You can't afford to lose a dot even briefly on an animal, or your attention will be drawn from making the shot to finding the reticle. If a dot in a target scope obscures more than half the X-ring, it's too clumsy for shading. On a rimfire rifle, it can keep you from seeing bullet holes appear. You'll be tempted to move the scope to see bullets hit, ruining your shots.

Dot size is given in minutes. The right dot size depends on 1) the application of the scope and 2) its magnification. To my eye, a 4-minute dot is about right for a 2.5x scope mounted on a Marlin lever-action for whitetails in the hardwoods. It would appear huge in a 6x scope you might prefer for your .25-

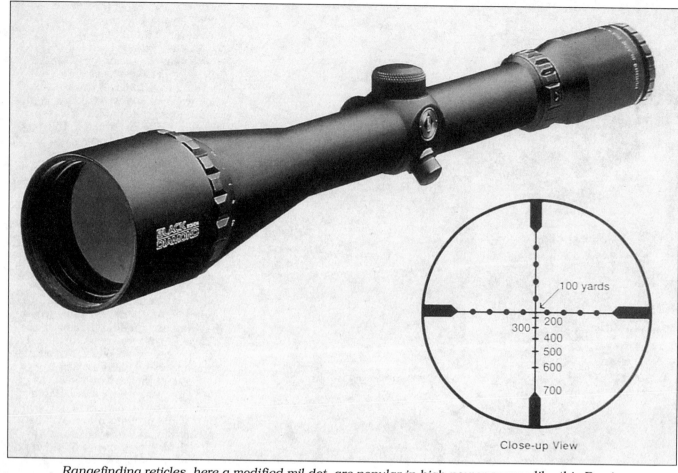

Close-up View

Rangefinding reticles, here a modified mil dot, are popular in high-power scopes like this Burris.

06 pronghorn rifle. A 3-minute dot works fine in a 4x scope, and a 2-minute dot will look about the same size in a 6x scope as the 4-minute dot in the 2.5x scope. *Subtentions of same-size dots don't vary among scopes of different power, but as a deer appears bigger in a 6x than in a 4x scope, so a 3-minute dot will appear bigger in the 6x because it must cover the same area on that deer.* Any non-magnifying dot in a variable scope will vary in its coverage of the target as you change power.

The "Leupold dot" hunting reticle includes four slender pointers in lieu of crosswires, ending just shy of the center. (Leica offers a similar reticle.) At 3x in a Vari-X II, the dot subtends 2 minutes, at 9x .8 minutes. Target dots typically cover 1/4-minute at around 10x. The Burris 8-32x is cataloged with a 1/4-minute dot. You get that coverage only at 8x. Leupold's target dot in its 36x scope covers a mere .1 inch at 100 yards. Dots were once the rage in target scopes. Dick Thomas tells me that Homer Culver's world record benchrest group with a dot from

Premier Reticle fueled the success of that firm in the early days.

A dot combined with a standard crosshair doesn't attract me. It's sort of like the best turkey gravy and sour cream: Either makes a potato palatable – together they're too much. The Leupold dot is acceptable because the prongs are slim and don't come quite to center.

Rangefinding reticles are another option. The simplest comprise stadia wires that bracket a known measure at a given distance. Typically the measure is the chest depth of a deer – 16 to 18 inches. If you know the wires span a buck's chest at 200 yards and the deer you're looking at fills only two thirds of the space, you estimate 300 yards, hold a tad high and squeeze off. Redfield's Accu-Trac range-compensating reticle provided a set of stadia wires near the top of the field. You fit the target just inside the wires by adjusting magnification then read a range indicator at the bottom of the field. Next, you turned a dial on the turret to the appropriate number (4 for 400 yards) and held center. Changing magnification after setting the tur-

ret dial did not affect bullet placement.

In the Shepherd scope (Box 189, Waterloo NE 68069) a series of circles on the lower vertical wire are sized and spaced so that if a deer's shoulder fits snugly inside one, all you have to do is keep it there as you pull the trigger. The Shepherd sight uses two reticles — one each in the front and rear focal planes. The system works well; however, since it not only finds range but compensates for bullet drop, the reticle must be right for the particular load you're using. The same holds true for the Redfield Accu-Trac and similar distance-compensating devices like the Bushnell Bullet-drop compensator.

Reticles with stadia wires are still available. Some are unobtrusive, like the Ballistic Plex recently introduced by Burris in Fullfield II models. Actually, this is both a rangefinding and drop-compensating device. The thin wire beneath the intersection on the plex reticle is a bit longer than the other three wires (so the post is shorter). There are three hash marks on it; each space between

Holding any scope still is bound to make the shot better.

The best-known range-finding reticle is the mil-dot, fashioned by the U.S. Marine Corps for sniper use. The mil-dot features a series of dots emanating from the center on fine crosswires. In some, there's a thickening of the wire toward the outside so the shooter can use it like a standard plex in near-darkness. A mil-dot (like other complex reticles) may be etched on interior glass instead of suspended. Premier Reticle supplies the suspended or mechanical mil-dot reticles for Leupold. The 16 dots are installed by hand.

The mil-dot reticle enables you to find proper holdover at great distances. A milliradian is part of a circle, which comprises 360 degrees or 2pi radians. So a circle has 6.28 radians, and one radian is 57.32 degrees. A minute of angle is a 60th of a degree; thus there are 3,439 minutes of angle in one radian, 3.44 minutes of angle in a milliradian. Dividing 3.44 into 60 (the number of minutes per degree) gives us 17.44. So a milliradian is about 1/17th of a degree. The spaces or interstices between the dots each subtend one milliradian or mil – a span of about 3.6 inches at a hundred yards or 3 feet at 1,000 yards.

To use the mil-dot reticle as a rangefinder, you divide the target's height in mils by the number of interstices subtending the target to get range in hundreds of yards. A deer (10 mils at the shoulder) that appears in the scope to be two dots high is about 500 yards away. A moose (20 mils tall) that filled two spaces would be 1,000 yards distant. Actually, the official method is to divide target size in yards by the number of mils subtended and multiply by 1,000. Naturally, scope reticles with mil dots are calibrated for only one magnification. In variable scopes, mil dot reticles are typically calibrated at top magnification or 10x.

An alternative to the mil dot is a reticle available in Schmidt & Bender's 3-12x scopes from Wes Harris (Harris Barrelworks, 11240 N. Cave Cr. Rd., Phoenix AZ 85020). Designed by Dennis Sammut of San Bruno, California, the Sammut reticle has a crosswire with mil hashmarks, plus 13 horizontal wires half a mil apart below the main horizontal wire. Each of these has hash marks too; in addition, there are dots between the hash marks. The upper left quadrant gives you a rangefinding scale, also marked in mils.

the marks is incrementally bigger than the one above it, to trace the trajectory of bullets from popular big game cartridges. Example: Zero at 100 yards with a .30-06, and you hit at the first hash mark (3 inches low) at 200 yards, the second mark (13 inches low) at 300 and the third tic (30 inches low) at 400. At 500 yards, your bullet strikes near the top of the bottom post. You can zero faster bullets at 200 yards and use the center wire for all shots to 250. You'll stay within 3 vertical inches of the hori-zontal wire. At 300 yards, your bullet will strike about 5 inches low, or close to the first hash mark. At 400, it will land near the second tic, or 18 inches low. The third mark is your aiming point at 500 yards (- 38 inches), and you'll hit 66 inches below the center at 600 – right at the top of the post.

The TDS Tri-Factor reticle marketed by Swarovski is similar to the Burris Ballistic Plex. Schmidt & Bender also lists a reticle with hash-mark spacing engineered to follow bullet trajectory.

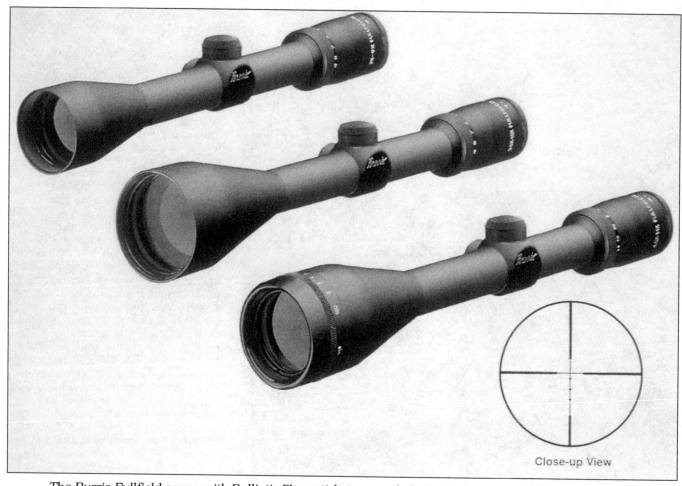

Close-up View

The Burris Fullfield scope with Ballistic Plex reticle is a good choice for long-range shots at big game.

Dennis Sammut says he used his reticle to kill at least 500 feral animals in the Australian Outback, as far away as 1,370 yards, and has "shot material objects to 1,800 yards." I've used a Sammut-equipped S&B on a Savage 110 in .300 Winchester and found it helpful for deliberate shooting to 700 yards. That's twice as far as I'll likely shoot at game. Still, it is an intriguing reticle. Not only will it assist in estimating range and maintaining holdover, its hash-marked horizontal lines enable you to correct for 90-degree winds to 30 mph. Also, you can correct for an errant first shot by using bullet impact as a grid marker. It becomes the subsequent aiming point. This is hardly a fast reticle to use, but it enhances precision at extreme range.

I'm not keen on complex rangefinding reticles that fill a field with lines, dots, bars, posts, circles and numbers. A reticle's primary function is to help you aim. Clutter impairs aiming. A reticle that helps you determine range accurately may be excused for imposing a little clutter in your field. Not so

reticles meant only for aiming. I prefer simpler reticles than the Simmons Diamond Mag, with a center diamond on a plex reticle, plus stadia-style hash marks on all four wires. Neither do I own what Bushnell calls its Circle X, a plex reticle with a circle encompassing the slim-wire center. Pentax calls it the Comp-Plex reticle on its Zero X/V Lightseeker SG Plus shotgun scope. Swarovski and Schmidt & Bender make a No. 24 reticle that's similar. One hunter who used a center-circle reticle in a low-powered scope on dangerous African game told me it is perfect for fast, close shooting. I must admit that a Sightron diamond in the middle of a plex reticle helped me shoot faster and more accurately than I thought it would on running game. And that a center circle in a Simmons scope worked beautifully on a turkey gun.

Burris hawks a Peep Plex that's a tiny, open circle in the middle of a plex reticle. The idea is to keep the reticle from obscuring small targets like prairie dogs. I think it's of marginal value because no matter how small an orifice, the eye looking

through it to a target searches for something to paste on that target. A fine crosshair or small dot is less ambiguous. Besides, for varmint hunting you hardly need the thick legs on the periphery of a plex reticle.

Europeans have had a long love affair with posts, partly because a lot of shooting there is done as the stars come out. Besides the American-style post (No. 2 to the Germans), there's a three-pronged reticle about as heavy as the thick section of a plex. The lower prong ends in the middle of the scope, the two horizontal prongs just shy of center. This reticle is known as the No. 1 or, if the horizontal prongs leave more space in the middle, the No. 1A. European No. 4 and No. 4A reticles are the same save for the addition of thin wires in the center, the vertical one extending up as a fourth prong. Typically, European dual-thickness reticles have a square step where thin wire gets thick. The heavy end of American plex reticles tapers to the thin section. I actually prefer the squared-off juncture because it gives me a clean terminus for rangefinding.

The author fired this group (one just over the shoulder) at 400 yards, using a Burris Ballistic Plex reticle.

Perhaps because there are more of them, European reticle designations are not so descriptive as ours in the United States. America's plex reticle *is* called the plex in Swarovski's catalog, which shows the similar No. 7A with its more open center. Schmidt & Bender calls the plex a No. 8. Adding to the

The Schmidt & Bender Flash Dot is for scopes used quickly and up close.

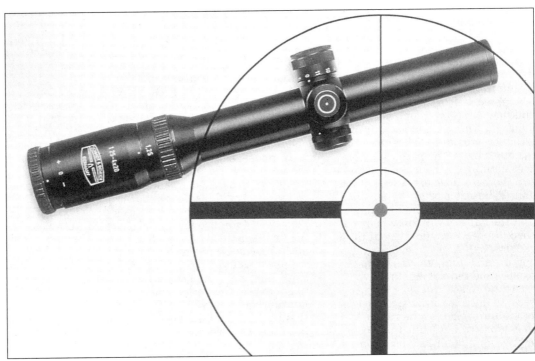

This Wyoming buck fell to a Swarovski scope and a Dakota rifle.

confusion, Zeiss calls its plex reticle the Z-Plex and the more open European design a No. 8. A crosshair is No. 6 in the Zeiss literature, which shows a heavy, tapered-prong version of the No. 1 as a No. 11. There's also a No. 25: a dot perched on a thin horizontal wire.

Because European reticles are normally placed in front of the erector tube, they must be finer than rear-mounted reticles. Otherwise they'd appear too bulky even at the low end of a variable scope's power range. Making mechanical reticles slender enough is difficult, so some European firms etch the reticle on glass. The problem with this is that it introduces another drain on light within the scope.

Lighted reticles are the rage now, and they do show up quickly in dim light. They'll also help you sift the reticle from a maze of branches. On the other hand, the battery bubble does nothing for the looks of a scope, and there's a little extra weight and bulk. Adjustable brightness means another dial. And there's a chance that the battery will fail when you need it most. I can do without these gadgets, but sales indicate a growing demand. Lighted reticles in scopes (and red-dot sights) have rheostats so you can vary brightness. In dark conditions you need *less* illumination for the reticle to show up. Brilliant sunshine floods out the glow of all but the strongest

of lighted reticles. Keep the brightness low, and reduce it as light fades. A glowing reticle can dilate your eye, making the target harder to see. The halo effect can also compromise precision.

Electronically illuminated reticles have become modestly popular, as modest numbers of shooters will always have to own the most sophisticated optics available. Zeiss offers one. So do Swarovski ,Kahles and Schmidt & Bender. You can get one at lower cost in a Bushnell or Burris scope. The industry leader in lighted reticles, though, is Lightforce. I've used its huge, Japanese-built, high-power variables. The reticles amount to slim variations of European three-pronged reticles. They float in the middle instead of extending to the periphery. They look a bit like the artificial horizon on an airplane instrument panel.

Of course, before you can get the most of *any* reticle, you must bring it into sharp focus. Adjust that eyepiece!

I'm surely old-fashioned, but it seems to me that with two reticles I'd be well equipped for all the shooting I'm likely to do. A standard plex (or European No. 7A or No. 8) will outperform anything else for big game hunting. A fine crosswire is tough to beat for target shooting, hunting squirrels with .22 rimfires or sniping at small rodents far away. Both these reticles are quick and easy for my eye to comprehend; they

put nothing unnecessary between me and the target.

Of course, if like me you have a soft spot for dots, you can write Dick Thomas at Premier Reticle in Winchester, Va. He might still have a local spider sequestered in a Dixie cup.

Wobble

We trailed the kudu until the blood stopped. Then we cast about like children hunting Easter eggs. *Miopo* litter lay thick and dry. The occasional patches of exposed soil held nothing; the bull had avoided them. We'd seen him once, standing tail to us in a thicket, pretending to be invisible. Kudu do that often, even when they haven't caught a bullet.

We didn't know where the bullet had struck. I thought the impact was too far back, judging by the animal's quick pirouette and reflexive kick to the paunch. But I hadn't held the rifle.

He'd given us just one chance for a finisher. It wasn't much: fragments of smoky flank behind a latticework of thorn. It wasn't what the hunter wanted. It was all he got.

The track drew us to a riverbed. Boysen glided over the sand like a bird dog compelled to cast where there is no scent. He moved to the high ground then, to the difficult places where a kudu might lie up.

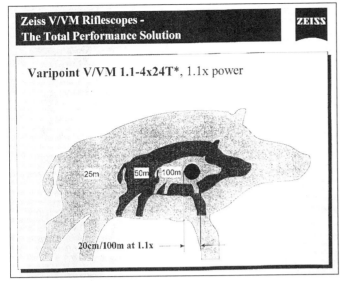

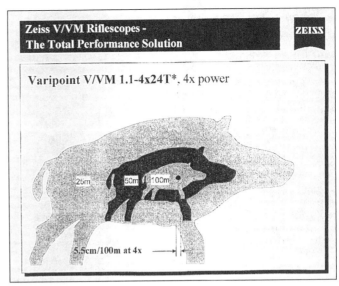

The Zeiss Varipoint reticle offers a relatively bigger dot at low power – useful in thickets.

He looked for small prints because even big kudu have small feet. He also looked for scuff marks, a freshly shattered leaf or brachestesia pod. Meanwhile the sun blistered the sand and blackened the specks of blood in the bull's wake.

Suddenly Boysen jetted ahead. We scrambled into line behind him, winding through the bush on a taut game trail. A spot of crimson winked darkly from a blade of grass. Then Boysen was down on one knee, pointing. Ben raced up beside him, and I saw the kudu move – a shard of smoke sliding through the *mopane*.

Bang! The bolt snapped down as Ben dashed forward and fired again. Boysen grinned back at us.

We found the bull dead. Ben apologized for the last hit, which had entered the skull and blown off a section of horn on exit. "The taxidermist will sort that out," he promised. His first bullet had lanced the paunch, ranging forward to the off lung. It had been enough, but the kudu had bounced up again.

A part-time professional hunter, Ben relies on his Model 70 Winchester in .375 for all his hunting. The rifle wears iron sights "because I seldom shoot beyond a hundred meters. With open sights, my rifle behaves like a shotgun." He points to the kudu and sweeps a browned arm at the surrounding thorn. "I'd have been too slow with a scope in here."

I might well have argued that iron sights aren't necessarily faster than a scope. Because the reticle

Reduce wobble with a rest, a sling or both.

appears in the same plane as the target, there's nothing to line up. Aiming with a scope is like pointing your finger. I looked at the kudu and decided to say nothing.

When scopes began replacing iron sights in quantity during the 1940s and 1950s, hunters resisting the switch pointed out that tight fields of view in scopes slowed their aim. Small ocular lenses *did* restrict field, and uncoated glass compounded the problem with dim images. Stocks built for iron sights offered no cheek support if you mounted a scope, so you had to move your head around in space to find a sight picture of any kind.

Modern scopes are much brighter, with wider fields. Rifle stocks bring your eye into the scope's axis right away. But there's one problem that better optics and stocks have not solved. It's wobble.

You see, what *really* makes a scope slower than irons – for beginner and accomplished rifleman alike – is muscle tremor and your efforts to deaden it. The higher the magnification, the more furiously that reticle hops about and the more determined you become to make it behave. The longer you delay, the more weary your muscles become. Eventually the reticle is jerking around with such speed and scribing

such wide arcs that you question firing a shot at all. While practice helps control tremors and gives you the courage to squeeze despite them, it cannot ensure against delay when you're puffing up a ridge and jump a whopper buck and the crosswire caroms from deer to sky to treeline to trail, then darts across an antler to trace another random path across the landscape.

While a quick shot may not snare venison, *delay will ensure failure*.

We're conditioned to believe what we see, to act on what we believe. If the crosswire is bouncing on and off the target, in and out of the vitals, we lose confidence because we see that our aim is true only a fraction of the time. We try to increase the "dwell" of the reticle by reducing the speed and amplitude of its movement. Either that, or we try to anticipate those dips and hops so we can trigger the rifle as the reticle dives into the target.

When I had even more to learn about shooting than I do now, I practiced the "controlled jerk" in smallbore competition. I eventually got it half right, mastering the jerk but failing any control. My scores didn't improve until I disciplined myself to crush ounces from the trigger slowly, holding pressure when the sights or reticle wandered off, increasing

pressure when the picture again looked right. This a tough assignment, because you frequently run out of breath before the trigger breaks, or your muscles become tired and start bucking violently just as you reach the trip point.

On the premise that knowledge is power, riflemen have demanded more and more magnification from their scopes. They want to see everything that's going on. After all, if they pick up more target detail and track closely the relationship between reticle and target, won't that make them better marksmen?

Uh-uh. Knowledge isn't always helpful. You won't convince young children to drink more milk by pointing out a herd of Holsteins swatting flies in muck outside a barn. Few people who eat sausage have watched it being made. A friend starting work in an ice cream plant was appalled to see strawberries swept off the floor into the vat.

Sometimes we must know and ignore. If you're a pilot, you don't react to every thermal bounce or gust of wind. You try instead to guide the airplane with a steady hand on the yoke, correcting not for the individual bumps but for their collective effect on your course. You want to stay in close touch with your airplane, either through instruments or

An adjustable objective eliminates parallax at the set range and hones focus. It also adds weight, cost.

From left: Lenses 50mm, 40mm, 32mm and 22mm. Author's pick: 32mm for 4x to 8x magnification.

feel. On the other hand, you must sift the inconsequential signals from those that matter.

So it is with shooting. A rifle equipped with a coarse front bead will not allow you to hit a small target because it denies you a clear view of that target. You need more information. But mount a powerful scope, and you may get more data than you can handle. Minding *all* the gyrations of your rifle causes you unnecessary angst and can scuttle your efforts to control the big bumps – the movements that matter. You can't eliminate pulse or muscle tremor any more than you can escape air currents in a Cessna.

Magnifying them, however, can be as detrimental to accuracy as pretending they aren't there.

When I started shooting metallic silhouette targets, they'd just come across the Mexican border. The first match I fired went to a fellow shooting a .30-06 Winchester with a Weaver K4. In a sudden-death shootoff for placing, I managed to topple a ram with a Henriksen-built Mauser in .270. It wore a 6x Pecar scope that showed me all the wobble I could handle offhand. Within a few years, however, the top-scoring metallic silhouette shooters had gone to scopes as powerful as 20 and even

24x (and to specially built rifles hardly in keeping with the spirit of the game).

Balancing sight-picture detail and wobble is crucial when you're buying a scope. Target size and probable yardage and shooting positions figure into your choice. Small targets don't always require as much magnification as many shooters think. If you can see target in all corners that define the intersection of the crosswire, you have power enough for a hit. If you have plenty of time and a steady position, you might use additional magnification to advantage – mainly to read conditions as you

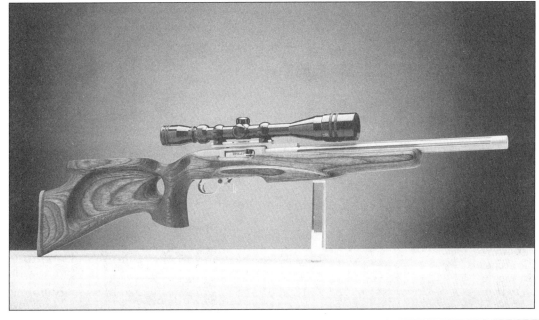

Even little .22 rifles like this customized Ruger are wearing big scopes. Sometimes it's a good match.

David Miller of Tucson, Ariz., used his own rifle and a Leupold scope to take this fine Coues deer.

squeeze and to shade accordingly. If recoil isn't severe, high scope power can also give you a clearer indication of the bullet's strike.

My Model 37 Remington that nibbles little groups in smallbore prone targets wears a 20x Redfield 3200 scope I bought used in 1970 and mounted first on an Anschutz 1413. I need that much magnification to quarter bullet holes at 50 meters while reading changes in mirage. But it is a difficult glass for offhand shooting because I'm not steady offhand, and I can't keep up with the reticle, or tame it.

On hunting rifles, wobble can become unmanageable at 8x, 6x, even 4x, depending on conditions. Using a bipod or improvised rest, or shooting prone with a sling, you can handle plenty of magnification. Shooting offhand on a shale slide in a stiff wind after a climb, you'll find even low magnification causes the reticle to leap all over the mountain.

In my view, wobble management is the strongest argument for owning a variable scope. Variable scopes allow you to dial up the most magnification you can handle, and to trim wobble when conditions deteriorate. The sensible alternative is to choose a scope low enough in power that you're never flustered by a bouncing reticle. That's better than choosing a scope that offers more precision and less control. When you must shoot fast and the crosswire won't behave, you will either lose the shot to delay, or miss by jerking.

Generous eye relief keeps you from getting clobbered during recoil.

"Easydot" is a luminous dot you can affix to most scopes. It's centered by clever screw adjustments.

Hunters commonly overestimate the magnification they'll need for effective shooting at big game. In prone competition, iron-sight scores come very close to matching those shot with scopes. It's no trick to shoot groups under a quarter inch at 50 meters with irons, and in favorable weather the best shooters do it routinely. So it seems odd to me that elk hunters insist on setting variables at 8 to 10x to shoot animals the size of a Honda Gold Wing. If high-power competitors can lob .30-06 bullets into the V-ring at 600 yards with irons, there's no reason you or I can't center a ribcage at half that distance with a 4x scope.

High magnification won't necessarily prevent you from finding a target quickly, but it can make the shot a long and bumpy ride!

Chapter 8

Simple Hunting Scopes

" …It's a sight. A rifle comes with it."

The virtues of fixed-power scopes

ANY SCOPE MANUFACTURER will tell you that the fixed-power scope is all but dead. Swarovski and Zeiss don't even offer a 4x anymore. Variables account for more than 90 percent of scope sales in the United States. Pity. I think the fixed-power scope is better. Here's why.

It's lighter. A fixed-power scope has fewer lenses, no power-adjusting mechanism. Less weight means a lighter, more responsive rifle. More of the weight is between your hands, not on top where ounces disturb balance.

It's shorter. Power-adjust rings add length to the ocular assembly. With some mounts you'll have problems getting a variable far enough forward for proper eye relief. Stock-crawlers beware!

It's less complex. Translation: It's more reliable. Given the sure-fire reliability of high-quality variables these days, this may be an academic point. Nonetheless, most military sniper scopes are fixed-powers.

It's cheaper. Fewer parts and less fitting and assembly save you money at the counter. Buy more ammunition with what you save, and become a crackshot.

It's brighter. Up to 4 percent of incident light can be lost at each air-to-glass surface in a scope. Lens coatings dramatically reduce these losses; still, no lens transmits *all* the light entering it. A fixed-power scope has fewer lenses, so more light gets through. Admittedly, the best variables transmit so much light that your eye may not discern a difference.

It's better looking. OK, that's *my* opinion. I prefer trim, clean stock profiles and streamlined rifle actions, too.

Do fixed-power scopes have a downside? Two, actually. Limited availability is one. Chris Lalik of Bushnell says that to justify its development, any new product should net $200,000 the first year of its manufacture. To stay in a catalog, requirements are less stringent; however, in the last decade, fixed-power scopes have been culled from several scope lines. The notable addition has been Leupold's 2 1/2x Compact (a reintroduction). Because shooters overwhelmingly prefer variables, look for continued shrinkage in the selection of fixed-power scopes.

The other problem with fixed-power scopes is their limited versatility. If you must use one rifle for woodchucks, whitetails and western game, a variable makes sense. On the other hand, the advantages of variables on rifles for general big game hunting are oversold. If you're like me, you'll find that power dial stays pretty much at one setting – probably between 4x and 6x. At 4x, a deer 200 yards away looks as big as a deer over iron sights at 50. I've shot a few big game animals at around 400 yards, and though more magnification would have been useful, most of them were taken with a 4x scope. High magnification not only gives you a bigger target image; but it also shows you how much your

The 6x36 Leupold on the author's Ruger No. 1 is a fine scope for long shooting at big game.

The Weaver K4, here on a Savage 111 in 7mm08, set the standard for post-WWII hunting scopes.

rifle is wobbling. Trying to calm that jittery reticle – minding all the movement you can't control – can slow your shot and encourage you to yank the trigger.

If you carry a variable scope set at the top end, you're asking for trouble. I've guided hunters who had to be reminded constantly to dial down. If you jump a buck at close range, you won't have time (or the presence of mind) to reduce magnification to boost field of view. Because long shots are most often taken deliberately at undisturbed game,

there's almost always time to turn the power *up*. When I'm hunting with a variable, I keep it at the lowest setting. Using the top setting of a variable scope to look for distant game is not only fatiguing but dangerous if you find yourself scoping another hunter. Carry a binocular.

To keep things simple, I rarely hunt with a variable these days. Call me old-fashioned or dull, the kind of guy who still eats oatmeal. Or join me. The only thing you might miss is fooling with that power ring while you chew on a raisin bagel and con-

template an ant because it's the only living thing in sight despite the rancher's contention that this hill was aswarm with elk last week and you are the first hunter he's allowed on it since Truman's presidency. Variables can entertain.

The one that works

It was Thanksgiving week, under iron Michigan skies. Snow had come as powdered sugar over freezing rain that had frosted the oak leaves and made each step an announcement.

Charlie Sisk built the .338/308 under this Kahles 4x36.

The 2½x Sightron on this Weatherby in .338/06 is ideal for elk hunting in timber.

the buck further. At 16, I couldn't track a dump truck through a strawberry patch.

Except for walking too fast, looking too little, letting my hands freeze, shooting before I had a sure target and pausing to congratulate myself after the shot, I didn't do much wrong. And I had a good scope. It was a Weaver K4.

A review of scope history can show the notable points of progress: internal adjustments, centered reticles, alloy tubes, lens coatings, fogproofing and the like. It doesn't tell much about the slow evolution between them – the subtle forces and market responses that make scopes the way they are.

Automobiles, for example, are sleek and rounded now. That was no clean decision to change from earlier boxy forms, which followed the bulbous look of cars in favor short model years before. Automobiles evolve in response to customer whims, which are malleable. Change is more like drift than shift. White has been the most popular color recently. Time was, you couldn't even buy a white car. When I was young, cars with manual transmissions featured a column-mounted stick because it seemed more chic than a floor shifter, the mechanism of trucks and tractors. Then tastes changed. Bucket seats and floor-mounted sticks took over. Just the other day, I saw a new sedan advertised with a gear selector on the column. A novelty!

So it is that big-eyed variable scopes have become the sight of choice on hunting rifles, that silver and matte finishes are supplanting glossy black and that shooters seem as willing to pay $300 for a scope as car shoppers are to accept sticker prices above $20,000. We consumers are easily manipulated, demanding what we've been told to expect from companies that tell us we need what is most profitable to produce.

Admittedly, this game has given us a stream of improvements. But a few old items, like the steel-tubed Weaver K-4 and the 1965 Mustang, merit a thought now and then. Instead of floating by in a current of new products, they lodged and stuck, changing the current as a fallen hickory might alter the course of a stream. Shooters learned about scopes with the K-4, and though scopes these days offer brighter, sharper pictures, the 4x as defined by Bill Weaver may still be the best all-around big game scope. I'd buy a

When the deer flagged off down the hollow below me, I couldn't believe I'd not seen them. Stiff-fingered, I struggled to bring the Mauser to bear. It came up like an I-beam on the gib of an underpowered crane. The whitetails, meantime, were pushing Mach 1.

By some woodland miracle, my eye found a hole in the scope just as its crosswire staggered across deer hide. I yanked the trigger and the buck skidded on its nose. I gawked.

Then my clothespin fingers struggled with the bolt. The deer beat me this time, arising to gallop up the hill as I futilely fought the rifle. My second bullet brought down only one luckless acorn.

I don't tell this tale very often because that animal escaped. There was less blood than snow, and none of either in the timber. A diligent sweep of the oak thickets above the hollow gave me a few scuffed leaves. Perhaps now I might have followed

An Iowa hunter killed this Utah elk with a Remington .30-06 and a Weaver K4.

designs, he kept the improvements affordable. The K-series, which would eventually boast fixed magnifications as high as 15, initially featured steel tubes that were not hermetically sealed. Reticles crawled to or from center when you moved the adjustment dials. Light transmission was poor. Many early Ks were clamped to the side of the rifle or in swing-over or detachable mounts so if the optics failed, the shooter could use his iron sights.

But mostly the K-4 worked as it was supposed to.

World War II brought the end to some scope companies, but Weaver survived. During the 1950s, when magnum rifles piqued shooter interest and wildcatters fashioned cartridges for long shooting, scopes became more popular. Especially 4x scopes. The Bear Cub by Stith and Kollmorgen eventually wound up in Redfield's house. Leupold's Pioneer served as a prototype for the M-8. Lyman's Challenger became the All-American. Bausch & Lomb broke with other firms by retaining external adjustments in its Balfor.

There's probably no more justification for the dominance of 4x magnification than for left-side steering wheels in American automobiles. Four-powers simply happened along, and nobody thought to invite 5x to try out. During the next three decades, a few hunters chose the Weaver K-2.5 and K-3, some the Redfield 2 3/4x and others the Leupold M-8 3x. Only hunters expecting to stretch their cartridge opted for a 6x. By far, most fixed-powers sold were 4x. Not until variables shed their shift-of-impact problem and makers convinced shooters that zooming in and out had spiritual significance was the 4x overtaken by variable scopes. Now fixed-power models are about as common as vacuum-powered windshield wipers.

bushel of the old models at their 1965 price – just as I'd borrow to get a fleet of new '65 Mustangs at $2,800 each.

The K-4 wasn't Weaver's first scope. That distinction belongs to

the 330, a crude, dim instrument that appeared during the Depression. Flawed by modern standards, the 330 was at least affordable. And when Bill Weaver improved his

This Weaver K4, like the Remington 700 rifle, dates to the early 1960s.

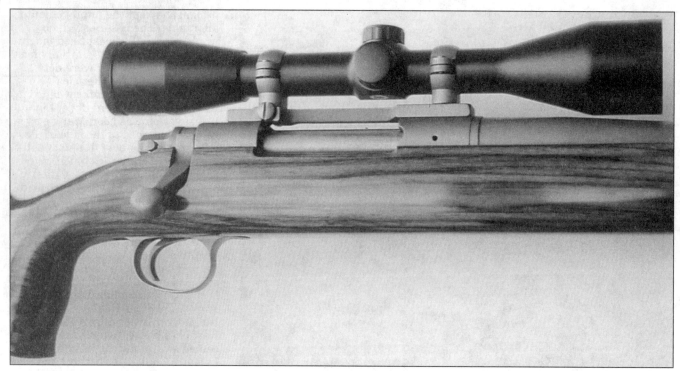

Medford, Oregon, gunmaker Kevin Wyatt built this .35/404. The author scoped it with a 4x from Cabela's.

Variables seem to make a lot of sense. Even hunters who eschew zoom lenses like the wide range of power available. They don't want to be caught in a thicket with an 8x scope or have to decline a long shot with a 3x. I thought this once, but found my variable stayed set at 4x or 5x nearly all the time. I've used 4x magnification on big game at distances from 20 to 450 yards. At the extremes, lower and higher power would have been better. But 4x worked, and for probably 90 percent of my shots – between 50 and 250 yards – it proved ideal.

In the late '60s, I read an article on mule deer hunting by a respected writer who praised the 4x. "It's about all you need to know about deer scopes," he concluded. Or something to that effect. I agreed then, and I'm afraid time hasn't changed my opinion. The writer has died, so his view won't change either. Lest you think me hopelessly mired in the past or too tight-fisted to buy a variable scope, I'll point out why my dead colleague and I still favor the 4x.

The B&L Balfor on this Model 70 has no adjustments so must be installed in adjustable mounts.

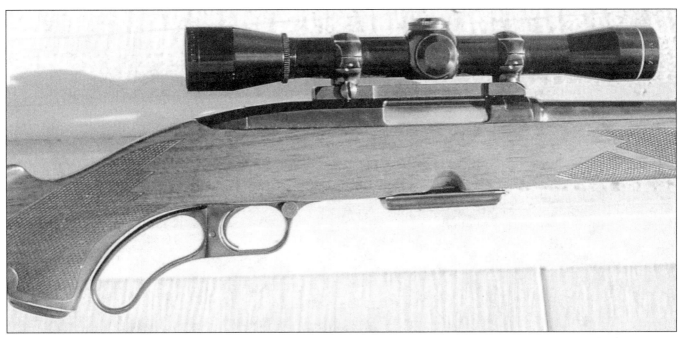

This Winchester 88 carries a 4x Leupold, one of the lightest all-around big game scopes available.

In a word, the 4x is a grand compromise. It combines adequate field with adequate eye relief and adequate magnification. It is not too powerful to hold steady from hunting positions, but it permits precise aim on deer-size game as far away as I feel justified shooting. It is a simple scope, with fewer lenses and, thus, better light transmission than variables of comparable quality. Compact and lightweight, a 4x can be mounted in low rings. It is relatively inexpensive. The only problem with it is that the thoroughbred scope stables are filling all their stalls with variables.

A 4x Zeiss on a .280 Remington Mountain Rifle accounted for this outstanding bull.

The author has a discontinued 4x Zeiss on his .350 Remington Model 700. It's one of his favorite scopes.

Bushnell, for example, doesn't offer one. That's right. Of the 19 scopes listed in the Elite 4200 and Elite 3200 lines, none are 4x. You must buy a Bushnell at slightly lower price (and, presumably, lower quality) to get a 4x from that company. Zeiss and Swarovski have abandoned their 1-inch 4x scopes.

Now, there are still plenty of 4x scopes around. Burris sells them in both Signature and Fullfield lines. Leupold builds 4xs in standard, compact and shotgun configurations. Nikon has a brilliant 4x, and Redfield catalogs one. Simmons offers a 4x scope in its Whitetail Classic Collection, others in less pricey lines. Tasco has several. And Weaver, from Japan, still markets the affordable K-4.

Perhaps the best 4x available is the Schmidt & Bender. I have one. It was a gift from a fellow who said I could pick any Schmidt & Bender scope I wanted. The company manufactures excellent sights, from high-power tactical instruments to low-power variables with lighted reticles. The 4x is the cheapest scope in the catalog. I chose it because it is such a fine hunting scope and because, though inexpensive beside its mates, it is expensive enough that I knew I'd never buy one. Besides, how would it look to extol the 4x to other hunters, then choose a big variable just because it was more expensive?

Current 4x scopes are, at all price levels, better bargains than compa-

rable old ones. They give you brighter, sharper images – the true measure of quality in optical sights. Leupold's M-8s cap several rifles in my rack. There's a Nikon and two Zeiss 4x scopes. I may have shot more big game with 4x Redfields than with any other type of scope, if you count the earlier Kollmorgens as part of the line. The old Balfor on a 1940s-vintage .300 H&H Model 70 was a revered scope in its time but cannot match the competition now. If it had the optics of the B&L 4200-series variable on my 6mm Remington 700, I would own more.

Field of view varies in 4x scopes from about 26 feet to 36. An average 30-foot field enables you to find game quickly and to lead any running deer without losing part of the animal. At 25 yards, a buck that's stretching out in a full-throttle race across the field will almost fill it – but, then at 25 yards, you need only swing with the animal and keep your crosswire on the forward edge of the vitals. Bullet flight time is negligible. At 100 yards, you'll have to lead; but at 100 yards that buck takes up only about 20 percent of the lateral field, giving you lots of room in front for the intersection of your crosswire.

As important as field of view to quick shooting is eye relief. Leupold's M8 4x is more generous in this regard than most scopes, but I haven't shot with a 4x that gave me too little eye relief. The only thing I don't like much about the M8 is

mushy coin-slot adjustment dials. Finger-friendly dials that click as crisply as cracking ice are available on more modern 4x scopes.

A 4x need not be big. Four-power scopes range in length from 8.5 inches (Burris Compact) to a tad over a foot. Weight depends on tube material as well as bulk. I favor alloy over steel. The lightest 4x on the market now, at least to my knowledge, is the 7 1/2-ounce Leupold Compact. Average weight for all 4x models is about 10 ounces. A 32mm objective is common, and more than adequate.

Price is a good indication of quality in optics, and because a scope should be a lifetime investment, it's a good idea to stretch to get the scope you really want. Hunters who buy 4x scopes because they're less expensive than variables are bound to be disappointed – first because they are paying for a bargain instead of perceived utility, and second because they will surely choose a cheap, inferior 4x scope rather than a costly model. You can save money by buying a 4x instead of a variable, but the best place to invest that savings is in the best 4x you can find! On the other hand, you can spend a good deal extra for a slight edge in real performance – in other words, some labels command a premium. That's why I compare closely the scopes I'm considering for purchase.

Shopping for a 4x scope is a bit like looking for basic transportation

The 4x Redfield on this lovely 1961 Mannlicher Schoenauer matches the period of the rifle.

on a car lot. Circling sharks in red slacks, Hawaiian shirts, trout-shaped ties and metallic blue sunglasses will croon to you the merits of special add-on packages from which the dealership derives most of its profit. If you hold fast, you'll get the same car for far less money and probably not miss the seat warmer,

official Indy wheels and self-tuning CD player. Likewise you must resist the curmudgeon behind the gun counter who immediately pulls out the biggest variable scope in the case and tells you it is just what you need. It may in fact be what he needs to sell you; it probably won't serve you any better than a good 4x.

Some hunters think the 4x is a primitive tool that got us from iron sights to real scopes that zoom animals in and out of our eyeballs. To others, it is still "about all you need to know about deer scopes." You don't have to take sides. After all, it's neither illegal nor immoral to carry a variable scope set at 4x.

Nikon's 4x, here on a Dakota Model 10, is among the brightest of fixed-power scopes.

The simple six

A good day should end well, I remember thinking to myself, just before I spotted the buck. I was not in the best place to make it end well. On a cold, featureless flat, prone behind sagebrush not much taller than croquet wickets, I was glassing west, into hills black with shadow. The sun had already left, and a weak orange sky was dimming by the minute. In the binocular, the four deer became six, then seven, eight …. Then I saw the buck and stopped counting. I'd have to take him quickly.

There was no approach cover. I might as well be sprawled on a beach. With the deer a jump from security in pinyon-juniper, I would have to shoot from here. It looked to be 300 yards. Good grief.

My rifle was chambered in 6.5mm Redding, a .243 Winchester necked up and given a 30-degree shoulder. The Remington action wore a Douglas barrel and a stock fashioned by Brent Clifton. A 6x36 Leupold scope completed the outfit. Behind the crosswire, steadied somewhat by a tight sling, those deer looked every bit as far as they were. More magnification might have shown me more detail, but it would have been very dark detail. I barely had enough light at 6 power.

As I tried to settle the crosswire on the buck's spine, the other animals started trailing up into the junipers. They weren't just drifting, but moving with purpose. They knew about me.

I tightened my finger, and the rifle's snap bounced back from the hills. Flame obliterated the herd, and by the time I recovered, the last of the animals were slipping into the trees. I kept the scope trained on the spot long after there was no more movement. At last I got to my feet and eased forward. The buck lay dead where the wicked little 120-grain Speer had struck him.

It seemed the 6x scope was a good choice for this rifle and western Colorado's mule deer.

Not long after that, I was poking along an elk trail in Idaho's Selway wilderness, keen to hear a rutting bull. My rifle: another Remington 700 with a Douglas barrel, this time chambered in .308 Norma. My scope was again a 6x Leupold. Instead of the standard 36mm objective, this one had a 42mm front glass, for a brighter picture at dawn and dusk. I'd trudged over broken country all morning and most of the afternoon when I heard the first elk bugle of the hunt. I hurried toward it, and presently spotted two cows. They crossed a timbered hill above me about 80 yards away.

The bull came at a trot. I had no time or place to sit and sling up. But even my offhand wobbles were manageable at 6x. There was plenty of field to get on the elk quickly, and when he stopped, I was ready. At least, I should have been. The first shot was off the mark, and a fast followup not much better. Graciously, the bull turned around and gave me another look at the ribs. When the last 180-grain Nosler took effect, the big five-pointer collapsed and rolled down the hill. He lodged in a depression, belly down and hard against a windfall. I couldn't budge him. I field-dressed him from the top, something I've not had to do since and can't recommend.

That elk might have been taken handily with a 2 1/2x Lyman Alaskan – or iron sights. A 6x scope is hardly what you want when elk are tripping through the lodgepoles a few yards off. On the other hand, the .308 Norma has great reach, and sometimes elk appear far away. Besides, if I'm to belittle a scope, I won't do it over a carcass. That's like examining a bullet that killed an animal and saying it didn't perform well. You might wish that the bullet looked different, or that you'd had a different scope. But it's properly charitable to spare the criticism.

Leupold brought back the Lyman Alaskan – briefly. The author's 6x is on a Dakota Model 10.

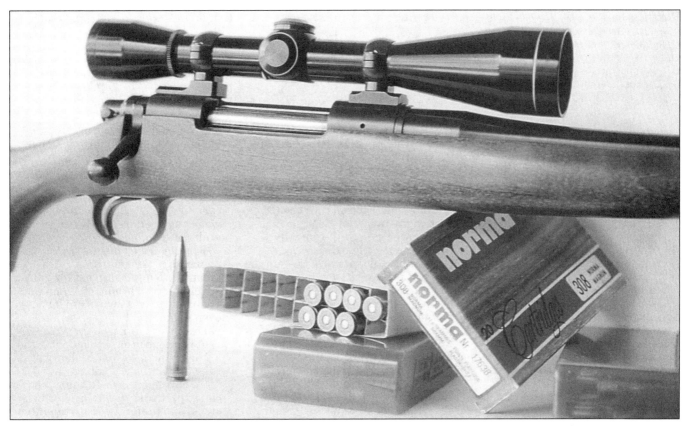

The author chose a 6x42 Leupold for his Remington 78 in .308 Norma Magnum.

The 6x scope isn't very popular now. Like the 4x, it used to be common but now falls far behind variables. Pity. I think the 6x is perhaps the best sight around for long-range big game rifles. Depending on where you hunt – that is, how often you must shoot quickly up close – it's probably less versatile than the 4x. But it is definitely better than the 4x at distances beyond 200 yards. It's easy enough to hold steady offhand except when the wind is very strong or you are very winded (just like a 4x!). Exit pupil for the 4x is greater for any given objective size, but you won't gain much if anything in brightness. Here's why: A 6x with a standard 36mm objective lens gives you an exit pupil of 6mm. A 4x32 gives you an 8mm exit pupil. Realistically, your eye (if it's young and flexible!) can

use an exit pupil as big as 6mm in dim light. The bigger the exit pupil, the brighter the picture, up to that 6mm diameter. Beyond that, the scope gives you a thicker bundle of light than your eye can take in. Older eyes may find their limit at 5mm.

You can get 6x scopes with 42mm front lenses, bumping exit pupil up to 7mm. Nikon's 4x scope is one of several with 40mm front ends and 10mm exit pupils. To my mind, 6mm is big enough. That's why I prefer the 6x36 and 4x32 scopes. They're the lightest and most compact versions to offer maximum usable exit pupil. Incidentally, the 6x36 gives you a significantly higher twilight factor (the square root of the product of the magnification and objective lens diameter). It differs from exit pupil in that it *credits* high magnification. Given equivalent lenses and

coatings, it shows how scopes of different specifications compare in dim light. The higher the value, the better you'll be able to distinguish objects. TF for the 6x36 is 14.7; for the 4x32 it's 11.3.

It may be that I have an unreasonable affinity for fixed-power scopes, and that my affair with the 6x has long outlived logic. But I'm not ready to change my ways. In fact, I just ordered a new Weaver 6x. It's a 6x38 with a one-piece tube and brilliant, fully multi-coated optics. It is handsome and lightweight, with enough tube to make for easy mounting on any rifle. It costs relatively little. In sum, I think it's a real bargain.

But it's not the only 6x worth a look if you're in the market for a trim, sturdy scope for a long-range big game rifle. Here are some other options:

Maker, Scope	Field (ft. at 100 yards)	Tube dia.	Length (inches)	Weight (ounces)
Burris 6x50 Black Diamond	19.0	30mm	13.1	17.7
Burris 6x40 Signature	20.0	1	12.6	16.0
Burris 6x38 Fullfield	20.0	1	13.5	12.0
Burris 6x28 Compact	17.0	1	9.3	9.0
Kahles 6x42	23.4	1	12.4	14.5
Leupold 6x36	17.7	1	11.4	10.0
Leupold 6x42	17.0	1	11.9	11.3
Leupold 6x42 AO Tactical	17.0	1	12.2	15.0

Maker, Scope	Field (ft. at 100 yards)	Tube dia.	Length (inches)	Weight (ounces)
Schmidt & Bender 6x42	21.0	1	13.1	16.6
Sightron 6x42 HBR AO	20.0	1	12.9	16.0
Swarovski PF 6x42	21.0	1	12.8	12.0
Swarovski 6x36 A	21.0	1	11.9	11.5
Weaver K6 (6x38)	18.5	1	11.4	10.0
Zeiss ZM/Z 6x42	20.0	1	12.8	14.1

This isn't a long list, compared to the myriad variables that include 6x in their power range. And many shooters will say the variables are justifiably popular. Why limit yourself to one magnification when you can have a choice of several? After all, the days are long past when turning a power ring changed your point of impact. Now, if you stick with high-quality variables, you don't have to worry about impact shift.

Well, the argument for variables is strong. But the fixed 6x has some advantages. First, the fixed-power scope is less expensive. Burris has the most extensive line of 6x scopes, and enough variables to fill two catalog pages with stocking numbers. Not long ago, a 6x Signature listed for $423, while a comparable (matte) 1.5-6x nailed you for $492. The 2-8x Burris Signature cost $565 and the 3-9x $578. If you wanted more power, you had to take more features, like Posi-Lock and an adjustable objective, and a price jump to $682 or higher. The economy Fullfield line showed the same price ladder. A matte-finished 6x scope cost $361, while the 2-7x listed for $418.

Oddly enough, Kahles prices its 6x42 scope higher than its 3-9x42 ($694 to $665). But this is an anomaly. If you compare scopes of similar construction (not the 6x tactical or target models), a variable-power sight will typically drain you a little drier.

Another advantage of the simple 6-power is its relatively light weight. Swarovski's 6x36 scales 11.5 ounces, while its 3-9x36 weighs 13. Not much difference, admittedly – but a little less inertia in the rings under recoil, a little less weight affecting the rifle's balance, not quite as much hanging on your shoulder as you climb to the elk. Incidentally, you'll notice that 6x scopes vary a great deal in weight. Discounting the Burris Compact and 30mm Black Diamond, there's a weight range of 10 to almost 17 ounces. Some of the differences can be traced to objective lens diameter. Lens weight also varies. Tube wall diameters and alloy types figure to a lesser extent (steel tubes excluded).

There's no need for a tube stout enough to billy a salmon on a boat deck, or pound pickets for the horses. It's easy to find a high-quality 6x scope that weighs 12 ounces or less. That's not much hardware to carry on top of your rifle, and it won't tug itself free of the rings under stiff recoil.

The clean look of a 6x scope complements most bolt-action rifles meant for long shooting at big game. While the trim profile of 36mm and 38mm objectives appeals to me, even 42mm front ends clear most barrels over low rings.

A 6x scope is easy to mount (as is a 2 1/2x and a 4x), with plenty of tube fore and aft of the turret – more on the ocular end than you can expect with variables. I crawl a stock, and prefer the scope mounted well forward. A fixed 6x lets me easily locate the tube so the ocular lens is more or less lined up with the rear guard screw. A lot of variables have so much machinery in front of the ocular housing that I must use extension rings or adjust my shooting style.

A Swarovski 6x42 tops the .30/338 built for the author by gunmaker Rick Freudenberg.

The extended eye relief of this Leupold scope makes for quick sighting.

As with any scope, I want my 6x with crisp, 1/4-minute, finger-accessible windage and elevation dials. The important thing is that the dials turn smoothly and with uniform resistance, that each click feels crisp. A loose dial, or one that hangs up, means you can't count on the adjustment.

Once you get the rifle zeroed, the dials shouldn't matter. I have an old 6x Tasco that I switch a lot from one rifle to another. Its elevation dial is very tight, and sometimes it doesn't move uniformly. But after I get bullet holes showing up in the middle, the scope does not shift zero. I recently installed it on a .338/378, and it weathered the punishment like a champ. When I picked up this scope at a gun show a few years ago, it probably cost me less than a couple of big pizzas. It's not the brightest scope, but the reticle is still in one piece, and the image is really quite sharp. I probably could kill all the big game I'm ever going to kill aiming with this scope.

Field of view shrinks as you increase power. At 6x, the field is tight enough that you'll notice small differences between scopes, and you'll want the biggest field you can get. A generous field helps you get on target quickly and stay with mov-

ing animals. It also shows you more of the animals in a herd, so you make the right decision when it's time to shoot.

Say, shouldn't field of view for any given magnification always be the same? Why then does the Leupold 6x42 have a 17-foot field and the Kahles 6x42 have a 23-foot field?

Well, it's pretty clear that objective diameter doesn't determine field. A lot of shooters think that 50mm front glass gives them a wider view; but if that were so, Burris' Black Diamond would give us the biggest field in our list, not a modest 19 feet. Neither is tube diameter the key factor. If it were, the 30mm pipe of the Black Diamond would show a bigger field than is possible with a standard 1-inch tube.

The truth is, for any magnification, field of view varies within a pretty broad range. Field is one leg of an "optical triangle" whose other corners are magnification and eye relief. As you can change the shape of a triangle without changing the sum of its angles, so you can manipulate field and power and eye relief in a number of ways to achieve a sum effect. That's how engineers design optical systems. Every improvement forces compromise. A useful scope is one with intelligent compromises.

So a 6x scope with a small field may have generous eye relief (the Leupold does). It may also be slightly more powerful than 6x, while comparable 6x scopes do not magnify objects a full six times. (It's common for the actual magnification of scopes to differ from the advertised magnification, and for "clear" objective diameter to differ from listed diameter.) While a range in field of view of 17 to 23 feet appears extreme for one magnification, it is not so large as to affect my choice of scope. First, I'd discard a 23-foot field as being unusually broad for a 6x, and expect my options to range from about 18 to 20 feet. (I phoned manufacturers the other day to confirm a couple of catalog listings for field of view; both were incorrect!) The 17-foot field of Leupolds wouldn't stop me from buying a Leupold any more than the 21-foot field of a Swarovski would compel me to buy scopes in green boxes.

Considering field, it's best to consider a *range* of field, 10 percent either side of what you might think ideal for your purpose. If you want a scope for shooting whitetails in woodlots, the 55-foot field of a 2 1/2x fixed-power scope is a benefit. Deliberate shooting at long range is quite easy with the 20-foot field of a 6x.

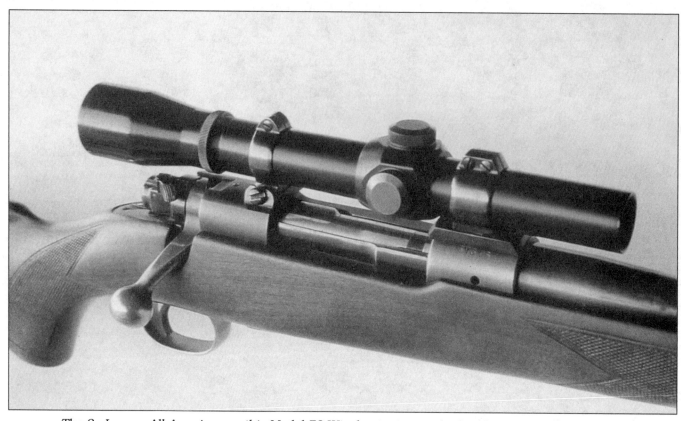

The 3x Lyman All-American on this Model 70 Winchester is attached with a svelte Tilden mount.

Remember that when a whitetail rockets across your front 25 steps away, the field of that 2 1/2x can show you *only 19 feet in the target's plane.* That's the same field you get at 100 yards with a 6x scope. At 300 yards, steadying a 6x on the chest of a buck, you're getting *60 feet of field.* The post-war popularity of the 4x as an all-around big game scope derived from its useful field. With 32 feet at 100 yards, you still had 8 feet at 25 – not a lot, not as much as the 2 1/2x, but enough for most shooting.

Though a 6x field may not compare well with the window you see in a 2 1/2x scope, a friend who's deadly on running coyotes uses only a 6x. "Lots of room there," he says. "And enough precision for those long shots." The last animal I shot was a reindeer (caribou) hustling across a mountaintop in Norway. The borrowed Sako .30-06 wore a Swarovski variable I'd set on 6x. I swung with the bull, fired and saw him collapse behind the crosswire. Obviously, there was plenty of field, even at 80 yards.

The 4x may still be the best all-around magnification for a big game sight. But as I get older and slower (make that more deliberate!), the 6x appeals more and more. It's still a trim addition to any rifle, and bright enough for shooting in any legal light. The 6x is ideal for long pokes across tundra, prairie or mountain basins; it's fast enough for all but the shortest and most urgent shooting.

A post-script: If you can't decide between a 4x and a 6x and, like me, prefer a fixed-power scope, look at Weaver's Grand Slam 4.75x40. Optically, it's top-drawer. Like most other Weaver scopes, it is also clean of line, lightweight and reasonably priced.

Chapter 9

Variable Hunting Scopes

"… You can change the way the world looks, but not how it is."

The trend

WHOEVER DREAMED UP the variable scope has been denied his (or her) due. History has lost the name. But then, good ideas seldom come to one person at a time, and who most deserves remembrance – the idea man, the builder of prototypes, the sales wizard, or the company whose resources ensure a market? Winchester is the name most people associate with lever-action rifles, but Mr. Winchester was a shirt salesman, not a gun designer. Winchester's early lever guns derived from the efforts of Jennings, Hunt, Smith, Henry, Spencer and others, including Winchester's son-in-law Thomas Bennett. John Browning designed the Winchester 1886.

So much for history.

The notion of dialing up various magnifications in your scope as you might change stations on the radio was appealing to shooters in the days following World War II. Scopes were just then becoming popular on bolt guns chambered for long-range cartridges like the .270, .30-06, .300 H&H Magnum and a new line of belted rounds from the California shop of Roy Weatherby. Several prewar scope companies – Noske and Litschert among them – had already folded or were forced to sell to larger

firms. By this time, Bill Weaver had designed a series of steel-tube scopes that offered shooters an affordable alternative to iron sights. Weaver was among the first to market a variable – a 2.5-5x that had no settings in between. Bausch & Lomb's Balvar 8, a 2.5-8x, came later. It cost more but had intermediate settings. Like other B&L scopes of that era, it had no internal adjustments; you used adjustable mounts.

In the early 1960s, a few companies came to dominate the U.S. scope industry. Weaver and Redfield, Leupold, Bausch & Lomb and Lyman boasted expanding scope

Elk country is both open and dense – a good place to carry a variable scope.

Variable Hunting Scopes **153**

Still hunting in heavy cover, keep that variable at its lowest setting!

lines and brisk sales. Zeiss and its European compatriots offered fine optics, but their high cost and inadequate distribution networks stateside kept them out of the running. Dave Bushnell, on the other hand, succeeded in planting a stake by importing Japanese optics – despite American disdain for Japanese products in general at that time.

During the 1960s and into the 1970s, the standard 4x scope that had for a generation been the most popular sight for all-around use lost substantial ground to variables. Manufacturers were working hard to fix the problems of early variables: fragility and shifts in point of impact between settings. They couldn't do much about the greater complexity and cost of variables, but they succeeded in focusing attention on their one great advantage: versatility.

With a variable scope, you didn't need to change scopes when hunting conditions changed. You could do everything with one scope and, if the chambering permitted, one rifle. A twist of the dial would give you enough magnification for shooting prairie dogs or the bright, wide field you'd need in thick whitetail coverts. You could hunt coyotes and deep-timber elk with the same scope, and if you wanted a close look at distant antlers you wouldn't even have to break out your binoculars.

Hunters bought this reasoning, and they bought variable scopes by the thousands. Now variables are so popular that some makers no longer offer 4x scopes in their

The author shot this buck at iron-sight range with a Swarovski variable.

premium-quality lines. In the most recent of surveys I've taken among elk hunters, 623 of 861 respondents used variables! The most popular were 3 or 3.5x on the low end (374), followed by what I call mid-range variables: 2 to 2.5x on the low end (214). Only 35 of the hunters responding preferred variables with less than 2x magnification on the bottom of the dial. The fixed-power 4x, incidentally, appeared 158 times on the response cards.

Is a variable the best choice? That depends on what you want to do with your scope. You wouldn't buy a radio without a station-changing knob, or a stove that had only one setting. But a scope is different. We don't feel handicapped with a rifle that shoots just one type of cartridge. The option of changing bullet weights intrigues

with a favorite load in each rifle. Dialing up a prairie dog one day and hunting a thornapple thicket for whitetails the next is likewise an appealing idea; but in truth the best dog rifle is poorly suited to still hunting in dense cover, no matter the cartridge or scope.

Below is a list of riflescopes from the year 2000 reflects the leanings of the U.S. market toward more power and bigger objective lenses. It also tells us that American shooters like variable power.

The .243 Winchester has been successful since its introduction in 1955, partly because it was hawked as a "dual-purpose" cartridge that could be used for deer as well as coyotes and smaller animals at long range. Variable scopes have ridden the same wave. If you have but one rifle and must use it for a variety of hunting, you'll be

needn't hunt a great number of species to justify a variable. It may be your best choice if you hunt only deer, for instance, because you can find deer at spitwad range in oak-brush and on the far sides of sage flats or beanfields.

But variables are not so versatile as to supplant binoculars. A scope set at 8x doesn't match a pair of 8x40 binoculars when you look for game. The scope provides only monocular vision, straining your eyes as they try to reconcile two images or, when you squint, different light intensities. Because it is attached to the rifle, bringing a scope to bear requires lots of movement, which can spook game. You must also hold the rifle to hold the scope – which gets tiring in a hurry if you don't have a rest. Finally, your rifle muzzle tracks the crosswire, so if you glass randomly with

Make/Model	Power/Obj. Dia. (in.)	Field (ft.)	Dia./Length (in.)	Weight (oz.)	Price
Burris Mr. T	2.5-10x50	35-10	30mm/13.5	29	$2,129
Burris	6x50	15	30mm/13	18	$683
Burris	8-32x50	13-4.5	30mm/18	27	$999
Burris Fullfield	1.75-5x20	65-23	1/10.5	10	$374
Burris Fullfield	3-9x40	31-13	1/12.5	13	$356
Burris Fullfield	3.5-10x50	28-11	1/13	15	$496
Burris Fullfield	4.5-14x42	25-9	1/14	15	$545
Docter Optic	3-9x40	31-13	1/12.5	17	$378
Docter Optic	3-10x40	34-12	1/13	18.5	$626
Docter Optic	4.5-14x40	23-8	1/13.5	21.5	$652
Docter Optic	8-25x50	13-4	1/16	26.5	$901
Kahles	1.1-4x24	108-32	1/11	15	$722
Kahles	1.5-6x42	72-21	1/12	16	$832
Kahles	2.5-10x50	44-13	1/13	17	$999
Kahles	3-12x56	38-11	1/14	19	$1,110
Leupold	6x42	17	1/12	15	$628
Nikon Titanium UCC	3.3-10x44	30-10	1/13	20	$899
Nikon Titanium UCC	5.5-16.5x44	19-6	1/13	20	$939
Nikon Buckmaster	4.5-14x40	23-8	1/15	19	$401
Schmidt & Bender FD	1.25-4x20	96-30	30mm/11.5	14.5	$1,480
Schmidt & Bender PH	3-12x50	33-11	30mm/13.5	20.5	$1,285
Schmidt & Bender PH	4-16x50	25-8	30mm/15.5	27.5	$1,555
Schmidt & Bender PH	2.5-10x56	40-12	30mm/15	22	$1,325
Sightron S II	6x42	20	1/13	16	$291
Sightron S II	4-16x42	26-7	1/13.5	16	$403
Sightron S II	6-24x42	16-4.5	1/14.5	18.5	$354
Sightron S II	6.5-25x50	15-4	1/14.5	19.5	$422
Simmons WE	1.5-6x32	72-19	1/11	15	$290
Simmons WE	3-9x42	40-13	1/13.5	17.5	$300
Simmons WE	4-12x42	29-9.5	1/13	21	$365
Simmons WE	6-18x42	18-6.5	1/15	26.5	$365
Swarovski PH	4-16x50	27-8	30mm/14.2	22	$1,440
Weaver Grand Slam	1-5x32	71-21	1/10.5	11.5	$430
Weaver Grand Slam	4.75x40	26	1/11	11	$360
Weaver Grand Slam	3-10x40	35-11	1/12	13	$380
Weaver Grand Slam	4.5-14x40	23-11	1/14	17.5	$500
Weaver Grand Slam	6-20x40	60-5	1/14	18	$500
Weaver Grand Slam	3.5-10x50	31-11	1/13	16	$460

us, but most hunters I know stick

well served with a variable. You

a scope, you are pointing the rifle

This Kahles 3-9x is a good match for the Remington Model Seven in .300 Short Ultra Mag.

at every Hereford, house and human that appears in your field of view.

Neither will a variable extend your effective range. Hunters who crank variables to their highest settings and lob bullets long distances at game that looks close in the scope miss and cripple a lot of animals. Properly used, the top magnifications on variables let you take more precise aim at small animals, or at big game that is partially hidden by brush. Finding a bullet alley through cover becomes easier as you increase power. So does antler judging. You won't always have time to assess a buck with your binoculars, then drop them and lift your rifle.

The best variable

Given that you want the versatility of a variable, which range of power is best? If you want to hit tiny rodents at long yardage, the scope should reach at least 12x. If you hunt only big game but often get shots at extreme range, a 3-9x or 3.5-10x will suffice. For all-around big game hunting, my choice is the 2-7x or 2.5-8x. While at one time I thought highly of low-power variables (1-4x), I'm less inclined to favor them now. The magnification range is small, and at 1x, I see a distracting length of barrel.

The 2-7x scope dates back to the early days of variables, when manufacturers didn't know what deer hunters wanted so decided on a power range that neatly bracketed the standard 4x magnification. A 2-7x with a 32mm objective lens delivers a field of view at 2x of 50 feet at 100 yards, an exit pupil of 4.5mm or bigger throughout the power range, a compact housing that lets you mount the scope as low as any 4x. Most 2-7x scopes weigh the same as comparable 4x models: 10.5 to 14 ounces. That's 3 ounces less, on average, than 3-9x scopes. Leupold's 2.5-8x36 weighs only 11.5 ounces.

You probably won't use more power than 6x for hunting. Granted, magnification of 9x or 10x can give you more precise aim, but it also reduces the size of the exit pupil and hence the amount of light

Here, the author shoots a Kimber 84M with a Leupold 3.5-10x50 scope.

The Zeiss 5-15x on this Winchester in 7mm STW equals the cartridge's great reach.

entering your eye. And it exaggerates that wobble you can't seem to stop. Too much of that spoils your aim because your eye can't find in those gyrations a pattern or center of movement. To prove this to yourself, find a hunting rifle that wears a 20x scope. Trot up a flight of stairs. Then, holding the rifle offhand, try to control that reticle. A 36x scope is intractable even when the rifle is sandbagged!

The light weight and compact profile of a 2-7x or 2.5-8x is a big advantage to me, because I want the weight of the rifle to settle low between my hands, not above them. A top-heavy rifle is slow to mount, feels awkward and can be hard to manage during recoil. Weight in the scope adds inertia, which resists the pull of the rings rearward at recoil. Powerful rifles can unseat heavy scopes during recoil.

Left-handed shooter, right-handed rifle. He has no problem using that 3-9x Bushnell!

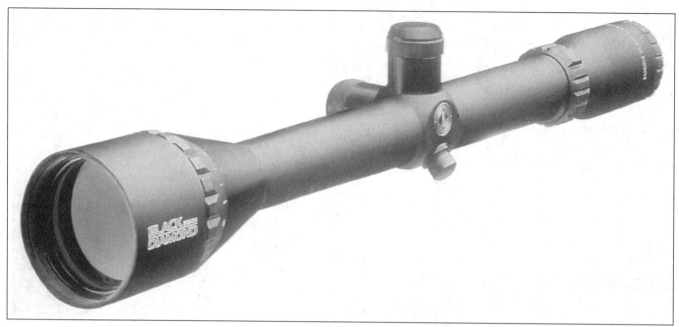

The Burris Black Diamond is top of the line, optically. It's also heavy and must be mounted high.

A scope with an objective bell the same size as the ocular housing not only looks balanced on a rifle, but accommodates the low rings that keep your cheek tight to the stock and put your line of sight close to line of bore. A 2-7x32 qualifies, with the look of a fixed 4x in profile, save for the power ring. If you want a wide field of view, you'll get it at 2x. The increase in field size as you drop from 3x to 2x is dramatic. For instance, Burris' 3-9x has a 35-foot field at the 3x setting, while its 2-7x scope boasts a 53-foot field at the low end. This may not be surprising; it is still a point worth considering. Would you trade two steps in magni-fication above the highest power you'd expect to use on a hunt for a field that's twice as big at a setting you'll likely use often?

The 2-7x has never sold as well as the 3-9x, but hunters must be showing some interest in mid-range variables because there's a new Kahles 2-7x36 on the street, and a spate of 1.5-6x scopes as well. You can still get a 2-7x from most companies. Those that list two or three lines of scopes may show a 2-7x in one and a 1.5-6x in another (Burris, for example). Leupold's Vari-X II is a 2-7x; its Vari-X III series includes two 1.75-6xs, one short and the other of tra-ditional length. While Redfield cat-alogs no 1.5-6x, it lists a 2-7x in the Widefield line. Bushnell has a superb 1.5-6x among its 4200-series scopes and a fine 2-7x in the 3200 series. Nikon lists a 2-7x with 32mm objective that weighs just 11.2 ounces. Pentax offers a 1.75-6x35 and a 2-8x39 in its bright Lightseeker line. Tasco and Sim-mons carry 2-7x scopes as well.

European scope-makers have traditionally had little to do with the 2-7 power range, but Swarovski, Zeiss and Schmidt & Bender build 1.5-6s, all with 42mm objective lenses. While a 42mm objective makes a scope noticeably

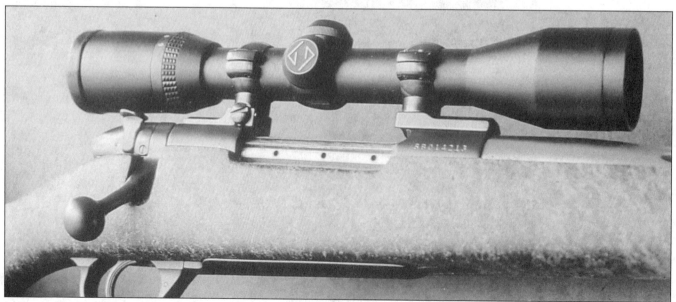

This sleek Zeiss 3-9x is among those the author likes best for big game hunting.

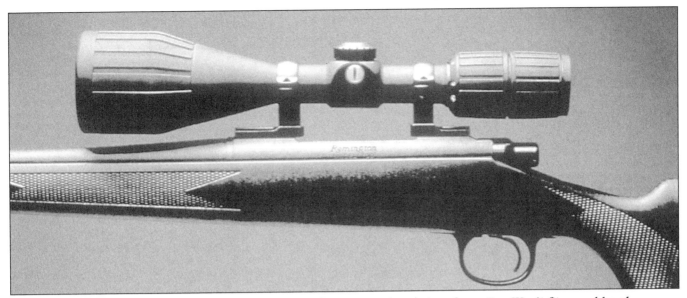

This BSA Big Cat variable overpowers the rifle, raising the center of gravity. Won't fit a scabbard.

heavier and bulkier than one with the 32mm lens commonly employed stateside, the big glass generates an exit pupil of 7mm at high-end magnification. In Europe, where hunters frequently shoot at night, light transmission matters more than weight or bulk. Weight gets another boost from the 30mm tubes of these variables. An aluminum 1.5-6x with 42mm objective scales an even pound, while a steel variant (a Swarovski option) weighs over 20 ounces.

So there you have one notion of an ideal variable scope. The 3-9x and 3.5-10x are still out front in sales. But perhaps because manufacturers realize that increasing magnification can't forever boost utility, they have begun to shore up their lines with scopes of modest proportions in a revival of variables that neatly bracket the 4x middle ground.

For the 20 years I knew him, a friend of mine hunted deer and elk with one kind of scope, though he had several of them on various rifles. His pick: a 2-7x Leupold Vari-X II. Bob carried it set at 2x when he was in heavy cover, with the idea that cross-canyon shots allowed him time to crank more magnification into the glass should he need it. "It's small enough, light enough, bright enough, quick enough, powerful enough. I like to carry it, and it helps me shoot well. I can't imagine a shot it couldn't handle." He tried others. "They came on used rifles, so I'd shoot with 'em till I could sell 'em and buy another 2 to 7."

At one time, I thought the best variable was one with the power dial stuck at 4x. But the antlers on Bob's living room walls were evidence to the contrary. "All my scopes have dials," he once told me. "Who wants a radio with just one station?"

How variable the variable?

Variable-power hunting scopes have beaten out fixed-powers. For those of us who teethed on the Weaver K4 and Lyman Alaskan,

Browning's A-Bolt is popular with Alaskan hunters. This one wears a Cabela's variable.

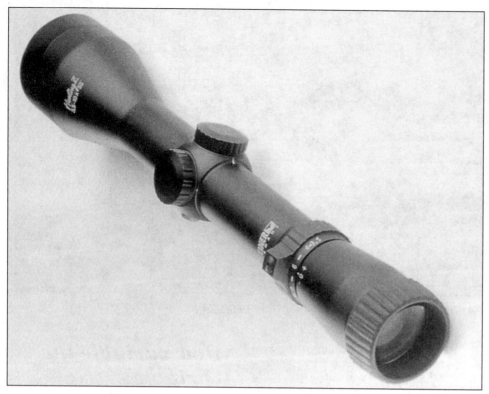

Steiner makes this 3.5-10x50 scope with 30mm tube.

this is sad news. But the evidence is irrefutable. Leupold, whose fixed-power line is the biggest in the industry, sells nine variables for each fixed-power model. Swarovski and Zeiss have dropped 4x scopes from their lines. When Blount resurrected the Redfield name, only variables surfaced. Over 92 percent of scopes sold by Tasco and Bushnell, the top-volume brands in the United States, are variables.

Versatility is the selling point. Why settle for 4x when you can have 4x, 8x, 2 1/2x and 10x at the turn of a dial? Initial concerns about reliability have pretty much been laid to rest. Recoil machines that simulate the pounding of magnum rifles now fail to shake variables apart. "We spot-check our scopes with the equivalent of 10,000 shots from a .375 Holland rifle," said Bushnell's Chris Lalik. "If a scope is going to

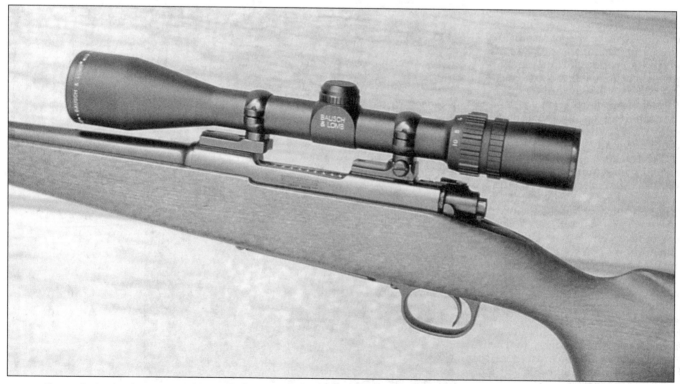

Bausch & Lomb (now Bushnell) Elite variables have Rainguard lens coatings for clear aim in the rain.

The author shot this Texas whitetail with a Pentax variable on a 7mm08 rifle.

fail, it will be right away. After a scope takes a hundred hits, it's almost always good for thousands. But we go the distance because the claim makes good copy."

Turning the power ring on a variable scope rotates a cam in the erector assembly. Two lenses then move different distances along the scope's axis. Off-axis movement used to result in impact shift, but tight manufacturing tolerances have now all but eliminated both. "There's so little shift that you probably won't detect it by shooting," one engineer assured me. "But nobody can guarantee zero shift."

The current trend to more magnification for long shooting with variable scopes raises questions. Is reticle shift more noticeable than it was decades ago when Weaver came out with a scope that gave you a choice of 2 1/2x or 5x? Does a broad power range – say, 6-24x – give you more shift than a narrow range – say, 1.5-4.5x? Is direction of shift predictable? Do expensive scopes have less shift than cheap models?

Certainly, high-power variables on rifles capable of one-hole accuracy can

make reticle shift more noticeable than it was for early post-war hunters using ordinary .30-06s with post reticles in low-power scopes. On the other hand, new manufacturing techniques and tighter tolerances have reduced shift over the last 50 years. Some makers claim they've eliminated it. They'd be safer saying you won't notice it.

Swarovski's Tom Hogan told me that shift tolerances for 4-16x and 6-24x scopes are tighter than for less powerful variables in green boxes. He reminded me that reticles set in the first focal plane give you *no shift at all* from low to high power. "European hunters prefer a front-mounted reticle for that reason, and because it can be used as a rangefinder at any power. Unlike the second-plane reticles common in the United States, first-plane reticles change size as the target image does, so *that* relationship remains constant." The main drawback to a front reticle is that you won't always like its dimensions. At low magnification, ideal for quick shots in thickets, you get a fine reticle that's hard to see. At high

power, when you want precision for long shots, you get a crosswire as thick as ship girders.

Logic would tell you it's hard to predict the direction of reticle shift, because moving lenses are subject to both vertical and lateral play. You might expect less shift in costly scopes, because tolerances in manufacture and assembly would seem to be tighter than in cheap scopes. But shift can occur in any scope with a second-focal-plane reticle. Individual scopes within a model can show different degrees of shift and no perceptible shift at all.

I've tested shift in a sampling of hunting scopes – not with a collimator, but under recoil from the bench, the way you'd shoot to zero your rifle. I used sandbags on an adjustable rest, with another sandbag under the toe of the stock. Except for .22 rimfires, a shotgun and short-range scopes, the shooting was done at 100 yards. There was no wind of consequence. I fired three shots per scope setting if the resulting group was tight, more shots to establish group centers with rifles that did not group well.

Rifle, Cartridge	Scope	Price	Groupshift, low to high x
Remington M700, .35 Whelen	1-4x Docter Optic (30mm)	$722*	1/2" to 6 o'clock
Savage M99, .308 Win.	1.5-4.5x Bushnell Banner	$117	none (50 yds)
Remington Model Seven, .308 Win.	1.5-5x Weaver Grand Slam	$383	3/4" to 12 o'clock
Ruger M77, .300 Win. Mag.	2-7x Redfield Five Star	$230*	none
Remington 11-87, rifled 12-gauge	2-7x Kahles	$532	none (50 yds)
Remington M78, .35 Whelen Imp.	3-9x Leupold Vari-X II	$432	none
Remington M78, .35 Whelen Imp.	3-9x Redfield Illuminator	$650	none
Winchester M70, .270 Win.	3-9x Zeiss Diavari C MC	$599	none
Remington Model Seven, .300 Rem. SUM	3-9x Kahles	$621	none
Remington M78, .270 Redding	2.5-10x Bushnell 4200 Elite	$643	1/2" to 6 o'clock
Winchester M70, .223 Rem.	2.5-10x Sightron	$222	3/4" to 2 o'clock
Remington M710, .30-06	3.3-10x Nikon Titan	$899	none
Ruger 77/22, .22 WMR	3.5-10x Simmons	$130	none (50 yds)
Remington M700, .240 Hawk	4-12x Bushnell Trophy	$301	none
Remington M700, 6mm Rem.	4.5-14x Leupold Vari-X III	$816	1/2" to 9 o'clock
Remington M710, .30-06	6-18x Swift	$255	1" to 2 o'clock

I got additional data from Ken Nagel and Rich McClure, both capable riflemen:

Rifle, Cartridge	Scope	Price	Groupshift, low to high x
Husqvarna, .270	2-7x Leupold Vari-X II	$448	1 1/2" to 6 o'clock
Kimber 82, .22 WMR	2-7x Leupold Vari-X II	$448	none (50 yds)
Ruger 77/22, .22 LR	2.5-7x Weaver Rimfire	$185	none (50 yds)
Husqvarna, .30-06	2-7x Redfield Frontier	$175*	1 1/2" to 6 o'clock
Kimber 82, .22 Hornet	3-9x Redfield (1968 vintage)	$300*	none
Remington 541, .22 LR	3-9x Tasco	$100	none (50 yds)
Sako, .270/308	2.5-10x Bausch & Lomb Balvar	$429*	3/4" to 12 o'clock
Browning M78, .30-06	3.5-10x Cabela's Alaskan Guide	$210	none
Sako, .300 Imperial Mag.	4.5-14x Leupold Vari-X III	$816	3/4" to 12 o'clock
Browning M78, 7 STW	6.5-20x Leupold Vari-X III	$861	none
Winchester M70, .223 Rem.	6.5-20x Leupold Vari-X III	$861	none

*These scopes are no longer available in the exact form tested. Prices are of equivalent models.

Most elk hunters use variable scopes with top ends between 9 and 14 power.

This is hardly an exhaustive test. Peruse the catalogs and you'll find literally hundreds of choices in hunting scopes. Swarovski and Schmidt & Bender both market high-quality variables, as do Pentax and Burris. But samples were not immediately available for this exercise.

Some rifles delivered tiny groups that made reticle shift more visible. My .223 M70, for example, punched out two half-inch clusters that gave the 2.5-10x Sightron no slack. Had that scope been on a less accurate rifle, group overlap might have hidden the shift. Also, aiming errors at low magnification surely influenced results. One scope wore a dot reticle that all but obscured the 100-yard target when the scope was set at 2 1/2x. Overall, groups shrank significantly when the scope power was increased. Collimator tests for shift are less trouble (once you have the laboratory!) and more reliable. The advantage of these trials over a collimator check is that they're a step closer to what you can expect from

Another 30mm scope: the carriage-class Zeiss VM/V 3.5-10x50 with lighted reticle.

the sights on opening day, complete with recoil and the pressure of your own scope rings.

These data suggest that you can't buy your way toward zero reticle shift. Shift was not correlated with price. In fact, the average list price of scopes with discernible reticle shift ($491) was higher than the average price of all scopes tested ($459). Nor did shift depend on range of magnification. The Docter 1-4x and Swift 6-18x both showed error. The 1.5-4.5x Bushnell Banner and 6.5-20x Leupold did not. When a shift occurred, it was mostly vertical, but the change was evenly split, up and down. And you can't rule out lateral shift.

If you're concerned about reticle shift in your scope, test it. Fire five rounds each at low, middle and high magnifications. If group centers are no farther apart than half the spread of an average group, you can dismiss shift as insignificant. Zero the scope at the highest magnification you expect to use in the field. That way, you'll get the most precision when you need it, for shooting little targets far away. So what if you get 3/4-minute shift when you crank that 4-12x scope down to flail away at a whitetail dashing through the alders at 30 steps? Actual error at the target is a quarter inch! The buck's vitals are the size of a camp frying pan, and your pulse is tossing the reticle all over the landscape. In this case, fretting about reticle shift is like contemplating the length of the loops in your bootlaces.

When you shop for a new scope, put reticle shift low on a list of priorities. Brightness, resolution, a flat field and precise, repeatable adjustments come first. Much of what you pay for in high-priced scopes is better glass and more sophisticated coatings that enhance brightness and sharpness.

If you lose sleep over shift, you can always choose a variable with a front-focal-plane reticle, or join a shrinking cadre of old-timers like me who prefer fixed-power scopes.

My favorites include Leupold M8s: the 4x and standard 6x. I like the Kahles 4x, the Burris Fullfield 4x, and the new Weaver Grand Slam 4.75x. Nikon's 4x Monarch is a brilliant scope, and a bargain. The best fixed-power big game scope? It could be the Schmidt & Bender 4x.

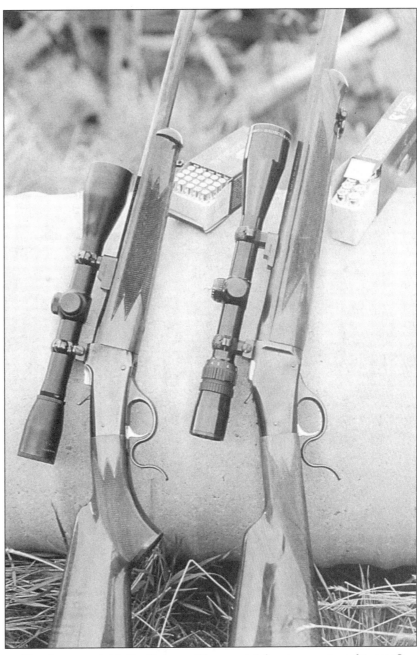

Fixed or variable? Do you like a pistol grip or straight grip? Browning Low Wall or High Wall?

Don't overlook 2 1/2x "shotgun" scopes, whose big fields of view, light weight and slim lines make them fast to aim and quick out of the scabbard. You'll like the way the reticle steadies itself. High magnification can show you more wobble than you can control.

It's easy to think you'll shoot better with a more powerful scope, or that a variable will make you more versatile. Or that zero reticle shift will eliminate misses. But a scope is only a sight. What matters most is your ability to aim at the right spot and hold the rifle still while you squeeze the last ounce from the trigger.

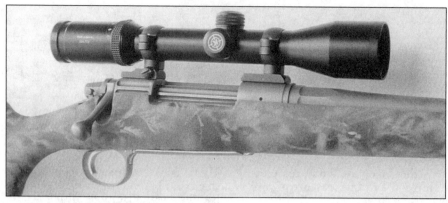

An early Kahles variable complements this lightweight Kevin Wyatt rifle in .300 Winchester.

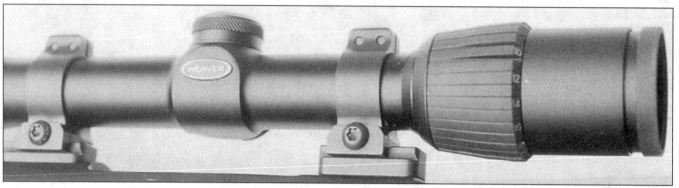

Weaver's Grand Slam variables have raised ribs on the power dial, to show numbers at the rear.

A Cabela's variable scope and a Browning A-Bolt rifle in .300 WSM accounted for this caribou.

Chapter 10

Specialty Scopes

Turkey sights ... and deer

USED TO BE, a shotgun had a bead. If you had a fancy shotgun, it had two beads. If, like me, you had to borrow shotguns, sometimes they had no bead. But that didn't matter much because you pointed a shotgun like you pointed your finger, and you made do nicely without a bead on your finger.

Then deer hunters started putting sights on shotguns. First open sights, then receiver sights, and then scopes. Sights made sense when you shot slugs, because even if the slugs weren't accurate, you could at least take more precise aim and get the slug *close* to where you wanted it. When sabot slugs and rifled shotgun barrels came along, improving accuracy and extending effective slug range to 150 yards or so, deer hunters started equipping their slug guns with scopes. That's logical. But now *turkey* hunters are aiming through glass. *That* doesn't seem logical at all!

Yes, you still shoot at turkeys with birdshot from a smooth bore, just like you do pheasants. But there the similarity stops. Turkeys sneak around like deer in the shadows, and you'll often spot them in dawn's dim light. Most of your shots will be at turkeys standing like deer, not flying like pheasants. And those shots could be long. You need a dense shot cloud to put the most pellets possible in that skinny neck, so a tight choke is in order, and centering your pattern becomes important. In sum, though you're hurling a column of pellets at Tom, he's making you shoot that smooth-bore like a rifle.

You want a sight that's clearly visible in dim light, and one that's adjustable so you can bring the sight to the center of your pattern.

A shotgun scope, like this Simmons, can make you a more effective turkey hunter. If you can call.

(Though shotgunners seldom think about it, the bead doesn't always bring your eye to where most of the shot is!) Quick shooting isn't as important as accurate shooting. Thus, a scope does make sense. It's better than iron sights because it gives you an unobstructed view of the target and a cleaner sight picture. It's much better than an illuminated bead or rear sight, in my opinion, because while a bright orange blob is easy to see, it doesn't make the turkey easier to see. In fact, it can reduce the sharpness of your vision. It can steal your eye from the target, and just as a flashlight in night woods makes everything outside its beam hard to see, a lighted open sight can obscure details on its periphery. Even in scopes, illumination can be a mixed blessing – mainly because hunters turn the brightness up too high. A turkey's head is small; you need sharp vision to aim well! Illuminated crosswires and red dots can help you aim fast and precisely if they're kept to just a faint glow.

Magnification, like illumination, is easily overdone. Indeed, there's nothing wrong with 1x glass! Still, you may be surprised at how much better you can aim at distant birds with scopes of 2.5x or 4x. Stay at that power level. If you're used to shooting scoped rifles, a 4x glass will be as quick as iron sights. And you'll get plenty of light to your eye through the smallest objective lenses. If I were to pick a scope, it'd be a 2.5x with a straight tube, mounted very low so a standard shotgun stock would put my eye on the optical axis as soon as the butt hit my shoulder.

Most repeating shotguns accommodate scopes these days. I had to drill an old 870 Remington to mount my first scope on a shotgun 30 years ago. Now you can get receiver mounts that use the two pins holding the trigger group. Many receiver tops are drilled for scope bases. Cantilever mounts that affix to the barrel are becoming popular. Shotgun recoil is stiff, so a mount must be secure. On the other hand, you won't be using a heavy sight. The lighter the scope, the less its inertia, and the more likely it will stay put.

Some scopes are made to be mounted ahead of the receiver (usually they're designated IER or XER, for intermediate or extended eye relief).

Optics companies have accommodated deer hunters with extra-heavy reticles for fast shooting in dark woods. These and standard plex reticles work fine, but special turkey reticles are also available. They typically have an open center that doesn't hide the bird's head. Some can help you range birds (the Pentax Deepwoods reticle has an inner circle that compasses 30 inches at 40 yards).

Scopes designed specifically for turkey hunters should be parallax-correct at 50 or 75 yards, not the 100 to 150 yards common for rifle sights. It won't make a lot of difference at woods ranges, but as my Mama observed, ain't no smart man passes up free biscuits. You'll find some turkey scopes in camouflage finish. Now, a 2.5x scope is a pretty small item and in black matte finish won't by itself spook turkeys; but hunters who like camo on their guns can now color-coordinate.

Here's a shopping list of turkey sights. There's no "field of view" data because all scopes of low magnification have more than enough field. Reticle selections may be broader than indicated; I've shown my preferences. You're smart to compare sights at the counter and get *all* the specifications.

Make, Model, power x obj. dia. (mm)	Tube diameter	Wt. (oz.)	Reticle	Eye relief (in.)
Aimpoint 3000 2x20	1 inch	9	illum. dot	unlimited
Aimpoint 5000 2x24	30mm	11	illum. dot	unlimited
Burris Speed Dot	35mm	5	illum. dot	unlimited
Burris Fullfield 2.5x20	1 inch	10	plex	3.5
Burris Fullfield 1.75-5x20	1 inch	10	plex	3.5
Burris Compact XER 1x20	1 inch	7	plex	4-24
Burris Compact XER 1-4x20	1 inch	10	plex	4-24
Burris Scout XER 2.75x20	1 inch	7	heavy plex	7-14
Bushnell Holosight 2x	NA	9	illum. dot	unlimited
Bushnell Banner 1.5-4.5x32	1 inch	13	plex	3.5
Bushnell Sportview 1.5-4.5x21	1 inch	9	plex	3
Bushnell Sportview 1.5-4.5x32	1 inch	11	Circle X	3.5
Bushnell Sportview 2.5x32	1 inch	10	plex	3
BSA Red Dot 1x	30mm or 42mm	5 or 7	illum. dot	unlimited
BSA Deer Hunter 2.5x20	1 inch	7.5	plex	6
Leupold LG-1 Red Dot	1 inch or 35mm	11	illum. dot	unlimited
Leupold Compact 2.5x20	1 inch	6.5	Turkey Ranger	4
Leupold Vari-X II Shotgun 1-4x20	1 inch	9	heavy plex	4
Leupold Shotgun 4x33	1 inch	9.5	heavy plex	4
Leupold Vari-X II Shotgun 2-7x33	1 inch	10.5	heavy plex	4
Leupold IER 2.5x28 IER	1 inch	7.5	plex	9.5
Nikon Shotgun 1.5-4.5x20	1 inch	9	TurkeyPro	3.5
Nikon Sabot/Slug 1.5-4.5x20	1 inch	9	plex	3.5
Pentax Lightseeker SG Plus 1x27	1 inch	8	Deepwoods Plex	4.5-15
Pentax Lightseeker SG Plus 2.5x25	1 inch	9	Deepwoods Plex	3.5
Pentax Lightseeker SG Plus 1-4x27	1 inch	10	heavy plex	3.5-7
Schmidt & Bender 1.25-4x20	30mm	15	Flash Dot	3.5
Sightron Shotgun	2.5x20	1 inch	8.5 plex	4.5
Sightron Shotgun 2.5-7x32	1 inch	8.5	Double Diamond	4.5
Simmons Shotgun 2.5x20	1 inch	7	plex	6
Simmons Shotgun 2x32	1 inch	9	Pro Diamond	5.5

Make, model, power x obj. dia. (mm)	Tube diameter	Wt. (oz.)	Reticle	Eye relief (in.)
Simmons Shotgun 4x32	1 inch	9	Pro Diamond	5.5
Simmons Shotgun 1.5-5x20	1 inch	11	Pro Diamond	3.5
Swarovski Nova-A 1.5-4.5x20	1 inch	10.5	plex	3.5
Swarovski PV 1.25-4x24	30mm	13	circle in plex	3
Swift 1x20	1 inch	10	plex	3
Swift 1.5-4.5x21	1 inch	11	plex	3
Tasco Pro-Point 1x30	30mm	5	illum. dot	unlimited
Tasco Shotgun 2.5x32	1 inch	9.5	plex	3.5
Tasco Wide Angle 1-3.5x20	1 inch	10	plex	3
Tasco Wide Angle 1.75-5x20	1 inch	10	plex	3
Weaver K2.5 2.5x20	1 inch	7	plex	3.5
Weaver V3 1-3x20	1 inch	9	plex	3.5
Zeiss Diavari VM/V 1.1-4x24	30mm	15	illum. dot	3.5
Zeiss Diavari ZM/Z 1.25-4x24	30mm	17	plex	3

Turkey scopes aren't just for turkeys. They're perfect for hunting whitetails in close cover, too. Or for mule deer that hide where they're not supposed to....

It happened during a hard rain. The woods had closed in on me. At the same time, there was that palpable loosening every woodsman has felt in a downpour. The forest sighs when it takes a bath.

I decided to relax too. Soaked even under my poncho, I slumped at the base of a great Douglas fir, prop-ping the rifle against it. I dug a can of sardines from my rucksack and ate, using a twig as a fork. Messy, but I got everything that wasn't mustard.

It came to me then that I should use the glass. With rain riveting the forest floor and screening even the close cover behind milky sheets, I peered into the 7x35 Zephyr.

I could hardly believe the buck was there. It was as if I'd picked up the binocular to get a better look, because he was in the field of view immediately. His eye and the thick, studded base of one antler didn't stay there long, because I lowered the glass immediately as I slowly snaked the rifle into my lap. The Model 70 came up smoothly. The safety was off, my finger taut on the trigger.

And he was gone.

When you don't have a shot, it doesn't matter what scope you're looking through.

Still, where the trees grow thick, where old bucks find security, you

The author shot this turkey with the help of a Simmons scope.

Weaver Shotgun Scope 1.5 x 7

Shotgun scopes may look like rifle scopes, but typically have thicker reticles, short-range parallax correction.

want a sight that delivers plenty of eye relief and a big field of view for quick sighting. You don't need magnification, just a bright, sharp sight picture that instantly tells you when to crush the trigger. Trim, low-power scopes work best, no matter if they're listed in the big game section of the catalog or as turkey sights. Here are some attributes I look for in a deer scope for the deep woods:

Light weight – up to 13 ounces without mounts; but no more than 10 percent of the weight of the scope and rifle together. Reason: weight on top of a rifle adds nothing to accuracy but can impair handling by making the rifle tippy. Shoulder a fine English shotgun to feel how a low center of gravity allows the barrels to point themselves. An old .30-30 carbine isn't quite as lively, but it still points well. Now aim a modern bolt rifle with a 3 1/2-10x50 variable scope. The ponderous sight, and a high mounting prompted by the big objective lens, give that rifle all the agility of salvaged plumbing. Most early scopes weighed little (though the tubes were steel, they measured only 7/8 inch in diameter, and they had no objective bell). The ocular housings were also small, to permit low mounting. Eye relief was so long that many were mounted ahead of rear-swing safeties on pre-war Model 70 Winchesters, further pulling down the center of gravity. Lightweight, low-mounted scopes still make sense, especially where shots come quickly. A sightline close to the barrel helps

you point a rifle as quickly as you would a grouse gun.

Wide field of view – say 24 feet at 100 yards. All 2 1/2x scopes and lots of 4x scopes will give you more, but 24 feet is what you get with a Leupold M8 4x. That relatively tight field is the price of long eye relief, a Leupold trademark. With a 24-foot window, you should still find your target quickly, and be able to swing easily ahead of sprinting game without losing it behind the trailing rim of the scope. A 24-foot field should show you other animals about to step in front of your target, or that are standing alert, ready to give you away. At 50 yards, the 24-foot field shrinks to 12 feet. But that's still enough. Even a whitetail with the afterburners roaring needs no more than a foot of lead, and stretched out across your field should be easy to keep inside it. Besides, most game surprised up close runs directly away or quarters away. In either case, you'll have plenty of air around your target. Variable scopes of 2 1/2x to 3 1/2x on the bottom end give you 26 to 43 feet of field when you crank them down. Which you should, whenever you move into cover. You'll generally have time to turn up the power when you see animals distant enough to require it. Up close, you must shoot *now*! Scopes left at high power give deer in the deep woods a chance to escape!

Generous eye relief – 3 1/2 to 4 inches. Eye relief is the distance between your eye and the ocular

lens when you see a full field of view in the scope. You want long eye relief so you can mount the scope well forward. A forward mounting gives you good secondary vision around the scope. Also, you may find it easier to look *through* the sight instead of *into* it, speeding up your shot. Finally, the scope won't then hit you in the brow during recoil if you must shoot uphill or from unorthodox positions. Generous eye relief comes at a price in field of view. Sights mounted forward of the action have what is called "intermediate eye relief" (between the eye relief prescribed for rifles and that suitable for handguns held at arm's length). Their field of view is smaller than you'd expect from similar magnification in receiver-mounted scopes. When you check for eye relief, make sure it's not critical. That is, see to it that your eye has some latitude, forward and back from its ideal position, without losing the sight picture to blackout. Critical eye relief slows you down by insisting that your eye be perfectly placed behind the scope. Check eye relief at all the magnification settings on variable scopes, because it commonly shrinks when you boost power.

Low power – but not too low. I like 2 1/2x to 4x magnification in scopes for woodland deer hunting. To get a big field of view, long eye relief, and light weight, you won't be using powerful glass. Why not less magnification than 2 1/2x? If you look through low-power variables turned down to 1x or 1 1/2x, you'll see a small target and lots of rifle barrel. I find the barrel distracting. If you buy a variable, consider a 2-7x or 2 1/2-8x for greater versatility. Given a 32mm or 36mm objective, they're light and compact enough for a woods rifle while affording the precision for long shots across clearcuts. I like the Bushnell Elite 1½-6x – and the Aimpoint red-dot sight, clever in design and tough as a splitting maul. Its lighted dot is especially useful in dark cover. You can get it in 2x magnification. Another option is the Bushnell Holosight, also with a lighted reticle. Both it and the Aimpoint 7000 are very fast.

Bold reticle – like a heavy plex. Where leaves and branches clutter the field, you may hesitate an instant looking for an ordinary crosswire or fine plex. As light fades, the problem worsens. Thick posts used to be favorites of woods hunters, but you don't see them much anymore. I've never shot well with them because the top of the post seems harder to define than the intersection of four posts. The heavy plex available now is immediately visible and directs your eye to the center. The dot is another option, but it must be a BIG dot, or you'll lose it in dark places. The first elk I shot almost got away as I tried to find the 3-minute dot in my 2½x Lyman Alaskan against his dark neck and even blacker lodgepoles at dusk. When specifying a dot, remember that its size in minutes is the number of inches subtended at 100 yards, and that a low-power scope needs a bigger dot than a high-power sight. That's because an inch looks smaller at low power. Except in red-dot sights, I'm not keen on electronic reticles. Battery bubbles on traditional scopes add weight and bulk and don't look good. You shouldn't need the glow in legal shooting light. If you use a red-dot sight or Holosight, keep the rheostat on the low end or you'll lose target definition.

Easy to see through. That's the ideal deer scope for the brush. Just like the ideal turkey sight, it's part of what can make you a successful hunter. But the biggest bucks and birds don't always go to hunters who shop smart. Woodsmanship and skill with the rifle or shotgun count too.

Red dots for quick shots

The main advantage of scopes over iron sights is their single-plane sight picture. You have only to focus at one apparent distance. That's lots easier than trying to pull together target, front sight and rear open sight. The main *dis*advantage of scopes is their limited field. When you see a bigger image, you're seeing a smaller part of what's around you.

If the whole world and sky in front of you – let's call it the kaboodle, because that's what people used to call everything when they didn't have the kit to go with it – got bigger, you'd see more detail in all its parts. But this idea of a bigger kaboodle is nonsense because there are boundaries to kaboodles that we can't change. One of them is spatial. If you make a kaboodle wider, you can't see the ends as well. If you could see one end well, you wouldn't see the other at all. The top of a higher kaboodle would get farther away as you got a better look at its lower end.

With a scope, you're tunneling into the kaboodle, magnifying a patch of it while blocking out the kaboodle immediately surrounding that patch. It would be nice if you could instead block out other parts of the kaboodle that you don't care to look at. But the law of kaboodles gives you no choice. What you can't see is the kaboodle right around your target, the part obscured by the scope tube, turret and mount. Higher magnification gives you a smaller field and hides more of its periphery.

In the mid-1970s, the Swedish company Aimpoint brought Stateside a novel aiming device that came to be known generically as the red dot sight. Aimpoint's version, with its short, compact tube, long eye relief and illuminated dot reticle, was as quick to use as a shotgun bead. Its broad application – rifles, pistols and shotguns – drew the interest of established optics firms like Tasco and Bushnell.

Most red dot sights operate this way: Light from the front passes through a lens with a partially reflective coating on its back surface. A battery-powered diode behind the lens emits a small, bright light that bounces off that lens and back into your eye. The red dot and target appear to be in the same plane, so your eye need focus only on the target.

Dot size is measured in minutes of angle. Many of these electronic sights offer a choice of dot sizes; a few even let you change reticles in seconds. Because there's no magnification, you want a big dot – at least 3 m.o.a. for rifles. To my eye, 6

The Aimpoint 7000 is a perfect match for this fast-shucking Blaser rifle.

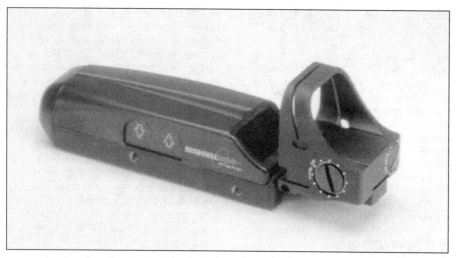

Bushnell's Holosight is lightweight and very fast to use.

m.o.a. is better. Remember that in a 20x scope a quarter-minute dot makes sense because a quarter-inch spot *magnified 20 times* is as plain as a 5-inch disk seen with the naked eye. In a 1x sight you must have a 5-minute dot to equal the apparent size of that quarter-minute dot in the target scope. The target will appear smaller through the red dot sight, of course. You need the big dot because dots are measured against the target *as it appears in the sight*. Big dots make a lot of sense if the range is short or the light dim. IPSC (International Practical Shooting Confederation) competitors, who shoot fast at big targets up close can well use 10-m.o.a. dots. So can shotgunners in whitetail coverts. One thing to keep in mind, however: An illuminated dot needn't be as big as a dot in a conventional 1x scope to catch your eye. You'll want to try several before deciding on a size.

The apparent size of a dot can vary with its brightness, which is adjustable on every red dot scope I know about. It's good to have a wide range of brightness, especially on a hunting gun that might be used in dim or very bright light. For dim conditions, you want that red dot at its lowest setting, as your eyes will have dilated to take in lots of light. A bright dot in dark timber has the effect of an automobile headlamp: It hides what's behind and a good deal of what's around it. Under a noon-time sun, however, you'll want to crank the dial to a high setting. Your pupils will have constricted to admit less light, and background glare will compete with the illumination of the dot.

Most red dot sights have the equivalent of a scope's erector tube inside the main tube, so you can change windage and elevation by moving the smaller tube with exterior knobs. The "C-more" sight has neither tube – just a lens with the diode set into the sight base behind it. You make windage and elevation adjustments by changing the angle of the lens.

Bushnell's Holosight, also tubeless, employs photographic film sandwiched between two pieces of glass. The film has a holographic image in the form of a reticle. The holograph seems to project itself when you aim, so the reticle appears not just *against* the target but *at* the target. This principle is not new, but Bushnell pioneered its use in sights. The 3D effect is remarkable. Introduced in 1996, the Holosight now has eight interchangeable reticles. There's also a 2x adapter that adds just 3/4 inch and 2½ ounces.

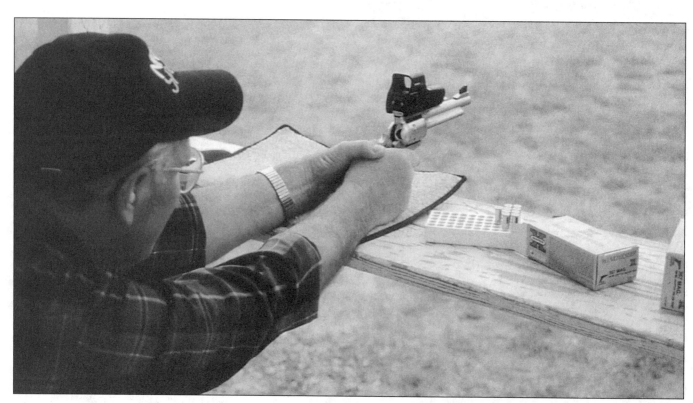

The author thinks the Bushnell Holosight is at its finest on handguns.

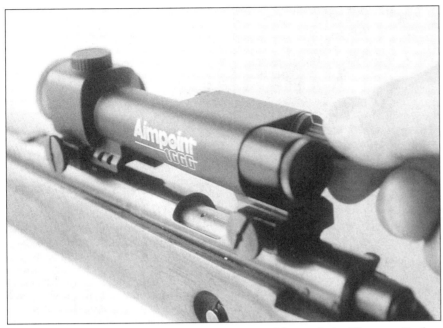

The Aimpoint 1000 is several generations old now but still a practical sight for the timber.

You needn't center your eye behind a red dot sight. The dot will appear even if your eye is some distance out of line. If you can place that dot on target – no matter the dot's apparent position in the sight – you should hit. The farther a dot appears from the center of the lens, the farther your eye is off-axis and the greater the parallax (difference between the apparent relationship of dot and target and the *real* relationship, discernible only when your eye is centered behind the lens). Red dot sights with tubes are slightly less vulnerable to parallax problems because the tube allows your eye less deviation from the sight's axis. The Aimpoint optical system all but eliminates parallax, according to engineers there.

Some people say red dot sights are unsuitable for big game rifles because at long range parallax can cause serious aiming error. The truth is, if your eye lines up with the middle of the lens, there is no parallax. The dot's apparent place relative to bore-line is just where it *is* relative to bore-line. Assuming you've zeroed properly, you'll hit the target. The same holds for conventional scopes. The difference is that a conventional scope won't let you see the reticle if your eye is outside a very narrow cone behind the ocular lens. The red dot sight gives you a lot more latitude in eye placement. This latitude is what makes a red dot sight especially useful on handguns. When time is short and your

position unsteady, it's better to get an imperfect hit quickly than to delay the shot. I have used several red dot sights on handguns, including the Holosight and Tasco's Optima 2000. They've all impressed me. My aging eyes don't shave the fuzz off iron sights like they used to, and I shoot with red dots much more quickly. That means less arm fatigue when there's lots of time, faster recoil recovery when there isn't.

A pistol scope can give you the same sharp sight picture, but eye relief is more critical. A red dot sight delivers a full screen of kaboodle whatever the length of your arm or however you have it bent while aiming. You can take a red dot sight off a handgun and mount it on a rifle or shotgun receiver and get the same view. In contrast, ordinary pistol scopes are as useless 3 inches in front of your eye as riflescopes are a sleeve-length away.

A red dot sight is a good choice for slug guns, assuming the stock comb puts your eye in line with it. Some shooters recommend red dot sights for bird hunting and clay target shooting. I can't, because for me it requires deliberation. Once, on a sporting clays course, I tried to hit a high incomer using a red dot sight. After several frustrating misses, I finally broke a bird. From then on that particular shot became easy, because I knew where to put the dot. But the occasional pigeon that took a different path at a slightly different speed often sailed on unbroken.

My success hinged on the rote relationship of dot to target. I'd lost my fluidity, any natural connection with the bird. The barrel and my left hand, now no longer visible, were together part of a remote apparatus guiding the dot.

Part of the problem with using a dot on a bird gun is the inevitable loss of stock contact. Though typically mounted tight to the receiver, a red dot sight still sits much higher than a bead or field rib on a shotgun barrel. Because of the diode apparatus, some ride higher than ordinary scopes. To put your eye behind a red dot sight is to take your cheek off the stock. If there's an easier way to miss flying targets than to take your cheek off the stock, I haven't found it. To be fair, I'll admit that many years of shotgunning habits limit my effectiveness with red dot sights. Using a Holosight left-handed, with no habit interfering, I managed to break more birds than I thought I would – more than I could break left-handed looking down the barrel.

One other liability of red dot sights on bird guns is their mechanical presence: the housing blocks out part of the kaboodle. When shooting stationary game, you won't notice that housing. But sweeping a blur of grouse feathers from a labyrinth of brown alders, or sifting wood ducks from swamp timber as they drop and bank, leaf-like but faster – these tasks call for clear vision. Eye and hand must act in concert and unimpeded. For shotgunning close, quick targets of changing speed and direction, *any* sight can be more hindrance than help. At least, that's my opinion.

On guns meant for sights, red dots speed up the shot. They're faster than iron sights because you just slap the dot on the target. They're faster than any scope because eye relief is less critical and the dot stands out against cluttered backgrounds. Though parallax and reticle subtention limit their utility at long range, red dot sights with 3-minute reticles at low power settings make sense for big game to 200 yards.

Before buying a red dot sight for hunting, you'll want to try several models and dot sizes under extremes of light conditions, tuning brightness to match. Weight and bulk matter too. Red dot sights are compact, as a class, but some are much smaller and lighter than others. Tasco's Optima 2000 is among the lightest and most compact of all

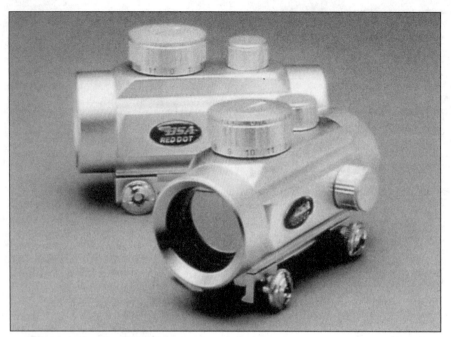

BSA's red dot sights are typical of those now popular with pistol shooters.

sights: It measures just 1½ inches long and weighs about the same as a trim receiver sight! But despite its compactness, it is not delicate. These days, you can't equate ruggedness with weight. The lighter the sight, the less its inertia and the less apt it is to come off the gun during recoil.

Some hunters shy from electronic gizmos, and I'll confess an aversion to batteries. They always seem to die when I need them. But the tiny batteries in red dot sights have light duty, and under normal conditions, they'll last a couple of years. We've gotten used to batteries in flashlights, cameras, hearing aids and watches. I don't suppose a sight battery is all that far-fetched.

Here are some addresses of companies marketing red dot sights:

Adco Sales
4 Draper Street
Woburn, MA 01801
781-935-1799

Aimpoint USA
7702 Leesburg Pike
Falls Church, VA 22043
703-749-2320

Bushnell Sports Optics
9200 Cody
Overland Park, KS 66214
913-752-3400

C-More Systems
7553 Gary Road
POB 1750
Manassas, VA 20109
703-361-2663

Crosman
Rts 5 and 20
East Bloomfield, NY 14443
716-657-6161

Leupold & Stevens
POB 688
Beaverton, OR 97075
503-646-9171

Millet Sights
7275 Murdy Circle
Huntington Beach, CA 92647
714-842-5575

Sightron
1672B Highway 96
Franklinton NC 27525
919-528-8783

Simmons (Blount)
201 Plantation Oak Drive
Thomasville, GA 31792
912-227-9053

Tasco Sales
2889 Commerce Parkway
Miramar, FL 33025
954-252-3600

Thompson-Center Arms
POB 5002
Rochester, NH 03867
603-332-2394

Ultra Dot
2316 Northeast 8th Road
Ocala, FL 34470
352-629-7112

Aimpoint: Sparking a red dot revolution

The forest reminded me of west-side timber in my home state of Washington. Towering conifers dripped rain to a forest floor soft with soggy moss. The gray sky hung solemnly over their spires. It had leaked since dawn, since before the fallow deer had ghosted by, since the first faint bellow of the horn.

Now, waiting for the second drive to sift through the swamp in front of my stand, I could hear the voices of the cheerful Danes pushing the highland beyond. I dabbed the sight's rear lens with an already-saturated Kleenex. Closer they came, and suddenly a dark flicker of movement winked between alders on the swamp's edge.

At 100 yards, in the rain and with lots of brush in the way, I couldn't tell if it was a bull or a cow, but it was surely a moose. I looked for a calf. Cow moose were

The Aimpoint is a favorite sight in Sweden, where it's manufactured.

legal game on this hunt only if they were without a calf. The animal had vanished by the time it was clear no calf would follow. I pivoted to cover the forest, where the alders gave way to big trees, and where open understory might give me another glimpse.

There! But the moose had almost passed me, crossing at 90 yards, before I could find a shot alley. Then I saw the antler, which wouldn't have mattered, except that here a bull that carried between 5 and 10 total points was protected. I could shoot a forkhorn. The red dot of the sight probed the gaps between the black boles as pieces of moose slipped between them. The animal stopped once with its shoulder exposed, but not the antler. Then I saw the antler again and decided to shoot and found no vitals. Just as the moose was about to vanish, angling away through the gloom, it paused one more time. The dot glued itself to the shoulder, and I triggered the .30-06. Instantly the bull lunged forward, a rear hoof coming up just a little higher than normal. It was a good sign.

I didn't move, because here in Sweden you didn't leave your stand until the drivers converged or you heard the final three blasts on the hunting horn. Finally they came. I raced over to where the moose had stood and saw the great animal dead a few yards down the trail. The Blaser's 165-grain bullet had hit a tad farther forward than I'd called, but still well within the boiler.

It was the first moose of the day at Claestorp, the first game I'd ever shot in Europe.

The notion of shooting driven game didn't appeal to me at first. I don't like to stand still for long in the woods, and I don't like other people doing my hunting for me. But the expansive forests of central Sweden give the game plenty of options. I saw moose sneak away from the drivers and sprint between the standers. A huge wild boar, which would have been the hunt's finest trophy, seemed to vanish in the mist.

Swedes hardly need to apologize for shooting a few moose. Closely managed on private ground, moose and other big game thrive north of the rich coffee-colored soils that nuture sugar beets and other cash crops east of a line between Malmo and Hoganas. A few years ago, when the big-nosed deer were at a population peak, there may have been more moose in Sweden than in all of North America! About the size of California, Sweden had to trim moose numbers. With typical Scandinavian care, it has: 100,000 a year.

You can hunt big game with lots of cartridges, but the not-surprising favorite among Swedes is the gentle 6.5x55. Next comes the .30-06, then the .308. From what I could determine, almost all of Sweden's moose harvest is taken with one of these cartridges. Mauser rifles are favorites. It seemed to me that the Finnish Tikkas and Sakos outnumber Husqvarnas. Big scopes are popular. Hunting wild boar from stands at the edge of night, Swedish hunters value pie-plate objectives.

"But you certainly don't need high magnification on drives," one rifleman told me before the hunt, seeing that I'd borrowed the Blaser with its Aimpoint sight. "In fact, I like a sight with no magnification at all, even for the qualification target."

The qualification target, I found, was the lifesize print of a moose on a frame that ran under motor power along a track. Scoring rings on the vitals were invisible from the line,

Red dot sights are a logical choice for slug-shooting shotguns like this Remington autoloader.

100 yards distant. The drill: Load with four rounds. Call for the target and fire once at the moose as it pauses, motionless. Then cycle the bolt and fire as the moose scoots along the track to disappear behind a barricade. Call for the target again, shoot once more at the standing moose and fire the last shot as it repeats its run in the opposite direction. You fire all shots offhand, for a possible score of 20. I managed 18 once, but not the first time.

There's no reason you shouldn't net 20 with a little practice. Unlike a real moose, the target runs smoothly and at a set speed. There's no brush in the way. The track is quite long. Though I wasn't very proud of 18, the Swedes assured me that many hunters fail to keep all shots in the scoring rings. Offhand is evidently as tough a position in Scandinavia as it is stateside.

I found in shooting the target, and then in killing the bull moose, that Aimpoint's red dot sight was indeed effective. Never fond of gadgets and wary of anything that requires batteries, I had to give this sight high marks. In the dim forest, that dot shown like the North Star on a frosty night. It was easy to pick up, and no matter where it appeared in the field of view, I could be assured the bullet would go there. I proved that at the range, moving my head to different positions on the stock. Offhand, I shot better than I normally do with a scope (thanks, also, to the Blaser's marvelous 2-pound trigger). I found the key to precision was keeping the dot at a low luminance. Some shooters crank up the dial to give themselves the equivalent of a brake light. As the dot gets brighter, it appears bigger, hiding the target. A halo effect reduces resolution around the dot. And your eye's pupil constricts, impairing its ability to see anything *but* the dot. Very dark conditions call for a very low setting – No. 3 was my choice on the nine-station dial of the Aimpoint.

Frankly, I hadn't given red dot sights much thought until the trip to Sweden. But after a couple of days at Claestorp, I contacted an engineer at the Aimpoint plant and asked if I could visit. Yaah.

Red dot sights are available from several companies now. But the idea was pioneered in Sweden back in 1975 by Gunnar Sandberg, inventor and entrepreneur. Sandberg formed the Aimpoint company shortly thereafter. In 1976, it comprised

four people. One of them was Kenneth Mardklint (now product manager), who graciously agreed to talk with me on a bright Saturday morning. He told me that 52 people currently work at Aimpoint's modern Malmo facility. It's an upscale place. The workers eat lunch in a glass-walled cafeteria served by an accomplished chef. The premise: If they eat together, they'll probably talk shop, and that will benefit Aimpoint. He pointed out that the company designs and specs everything for its sights but outsources most of the 60-odd components. "It's more cost-effective that way. Of course, we assemble and proof all the sights here." The facility has state-of-the-art optical testing devices.

"The first red dot sight we called the single-point sight," said Mardklint. "You saw the dot with one eye and the target with the other. You couldn't see through the sight at all!" Things improved from there. In 1975, the first-generation Aimpoint Electronic appeared. Windage and elevation adjustments protruded under the 3/4-inch tube, so it sat high on Weaver-style bases. "Its five light settings were all too bright for a dark day," he laughed. "We produced only 2,000 of them." In 1977, an improved version came out, with more latitude in the brightness dial, and no detents. A year later, the second generation of Aimpoint sights made its debut in a lower sight, with windage and elevation clicks in front. It featured a better diode and a detachable 3x or 1-4x lens to magnify the target. It was the first Aimpoint sold in the United States.

Aimpoint refined its "G2" sight and in 1983, brought out the Mark III, with internal adjustments and a dot that automatically dimmed for dark conditions after it was adjusted to the eye in daylight. The Aimpoint 2000 came in 1985. Unlike its predecessors, it had no base. The 1-inch tube could be mounted like an ordinary scope. Long and short versions were manufactured to accommodate various ring spacings on rifles and handguns. Stainless finish became available for the first time.

In 1987, Aimpoint introduced its Model 1000, designed as a penny-wise alternative to the 2000. It offered nine click-stop light settings and an integral Weaver-type base, with less costly electronics than the 2000. That year, Aimpoint also introduced a red dot bow sight. It fared poorly at market, because there is essentially no bowhunting

in Sweden, and U.S. bowhunters weren't sold on it.

In 1989, the Aimpoint 3000 supplanted its predecessors. Its battery case was much smaller, so this sight was lighter and more compact than the Model 2000. It featured 2x magnification and a 1-inch tube with an extension for wide ring spacing on rifles. The company dropped the automatic brightness adjustment in this sight. Though the 3000 is still available, it was upstaged in 1991 by the 5000, which is really a 3000 with a 30mm tube. Field of view increased by 20 percent. In 1998, Aimpoint announced the XD (extreme duty) diode in the 5000. It generated three times the brightness of the old diode, using a fifth of the current. Battery life jumped from 100 to 500 hours. The technology was carried over to the 5000 Comp, introduced four years earlier specifically for handgun competition. In fact, the XD diode was engineered for the target range, where shooters needed a bright but "clean" dot on white paper in midday light. Hunters benefited from the switch. The No. 6 setting on an XD sight is as bright as the No. 9 (highest) setting on a pre-XD model.

Incidentally, one difference between the Comp and hunting-style 5000 is the brightest setting on the dial. It is right next to the "off" position on the Comp, but farthest from "off" in a standard Aimpoint. Intelligent.

Mardklint, and the firm's U.S. representative, Mike Kingston, assured me that Aimpoint is a widely-recognized name in the red dot sight industry, but pointed out that fame is a mixed blessing. "Aimpoint has been unlucky in that some shooters think of it as the *only* red dot sight," said Kingston. "Sort of like Xerox has become a synonym for copier. Trouble is, not all sights or copiers are made to equal standards. Aimpoint sights cost more than most red dots produced by companies following our lead. That's because Aimpoint is better. Hands down. Many hunters who have tried and rejected red dot sights have never used ours."

The main difference, he explained, is in the front lens, whose red tint means it reflects red light so the dot appears brighter. That's a common feature. What isn't so common is the compound objective lens, which corrects for parallax. A single lens up front will still reflect the dot produced by the diode in the rear

Offhand qualification at the Swedish moose hunter's target is easy with an Aimpoint sight.

bottom of the tube. But its reflective path can spread fanlike as your eye changes position behind the sight. Result: If the dot isn't centered in the sight, you get parallax error at distances other than the one for which the sight was parallax-corrected. In contrast, the Aimpoint's doublet bounces the dot back to your eye in a line parallel with the optical axis of the instrument. With an Aimpoint, if you see the dot, you'll hit where the dot appears to be.

The field of view of an Aimpoint 3000 is about the same as that of a 4x scope. How so? Well, the 1x Aimpoint has a straight tube and is not designed to maximize field. You don't need extra field if you have no magnification, because there's plenty of woods around your target anyway. While the 4x has an edge in resolution, it gives each eye a different perspective downrange. You can't shoot as well with both eyes open because there's an area you see

with your left eye, immediately around the field of view, that's invisible to your right. And the images differ in size. Your eyes can't believe what they're seeing – which is why some shooters insist on squinting. The Aimpoint's field border is simply a narrow physical shadow caused by the sight's body. You can shoot as you might with a shotgun bead, with both eyes wide open.

Except in models with magnification (I prefer those without), Aimpoint red dot sights impose no limits on eye relief. Your eye can be 2 inches back, or 10, and you'll see the same field. The dot will be there for you too, in the same apparent focal plane as the target. There simply is no faster sight. And if you keep dot brightness at low settings, you'll shoot as accurately as you can hold under hunting conditions. A couple of hunters who have used Aimpoints have told me that they lose precision beyond 100 yards, that in effect they're a fine substitute for iron sights but not as precise as scopes farther out. My shooting suggests that 200-yard kills should be easy. That's about as far as you'll zero a big game rifle, or as far as you'd fire at animals without the benefit of magnification.

Early red dot sights were heavy and hard to mount. The detachable magnifiers added length and decreased eye relief, while reducing precision (in the rear focal plane, they magnified the dot, too!). Battery life was limited. But the advent of XD Aimpoints, which have wider fields but weigh less than the molded-body models of the 1980s, make this sight a practical choice for hunters. A new Aimpoint, the 7000, came out last year. It's a smoother, "prettier" sight, with a diode that offers 20 times the battery life of previous LEDs. A standard 3V lithium camera battery gives you a visible dot for *20,000 hours* on the low setting. That's a lot of hunting! Figure 1,000 hours at the highest setting. Batteries go to work only when the dot switch is on, and Mardklint says they last the same number of hours whether you use the sight intermittently over 10 years or leave it on for weeks at a time. The Comp 7000 features double the range of windage and elevation adjustment of earlier sights – 4 meters at 100 meters. That's more than 140 inches at 100 yards! The 2x objective housing on the 5000 was attached to the inner tube but on the 7000 fastens to the outer tube for greater strength.

As you might expect, Aimpoint has courted military and police contracts. The Comp M and ML are heavy-duty sights for service rifles and pistols. Band-pass coatings on objective lenses suit them for use with night-vision equipment. The first two stops on a night-vision red dot sight dial bring you no red dot. It's there but invisible to the unaided eye. Military sales account for a whopping 75 percent of total revenues at Aimpoint. Mike Kingston added, however, that if you left out the considerable commitments to U.S. and French armies, Aimpoint's hunting market share would be much bigger. Currently, Aimpoint exports hunting sights to 40 countries, and equips one of every 10 Swedish hunters using optical sights. Other red dot sights, most notably from Leupold and Tasco, have made progress in the American market, mainly among handgunners.

No Aimpoint sights are nitrogen-filled. "It's not necessary," said Mardklint. "We assemble these sights under controlled conditions. In fact, from the beginning, we've advertised our sights as submersible. First that was with caps on, but now it's with caps off. Aimpoints don't fog, and they don't leak." After two days under near-constant rain in Sweden's forests, I'd seen no evidence of either. The only moisture problem I had came on the last afternoon, just before dusk, in a swale overhung by dripping conifers. The rain drove through them, and I tucked the Blaser under my arm to keep water off the Aimpoint's lens.

My body heat would eventually fog the outside of the lens, but I'd give it time by airing the glass as soon as I heard the hunting horn.

Dusk came, a gradual deepening of the gloom. Then the faint moan of the horn sifted through the timber. I pulled my rifle across in front of my rainsuit – and immediately heard a branch break. Moose! The first was gone before I could raise my rifle. The second paused behind a tree 70 yards off. Hastily I rubbed the condensation off the lens with my thumb. Still, it was like looking through a bass pond: black moose in black timber behind a sheet of rain thick enough to part with a pitchfork. A crosswire or ordinary dot would have vanished in the murk. But that red dot stood out immediately. I fired. The moose bolted back toward the horn.

When the drivers came, I expected them to have found a kill. None had. "We'll bring the dogs," one said. Tracking dogs are not only popular in Sweden; the law requires that big game hunters have quick access to them. Still, I paced in the wet as the dog handlers waited for an hour for the woods to "get quiet" – and as rain washed the trail and darkness descended. "If you hit the moose, the dog will find it," said one simply. "Don't go near the place where the moose was. Your scent there will confuse the dog."

It was near flashlight-dark when we harnessed up a couple of Norwegian hounds that looked like compact versions of sled dogs. One was just a pup. The other appeared to be

all business. Behind the tree that had half-hidden the moose, she went to work like a setter on a hot pheasant track. Over a knob, down again into the swamp. Then she hooked back toward where I'd shot the moose. This wasn't good. Surely the drivers that came through would have seen a carcass. Had the moose circled, I'd have spotted it....

"There she is." The dog handler pointed. In a narrow, water-filled depression lay the cow, belly down, her hump blending with the swamp grass and hidden from the side by tangles of brush. I'd never have found her. She had been shot squarely through both lungs and had obviously died on the run, falling where even seasoned woodsmen only a few yards apart had passed her by. There was no exit wound, and none of us found blood on the ground.

The dog tore a little hair from the hump. I let her.

Tactical scopes

Long before scopes became popular with hunters, they became useful to soldiers and policemen. Snipers used them during our Civil War. During the world wars, Springfield and Garand rifles were issued with scopes. Unlike the long, heavy barrel-mounted tubes of the 1860s, these receiver-mounted Weavers, Redfields and Lymans did not impair a rifle's handling qualities. Essentially hunting scopes, they were of modest power (4x seemed standard) and had ordinary reticles. During the Viet-

This Leupold tactical scope looks right at home atop a Dakota Longbow rifle in .338 Lapua.

nam War, sniping became an important part of the offense on both sides. Among the most celebrated American riflemen was Marine Sgt. Carlos Hathcock, who used not an infantry rifle but one built for the civilian market: a Model 70 Winchester chambered in .30-06. It wore a barrel-mounted target scope with external adjustments. Other U.S. snipers carried Model 700 Remingtons, some chambered for the .308, others in .300 Winchester.

Scopes gave sharpshooters greater reach. While accuracy from an ordinary GI with an ordinary service rifle deteriorated badly beyond 100 yards, trained marksmen with accurate rifles and optical sights could be deadly to many hundreds of yards.

Police use of optical sights became commonplace in the United States after Vietnam. The SWAT (Special Weapons and Tactics) team emerged as the premier urban strike force, a law enforcement counterpart to the Army Rangers or Navy Seals. Heavy-barreled .308 bolt rifles and match-grade ammunition justified high-power optics. Scopes that looked a lot like hunting scopes (but with notable differences) became standard issue for SWAT teams. In the last decade, these scopes have appeared in optics catalogs that used to feature only hunting sights.

The recent proliferation of so-called tactical scopes can hardly be attributed to ballooning police or military budgets. Many civilian target shooters and some hunters buy tactical scopes. Oddly enough, the differences between tactical and sporting optics are seldom clarified. Tactical models can cost a great deal more, so they're superior by implication. But in what ways? Shooters have had to dig for particulars.

That's changing. Schmidt & Bender does a fine job of describing its tactical scopes, even telling how the reticles work. In an interview, Markus Schwarz of the Austrian optics firm Kahles told me more. He said that a tactical sight claims some distinguishing features. "They aren't all visible at a glance, and you can't say they're exclusive, because a few hunting scopes have them." But here they are: 1) matte or parkerized finish, 2) mil dot reticle, 3) bullet drop compensating device that can be set for any given load and 4) sturdiness to meet demanding military specifications.

"The modern tactical scope was developed by the U.S. Marines," continued Schwarz. "You'll see scopes of various dimensions and optical specs now. But the classic version is a 10x42 with quarter-minute clicks." He notes that the Marines also fathered the mil dot, a reticle now widely accepted in military and police communities. To recap, a mil dot reticle looks like a crosswire with flies on it. The spaces or interstices between dots are typically 3/4-minute in size, and each subtends (encloses) one milliradian, millradian or mil. That's equal to 1/6,400 of a degree in angular measurement. The span is about 3.6 inches at a hundred yards or 3 feet at 1,000 yards. So at 1,000 yards, two mil dots subtend approximately 6 feet.

To use this reticle as a rangefinder, you divide target height in mils by the number of interstices subtending the target to get range in hundreds of yards. A man or a moose (20 mils by linear measure) that appears in the scope to be four dots high is thus 500 yards away. Actually, the official method is to divide target size in yards by the number of mils subtended, and then multiply by 1,000.

In variable scopes with rear-focal-plane reticles, mil dot reticles are generally calibrated for the highest magnification, though some variables with very high top ends have the reticle set at a slightly lower power.

Swarovski's laser rangefinding scope is one of a kind. Big and heavy, it's a specialist's sight.

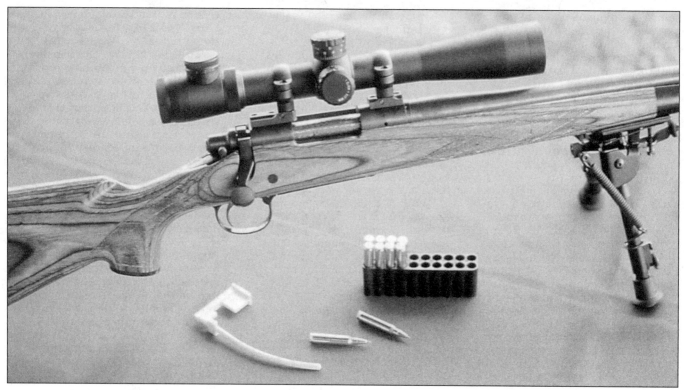

Ordinary rifles are increasingly paired with tactical sights like this Leupold with lighted reticle.

Schwarz told me that Kahles makes 25 percent of tactical scopes used throughout the world. "But we employ the same manufacturing methods and materials as for hunting scopes. We fashion all our tubes of steel, because many military organizations demand it. Hunters deserve no less than soldiers. We build all our products to rigorous standards." According to Schwarz, 95 percent of Kahles scope building is done in-house. When I visited the Vienna plant some years ago, Kahles people acknowledged their corporate ties to Swarovski but emphasized that the larger firm did not control their production or optical standards.

At least, that's what I gleaned through the interpreter. Kahles scopes have since joined the Swarovski line.

Military contracts are a boon to any manufacturer, but scopes don't wear out during peacetime, and I'm told overall military demand is declining. Swarovski concentrates increasingly on sports optics, Schwarz said. "Kahles will continue to supply police and military institutions with its 6x and 10x tactical scopes." At the time of my interview, Kahles manufactured only three

Target knobs on this Leupold variable allow for quick adjustment. The rifle is from Olympic Arms.

Coarse elevation clicks enable you to dial for bullet drop at 1000 yards with just one spin. The left-hand knob is for parallax adjustment.

variable-power scopes for hunters: a 1.5-6x42, a 2.2-9x42 and a 3-12x56 – all with 30mm tubes. The company now has a complete line of fixed- and variable-power scopes with 1-inch tubes for the U.S. market.

Schmidt & Bender, another prestigious European optics firm, offers five scopes in what it calls its Police/Marksman II line. The 6x42 of the original P/M series has been dropped (you can still get a hunting 6x42), but the 10x42 remains. It has the traditional 30mm tube, and the brilliant optics for which Schmidt & Bender is famous. The P/M II variables include a 3-12x50 and a 4-16x50. These have 34mm tubes, the biggest tubes available through ordinary channels. Parallax correction is via a third knob on the turret.

You get a choice of three reticles. P-3 is the mil dot, P-3L an illuminated mil dot, with the dial on the left side of the turret. P-1 is called the Bryant reticle after the SWAT team member who designed it. It is a busy image, with a crosswire and circle in the middle and heavy tapered bars pointing to it from the bottom and two sides. There's a clean perimeter. Horizontal stadia lines form a platform below, while the horizontal bars have hashmarks designating 6-minute increments. Another reticle, the P-2 Sniper, featured hashed horizontal bars on an otherwise-standard German three-legged plex reticle. It is not available in the P/M II series of scopes.

I imagine you can still special-order a MIL scope from Schmidt & Bender. The MIL is designed for shooting to 1,000 yards, as the elevation ring on the bullet-drop compensating dial indicates. It features 1/2-minute windage increments and full-minute elevation clicks (as opposed to the standard 1/4-minute clicks on other tactical scopes in the line). Every MIL scope comes with two elevation rings: a "neutral" ring that allows you to record settings for your particular load, plus a ring already calibrated for the 168-grain .308 match load that's standard fodder for many tactical rifles.

American hunters are probably more familiar with tactical scopes offered by Leupold & Stevens. These comprise two lines. The Mark 4 series includes a 10x and a 16x scope with 40mm objectives and a 10x40 "M3" whose elevation knob doubles as a bullet-drop compensator. The dial is calibrated to track bullet drop to 700 meters (1,000 on some models) with specific loads most commonly used by police and the military. Like the Schmidt & Bender MIL, the Leupold M3 has 1/2-minute windage clicks and 1-minute elevation detents. The two M1 models have target elevation knobs with 1/4-minute clicks. These tactical scopes differ in appearance from standard hunting models because they have a third turret knob for parallax adjustment. Mark 4s feature 30mm alloy tubes. The mil dot reticle can be ordered only in the M1 10x40.

This Leupold variable is a good example of a modern tactical sight "all tricked out."

Vari-X III 3.5-10x40mm Long Range M1
Illuminated Reticle with
Mark 4 Mounting System

Leupold's Tactical-series scopes include eight variables in magnifications of 3-9x, 3.5-10x and 4.5-14x. M1 and M3 adjustments are available. They are offered in 40mm and 50mm objectives. All models can be ordered with a mil dot. All have 30mm tubes. Two Long Range models come with illuminated reticles.

Incidentally, the U.S. Army incorporates 10x Leupolds in its Model 24 tactical outfit: a Remington 700 with H-S Precision stock and Harris bipod. These rifles initially cost $5,000 apiece, reportedly because the government specified a changeover capability from .308 Winchester to .300 Winchester Magnum. The current burden to taxpayers is only about half that.

Bushnell no longer catalogs its tactical 10x40 scope. It had a one-piece 30mm alloy tube, quarter-minute clicks on target knobs and a whopping 144 minutes of adjustment. Standard reticle was a mil dot, and bell overhang in front was long enough to shade the objective lens unless you were aiming at the sun. I shot with this scope once and managed a sub-quarter-inch group with a .308 tactical rifle custom-built on a Remington 700 action. The B&L scope delivered an uncommonly bright image. I liked the eye relief too: a generous 90mm (3.6 inches).

Other companies offer mil dot reticles in scopes with target-style adjustment knobs. Few of these meet Markus Schwartz's definition of tactical because few have bullet drop compensating mechanisms or are tested to meet military standards for durability. But for hunting, these quasi-tactical scopes work fine.

Tactical scopes can be heavy. Not that weight matters much on a tactical rifle. If it did, military contracts wouldn't specify steel tubes. Outside dimensions too are of secondary importance; but as with anything, you can find extremes. Scopes from U.S. Optics are custom-built (that's right, to buyer specs) and typically feature bigger tubes and lenses than are available through standard market channels. You can, for example, order a 3.8-22x variable with a 58mm objective bell and 35mm carbon graphite tube. If that doesn't give you enough reach or light, you might try a 6-30x with an *88mm* objective!

You'll need a 40mm tube to keep that big lens from sagging, and since you don't want this to look like every other scope at the range, you might as well order it in titanium. (That's not the finish; it's the tube *material.*) You also get to choose from 200 reticles. Rings are no problem: Autauga Arms, which markets the U.S. Optics line, will provide them, big enough and high enough.

Incidentally, despite their imposing size, these scopes weigh just a shade more than the traditional high-power hunting variable or a 30mm tactical scope: as little as 27 ounces. You get an 80-year warranty.

In my view, tactical scopes sell outside police and military circles largely because they're called tactical scopes, not because they perform better than ordinary scopes. The name has the flavor of life on the edge. It evokes images of square-jawed sharpshooters making society safe for the weak, of *real* men cool under pressure, risking all on a skill that's as old as gunpowder.

OK. Maybe image isn't the issue. But why then so many "safari" rifles and cartridges?

Chapter 11

Mounting And Zeroing

"...The scope has to look where you do."

What makes a good scope mount?

WHEN I WAS a lad, I volunteered to work on local farms for nothing. The farmers were astonished, because their children detested chores. To me, learning about animals and big machines, how to weld and plant crops and build grain bins – all that was fascinating. It seemed criminal at the time to accept wages.

While I've since learned to open my palm a bit, I've not forgotten the lessons of the farm. One of them: Simple things work best. I recall the two-lung John Deere tractors we used. I started the "B" model by hand, fitting the removable steering wheel to the flywheel on the side, then opening a petcock to relieve cylinder pressure and heaving the steering wheel round until the beast fired. Its raspy flutter at idle would become a sharp pop when I engaged the clutch by pushing forward on a long iron rod. Lug

it down, and it would bang a little louder, but the thick axle kept turning with the plodding certainty of Earth's spindle.

Those tractors were 25 years old when I used them, and I can't remember ever having to send one away for repairs. They were just too simple to come undone.

It seems to me that the best scope mounts are simple too. While you can choose from many clever designs, the most reliable way to attach your scope may not appear clever at all.

One of the first American scope mounts was developed during the 1930s by Bill Weaver to fasten his new "330" scope to a rifle. Aptly named the grasshopper mount for its shape, it did not last. Inventors came up with many bizarre, and some practical, alternatives. Among the latter was a machined-steel mount John Redfield designed in 1916. The original model had a dovetail slot cut in the front base (or the front of a one-piece base) into which an extension of the front

ring turned. The rear ring was clamped on by two "windage" screws that secured the ring and enabled you to leave the scope's internal windage adjustment alone – an advantage in the days when reticles moved out of center as the dials were turned. Redfield scope rings were then commonly one-piece affairs, split on the side or on top. You slipped them over the scope tube, removing the ocular housing for the rear ring (the turrets as well if the objective end was bigger than the tube diameter). This was no problem at first, when scopes weren't nitrogen-filled. Fogproofing made disassembly impossible. Shooters improvised by forcing one-piece rings open wide enough to mouth the scope tube. This caused some rings to weaken or break.

Buehler, Leupold and Bausch & Lomb built adjustable mounts for scopes that didn't have internal adjustments. Stith mounts, heavy enough for grenade practice, made use of existing barrel dovetails and the holes drilled for receiver sights in bolt rifles, at a time when few receivers were drilled for scopes. Griffin & Howe double-lever detachable side mounts were popular among affluent riflemen. Echo and various swing-over side mounts served blue-collar hunters who wanted quick access to iron sights should a scope fail.

Weaver eventually came up with a simple but strong arrangement: rings that clamped on dovetail bases. They're still very good. The alloy bases weigh almost nothing, and there's nothing to go wrong with them. The steel rings hug them securely. The assemblies are inexpensive and made for almost every rifle that's ever been drilled and tapped for a scope. The only fault I can find with a Weaver Tip Off mount is the penchant of the rings to pinch the scope tube where the two ring screws snug down.

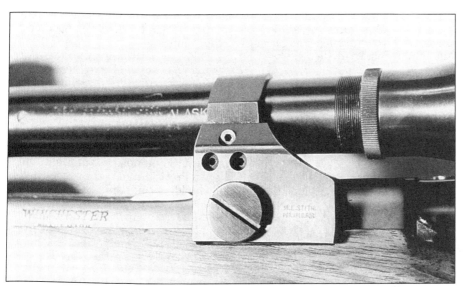

The old Stith mount holding this Lyman Alaskan fit the receiver sight base holes on a Winchester 70.

The adjustable mount securing this Leupold Westerner was also made by Leupold.

Weaver's main competition in the early post-WWII years was Redfield's dovetail mount, by then offered with two-piece rings that required no scope disassembly. With slight cosmetic changes, it is now offered by several companies under their names. Leupold was the first with a "Dual Dovetail" mount, with no windage screws. Because scopes now have constantly-centered reticles, and because a second dovetail attachment is neater and stronger than the clamping of windage screws, this design makes a lot of sense.

The sleekest mounts available are Conetrols, with their smooth covers that hide the top attaching screws in the vertically-split rings. Conetrols are a bit more work to install than the Weaver and Redfield, but this is almost a non-issue, because one installation is all you need. The Conetrols on two of my favorite hunting rifles seem rock-solid. You can't find a better-looking mount.

Quick-detachable mounts, first popularized by pre-war makers like Griffin & Howe, have made a rebound. A double-lever release is not particularly complex, and if the machinist has minded his tolerances, the scope will retain zero when replaced. My dislike of QD mounts is probably a result of examining too many early Model 70 Winchesters. Griffin & Howe stuck its big base to the side of these lovely rifles with five screws and pins. The defunct Echo mount was equally destructive. Both added considerable weight and bulk to the receiver. I probably should have kept a rifle or two with these mounts, but sold all I owned at bargain prices when I could no longer bear the loss of their virginity.

Current QD mounts are less obtrusive, with trim rings and bases that employ factory-drilled screw holes. Return to zero can be downright positive, depending again on closeness of fit.

One of the best-known QD mounts is fashioned by Dave Talley of Glenrock, Wyo. A native of South Carolina, Talley and his wife, Deb, moved west 13 years ago, after managing a machine shop that made textile parts. He'd been working on gun metal since 1956, just after he finished high school. But his gunsmithing career really took off in 1982, when he sold his interest in the textile shop so he could design gun parts.

During the next 10 years, Talley turned out a wide variety of metalwork. "I got my start by drilling and tapping Mausers for scopes," he says. "But I eventually made bigger changes." Like cutting actions in half and welding them back together so they were just the right length for .250 Savage cartridges. Once he mismeasured an action and took out too much metal. The result: a .223 for Deb, who shoots as often as he does and hunts with him. He did some work for Jack O'Connor and Les Bowman and quickly became known for his machining skills and artistic eye. In 1992, Talley eased out of gunsmithing to devote all his attention to making accouterments: swivel studs, grip caps and scope mounts.

Dave's youngest son Gary has worked with him full time for eight years. When I visited the shop for the first time a few years ago, Gary was running their newest CNC machine. "We've been using CNCs since the '70s," he told me. "But they keep getting better, so we have to keep pace." This one was chewing away on 20 metal blocks held in four fixtures. Each block would become a scope mount base.

Gary is still turning out scope mounts, but he and Dave have more machines now, in a new facility in Glenrock. They've expanded their operation in part to honor contracts with firms like Weatherby that use Talley mounts and rings exclusively. Dakota rifles wear them, and they're on the recommended list at McMillan, Brown Precision and other respected rifle-building companies. QD and traditional styles are available for most rifles. According to Dave, the mount is essentially a Weaver design done in cold-rolled steel. Well, not quite. Similar, it is hardly the same. The Talley base has a recoil shoulder front and rear, plus a flat saddle between them with a cutout in the middle so the ring doesn't rock. The ring abuts the front

George Miller's Cone-Trol mount has sleek lines, a great complement to a compact scope.

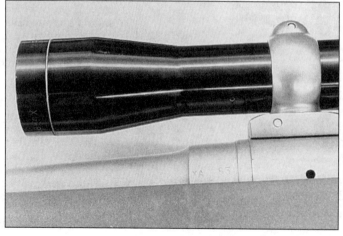

Griffin & Howe QD double-lever mounts attached to the side of the receiver – which had to be drilled.

Some early front rings were actually sleeves that attached the scope to the rear sight dovetail.

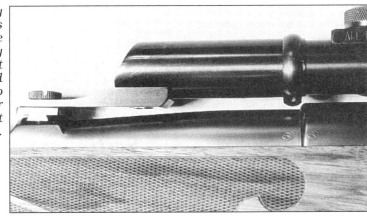

A European-style claw mount is complex and expensive but, properly made, effective.

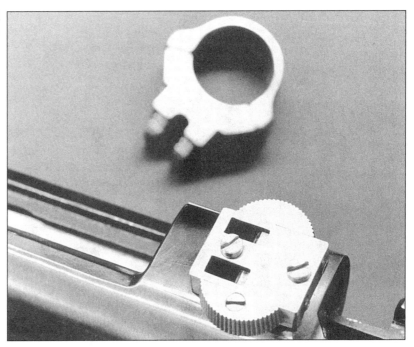

shoulder; the rear shoulder is for safety. I like that idea because a scope once flew off and hit me in the head after working free of another firm's bases that had only one shoulder.

The rings are vertically split, attaching at the bottom with two 6-48 screws and at the top with one or two 6-48s. Rings for 1-inch scopes come with your choice of single or double top screws, while 7/8-inch rings are single-screw and 30mm rings double-screw in design. A 10-32 screw holds the clamp tight on the base. The standard clamp screw has a hex head. For an extra $20, you get a lever-lock assembly that allows you to detach the scope without tools. Hexagonal contact between lever and screw enables you to index the levers so they point the same way when you've tightened the rings onto the bases.

Dave recommends 8-40 base screws for attaching mounts to rifles of heavy recoil. "You can also clean up off-center holes when you drill for big screws," he said. "Not many rifles come from the factory with mount screw holes perfectly lined up." Getting things lined up just right is one of Dave's obsessions.

Like many gunmakers, Dave Talley has strong opinions about the way other makers and shooters assemble their firearms. "I can't see why Winchester drills rear bridge holes just .330 apart," he said. "The new rifles have bridges 1.350 long. Even the old M70 magnums gave the screws a .435 gap. Wider hole spacing makes for straighter, more secure mounting."

This early Tilden mount is neat and trim and lightweight – and has a windage adjustment!

Another thing that bothers Dave Talley is the trend toward bigger scopes. "The more weight you have up there, the greater the inertia during recoil. Big scopes try to tear free of the rings, tear the rings off the bases, tear the bases off the rifle. On a varmint rifle, recoil isn't a problem, but rifles bored for hard-kicking cartridges are best fitted with small scopes. You don't need a lot of magnification if you're hunting large animals, so you don't need a king-size bell up front. A fat tube adds strength, but a 1-inch tube has always been strong enough for me."

For hunters who insist on heavy scopes for hard-kicking rifles, Dave suggests they coat the insides of the rings and the bottoms of the bases with "Plastid," a liquid compound that dries to a rubbery film. It's the stuff used to coat hanging pegs and the handles of small tools. "You can also smear contact surfaces with valve-grinding compound," Dave points out. "But that will mar your metal finishes."

Talley mounts are sold directly and through dealers. You *can* get these mounts in the white. Bases are available for most actions, even BRNO dovetails. Dave has hewed to simplicity as a guiding principle. "We make essentially one product here, and we think it is the best product for its purpose on the market. We make sure each mount is machined to tolerances most manufacturers wouldn't even consider, because we want shooters to think of Talley mounts as the best there is."

The cost of Talley mounts is less than you might expect of a product carefully fashioned and sold to the custom gun trade. When I was driving two-cylinder tractors, you could buy a top-quality 4x scope for $59.50. The same model now costs six times that. A $15 mount in 1965 would, by the same measure, list for $90 today. Given that a mount, like rifle and scope, will last a lifetime, spending a little extra for the very best performance makes good sense.

The longevity of simple, rugged mounts works against people like Dave Talley, who, last I knew, was still hunting with a .270 FN Mauser he bought used in 1953. It wears a Stith Bear Cub in Redfield rings. Ask him about it, and he'll grin. "One of these days I gotta get rid of that mount."

Setting up a scope

Upon recoil, a scope wants to climb off the rifle. Stress is greatest on the front ring, which is forced up and back violently. The scope's objective end, then, exerts a force down and forward, while the back end wants to flip up and forward. If the scope were free to move, it would somersault over the muzzle. Mount and ring screws must hold things together. And ensure that the scope stays in the same relationship to the bore, shot after shot.

Most rifle receivers are drilled and tapped for 6-48 screws, the 6 denoting outside diameter, but not in a unit of measurement. It's like a number 6 shot size (though not the same diameter). The 48 means there are 48 threads per inch. The higher the tpi count, the stronger the screw, because you get generous surface contact without having to make a deep thread cut. I'm told the 6-48 screw was developed by Winchester for sight and scope mounting.

In a perfect world, 6-48s would be adequate. But variations in receiver dimensions and contours

The front mount on this Mauser is of European design.

Ruger's rings are made to attach directly to Ruger receivers or quarter ribs.

mean that bases don't always hug gun steel like skin on a peach. If a radiused receiver is too flat, only the base edges will contact it; should the radius be too steep, the base will touch only in the middle. In either case, the screw gets little help from friction between base and rifle. Vibrations of the rifle and shear forces of recoil upon firing work to loosen the screw.

Tight screw fit is important, but drills and taps are manufactured to specifications allowing for some dimensional variation in screws. And screws are made so they'll fit in every standard hole. Most of the time, screw fit is sloppy. Custom gunmakers who take pride in seeing to every detail make their own screws if the fit is *too* loose. D'Arcy Echols, of Providence, Utah, does so. He also surface-grinds receiver and base to a perfect match. Companies manufacturing guns and screws for the hunting masses cannot afford to fit components this way. Nor can they guarantee that every receiver will have the same hole spacing. Hence, you'll find that screw holes in bases are also oversize, to enable you to start all the screws if the holes don't line up exactly. Rigidity and strength are again compromised.

Another problem on some rifles is hole depth. A 6-48 screw is .130 in diameter; its hole need be no deeper than .130 to give you maximum resistance to screw failure. But the rear bridge on one of my rifles, for

example, is only about .090 thick, or .040 less than necessary to give that screw maximum usable purchase. You'll find a kindred flaw in extremely thin bases, where countersinking for the screw head leaves a wafer-thin web between it and the receiver. Given that both head and shank are smaller than the base holes for them, the underside of the head and a sliver of base material must stand fast against the sudden eruption, inches away, of 50,000 pounds per square inch of pressure.

To better appreciate the task of tiny screws and slim bases, try to

hold a scope on top of your deer rifle by clamping the base with your fingers as you pull the trigger. Wear a helmet.

Screws can break and bases crack under the strain. I have a Tilden mount whose machined rear base split because it was too thin to weather the stress of recoil (and perhaps a less-than-perfect fit to the rear bridge).

Oval-head screws, such as on Weaver bases, give as much or more head-to-base contact as machine screws whose heads have flat undersides, without requiring that as much base material be removed in counter-boring. They seem to me the best option for thin bases.

While steel bases look best, there's nothing wrong with alloy (aluminum) bases. Neither is there a significant difference between one- and two-piece bases. I used to prefer one-piece "bridge" mounts, thinking they were more rigid. Eventually I decided a receiver was rigid enough by itself. Two-piece bases have one more screw – the weak link in a scope mount. They give easier access to the breech and, depending on style, can be marginally lighter in weight. Truth is, you'll be as satisfied with one style as with the other.

Short of custom screws and bases, you can substantially boost the strength of your mount by enlarging base and receiver holes to accept 8-40 screws (.140 diameter). This is a one-way alteration, so be sure that you want to do it before you begin! I must concede I've not yet drilled any of my rifles for 8-40 screws. Standard 6-48s have held

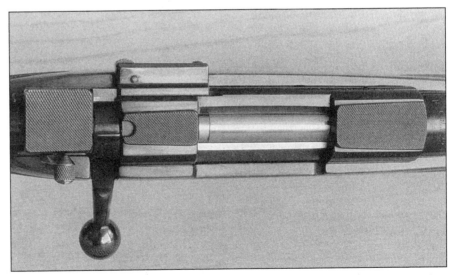

Tapered dovetails on the receiver top of this Sako accept special Sako rings.

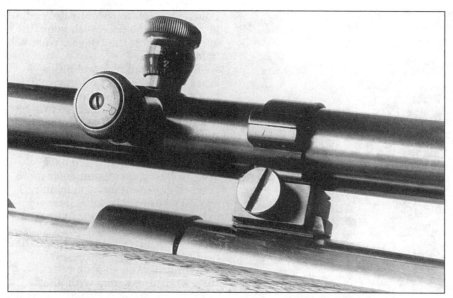

The rings on this Redfield target scope are mounted on barrel blocks, not the receiver of this .22 rifle.

Weatherby rifles were for many years served by mounts fashioned for the Remington 700. But the Weatherby's rear bridge is slightly lower, meaning the scope points up relative to the bore and cannot then provide enough vertical adjustment for long shooting. Now Leupold and other manufacturers offer a rear base just the right thickness for long shooting with Weatherby Mark Vs.

If a scope runs out of adjustment before you think it should after you get it on the rifle, you may have to remove it and have the receiver top remachined, or the mount holes redrilled. Enlarging the mount holes from 6-48 to 8-40, you can line them up while giving the mount more purchase in the bargain. If you need to tip the scope up in the back to get more distance from it, consider brass or steel shim stock. A little goes a long way, and you may not even need longer screws. "An alternative for Remington 700 owners," says Garth Kendig, "is to substitute a Winchester 70 front base for the 700 base. Hole spacing is the same, but there's .020 difference in base thickness."

my bases in place. Partly that is because I have few rifles that kick nastily. My .458 wears iron sights; so does my .375. I've not had trouble with .375s or .340s or .338s throwing their scopes into the bushes. One .416 Rigby put its scope into orbit – but that was because the detachable rings had inadequate contact with the bases. The base screws held.

If you do decide to enlarge base or receiver holes, find someone who can do it right! This is no job for a hand-drill. Pick a gun shop black with the greasy machinery that might have been used to build 1917 Enfields, manned by an equally greasy machinist with gray hair. If he growls at you, so much the better.

Improper drilling can cause real problems. I once examined a Swarovski scope with a neat hole in the forward tube. It had been perforated by the front base screw when the rifle fired. Turns out a weekend gunsmith had drilled the base hole all the way through to the chamber. The case ruptured, sending the little screw skyward like a bullet.

Before attaching a base, I double-check that I've bought the proper one for the rifle. And sometimes even this won't keep me from having difficulties with fit and alignment. Garth Kendig at Leupold tells me that many of the problems that customers report with scopes are really mounting problems.

"For instance, we've found receiver dimensions vary a great deal. In one test, we zeroed a scope on a rifle, then used the same rings and bases to mount that scope on two identical rifles. Well, we *thought* they were identical. Point of impact changed 2 *feet*! A quarter degree of slope in a receiver top amounts to 15 minutes of angle."

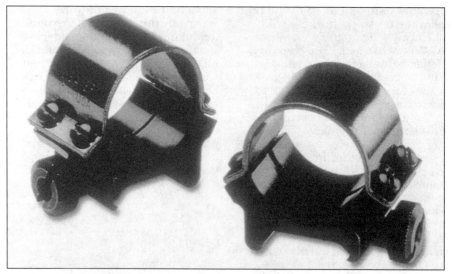

Weaver Sure Grip rings have a groove on the bottom half.

Leupold rings are made from solid billets of steel.

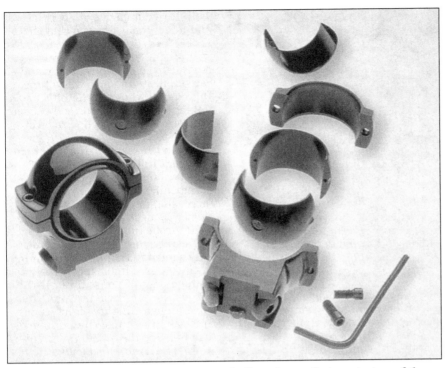

Burris Pos-Align rings grip well and allow for perfect centering of the scope over the bore.

Rings should be the lowest that will allow your scope's objective bell to clear the barrel and the ocular bell to clear the bolt handle. Low-mounted scopes keep a rifle's center of gravity low between your hands and put the target in front of your eye when your cheek comes tight to the stock. Tucked to the rifle, they're less susceptible to banging on rocks and trees, and they slide in and out of scabbards more easily than high-mounted scopes.

Ring spacing is important. You want the rings to give the scope as much support as possible. You don't want them crowding turrets or bells or forcing you to compromise on eye relief. Extension rings are some-times necessary, more often these days with short-coupled variable scopes. I shy from them, mostly for cosmetic reasons. They're no less solid than ordinary rings.

When I have all parts at hand, I remove the grease from them. Then I wipe everything with an oily rag, next a dry one. Or I use a silicone cloth. On hard-kicking guns, includ-ing big-bore pistols and slug guns, washing the metal squeaky clean with solvent makes sense. I've not found that measure necessary; a cloth-dry surface is generally dry enough, and the trace of oil remain-ing can help prevent rust.

It's a good idea to first run your finger lightly over the clamping sur-faces of each new ring set. Doing this, I've found burrs that would have marred the scope. Careful stoning will eliminate rough spots. Burris supplies thin strips of adhe-sive paper with its rings. You stick the paper on the ring interior. Its purpose is to increase friction, but it also helps protect the scope tube.

To install the bases, snug the screws alternately with a tight-fit-ting screwdriver. (If you don't have a gunsmith-quality screwdriver with a large assortment of magnetic tips, buy one! This is a modest invest-ment, which over the years will spare you much recrimination for marring valuable guns with tools you last used to open paint cans.) The type of screw head recess – slot or hex – doesn't matter, as long as

you have the proper tool. Many Allen screws have been stripped by cheap wrenches, and once stripped must be drilled out. I prefer tradi-tional slots and the newer Torx screws with deep, star-like recesses to grab the bit.

You can tap the screwdriver with a mallet as you make the last turn, to get base screws a little tighter. Usually, that's not necessary (6-48 screws *will* eventually snap under pressure!). You shouldn't need chem-ical locking agent to prevent the screws from backing out. Iodine is taboo; it seizes the screw by rusting it in place.

If you're using dovetail rings, the next step is fastening the rings to the bases. Clamp a section of one-inch dowel in the rings and turn them into their mortises. If the rear ring is gripped by windage screws, you of course won't need the dowel for that. Lots of shooters have man-aged to turn rings into their mor-tises using the scope tube. I don't do this any more because the pressure can mar, even bend the tube.

If you're using an old Bausch & Lomb spring-loaded mount, or a set of rings split vertically, the scope must be clamped in the rings before you mate rings to bases. With quick-detachable rings, you can make either the base-ring or the ring-scope connection first. Some scope rings, split horizontally, have one 8-40 screw on each side. Others wear two 6-48s. Both designs have merit. One 6-48 per side is less desirable, in my view. The Weaver Tip-Off mount, with its stamped rings that you hook on one side and clamp with a pair of 6-48s on the other, still works. Hints: Insert a thin cloth between ring and scope to protect the tube when you snap the ring over it. Before you tighten the rings on, say, the right side, twist the scope slightly to the left. Tightening

Tasco® See-Thru Aluminum Mounts

See-through mounts allow you to use iron sights. The author doesn't like them because they put the scope high above the bore, impairing rifle balance and slowing your aim.

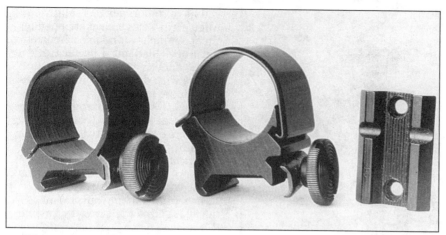

Weaver Tip Off rings are among the oldest still in widespread use. They're sturdy, cheap, lightweight.

from one side rotates the scope, so your crosswires will be tilted if you don't compensate.

Weaver Tip Off rings can put dimples in the scope tube if you over-tighten the screws. However, *any* ring improperly installed can damage a scope. It's important when using early machined-steel split rings to keep the pairs together. Halves that don't meet precisely bite into the tube at the split. Leupold people tell me that now their machining is so uniform that any bottom half can be mated with any top half of the same style.

At first, snug the rings only tightly enough to hold the scope in place, using all screws. Then mount the rifle. Loosen the screws slightly and push the scope forward far enough that when you cheek the rifle stock quickly you don't have to pull your head back to get a full field of view. Many hunters mount their scopes too far back. Slide it a half-inch farther forward than you think appropriate. You'll aim faster and

keep the ocular housing a safe distance from your brow when you must shoot uphill or from a prone position.

You'll want the reticle square with the rifle. Line up the vertical wire or post with the buttplate (unless your stock has been custom-crafted with a "bend") by securing the rifle in a rest or vise, then backing off until you see only the exit pupil in the scope. The crosswire will appear as a negative against black, but you'll see it clearly enough to align it. Again tighten ring screws just enough to hold the scope, then shoulder the rifle with your eyes closed. When you open them, you should see a full field, and a crosswire square with the world.

While I'm not a gadgeteer, an ingenious device recently caught my eye. It shows when the crosswire is square with the top of the scope base. Not all scope bases are level or at right angles to the stock center-line, but most are close. The "reticle leveler" (Segway Industries, P.O. Box 783, Suffern, NY 10901) works

well. I tried it on one of my rifles and found to my chagrin that the reticle was slightly tilted. Shooting with a cant does not cause misses – provided you zeroed that way and can duplicate the hold every time. But overall, you're better off when a top-mounted scope is directly above the bore, its horizontal wire level enough to puddle water.

When the scope is exactly where you want it, tighten the ring screws as you would the lug nuts on an automobile wheel: alternately, by increasing torque a little at a time. That way, even pressure is applied to the scope tube.

Despite your best efforts, you may someday find a scope slipping in the rings. This is most likely to happen on rifles of stiff recoil with scopes that are heavier than you need anyway. Lightweight scopes are least likely to come unhinged. The heavier the scope, the greater its inertia. Another disadvantage of scopes with fat objective bells is that they must be mounted high, increasing the leverage of the scope as it tries to flip forward during recoil.

Simmons 4x4 rings are split in the middle.

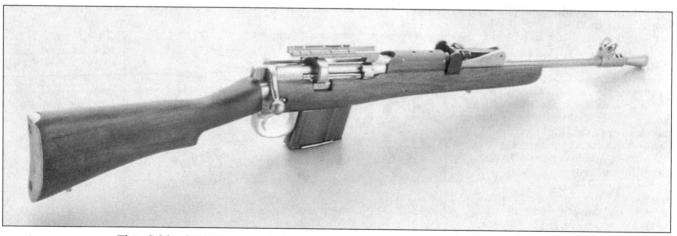

This Gibbs SMLE has a rail for easy scope mounting with Weaver-type rings.

Installed, the Pos-Align ring adds just a little bulk but won't mar the scope finish.

Burris Pos-Align rings," says that company's Patrick Beckett. "Clamp them as tight as you want. You can't hurt the scope. They also act to dampen high-frequency shock waves to the scope during recoil. We tested their holding power by mounting sections of pipe and dropping the base unit on a cement floor from a ladder. They hold better than any steel ring. You can get the inserts center-bored, or in pairs of +/- .005, .010 and .015 to compensate for off-center mounts and keep your sight-line through the optical axis of the scope. Or use 'em to jack up the rear of the scope for more long-distance elevation adjustment."

Zeroing

Zeroing, or sighting in, is what you do to make your line of sight intersect the bullet's trajectory at some distant point of your choosing. "Zero range" is actually the second intersection; you ignore the first. As soon as a bullet leaves the barrel, gravity starts pulling it toward the earth. As the bullet decelerates, the force of gravity has longer to work on it over any given distance. That's why a bullet's trajectory is not the shape of a rainbow but is instead parabolic. It gets steeper at long range. Your line of sight, in contrast, is straight, following the optical axis of the scope (at a slight downward angle) to pierce the bullet's trajectory a few yards from the muzzle and again when gravity brings the bullet through the line of sight at a distance. Scopes are

D'Arcy Echols advises against heavy hunting scopes, but some customers insist on them. Once, after mounting a weighty German variable in vertically split, quick-detachable rings, he could not stop the slippage. Part of his problem was that the bottom halves of the rings kissed each other before the tops drew snug. Having used a micrometer to measure diameters of many scope tubes, D'Arcy was not surprised. "There's incredible variation, even among scopes by the same maker!" Sometimes shimming or friction-enhancing compounds will solve a slippage problem. Sometimes not.

What if you *like* big scopes, or get one for your birthday from someone who wants to see you use it? "Use

The front mount here more securely holds the scope than would a ring behind that heavy bell.

Before zeroing, adjust the reticle focus.

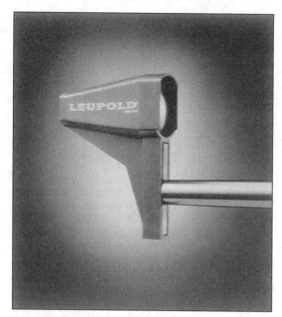
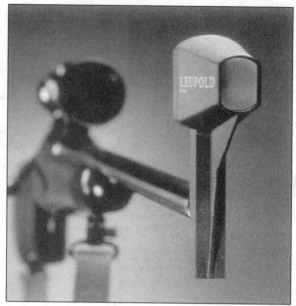

A bore-mounted collimator, like this Leupold, makes bore sighting easy.

adjustable, so you can align the scope's optical axis at the proper angle to the rifle's bore. Fine-tuning that angle, you can put your line of sight where you want it in relation to the bullet's trajectory.

After attaching the scope, you're ready to zero. The first step is to bring the reticle roughly onto the bore's axis. A muzzle-mounted collimator, with its calibrated screen, helps. Carefully ease the spud into the muzzle. Adjust the crosswire so it centers the screen. When it does, the line of bore will be very close to your line of sight at any range – close enough to put you "on paper." You must shoot to get a final zero; collimation is just a preliminary adjustment to save ammunition.

Lacking a collimator, you can bore-sight if you can see through the barrel. Lay the rifle on sandbags or a rest, or clamp it in a vise where you can point it at a small, distant object. I bore-sight through the living room window, aiming at a white

Zeroing is best done from the bench, to minimize human error.

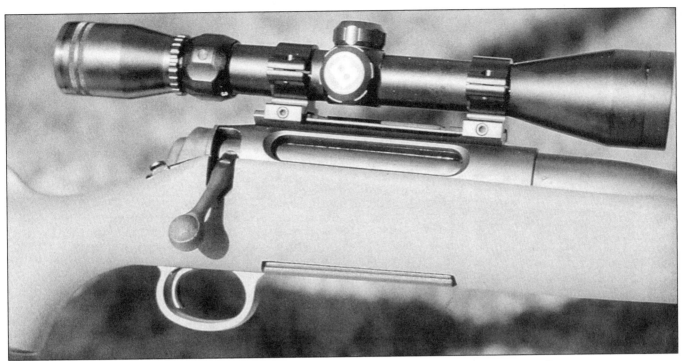

This Bushnell scope came with the rifle. That doesn't mean it's zeroed!

rock on a far-away hill. Bore-sighting poses no threat of accidental discharge, as the rifle's chamber must be empty and the bolt removed to get it done. Still, you won't want to point the rifle where people might cross in front of it. Position the rifle so you can see your "target" in the middle of the bore. Then, without moving anything, adjust your reticle onto the target. Your rifle is now bore-sighted.

You've just begun to zero. Here's how I finish:

At the range, I place the rifle on sandbags, using either an adjustable rest under the front bag or building a stack of bags so that with the rifle at rest, the crosswire quarters my 100-yard target. Having bore-sighted, I'm confident those first shots will be on the paper at 100 yards, so that's where I start. I position the front bag where my hand would be under the barrel, and the rear bag just ahead of the toe of the stock. The barrel never rests on the sandbag (it will bounce hard off the surface), nor does the bag go where the swivel or swivel stud will tear into it on recoil. I hold the stock's grip firmly with my right hand, using my left to squeeze the rear bag to make slight adjustments in my sight picture.

I fire one shot, then adjust the scope and repeat, my goal being to land the bullet 2 inches above point of aim. After I'm there, I complete a

three-shot group. Next I go to a clean paper at 200 yards. At this range, I want bullets hitting center. I shoot three-shot groups, letting the barrel cool between groups, adjusting until one cluster shows up in the middle.

With most big-game and varmint rounds, I then shoot at 300 yards to confirm a 6- to 8-inch drop, depending on the load. If I had a 400-yard range, I'd shoot at that distance, too. It is not good enough to shoot only at 100 yards (or as some shooters do, at 25 to 35, catching only the trajectory's first intersection with the sightline!). Nor will an ammunition chart show you exactly where your bullets will strike at long range. For one thing, small differences in loads and conditions become significant far from the muzzle. For another, the height of your scope mount affects the relationship of bullet trajectory and line of sight.

Not long ago, a fellow came to hunt with me toting a rifle he said was zeroed for 200 yards. He missed an outstanding elk. Later at the range, I benched the rifle and found it was zeroed at 325 yards. He had popped a few rounds through paper at 100 yards and figured that since most landed about 3 inches high, they'd hit center at 200. That's what everyone had told him. But the scope's big objective bell had forced the use of high rings. The flat trajectory of a hot .300 Weatherby load,

combined with the sharp pitch of a high sight-line, pushed his zero far from the muzzle.

Zeroing is properly done in such a way as to minimize human error. But you won't have a bench to shoot from on the hunt, so you must know where the bullets are likely to go

Zeroing, you sometimes get pleasant surprises (Winchester M70 in 7 STW, Weaver T-16).

A 200-yard zero is best for most big game rifles; this dangerous-game rifle may be zeroed closer.

from a hand-held rifle. Step to the side of the bench and fire two three-shot groups each from sitting, kneeling and offhand at 200 yards. Sitting and kneeling, you'll want to use a sling – one with a shooting loop so you can snug the rifle hard against your shoulder and take some weight off that forward hand. Sling tension steadies the rifle, reducing wobble. But it also pulls the forend away from the barrel and tugs against the upward thrust of recoil. That means your bullets may strike lower than they did when you shot from the bench. If the forward swivel is mounted on the barrel, the effect can be great indeed.

Some years ago, I zeroed a Ruger No. 1 in .300 Winchester Magnum. At the zero range of 200 yards, I was astonished to find its point of impact drop *9 inches* when I shot sitting with a tight sling! I managed to cut that disparity in half by relieving forend pressure up front and cushioning the pull of the forend screw in the rear. Most rifles don't show such a dramatic difference, but almost every rifle I've shot with a tight sling prints lower as a result. It's important to know that, because you won't have a bench in the field. Maybe you'll want to adjust your zero to compensate.

One last tip: When checking zero, reserve one target for "cold, clean-barrel" shots. Shoot only the first

bullet per session into this target, duplicating the first shot you'll fire at game. After five sessions at the range, with cleaning in between, compare that five-shot group with others you've compiled. It should be a relatively tight cluster and, more importantly, in the same place as warm-barrel groups relative to your point of aim. If first shots from that clean, oiled bore go "wild," you may want to consider hunting with a dry or even a dirty bore.

After you're done shooting – or before – check the dimensions of your reticle against a target of known measure. You don't need a mil dot or other range-finding reticle to help you judge distance in the field. An ordinary dot or plex can work. Obviously, a 4-minute dot subtends 4 inches at 100 yards. If the dot in your scope covers a 4-inch paper disc, it will cover 8 inches, or half the depth of a deer's chest, at 200 yards. If the dot blankets the deer from back to belly, you're looking at a 400-yard shot – which you might want to pass up.

Likewise, the thin section of a plex reticle can be used to estimate range, if you've determined the subtention, say, between the top of the lower post and the intersection of

the wire. Be aware that if your variable scope has the rear-plane reticle popular in the United States, reticle subtention will change as you change the power. Suggestion: Record reticle subtentions at the highest power you expect to use. That may be 6x or even 8x. For shots long enough to require a good estimate of range, you should have time to crank the scope to that power – which you'll probably want to use anyway. At low-power, the thin central wire will span too many inches far away to be of much value.

You may discover that at a certain magnification, your plex reticle will allow you some tricks that can extend point-blank range. For example, one of my low-powered riflescopes has a plex reticle with a vertical post-to-post gap of about 32 inches at 200 yards. An elk filling this gap is thus 200 yards away and dead when I shoot because my rifle is zeroed at 200, at the intersection of the crosswire halfway between top and bottom post. At 300 yards, I know the elk will appear about 2/3 as big. I can figure out holdover if I want – or again rest the top of the bottom post against the bull's brisket. The horizontal wire then cuts across

For hunting, you must know where the cold-barrel shot will hit. Circle it on practice targets.

About 1 1/2 inches high at 100 yards. The bullets should hit center a little beyond 150. That's fine if you'll be hunting at modest ranges. Most game is shot closer than most hunters admit.

Right in the middle! But if you want to hit center at 200 yards, you should be a bit high at 100.

After zeroing, shoot from hunting positions to check that zero. You won't have a bench in the field!

the elk about 2/3 of the way up the ribs. At 300 yards, the bullet drops about 7 inches, or 1/4 of the depth of the chest. So I hit only slightly below where I did at 200 yards, *given the post tip as my aiming device.* Another fatal shot. No range estimation necessary.

At 400 yards, a bull elk will just fit between the horizontal wire and the top of that bottom post. Again, I could estimate the 20 inches my bullet will drop, but I can also keep the tip of the post against the brisket, just as I did at 200 and 300 yards. The intersection is now on the bull's back, where it would be if I were to purposefully hold high. The bullet drops into the lungs.

This technique also works at 100 yards, incidentally. It breaks down beyond 400 yards where trajectory becomes very steep. But shooting beyond 400 steps rarely makes sense anyway, because even if the hold is perfect, slight errors in shot execution magnified by that distance can easily move your bullet out of the vitals. Wind also becomes a problem. If you're sure of wind conditions *all the way to the target,*

plus your bullet's rate of deflection under those conditions, and have lots of time and a steady position, you can snake a bullet to the bulls-

eye through wind beyond 400 yards. Usually, however, wind causes misses and crippling at such long range.

A lousy group? Well, yes. But not as lousy as it looks. The author shot it from the sit at long range.

Chapter 12

THE LONG SHOT

" ...a 450-yard kill? Don't worry, you'll get closer next time."

Precision at a distance: Big scopes for big game

I DIDN'T SEE all of the bone at once. Rather, I pieced together the bull's antlers over the course of many minutes. The thick foliage enabled me to sneak within 30 yards or so, but the milling cows stopped me there. If one of them got suspicious, the herd would smoke, and I most urgently wanted it to stay. After peeking through several narrow, leafy alleys at the loafing elk, I felt the wind swing on its hinges. Puffy, but dangerous at this yardage. I already feared my scent pool would reach the old man. A prize, he was, if I'd added correctly.

I backed out.

My client came in the next day. Though he had indeed seen many Januarys, he looked trim and moved with vigor. Capital. We had time this evening, I told him. Did he want to hunt?

"That's what I came for," he grinned. "Seen anything promising?"

"Mr. Main Beam," I said, helping him with his duffle.

He told me on the trail that he'd just returned from the far North, where he'd worn grooves in tall mountains looking for a ram. The iron would still be in his legs.

"We can arrow in," I said. "But it's safer swinging wide. Down this ridge," I pointed, "then west off the face into the bottom, then along treeline up yonder fork. There's a cut with a wallow. We'll come in downwind, the sun to our left."

We got there half an hour before dark, going slow the last few rods because elk song was sifting out of the timber close by. We narrowly missed bumping a silent bull. I spotted the rump just as he swung around to have another go at a shredded aspen. The walking got noisy in

The author shot this pronghorn using a Burris rangefinding reticle. He later checked the yardage with a Leica rangefinder: 394. The Magnum Research rifle in .280 was shooting 140-grain Barnes bullets.

At long range, you may need bigger targets, depending on scope reticle and magnification.

thick second growth above the cut. We crunched forward in a kinked route that delayed progress. But on the rise where we shucked our packs, a red sun still stabbed through the quivering tops of the quakies.

The wallow had already opened for business, and a five-point bull, black halfway up his barrel, hooked at one of the few green hummocks remaining on its perimeter. Junior.

"You make an appointment?" Joe whispered.

I shook my head. "I've tried before. Cud-chewers never show up on time."

He grinned. It was the first day, a pleasant evening with a bull in our laps. I read Joe's thoughts:

"We'll find a keeper."

Optimistic clients made hunting fun. But I could tell this man also expected results. The bull I'd pieced together could stay bushed up in this heat. Every day would be a new coin toss.

Shadows purpled the dry grasses and sedges, and blackened the dirt torn by elk hooves. The little bull moved off, alerting me. Then Sir Bone popped out of the boles behind him and stalked across the far edge of the cut. Maybe 250 yards off. I glassed him, saw lots of beam aft of the fifth and nodded. Joe pressed his Remington against a tree. It looked still.

But the elk didn't stop. The rifle moved to track it. "Wait," I rasped. Moving targets, even slow ones, had an annoying habit of snagging bullets in the wrong places.

Then the bull was gone. He bugled from the forest and it seemed to shake. His voice had lots of gravel but also a metallic twang that I remembered from my stakeout in the thicket.

We sat until almost all the light leaked from the day. Two other bulls tempted us, but Joe had no mind to shoot either. The bugling faded away. Then, just as we got ready to leave, it grew louder. My eyeballs strained against the binoculars. Something crawled in the black wainscoting across the cut.

The animal slid out along the forest hem and stopped. Joe had a rest again. "Is it him?"

The binocular dished up a big-shouldered bull with long beams. "E-e-ya-u-uh!" Like a steel guitar in the middle. It had to be him. But this was the first night, and the bone fuzzed into the dark firs behind. It might, just might, *not* be him. And even if it was the bull we'd come for, I wanted to check yesterday's math. Sadly, the light would only get worse.

Hitting at long range requires a great deal from the equipment, and ammunition – and the shooter.

Sometimes you have to shoot far or not shoot at all.

"He's big and he's 350 yards."
"Is he the one you saw?"
One question at a time.
"I think so. Yes." Then doubts. Antlers always shrank when they hit the ground, and in dim light they could shrink a lot. "Your call."
Joe didn't want the football. He wanted a decision.
"Will we find a bigger one?"
The Question.
"Dunno." Then, to be safe: "Better pass. We might get lucky and find...."
The bull moved across our front as Joe slung the rifle and turned to follow me out. I gave the elk one more look as it passed in front of a clump of yellow grass. The beam showed black against it, long and thick, hanging out far behind the fifth like irrigation pipe from a pickup bed. My throat felt dry; my heart quick-stepped. Binocular to my eye, I said, "Maybe we'd better...."
BLAM!
"... reconsider," I finished meekly as the bull buckled and the harsh echoes died.
The elk looked as big up close as it had in the glass, as when I'd pieced it together in the brush. Joe's bullet had taken it cleanly through both shoulders – a great shot in poor light. He told me as we got out the knives that you just couldn't beat a bright, high-power variable scope and a Weatherby cartridge.
We finished dressing the bull in the dark, then climbed out of the basin by thin starlight.
Joe's kill showed that sometimes high scope magnification makes

sense. A counter argument is that it can encourage shooting at unconscionable ranges. Hunters who would not shoot at distant game with a 4x scope might try if they could get a 12x picture. Powerful glass can give the illusion of an easy chance when in fact the shot is very difficult.
Last fall, I met a couple of young men on a snowy mountain. They were hunting elk, and I'd heard shots.
"Naw, we didn't git any," one said in answer to my question. "We shot a couple o' times, but they were four, maybe five hunnerd yards. We didn't knock any down."
It turned out that they hadn't walked into the canyon to check the track, either. Magnification and potent cartridges *can* prompt dolts like this to flail away at extreme range. But misuse (of scopes, station wagons, handguns, kitchen matches or sleeping pills) builds a mighty thin indictment against the product.
As riflescopes have evolved, the definition of high power has changed. A 3-9x variable no longer qualifies as a powerful sight. It and the 3.5-10x have replaced the 4x as standard fare on bolt-action big game rifles. Most hunters I've seen in the field leave the dial at or near the top most of the time. Variables that used to be hawked primarily to rodent-shooters – the 4-12x and 6-18x – have become popular with deer hunters. Hardly any new fixed-power scopes have come off the drawing boards in the past few years and only a few low-power variables. But the number of hunting-

style variables with high magnification continues to grow.
For example, Nikon's line now includes a 6.5-20x Monarch UCC Varmint scope. While its name reflects its purpose, I'm certain a lot of big game hunters will use it – as they use Leupold's 6.5-20x. Friends of mine in the Desert Southwest think this a perfect choice for Coues deer, and the dial rarely gets turned down. I borrowed a rifle so equipped one morning in Arizona and clobbered a buck at 410 paces. The rangefinding reticle, a bipod and 20x magnification made the shot not only possible but perfect. The bullet hit exactly where I was aiming, despite my rush to shoot before the buck stepped through a small opening. Unlike the 20x Lyman Super Targetspot scopes of yesteryear, the Nikon and Leupold mount on the receiver. Less than 15 inches long and weighing just 20 ounces, the Nikon is more compatible with a trim hunting rifle than many fixed-power scopes used to be. Some 6.5-20xs have 50mm objectives, which can brighten a sight picture at high magnification when light is poor. But I prefer the Nikon's 44mm front end. It's big enough to yield a 5mm exit pupil at 9x but will allow the use of low rings on most rifles. I also like the UCC's matte black finish. As is warranted on a long-range sight, this scope wears a parallax-adjustment sleeve on the objective bell. Leupold recently pioneered a turret dial for parallax adjustment, which allows you to allow for a sudden change in yardage from a shooting position.

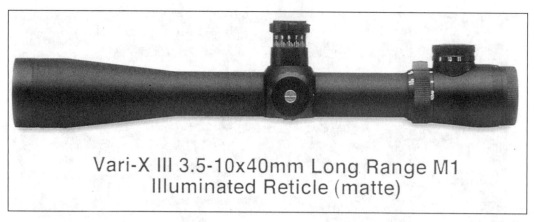

Vari-X III 3.5-10x40mm Long Range M1 Illuminated Reticle (matte)

Leupold and other manufacturers offer an increasing number of scopes for long-range shooting.

These two scopes are hardly anomalies. Swarovski and Pentax both list 6-24x scopes, as does Bushnell, which also markets an 8x32. There's an 8x32 at Burris as well – *and* a 6-24x and a 6.5-20x. In fact, most firms that field enough scopes to interest hunters have sights with more magnification than was thought useful for long-range target shooting in my youth.

For years, I've maintained that 4x is all the magnification needed to shoot big game. I've killed several animals at around 400 yards with both 4x and 6x scopes. At that range (which seems to me long indeed – a practical limit for even accomplished marksmen), I naturally prefer the 6x, but the 4x seems adequate. After all, most hunters would consider iron sights acceptable for shots at big

game to 100 yards, and through 4x glass at 400, the target appears the same size. The reticle also has an advantage over a bead, which is less distinct and must be aligned with the rear sight.

I still like 4x and 6x scopes, but am compelled to admit that the best variables these days are built to such close tolerances and so sturdily that impact point stays constant through power changes and nothing short of a bomb will cause mechanical failure. And I'll admit that as my eyes age, high magnification is becoming more attractive. A deliberate shooter by training, I'm not going to gun down many bounding bucks. Most of the shots that come my way are at undisturbed game, and I take them from a tight sling. I seldom shoot at moving animals. The average magnification of scopes in my rifle rack is creeping up.

The current market success of high-power variables – the 4-12x, 4.5-14x, 6-18x, 6.5-20x – indicates that most shooters like to see their target *big*, and that they expect to shoot at long range. Rifles and cartridges that make headlines are those that can deliver accuracy and punch far from the muzzle. Bipods, once exclusively the tool of prairie dog enthusiasts, are showing up more and more on big game rifles. David Miller's super-accurate (but hunting-weight) Marksman rifle comes with a Harris bipod. Unless you specify otherwise, it also wears a 6.5-20x scope.

Most variables are still designed in accordance with the "three times" rule. That is, the top-end magnification is no greater than three times the bottom-end magnification. You can have a "four times" scope if you make certain mechanical or optical concessions that until recently did not make sense. Scope designers plodded the same path for a long

time, improving the 3-9x but not supplanting it with scopes of higher power or wider power range. Now the 3-12x, 4-16x and 6-24x give hunters a low end that's useful in a wide range of hunting situations, with a top end that picks the eye of a ground squirrel from a grass tuft a quarter mile across a cow pasture. Leupold's new 30mm LPS scopes include a 3.5-14x50 model that's not only a much better scope than the first LPSs; it has a turret-mounted focus (parallax correction) dial and looks good on rifles built for long shooting at big game. Two other new LPS scopes offer slimmer profiles and lighter weight.

I've come to accept high magnification as a useful feature in big game hunting scopes. But when someone brags about shooting long, I'm still tempted to ask him if he's out to see what his rifle can do or to test his hunting skills. I'm tempted, when he claims a kill at great distance, to put a consoling arm around his shoulder and say, "That's all right; you'll get closer next time."

Rangefinders: Gadgets or gear?

"It was 500 yards," marveled the hunter. "He held right on the shoulder with that 7 Magnum and wham! – the elk dropped. Then I fired with my ought six and hit underneath another cow...."

"It was about 200 yards," interjected the other hunter.

I must have looked quizzical. Both men fell silent. They might have realized, suddenly, that their range estimates were 300 yards apart. That's nearly a thousand feet, three football fields, nearly 4 feet of bullet drop, farther than the point-blank range of a .30-06 with a normal zero. How could two people look

A lightweight bipod can be a help on the prairie when you're hunting pronghorns.

Prone, with a bipod to steady the rifle and a Swarovski 6-24x scope, this marksman has reach!

at the same animal and come to such different conclusions?

Well, distance can be pretty hard to judge, depending on terrain, light conditions, target visiblity, intervening brush, vertical angle and the actual yardage. With practice, most of us can come within 20 yards of guessing the distance to targets around 100 yards off. At 200 yards, the same level of precision gives us a 40-yard margin for error; at 300 a 60-yard window. However, our ability to determine yardage deteriorates as the range increases. At the same time, the parabolic arc of a bullet makes accurate range estimation ever more critical. A 50-yard error up close – say, a 150-yard estimate over a 100-yard distance – means little if you're shooting a big game rifle. The bullet will hit within an inch or two of where you thought it should. On the other hand, if you're 50 yards off when the target is actually 400 yards away, the error will cause a bullet displacement, high or low, of several inches. A miss or a crippling hit could result.

The same problem has plagued armies for centuries. Accurate range assessment made primitive artillery deadly; a bad guess could turn the battle around. It's no surprise that the development of optical rangefinders got enthusiastic military support. As the reach and destructive force of weapons increased, so did the importance of accurate range determination. You didn't want to hit a school or a hospital when you were assigned a

munitions target. You didn't want to rain shells onto empty ground while you gave your position away to the artillery emplacement you were supposed to demolish.

Hunters who wanted help from rangefinders had no place to get it when I was growing up. The first military instruments were not available to the public for some time. And they were better suited to tanks than to treestands. Heavy, complex and expensive, they eventually found their way to the surplus mar-

ket – and a lukewarm reception. Then Ranging, a company now defunct, adopted the split-image or coincidence rangefinding principle in a lightweight pocket rangefinder for hunters. These devices had plastic housings and two windows with lenses and prisms inside. Looking through the sighting window, you'd see two of everything. That is, any distant object would appear to have a double beside it. To find the range, you turned a dial to merge the two images, then you read the range on a scale. The split-image rangefinders were a boon to bowmen who used them to get precise readings at modest yardage. They were of less value to riflemen who fired at targets far away, where the accuracy of the system diminished. Still, Ranging products were handy and affordable, sparking widespread hunter interest in rangefinders.

By this time, split-image technology had already been supplanted in the military sector by lasers. More expensive laser rangefinders were also more precise. In fact, they could come within 1 *yard* of pin-pointing the distance of objects even at hundreds of yards. Laser rangefinders are battery-operated instruments that send a laser beam to the object that you "aim at" with the reticle in the viewfinder. The beam bounces off the object, returning to the instrument and its internal electronic clock, which calculates elapsed time instantaneously. Since

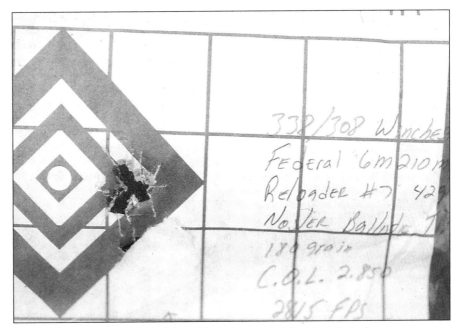

At long range, groups like this are rare. Natural bullet dispersion is compounded by wobble and by human error in compensating for range and wind.

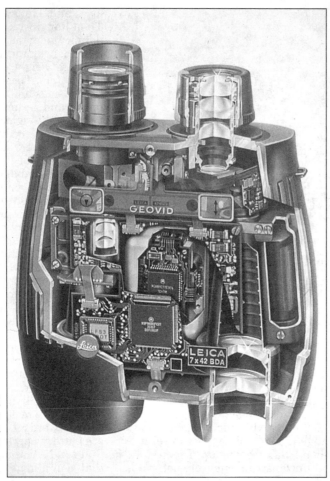

The Leica Geovid is a first-class binocular and a laser rangefinder. It's a complex, costly instrument.

Swarovski also makes an expensive rangefinder, the RF-1. For $2,900 you get this 2-pound, 6-battery monocular with 6x magnification. Accuracy: spot-on to 1,000 steps. While I'm very taken with Swarovski riflescopes and binoculars, I haven't warmed to this rangefinder. I prefer the Geovid. Mainly that's because the Geovid lets me use both eyes. It is truly a useful binocular; the RF-1 is a rangefinder only. I have also found the RF-1a bit unhandy to use, though the optics are beyond reproach.

Swarovski has pioneered rangefinding riflescopes, coming out a few years ago with the LRS, a 3-12x50 variable. This 2 1/2-pound scope accurately measures distances to 1,100 yards. Powered by four AAA batteries, it retails for $4,500. I've not shot with this scope, but a few years ago in elk camp, a hunter let me examine one. He had it mounted on a Dakota Longbow tactical rifle chambered in .338 Lapua. The outfit weighed 16 pounds with bipod. He was truly set up for long-range shooting! While I would not have taken this rifle into the steep country I like to hunt, I had to concede that the rifle, cartridge and scope were well matched, a shining example of the technology that appeals to lots of big game hunters these days.

More affordable rangefinders are available from Bushnell, which not long ago held a whopping 95 percent of the market in these instruments.

light travels at the constant speed of 186,000 miles per second, time can be easily converted to distance. The rangefinder does this and tells you the yardage via an electronic display. Laser rangefinders are very fast. You aim, press a button and get a reading right away. The most recent models also have options that tell the laser to ignore interfering reflections from raindrops or solid objects closer than a certain distance. So you can find the range to an animal on the other side of a clearing while you stay inside a boundary woodlot.

The best rangefinder in my opinion is the Leica Geovid. As regards performance, there's nothing even close. Actually, the Geovid is a superb 7x42 binocular with a laser rangefinder inside. It is lightning-fast, accurate to 1,000 yards and all but bombproof under its rubber armor. The BDA model incorporates an electronic digital compass. The Leica has only two drawbacks: its 3 pounds of heft require a harness, just like a heavy binocular, and its retail price of $3,295 ($4,395 for the BDA) is hundreds of dollars more than a new Mustang cost when

I got out of high school. Of course, in this age of $50,000 Land Cruisers, three grand ain't what it used to be.

A Dakota Longbow with Swarovski rangefinding scope is quite a contrast to one long-range rifle of a century ago: a Model 1886 Winchester with iron sights.

Since the introduction of the Yardage Pro 400 in 1996, the folks at Bushnell have been busy upgrading. The 800 model offered more reach. Now there are Yardage Pro 500 and 1000 models, plus Sport and Scout models with a range about like that of the 500. The numbers denote the approximate maximum yardage for ranging a modestly reflective target like a tree. Yardage Pros weigh from 7 to about 14 ounces and feature magnifications of 4x, 6x and 8x.

I've used several of the Bushnell rangefinders and found them quite accurate. While they don't match the Leica or Swarovski models optically, they are much lighter and much less expensive. The 600 Compact fits handily in a pocket and offers all the reach you'll likely need.

The growing popularity of rangefinders will certainly lead to heightened competition for market share. After a bumpy introduction, Leica's 11-ounce, 7x LRF 800 is back with improved innards. I used it last fall to range a pronghorn buck at 394 yards. The animal crumpled to a 140-grain Barnes bullet from my Magnum Research rifle in .280 Remington. I was using a Burris scope with Ballistic Plex reticle. If I felt over-teched, I also felt confident when I bellied onto the rimrock. The LRF 800 is not only a practical rangefinder for long hikes where long shots come often, it's eminently affordable. Hunters will benefit as new models proliferate and prices are trimmed to woo buyers.

But some sportsmen have taken a step back and questioned the use of rangefinders in the chase. Is the application of ever-more-sophisticated technology going to change the character of the hunt? Does the rangefinder obviate a hunter's need to develop skill in judging yardage?

The LRF 800 by Leica is one of the handiest of its type. Accuracy: within 1 yard to around 800 steps.

Are instruments that make hunting easier good for hunters or hunting?

Like high fences and four-wheelers, rangefinders provide fuel for talk over camp stoves. Records-keeping organizations have taken a stand on the rim of the issue, prohibiting records-book entry of animals taken with the aid of electronic devices that attract or locate game or guide the hunter to it. Rangefinders have not yet been put in the same category as two-way radios. We have yet to determine just how much of a crutch the rangefinder is and whether such a crutch undermines the nature of the hunt. In some instances, laser rangefinders have no doubt contributed a great deal to the kill. Should the hunter be credited as if his shooting were unaided? Is this fair chase? It could be argued that a whitetail buck in a brushy enclosure has a better chance for escape than a mule deer buck on open range several hundred yards from a practiced marksman with an accurate rifle and a rangefinder.

Me, I'm ambivalent. Rangefinders can't tow you up hills or see bucks peeking through the foliage or hold your rifle still. When I guide elk hunters, I try to get within 200 yards, rangefinder or not. I've learned that field accuracy drops dramatically beyond 200, even if the range is precisely known. Shooters just can't hold the rifle still while they squeeze the trigger. Even at ranges between 200 and 300 yards, my notes show that only 50 percent of the shots hit vitals. And these are *elk*, with vitals as big as a V-8 engine block! Furthermore, most of the shots are taken over my spotting scope or a similar rest!

My main concern with rangefinders is that they encourage shooting beyond the effective range of the hunter. Most hunters overestimate range more often than they fall short. The man who told me a center hit on an elk 500 yards away resulted from a center hold with a 7mm Remington surely overestimated the range – actual yardage may well have been less than half that distance. A hunter who thinks the range is 600 yards but finds from his trusty rangefinder that it is instead 375 might be inclined to shoot, no matter that from hunting positions, he cannot keep bullets on the side of a small tool shed at 375 steps. A hunter told me the other day that he'd seen another fellow pass up a shot at 400 yards. Shaking

Too heavy as a binocular, the Geovid has also been upstaged by lightweight rangefinders.

his head, he said he couldn't understand such a decision: "Heck, four hunnerd's not that hard a shot."

Maybe not for him. But I've bungled shots at less than *one* hunnerd and have seen others do the same.

I don't own a rangefinder. But I'll admit to having used the rangefinders of clients and hunting companions. These gadgets are fun. More to the point, they have made me more accurate in estimating yardage. While waiting at a trail crossing or saddle, or between intense glassing sessions, I've pointed rangefinders at rocks and trees and animals I didn't want to hunt, after letting my eye come up with the range. Sometimes my estimate is close; more often it is not. The rangefinder provides a check that doesn't require long pacing sessions that would take time and disturb game. Also, I can determine shot distances across gulches and canyons, where pacing would not tell me the yardage at all. Shots over rough terrain are common in the West, so it's important that I be able to estimate the actual distance covered by the bullet.

Shooters commonly overestimate cross-canyon range because their eye gobbles a great expanse of ground and tells the brain that "you'll use a lot of steps getting there." Steps are the measure of distance we've used since childhood. But bullets don't care how many steps we must take to get from here to there. They travel straight, and bullet drop depends only on the shortest distance from muzzle to target. By the same logic, distances

Long range is what Lazzeroni rifles are about. The 6-24x Swarovski scope makes a good match.

on the prairie often seem less than they really are, because our eyes see little ground.

Poor light makes animals seem far away because they are hard to distinguish. Animals partly hidden by brush also fool us. Conversely, a deer or elk silhouetted on a skyline, or a pronghorn brilliantly front-lit by a low sun, can appear closer than they are. Even if we don't use rangefinders to help us shoot at game, practice with them can train our eyes to more effectively judge yardage under varying conditions.

Not long ago, a fellow and I crept to the top of a ridge to glass a small band of elk I'd spotted on the opposite hillside. The animals were still there. My pal picked the cactus from his palms and wiggled into a prone position. The rifle steadied. "Golly, they're far," he rasped.

"Two fifty," I said. At least, they seemed 250.

"Where should I hold?"

"Center, tight behind the shoulder. Take your time."

He said something else about the distance. I thought that strange

because he had told me earlier that his rifle was zeroed at 300 yards. These elk were clearly closer than he had expected to see them... Weren't they?

The rifle banged, and the big elk in the middle humped. The others scattered.

"Shoot again," I hissed. He did, to no effect. Another shot hit the hillside to the right of the elk.

The animal went down, got up again, took a couple of steps. Bang! No reaction. Then the elk sank once more into the sage and didn't get up.

"That was a very long shot," said the hunter. We couldn't pace it, and I didn't have a rangefinder, but when we got across the canyon, we found the first 200-grain Sierra from his .300 Winchester Magnum had struck just slightly high in the lungs.

"Perfect," I said. It was. I didn't ask him why he'd zeroed at long range when he obviously felt uncomfortable shooting 250 yards from prone. The answer was pretty plain: From the bench, his 100-yard groups were tight, and he considered himself highly skilled. Had he risked humiliation by shooting from hunting positions at 300 steps, he might have taken another view and zeroed closer. Had he hiked into the hills and used a rangefinder on game to determine how far 300 yards actually was, he might have reached the same conclusion.

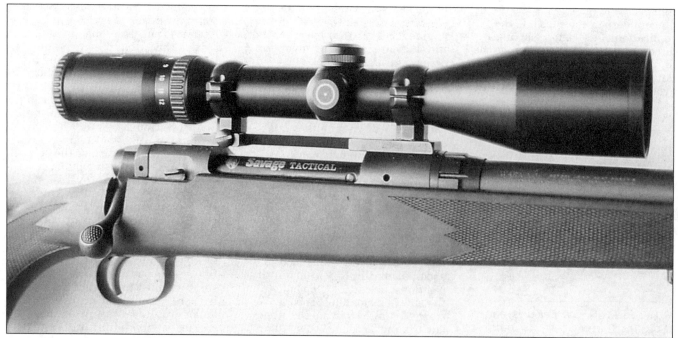

This 3-12 Schmidt and Bender scope has a rangefinding Sammut reticle.

Stretching rifles, optics ... and your marksmanship

One bitter November long ago, a kid in a hooded sweatshirt took aim at a whitetail buck standing in a stubble field. Shivering in the cold dawn air and shaking from excitement, he couldn't hold the crosswires still, even when he leaned against the snow-capped fence post. "How far?" he wondered. A long shot; the deer looked awfully small in the Weaver K4. The kid just *knew* he'd have to hold high. His reticle bobbing way above the buck's shoulder, the kid yanked the trigger. The rifle belched – and the buck kept eating. Two followup shots also received no reaction from the deer, which, it seemed to the kid, might as well have been cropping wheat on the moon.

Down to his last cartridge, the young hunter finally held on the buck's ribs and forced himself to squeeze. Down went the deer.

The kid was elated but as embarrassed with his shooting as with his failure to mark where the buck had stood. He scoured the shin-high stubble for 20 minutes before he found the animal only 160 yards from where he'd shot. The fast spitzer bullet would have hit the buck with a dead-on hold out to 250 yards.

Since then the kid (me) has been cautious about holding over. I've found that with a 200-yard zero, there's hardly ever a need to hold high on an animal. If my quarry seems too far for a center hold, I work a bit closer. I seldom shade higher than the backline, because a backline hold will ensure a kill from 250 to 300 yards. Game farther than 300 looks impossibly small, and is almost always approachable.

The place to test the limits of your equipment, as well as your own skill, is on paper. I've found that not many hunters like to do this in public, at least from hunting positions. I suspect that many of these hunters have a distorted view of shooting: They think it a reflection of their manhood, a measure of their competence in a field where every man is supposed to be competent. They hang their ego with the target. It's easy to brag about a kill, because details can be fudged: distance, number of shots

Pronghorns provide most of the long-distance shooting to North American big game hunters.

Photo by J. R. Hunter

fired, where the bullet hit in relation to where it was intended to hit. A lot of animals die despite poor shooting.

Truly, shooting is a skill that must be learned and honed. It cannot be inherited or bought. People who know anything at all about shooting know that the best marksmen are never reluctant to shoot at paper. Hunters who prefer to talk up their prowess without punching holes in a target are, almost without exception, unskilled. A super rifleman can make a poor shot; an accurate rifle can print an embarrassing group. But there are lessons in errant bullets. An accomplished shooter learns from them and loads up for one more string.

One October day a few years ago, an elk hunter and his guide worked their way into a promising canyon. I tagged along. We glassed the off-side and found elk, but none that we could reach. Finally I spied a branch-antlered bull on our side, down-canyon about a half-mile. We hurried around the head of a big draw and sneaked to the top of a rise 250 yards from the animal. The hunter got set, using the guide's spotting scope as a rest. Still, the rifle shook.

Boom! The bull buckled at the impact of the 210-grain Nosler and skidded downslope into heavy ceanothus. In the time it took our hunter to chamber a second round, however, the elk scrambled to its feet. The man sent four more bullets into the hillside around the standing bull before it limped into the woods. Five hours later, we downed that elk.

This hunter was using a borrowed rifle because with his own, he had missed another bull and thought a change would help. He hadn't shot this rifle at all – a colossal mistake. By coincidence, the axis of scope and rifle were so aligned that a hit resulted when he triggered the first round. But he couldn't repeat that hit because he hadn't called his shot, and his wobbles had taken the crosswires over a lot of country. He didn't know where the reticle had been when the rifle fired, so he couldn't know its relationship to the bullet path.

Long-range zeros account for a lot of missed shots. A 200-yard zero works well for most big game cartridges because it keeps your bullet within 3 vertical inches of your line of sight out to 250 yards or farther.

Use a rest whenever you can. Pad the forend with your hand. Never rest the barrel.

Hit 3 inches high or low, and you'll still strike well inside a deer's chest.

A 200-yard zero seems close for a magnum cartridge. Why not make that 250, or even 300? After all, for a .270 Weatherby, a 200-yard zero means the bullet rises only 1 1/2 inches over the sight-line at 100. Adjust the scope so the rifle shoots 3 inches high at 100, and you'll reach 300 yards with just an inch of drop! Well, some hunting rifles could well be zeroed for 250 yards. But beyond that, you run into problems near midrange. A bullet's arc is parabolic; the highest point above sight-line is not in the middle of that arc, but past the middle. For example, the .270 Weatherby zeroed at 300 yards with a 130-grain, pointed bullet will print 3.3 inches high at 100 yards and 3.8 inches high at 200, where it is nearer its zenith. Four inches is, to my mind, too much to ignore. In this case, maximum deviation occurs between 170 and 230 yards, where you can expect a lot of shooting at big game. It's silly to zero for extreme range, where you'll seldom shoot, if by doing so you incur a midrange gap that forces you to adjust your aim.

A few cartridges are best zeroed at 100 yards because most of the shooting they're designed for will be at that range, or because they lack

sufficient energy to be effective much beyond 150 yards. The .30-30 is a woods cartridge. So is the .35 Remington, the .444 Marlin, the .45-70. Even rifles chambered for 200-yard cartridges can benefit from a shorter zero if most of your shooting will be close.

Once, I was sneaking through second-growth Douglas fir, on the trail of a whitetail buck. Suddenly I spotted him, 60 yards away. As he turned, I shouldered my Savage 99 and found his forward ribs in the 3 X Leupold. The bullet was on its way almost before I realized my finger was applying pressure. The deer ran hard for a short distance and collapsed, both lungs destroyed by the 150-grain Winchester Silvertip. A lot of game is shot like that: right now, right here, with a center hold. A 200-yard zero makes center holds deadly at short and middle ranges so you can forget about shading.

Another time, I found the dot in my 2.5 X Lyman Alaskan bobbing around in a tight alley between me and a fine buck that was showing only its ear and eye. Because my zero kept the bullet close to my line of sight at this modest distance, I was able to hold where I wanted to hit, threading the 165-grain .308 softpoint through the alley to the buck's brain.

Part of the reason many hunters like to zero long is that they overestimate yardage in the field. One fellow told me recently that his .30 Magnum could outshoot any rifle between 800 and 900 yards, and that he'd toppled a grand muley buck at 700 steps by holding a tad over its withers. Now, I'm a country boy, but even a congressman would have blushed spinning that yarn. The flattest-shooting cartridges around lob their bullets nearly *3 feet* low at *500* yards when zeroed at 200. To keep a .270 Weatherby bullet (muzzle velocity 3,375 feet per second) from sagging more than a foot at 700 yards, you'd have to zero at over 600. That would put the bullet roughly 2 feet high at 300 *and* 400. The bullet would be plunging so rapidly at 700 steps that if you misjudged range by 50 yards, you'd miss the deer's vitals.

Zeroing at 200 yards gives you a solid reference point from which to calculate holdover if the animal is farther. Usually the long shots afford you plenty of time – time you might use to convince yourself to hold center or estimate the effects of wind or a steep shot angle. Close shots must often be taken quickly. Holding center is your quickest option, and knowing your bullet will strike within 3 inches of the point of aim inspires confidence.

But no matter how confident you are, or how precisely your rifle is zeroed, you're still hardly the perfect shooting platform. Pulsing blood, twitching nerves, muscles that tire and joints created to slip can make a steady hold little more than a dream. Consequently, a lot of hunters are discovering the value of a bipod. A bipod puts the rifle in contact with the ground, replacing slippery joints, pulsing arteries and quivering muscles with a couple of dispassionate steel pegs that don't move. At all. What could be better? Well, the best bipod is one that allows some movement at the attachment point. The Harris bipod that I favor is cleverly designed to allow the forend to roll slightly. When you have to take a shot from a place that is not perfectly level, you can quickly extend the legs to the proper length, then make up for induced cant by tilting the rifle to vertical as you aim (Harris Engineering, Barlow, KY 42024).

Shooting sticks are an alternative to the bipod. Buffalo hunters used crossed shooting sticks to steady their heavy rifles. Lighter,

The Simmons 4.5-14 V-Tac scope has been given high marks for optical quality. Note target knobs.

stronger fiberglass versions are available from Stoney Point Products (P.O. Box 238, New Ulm, MN 56073). The firm's Steady Stix and taller Safari Stix collapse for carry in a belt sheath. From the sit or kneeling, plant the stick legs well forward and pull the intersection toward you as you push into it with the rifle. The rifle shoves the legs more firmly into the ground as your hand (or a tight binding of some sort) keeps the sticks at a constant angle to each other.

A monopod offers some support, but not as much as crossed sticks, because it allows left-right wobble. Mainly, it keeps your left arm from getting tired. It is easier to carry and quicker to deploy than a bipod or crossed sticks, however, and is considerable help when you're winded and the muzzle wants to dip and soar at each breath.

In my opinion, the best shooting brace is a sling – not a carrying strap, but a 1-inch or 1 1/4-inch leather shooting sling with an adjustable loop that snugs around your left arm above the triceps. The loop hauls the rifle back toward you, transferring rifle weight from your left forearm to your left shoulder

A Brownell's Latigo sling can steady your rifle from hunting positions.

while pulling the butt into your right shoulder. If you simply wrap a strap around your arm, you tug the buttstock forward, because the strap is as tight *behind* your triceps as in front. Also, the pull on the butt is to the side, inducing a cant.

To my mind, Brownell's Latigo sling is the best commercial shooting sling (Brownell's Inc, 200 S. Front St., Montezuma, IA 50171). It has little hardware (a button and a ring), so it is quiet and lightweight. You can adjust overall length with a couple of tugs. A series of opposing holes give you almost limitless loop adjustment. A Whelen-style sling is less readily adjustable for length but offers the same advantages when you shoot. Any nylon sling is bad business because under tension it can slip.

Though a sling won't steady your rifle as effectively as a bipod, it is quicker to use and better for shooting on steep or uneven terrain. It adds no extra weight or bulk to the rifle and can be used in prone, sitting and kneeling. From prone, you should be able to keep all your shots inside 3 minutes of angle. That means killing shots on deer to 400 yards. From the sit, you'll do almost as well. Kneeling typically puts a 3- to 9-o'clock wobble into the reticle, but practice can shrink your groups to 3 inches.

Of course, if you find a natural rest, use it! Often I use a sling *with* a rest. Nobody will take you to task for an ugly position if the bullet lands in the middle. When you have

the choice, pick a horizontal rest over a vertical support. Your rifle will bounce away from a rest before the bullet leaves the muzzle. A bounce most like the bounce you got zeroing is upward off a horizontal rest. Never rest the barrel. Always pad the forend with something soft to minimize harsh vibrations.

Unsupported positions are not only unsteady; they *feel* unsteady. That is, you feel compelled to make your muscles direct the shot. If you muscle the rifle toward the target, without enabling it to find its natural point of aim, you'll be fighting it during the shot and while the bullet is moving up the barrel. You will miss. Shift your entire body so the rifle points toward the target naturally, minding body position and letting your skeletal structure take over as much as possible. Bone support is the foundation of accuracy.

Up, down and sideways

If you do things in a natural sort of way, you hold a rifle with the sights on top and the trigger on the bottom, just as you drive a car with the shiny side up. But unlike automobiles, rifles aren't connected to the ground. Rifles can be tipped as easily as you tip your hand. They can be fired at a tilt or even upside down. While most shooters keep the sights on top, many do not. Those who tip their rifles are said to be canting.

"A cant isn't bad," a shooting coach told me long ago, "so long as you do it the same each time." Doing it the same each time presupposes that you know you're doing it in the first place. Riflemen who don't think about cant either tip the rifle at pretty much the same angle out of habit, or they allow the angle of the sights to change slightly with each shot.

It's pretty easy to spot a cant if you're coaching, just as it's easy to see the tilt of a truck loaded too heavily on one side if you're driving behind it. In the truck's cab, you might not be able to tell; and when you're looking through the sights, you often can't tell cant.

A shooter used to canting a rifle will likely mount a scope so the crosswire is tilted off the vertical axis of the rifle. You've probably thrown a friend's rifle to your shoulder and had to consciously rotate the stock so the vertical wire would appear to be straight up and down.

"Good gravy," you say to your amigo. "How can you shoot with the reticle falling over like that?"

"Here, lemme see," he replies, grabbing the rifle and aiming it. After a pause: "Looks square to me. You're prob'ly just tippin' it."

"Ha! Not likely!" you shriek, slapping your knee for effect. "That scope's as crooked as your brand of poker."

"You callin' me crooked? Just because you can't hold a rifle...."

"Now wait just one minute, you...."

Discussions about canting can get animated in a hurry. About the only way to settle them, short of spiking the stew with cigar tobacco at hunting camp, is to lay the rifle in a rest on a bench and square up the stock by nudging the butt so a plumb line or carpenter's level shows it to be vertical. Now, without moving the rifle, look into the scope. The crosswires should appear to be vertical and horizontal. If they are not, you simply loosen the scope rings and twist the tube.

That is, unless you want to leave the reticle as is.

A canted reticle will not cause a miss. In fact, you can rotate the scope so the crosswire looks like an "X" and use it as effectively as before. A small disadvantage is that you won't have a vertical wire to help you hold off for wind deflection or show you the line of bullet drop at long range. You won't have a horizontal wire to help you lead running animals.

A tipped rifle is said to be canted. Cant will affect bullet placement, especially at long range.

A canted *rifle*, however, can give you problems. Regardless of how the reticle appears, if the rifle is tipped, you'll have problems hitting beyond zero range because the bullet path is not going to fall along the vertical wire or directly below the intersection. If your line of sight is directly over the bore, a long shot requires you only to hold high. If a canted rifle forces your sightline to the *side* of a vertical plane that passes through the bore, you'll not only have to hold high, but to one side.

Here's why: Given that your scope is mounted directly above the bore, your line of sight crosses the bullet path twice. The first crossing happens at about 35 yards; the second is at zero range. If the rifle is rotated so its scope falls to the side of the barrel, the sightline will cross only once, because gravity sucks the bullet straight down, while the line of sight has a horizontal component. Whether the scope is on top of the rifle or a bit to the side, the line of sight will converge with the bullet path, slice through it, then angle away. If the scope is on top of the rifle, gravity pulls the bullet in an arc back into and through the

straight line of sight. If the scope is not on top, the bullet path still dips below the horizontal *plane* of the sightline; but when this happens, the trajectory is well to the side of where you're looking.

How much practical difference will canting make? Not much. A cant that escapes your notice won't cause a noticeable shift in bullet impact at normal hunting ranges. As the targets get smaller and the range longer, and as you impose stricter accuracy standards, cant starts to matter.

When I was on the Michigan State University rifle team, I marveled at a colleague who shot very well but used a cant that would have spilled coffee. Standing, he looked straight ahead through sights that fell into his natural line of vision when he rotated the rifle on his shoulder. The adjustable butt let him do that without changing the contact angle of the butt hook. So his rifle tilted in toward him. Not only the line of sight but the rifle's center of gravity fell closer to the centerline of his torso. From a mechanical perspective, this made perfect sense. I

tried shooting that way and found it darned near impossible.

In traditional bullseye rifle competition, targets are very small and the rifles supremely accurate, so shooters must correct for cant. (Some globe sights for target rifles have tiny bubble levels that show you the slightest cant at a glance; similar devices are now available for scopes.) On the other hand, my amigo on the smallbore squad didn't have to worry about horizontal angles because his shooting was up close at one precisely measured distance. It is easy to accommodate cant at a single distance. You simply move the sights to put the bullets where you look. Forget about how sightline and trajectory converge, and what they do beyond the target. It doesn't matter.

We hunters don't shoot at just one distance, however, or with adjustable stocks. So although small degrees of cant seldom affect our performance on game, it's a good idea to shoot with the sight squarely on top of the rifle. Cant is just one more thing to worry about, one more distraction, a small but thorny threat to the self-confidence that

A scope level shows you when you're canting. Levels have long been used by competitive marksmen.

can help us shoot well. It's easy to see if you have a cant. Simply loosen your scope rings and line up the vertical wire with the butt of your rifle. Now tighten the rings. Throw the rifle to your shoulder with your eyes closed. Open them. The wire should appear vertical. If it does not, you're tipping the rifle. Practice holding it with the sights at 12 o'clock, where they belong.

Now, sometimes shooters slip a cant into their shooting routine without knowing it. They mount the scope carelessly and subconsciously adjust their hold on the rifle to correct for a reticle that's tilted. A culprit here is the ubiquitous Weaver Tip-Off scope ring. This inexpensive ring has been around a long time – and for good reason. It's strong and lightweight. But because the top half hooks the base on one side and its two screws take up all the slack on the opposite side, tightening a Tip-Off ring can rotate the scope tube down toward the screws. If they're installed on the right-hand

side, you put a clockwise tilt into your reticle as you cinch them up. Solution: Back off on the screws and twist the scope counterclockwise about as far as you think it moved. Tighten the screws again, and check the reticle.

Canting isn't the only way you can complicate your aim at long range. When I was growing up, side-mounted scopes were common. With them, you could affix a scope to a top-ejecting Model 94 or 71 Winchester, or so you could use your iron sights *and* a scope without removing the scope. If it holds the scope off the vertical axis of the bolt, a side mount introduces the same sighting error you get with a cant. Side mounts that put the scope over the receiver are best. A Remington 870 shotgun in my rack wears a side mount, but the scope lies almost directly over the center of the bore. Side mounts installed before rifles were routinely drilled for scopes made hash of collector-quality rifles. Many Winchester Model 54s and

70s, and untold numbers of lever-action carbines, were assaulted with drills in the decades of innocence after World War II. After it dawned on shooters that a pre-war hunting rifle might someday be worth more than $100, and that holes in the receiver were like rust pockets on Duesenbergs, drilling stopped.

Top mounts centered above the bore can give you problems with sight angles, too, if the bases are extra high. It's easy to see this in exaggeration. Picture a scope with ring bases 3 feet high. If you adjust that scope to put its bullets on point of aim at 35 yards, you can't expect a 200-yard zero. Directing the line of sight to intersect bullet trajectory at 35 steps puts the two paths at steep angles to each other. Entering and exiting angles are naturally the same. Your sightline now diverges quickly from the bullet's trajectory, diving under it in a straight but steeply descending path. The bullet will come down to meet it, courtesy of gravity. But that won't happen for some distance.

Truly, errors caused by cant and steep sight angles pale beside those caused by rifles that don't hold still. Shot angles are another cause of poor shooting.

Bullets react to gravity predictably because gravity is a predictable force. But because gravity works only perpendicular to the earth's center, shots taken uphill and downhill don't show the same rate of drop as those fired horizontally. That is, they don't drop at the same rate over a given distance of bullet travel. A 350-yard shot across a flat field allows gravity its tightest grip on the bullet. A 350-yard shot at a 45-degree angle up or down (direction doesn't matter) requires a lower hold.

For example, my .270 Winchester puts a 150-grain spitzer about 12 inches low at 350 yards, given my 200-yard zero. That means a top-of-the-back hold will hit an elk high in the lungs. If the bull is standing the same distance away but on a ridge or in a canyon, changing the shot angle to 45 degrees from horizontal, my hold should be dead on. That's because, though the bullet is travelling the same distance, gravity's effect is limited to the horizontal component of that distance: roughly 250 yards. At 250 yards, my bullet hits 3 inches low, not 12. It's easy to figure this out. Just imagine a triangle with the hypotenuse (long side) being the bullet's flight path.

Leupold's Vari-X III scopes are popular on long-range rifles like this .300 Jarret, by Kenny Jarrett.

Shooting at steep angles, up or down, you'll hit higher than if you shot as far horizontally.

One leg is perpendicular to the ground (from the target, a vertical line up or down). The other leg, extending horizontally from your position, meets it at a right angle. That second leg represents the horizontal component of the shot. You can calculate it if you know the shot distance and angle. These multipliers make it easy.

As a rule, you can ignore shot angles of 25 degrees or less if you're shooting within the point-blank range of your rifle (for most rifles zeroed at 200 yards, point-blank range is about 250 yards). You can ignore steeper angles if the animal is very close. Mostly, I've found that shot angles serve as excuses more often than they cause misses.

Not so the wind. Wind results from a draining of air pressure from one area to another. Think of it as a turbulence within the sea of air your bullet must drill through to get to the target. Always there is pressure, but often there's no discernible wind. If you zero for a no-wind condition, then any wind will move your bullet from your point of aim. Reading mirage is one way to tell what wind downrange is doing. Mirage boils straight up from the ground, like steam from hot soup, when the ground is warm and there's no wind. A breeze makes mirage lean, and gives it a more purposeful, less bubbly appearance. When undulations in mirage disappear, or when they flatten out parallel to the ground, wind is strong enough to matter. If you're shooting in hot, humid conditions and close to the ground, wind can also move the image of your target as it pushes the thick mirage. Apparent displacement of the target can exaggerate bullet displacement. Competitive shooters who ignore the wind or the mirage don't win.

Wind direction is as important as wind speed. A headwind makes little difference to a bullet that's cooking along at 50 times the speed of a gale. Drag caused by air friction, wind or no wind, is already 56 times the force of gravity! You can ignore all but the strongest headwinds and tailwinds when shooting at game.

The wind to watch is the side wind, because it is acting on a bullet whose relative velocity is zero. How far a side wind shoves your bullet depends not only on wind speed, but the speed, shape, weight and ballistic coefficient of the bullet. Fast bullets spend less time aloft than slow ones, so the wind has less time to work on them. Lag – the velocity lost between muzzle and target – also figures in. Bullets with less lag, or slower deceleration, are less affected by wind. That's partly why competitive smallbore shooters don't use high-speed ammunition. Standard-velocity .22 match cartridges have less drag than high-velocity rounds. Despite a quicker launch, the high-speed bullets drift farther in wind.

A wind far from the muzzle moves a bullet farther off course per unit of distance than does the same wind close up, because downrange the bullet is traveling slower. On the other hand, wind at the firing point can change flight angle of the bullet, whose altered course then multiplies the wind's effect over distance.

Bullet rotation speed and direction affect shot displacement, too. A 9 o'clock wind does not push bullets to 3 o'clock, but to 4 o'clock. A 3

Shot angle, Degrees (up or down)	Divide range by:
0-5	1.00
10	1.02
15	1.04
20	1.06
25	1.10

Bighorn sheep may be visible at a great distance, but they can usually be stalked and shot close.

o'clock wind shoves them up to 10 o'clock. Most hunters won't see this except with careful shooting at paper targets at long range.

You can calculate the wind's effect on your bullet with a formula: D=RW/C, where D is deflection in minutes of angle, R is range in hundreds of yards and W is wind speed in miles per hour. C is a constant for a given bullet at known velocity. For most game bullets with pointed noses, this constant is about 10. So if you boot a 180-grain spitzer from your .300 Winchester through a 15-mph crosswind toward an elk 300 yards away, you'll first think: D=3(15)/10. That's 4.5 minutes of

angle, or 13.5 inches. Hold a foot into the wind, and you'll be close enough. Disregard the wind, and you'll either miss or cripple.

Velocity differences between a .30-06 and your .300 Winchester give the magnum an edge that's not shown in this formula. Another, more precise way to figure drift is: D=W(T-Tv), where D is deflection in feet, W is wind speed in feet per second, T is time of flight and Tv is time of flight in a vacuum. It's impractical on the mountain, where you won't have two chronographs, an anemometer and a calculator.

Estimating wind speed, like estimating range, takes practice. You

can't see wind, so you must learn to judge by feel and by watching how wind moves grasses, leaves and limbs. Disregard the clouds; even the tops of tall conifers show much more wind than will affect your bullet near the ground. A sensitive anemometer helps teach you to gauge wind speed. Watch the light vegetation nod, swing and flutter. Then take a reading. It's like using a rangefinder to teach your eye to judge distance.

Winds of less than 5 mph can feel strong if the day has been dead still. They'll feel much softer if they come as a lull during a hard blow. Most of the time, you can forget about wind

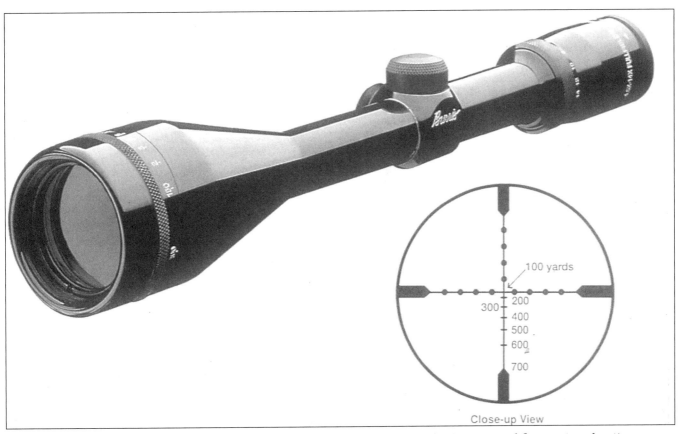

The Burris Ballistic Mil Dot helps you estimate range accurately. That's essential for precise shooting.

Having someone behind you with a binocular can confirm bullet strikes.

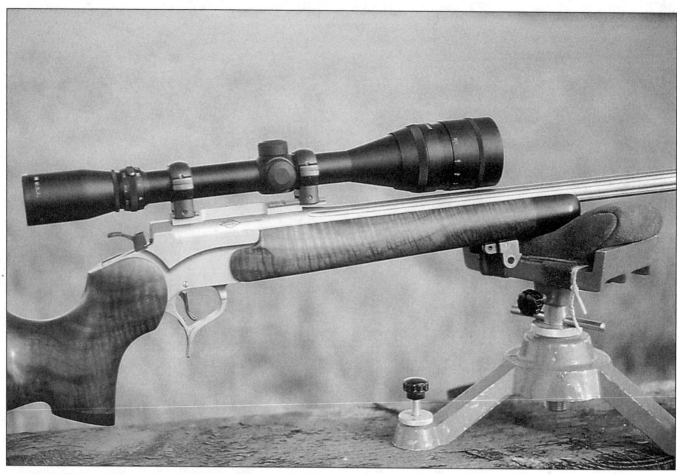

Virgin Valley Arms built this rifle on a T/C Encore action. It's a 7 STW with a Burris AO scope.

under 5 mph; only at very long range, and when your bullet cuts directly crosswind, will such a light breeze displace your shot enough to be a problem. A 5-mph wind will make grass nod and dislodges thistle down. A 10-mph wind blows leaves and unfurls flags. Those flags are flapping at 15 mph, and straightening out when the wind hits 20. You'll lean into a 25-mph wind, and squint. Unless the target is very close or the wind almost parallel to my sightline, I don't shoot in winds over 20 mph.

No matter the wind speed, pickups and letoffs are deadly. So are fluctuations in wind over distance. During rifle competition, I've often seen mid-range wind flags blowing the opposite direction from those near the targets. Sometimes one will sag while another snaps furiously in a gust. "Doping" these differences on a range is hard; in the mountains, where cliffs and canyons exaggerate thermal flows and trees and rocks boost wind speeds while they funnel the air across prevailing currents, you have a tough job indeed. The stronger the wind and the longer the range, the more effect these strange buffetings will have on your bullet.

Some will cancel each other. Others act cumulatively.

Most of us take great pains not to practice in wind. Wind makes groups bigger. It blows dust about the range and grabs the target off the frame. It wrestles with chronograph screens and rifles the notepad you're trying to write on. Wind is a close second to heavy rain as a pest. If your range has covered firing points, wind is worse.

Riflemen who try to avoid shooting in the wind don't shoot very well in the wind.

Chapter 13

Spotting Scopes, Accessories

"… So you don't have to walk so much."

A specialist's glass

A SPOTTING SCOPE has high magnification for long-distance viewing. Whether on the target range or on the hunt, it's best supported by a tripod. Magnification accentuates movement; even a giant image is hard to see well if it's bouncing around. High magnification also requires a big front (objective) glass, to deliver bright images in dim light. That big lens also delivers higher resolution than smaller glass, a more important factor in spotting scopes than in binoculars or riflescopes.

High resolution means that the lenses can keep separate tiny objects that appear blurred or joined when viewed through a smaller instrument or one of lesser quality. The naked human eye can distinguish about one minute of angle (60 seconds of arc, or roughly an inch at 100 yards). A fellow named Rayleigh came up with a constant that, divided by the objective lens diameter (again in mm) yields actual resolution in seconds of angle. The constant, 114.3, divided by 60mm (on a hunting-class spotting scope) yields a maxi-

A Utah hunter glasses for deer with a spotting scope. Small field, big magnification.

Spotting scopes give you detail binoculars can't and enable you to spot game where it's almost hidden.

mum resolution of 1.9. To find the highest power at which the eye can use this resolution, just divide 60 seconds of arc by 1.9 seconds of arc. Result: 31x. Beyond this, images will get bigger but not clearer. Larger front glass will boost both resolution and highest useful power, all else equal.

But all else is not equal. Scope lens quality and coatings vary. For spotting scopes as well as riflescopes and binoculars, you're smart to insist on fully (all air-to-glass surfaces) multi- (many layers) coated optics. You might also consider ED (extra-low dispersion) glass, which corrects for color fringing and gives you the sharpest possible image. ED lenses, which include fluorite glass, are available on top-quality full-size spotting scopes.

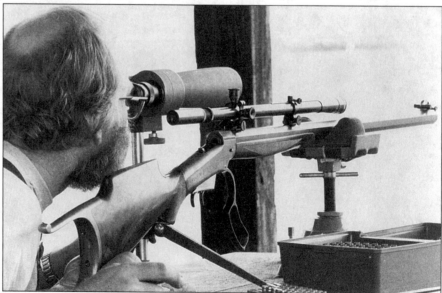

Shooting a blackpowder rifle at 200 yards, a marksman checks his target with a spotting scope.

Make/Model	Power/Obj. Dia. (in.)	Field (ft., 1000 yds.)	Length (in.)	Weight (oz.)	Price
Nikon Sky and Earth	20-60x80	99-50	16	53	$851
Bushnell Elite	20-60x80	98-50	17	53	$1,213
Fujinon Super 80 ED	20-60x80	102-60	19	49	$1,650

Prices and features of spotting scopes vary a great deal. Big objective lenses are costly, so you'll pay most for a full-size scope. But even in this narrow product field, you have a choice. For example, above are three very serviceable spotting scopes by reputable makers:

What are the differences? You'll have to find them yourself, by looking through the glass, as you would with a binocular or riflescope. And by reading specifications sheets. The ED objective of Fujinon's Super 80 boosts the price, of course. If you order ED glass on the best Nikon or B&L scope, count on that premium. Some features you'll want to pay for; others won't be of much benefit, and

you'll wisely save money by spending it elsewhere.

At the shooting range, your best bet is a scope of 30 to 40x, with a 75- to 80mm objective and an angled eyepiece so you can view a target without getting out of position. Hunting, you may want a lighter, more compact scope, with a 50- or 60mm objective and a straight eyepiece so you can sight down the scope to find game. As this is written, Swarovski is about to announce a 65mm scope of modest weight (and with a compact, removable sighting device) that should also appeal to hunters.

Variable power is an asset in spotting scopes. You pick up land-

marks with the wide field afforded by low power, then you zoom in. I hunted and guided for decades with a 25x Bushnell Spacemaster, which also saw service in rimfire competition. I like the scope a great deal, but a variable eyepiece would have put me onto game quicker and given me higher resolution in good conditions. Lately I've used Leupold's 12-40x variable. The low end helps on windy days, in thick mirage or poor light. The high end allows a close look at distant antlers. The 30mm rule applies, but sometimes bigger is better even after resolution tops out.

Here are my current picks for the "top 10" spotting scopes:

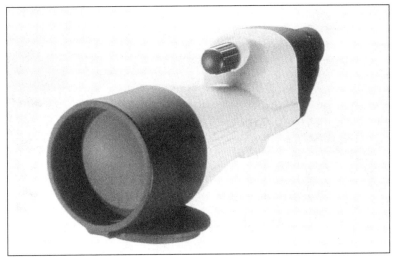

Nikon's affordable Sky and Earth Spotting scopes (shown) come in 60mm and 80mm sizes. The best-quality Fieldscope is available in 60mm and 78mm versions.

This trim B&L 60mm Elite scope with its Rainguard lens coating is a good choice for hunting in the mountains.

Full-size:	Bausch & Lomb 80mm Elite ED
	Fujinon Super 80 ED
	Leica Televid 77mm APO (like ED)
	Nikon 78mm Fieldscope ED
	Pentax PF-80ED
	Swarovski ST-80 HD (like ED)
Backpackers:	Bausch & Lomb Elite 70mm (at 40 ounces, 26 percent lighter than 80mm)
	Kowa 50mm (at 13 ounces, a real sweetheart, and optically fine)
	Leupold 60mm (36 ounces; a mirror mechanism keeps it short)
	Nikon 60mm Fieldscope (may be sharpest 60mm available)

This compact Bausch & Lomb spotting scope is a fine hunting glass, the long tripod handle an asset.

A smallbore shooter swallows the bitter news – and checks the mirage for the next stage.

Eyepiece selection (power and angle) is greatest with the full-size scopes. Other considerations: Will the eyepiece accept a camera adapter? (The Burris 60mm Signature and some others do.) How close will it focus? (Window birdfeeders can entertain you in winter.) Shop for low price. Read the warranties. In the 60mm class, compare scopes by Bushnell, Burris, Sightron, Swift and Weaver. You can buy scopes from these makers for less than $300 – scopes that may give you all the features and performance you need.

An occasional need for a spotting scope can also be filled by a powerful binocular like the 12x50 Pentax PCF, 12x50 Leica Trinovid, 12x50 Nikon SE or 15x56 Swarovski. The "doubler" available from Swarovski and the "tripler" from Zeiss give your binocular the reach of a spotting scope. Any binocular of 12x or higher should have a tripod adapter. You cannot hold a spotting scope or high-power binocular still enough for serious glassing without a tripod.

Optics accessories

Most talk about optics now is about what makes them expensive: lens quality, size and coatings, magnification, mechanical fit and special

Heavy 50mm binoculars like this Swarovski are best carried with an elastic harness.

features that let you focus and zoom, lock, illuminate, determine range and then adjust for it and tune out parallax. Beyond all that, however, are accessories, some of them very simple and inexpensive, that make optics more useful.

One of these items is a strap that makes a big binocular a smaller burden. As the magnification and objective lens size of binoculars have increased, narrow straps have become less comfortable. They'll do for occasional use, when you're toting the binocular on a pickup seat or in a pack. But if you hike the hills with your glass at the ready, you'll appreciate a wide strap. The strap needn't be wide its entire length. In fact, any extra width from the binocular to your neck is just useless weight and bulk. I've found a strap 1 1/2 inches wide in the middle 8 inches gives significant relief from the tug of stout binoculars over the course of a day afield.

Binocular and camera straps that stretch also ease the burden, though excessive stretch produces a disconcerting bounce. Some straps baby your neck with a thick, soft, foamy material that gives just enough to cushion the bounce and sway. Butler Creek Corp. (290 Arden Dr., Belgrade MT 59714, 406-388-1356) sells these straps, as well as other optics accessories that I've found useful. To try stretch suspension without springing for a commercial strap, splice surgical tubing into

your current strap where it attaches to the binocular.

Many hunters leave binocular straps too long. A long strap lets the instrument sway and jerk and bang against or hook on objects. In my view, a strap should be just long enough to allow the oculars an inch or two of clearance as they pass your chin and nose when you lift the glass. You can shorten most straps by cinching them up with double-pass fittings. Leather straps with tongue buckles warrant a few extra holes. I've simply tied an overhand knot in the center of narrow straps for a quick fix. It's wise to clip off or tape closed the loose ends of adjustable straps.

Another step toward better binocular control is a harness. Generally of nylon webbing with high-impact, quick-release buckles, a harness keeps the binocular close to your chest while taking the weight off the back of your neck. It enables you to carry a heavier binocular than you could manage with a traditional neck strap and limits the incidental movement of the instrument. Some models incorporate an ocular cover. One of the best I've seen is also one of the simplest: BinocSock (Antelope Trading Co., POB 317, Kaysville, UT 84037-0317, 801-723-1782) incorporates a soft cloth cover held gently on the binocular by an elastic band. A standard strap suspends the glass with help from the simple harness holding the cover. To use

A window mount enables you to glass for big game or watch birds conveniently from your pickup.

the binocular, you simply strip off the cover, which the harness then snugs to your chest. Because the harness is not attached directly to the binocular, it does not interfere when you're glassing.

R.C. Enterprises (508 Arch Bridge Road, Ghent, NY 12075, 518-672-5736) offers a sophisticated harness called the Bi-Tote. Though I've not used one in the field, it appears to be well designed. You can buy Swarovski's harness direct from the company (2 Slater Rd., Cranston, RI 02920, 800-426-3089).

One disadvantage of any harness is the minor inconvenience of removing it when you peel clothes or want to don a sweatshirt. Still, the increasing number of hunting-style binoculars with objectives of 50 to 60mm is reason enough to give harnesses a second look. You can't very well let a 3-pound glass dangle from your nape like a set of foam dice from the mirror of a '57 Thunderbird. After a few hours on the trail, your neck will feel like it's been all day in the jaws of a cattle chute.

Any binocular more powerful than, say, 12x, also needs a tripod. Here is where lots of money will *not* buy you more performance. The most expensive tripods are studio models too heavy and bulky for the field. For binocular and spotting scope use you'll want one of modest weight. Rigidity is a trade-off. The lever-lock legs are my choice (not the threaded-collar type). I can slide them in and out and secure them quickly without looking. Extended, tripod legs should put your line of vision above tall grass

An Alaskan guide looks for caribou with his Cabela's spotting scope.

A tripod is one accessory that makes every binocular more effective.

Leupold's 12-40x60 mirror-and-lens spotting scope is the firm's best.

and bushes. The stem must be substantial and have enough vertical range to permit you to stand erect (or, if you're tall, *almost* erect) to glass. The platform should pivot to let you take vertical photos with a camera or level your binocular quickly on uneven ground. It should have a quick-release plate so you can take your scope off in a hurry or switch scope and camera easily. Large knobs are an asset if you must turn them with cold or mittened hands. Beware small joints and parts that might come loose or drop off (some rubber "feet" slide off the legs easily and should be glued on before you go afield). Make sure there's an extension lock for the head. Such a tripod shouldn't cost over $70 or so – but don't play the Scrooge. You want the tripod to work properly and hold up under field conditions. Incidentally, color or plating doesn't matter; you'll spray-paint that tripod a drab tan or olive if you're taking it on a hunt.

You're smart to equip your tripod with a sling. A 1-inch nylon strap will do. The idea is to free your hands so you can carry a rifle or, if you're a birder, a binocular in your hand at the same time. If you hunt from a stand and carry your equipment only a short distance, you can stow your optics in a backpack and sling the tripod alone. You'll rig the sling differently for an empty tripod.

Another useful modification is the installation of rubber boots over the tripod feet. Boots quiet the metal feet on some tripods and prevent loss of rubber ends poorly affixed to the legs of inexpensive models. Simply fold a small square of inner tube around the leg tip and bolt it in place.

A friend has added versatility to his spotting scope by strapping a bench-rest sandbag to its top. He fills the bag with the foam "popcorn" used in shipping containers. The bag weighs almost nothing and serves as a rifle rest in open country, where sage or grass is too tall for a sitting position. All the shooter has to do is plant the tripod (or turn the scope at right angles if he's been using it) and crank the platform to the proper height. I've seen hunting clients use this rest and am convinced that in some cases, kills would not have been made without it. The disadvantage of using an *un*padded scope for a rest is that you must cushion the rifle with your left hand. So you cannot use that hand to steady the tripod in the wind or hold it upright on a steep hill when you haven't time to set it properly.

Before the days of rubber "armor," competitive shooters protected their spotting scopes by fitting them with fleece-lined jackets that zipped open at both ends conveniently but did not interfere with a tripod mount. Now few scopes come with jackets, and those without a rubber sheath are susceptible to damage on a hunt. Last fall, one of my amigos left his spotting scope on the top of my vehicle as we loaded an elk into it. Neither of us remembered the scope until we had driven 16 miles over rough roads. We backtracked and found the scope. The lenses were undamaged, but its focus ring had been dented when the scope sailed onto a roadside rock. Had this spotting scope been armored, it would have shown no bruises but may still have sustained damage to the focus ring, which is typically not padded. A jacket offers more protection.

A jacket should accommodate a tripod head. Leupold's variable 12-40x spotting scope is a lovely instrument, but the first jacket wasn't made to fit over a tripod. The

The Burris 15-45x60 Landmark spotting scope offers a reasonably sharp image at an affordable price.

Sheep hunters are well acquainted with spotting scopes, and prefer lightweight models!

eted with strips of tanned deerskin taped around shoulders and objective housings. The deerskin will cushion and muffle any bumps against rocks. It will protect the binocular and your rifle if the two bang into each other. The deerskin on my old Bausch & Lomb 7x35s is still supple after 30 years.

Binocular lens covers are a nuisance. When hunting, I leave the front caps off. That end is down so it can't catch rain or snow (front glass is still susceptible to dust – a hazard to tolerate if you want ready access to the bincular). The ocular caps stay in place. They catch all the weather and debris. I prefer one- piece ocular covers to individual caps. Swarovski supplies such a cover. It's slotted and slides up the neck strap when not in place so it can't be lost. I've taken a tip from a friend and slipped the strap off one side of the cover so it flops out of the way when I glass. If your binocular doesn't have a one-piece cover, you might try making one with a strip of hard rubber rimmed with duct tape folded against itself to form a cup.

Relatively few hunters keep lens covers on riflescopes when they're hunting. I seldom use them. But they're good protection for that valuable glass. The days of the leather caps are long gone, and most scope covers now are designed for quick removal. I like the simple see-through plastic caps you can wipe clean and leave in place for an urgent

jacket's zipper worked the wrong way, so you couldn't close it against a tripod either. That meant the jacket didn't get much use. Leupold's new scope jacket for the 12-40x is cleverly designed so it can stay on the scope even with tripod

attached. If the scope you're using has no jacket, it should have lens covers – which are worth tethering to the scope.

Rubber armor is an asset to spotting scopes and binoculars. Those without it can be protected and qui-

A shooting bag filled with plastic foam turns a spotting scope into a rifle rest.

Leupold's 12-40x spotting scope is shorter than most and a favorite of big game hunters.

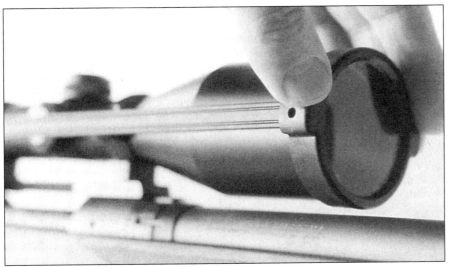

Scope caps protect the lenses and ensure that you'll get a sharp image when you aim.

Scope caps that stay attached to the sight don't always look good, but you won't lose them!

shot. Quake Industries (19 East Main, Belgrade, MT 59714, 406-388-3411) offers a see-through cap that's hinged to a rubber sleeve that fits over the scope bells. Flip-off disks attached by a common rubber band to the rifle barrel are also fast on the dismount. Spring-loaded lever-actuated caps are not my choice, though the few I've used have worked well enough. Be aware that ice and dust can make anything mechanical fail. Soft rubber caps with tabs you jerk against the tension of a rubber band that holds them to the scope tube make sense. The wide range of options should give you something you can live with, and testing alternatives is as easy as visiting a well-stocked gun shop.

Hunting big game, you may be on horseback, which means your binocular and rifle will be, too. You can get hurt on horses. So can your glass. The manner in which you carry your scabbard affects not only your rifle's security and your access to it, but the degree of protection you give your scope. Scabbard placement has generated lots of debate. Here's my view:

The scabbard, not the scope, should bear the weight of your rifle; it makes no sense to sheath the rifle horizontally upside down so it bounces on the scope's end housings at every hoofbeat. Neither does it seem wise to carry the rifle vertically; its weight wedges the scope's objective bell tighter and tighter against the restraining scabbard. Besides, an upright carry puts the buttstock above the saddle horn where, exposed, it can get whacked by limbs or snapped off if your horse takes a roll. A hood can deflect the

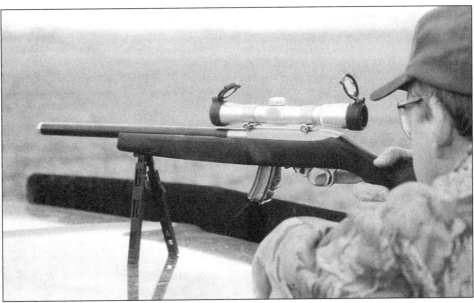

In general, a straight eyepiece is more useful for hunting, an angled eyepiece for target shooting.

branches, but it won't keep the wrist from yielding to 1,100 pounds.

Too, a long-barreled rifle can be hard to pull quickly from a vertical scabbard, especially after it has "settled" during a long ride. A rifle slung horizontally on the horse's right side is slow to reach because you dismount on the left, generally, and then must scurry around the beast. That leaves a horizontal left-side carry as the most sensible choice.

With a horizontal carry, you can point the muzzle fore or aft. I'll take the muzzle-forward option, the stock angled up to cantle-height in the rear. That way, brush sweeps easily along the scabbard without hanging up on it or the rifle. With the hood off, the scabbard mouth is less likely to catch debris than if it were facing forward. And the buttstock doesn't impair the horse's neck movement. Dismounting, I can grab the stock and pull the gun out to the rear very quickly. If the horse runs off, I still have my rifle.

Perhaps the most telling advantage of the left side-butt-to-rear horizontal carry is the protection it affords the scope. Your leg as well as the scabbard shields it from blows, and there's no rifle weight stressing the tube.

If you're using your own horses, you'll have had time aplenty to rig your scabbard to the saddle. But as a hunting client, you may have scant opportunity before opening morning. *Make* time the day before! Don't assume the outfitter's saddle

will accommodate your scabbard, or that his scabbard will accommodate your rifle! In fact, most scabbards provided by outfitters are poor protection for your rifle. They're either too big – in which case your rifle bounces around in them like a golf club – or they're so tight that you need a mallet to seat your gun and a jack to wrench it free.

Many fine saddle scabbards are available from commercial firms

now; and if you don't see any you like, you can have one fashioned to your specs by a competent saddlemaker. That's what I did. Gun fit is important, but so is scope fit. If you're partial to scopes with big objective bells, make certain the scabbard grips the bell snugly but doesn't clutch it in a rivet-popping embrace. Long, fat bells add leverage to any lateral force, and you can bend a scope by energetically shoving it into a tight scabbard.

Like rifles, binoculars need protecting in the field. Hard cases are better than soft, because they keep the hinge protected from stresses that can spring it. You'll wear your binocular while you hunt, whether afoot or on horseback. If you have an hour's ride in the dark to ridgetop, you may want to stow it. Saddlebags, the obvious place, can be easily overloaded. Horsemen sensitive to the limits of pack and saddle stock tell me that, while a horse or mule can tolerate great weight on its shoulders and forward spine, loading the kidney area is bad business. An SLR camera, plus a 7x50 binocular, plus a slicker, plus lunch, plus extra cartridges and film can be too much. Add a spotting scope and an assortment of camera lenses and you risk injury to the horse.

Some horses routinely bear up under burdens like this. But it's a good idea to keep rear-saddle loads to a minimum. Your outfitter may

Bushnell 18x-36x (50mm) Camo Sentry® Spotting Scope. Model No. 78-1519

Spotting scopes under the Bushnell and Bausch & Lomb names have earned a fine reputation among shooters.

A spotting scope can enable you to watch a prairie chicken perform its mating dance without disturbing the show.

well insist on it. Don't use saddlebag capacity as a gauge; those bags were made for sandwiches and clothes as well as cameras, binoculars and ammunition. Pickups can handle as much bark dust as you can pile in them, but you won't make friends filling a loaner truck to the rails with rock.

If you do put hard objects in saddlebags, pad them with extra clothes to protect both gear and horse. It's better to put heavy items in a daypack and wear it, leaving saddlebags for lunch and maps, then tying your slicker across the top. Be sure loaded bags are closely matched in weight and positioned the same on each side. Remember that, to a horse, a rider is a less onerous load than an equal measure of dead weight. That's because a rider can shift in the saddle, helping the horse maintain balance and momentum. Inert cargo bounces and tugs and slips at the behest of gravity and inertia, assisting the animal not at all while chafing and bruising its skin.

After a kill, your hands get bloodied, so the time to cap your binocular and scope is right after photos, before you even touch a knife. Slip the glasses back into their hard case and that into your pack so you won't dirty them later. Bloodstains quickly removed won't hurt binocular glass or optical housings, but you can avoid having to wash them or your camera gear by packing all these items away before tending to the carcass.

In camp, clean water spots or blood tarnish from lenses with a lens cloth dampened in warm water. Swab gently with a circular motion. To remove a light coating of dust, use an air bulb and camelhair brush. The

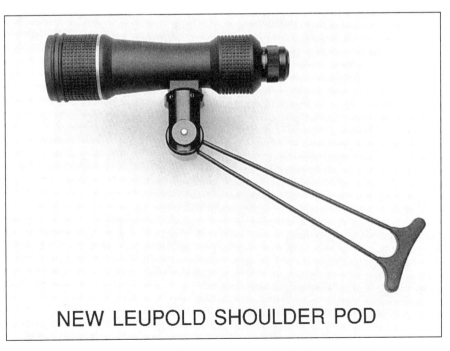

NEW LEUPOLD SHOULDER POD

One useful accouterment for hunters is a stock for a spotting scope. It's faster than a tripod.

bulb-brush combination is inexpensive and lightweight; you'll find it at camera stores. Soft lens cloths protected by a sealed pouch are inexpensive insurance for expensive optics. Carry one in the field, and use it instead of your shirtsleeve to wipe glass. As with cleaning rifle bores, over-zealous scrubbing does more harm than good.

Keep gun oil and bore solvent away from glass!

Babying your optics helps ensure that they'll perform as you expect them to when you need them.

Optics firms continue to spend many more development dollars on expensive internal changes and senseless cosmetic ones than on such mundane (but useful) accou-

terments as better lens caps and binocular straps. Generally, we get what we pay for. But we also pay for what isn't necessary to get, and some of the best ideas are still evident only in homemade accessories that manufacturers just don't want to bother with.

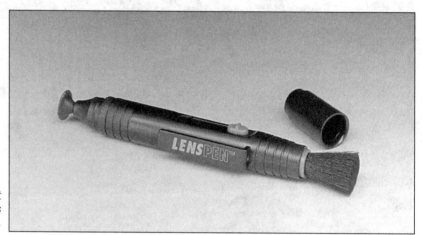

Clean lenses with a camelhair brush, not with your sleeve. This little Lens Pen is from Leupold.

Chapter 14

And Finally...

"...It's not what we see but what we remember."

Photographing your hunt

SOMETIMES HUNTING DOESN'T end in killing, and there's nothing left of a trip but memories. To save those, you can either write them in a diary or take photos. To share memories with others, you need the photos. Ironically, many hunters who spend profligately for trips, who travel far on precious vacation time, do nothing to ensure a photographic record of their exploits. Of those who take cameras, few know how to use them.

Photography used to be a complex mix of artistry and chemical wizardry, with enough mechanical devices to ensure that something would always break, stick or malfunction. Not so anymore. Great photos are available to anyone who can think about what he or she sees. While some cameras and lenses are frightfully expensive, the kind most useful on a hunt are bargains. A discerning eye is your key asset. You needn't be a technician or have an uncle on Nikon's board of directors to take outstanding photos. Here are some tips:

No. 1: Buy one moderately priced 35mm single-lens-reflex camera that accommodates high-quality lenses. You don't need automatic focusing or film advance. In fact, you'll have more flexibility with a camera that has no automatic features at all. Exposure set by the light meter may be what the light meter wants but not what you want. A timer is a useful feature, because if you're alone in the woods, you can set up the shot, then delay the shutter release with the timer until you can jump into the photo. The camera must have a tapped hole for a tripod screw. And you'll want to equip it with a wide neck strap.

A pocket camera with automatic everything and a zoom lens that pops in and out as if it had a will of its own will suffice as your backup, and the camera to carry when weight and bulk must be pared. With it, you can shoot mindlessly and get adequate photos. It is also easier to keep handy than is a full-size SLR, so you'll get photos that escape your conventional camera. Models with short zoom lenses, timers and built-in flashes are worth the extra money.

No. 2: For the SLR, buy one high-quality zoom lens with a range of about 35 to 70mm. A twist of the collar gives you several perspectives, so you can take a variety of shots without moving. A 55mm lens shows you the image you see with the naked eye; so the 35mm setting offers a wide-angle perspective, and the 70mm setting makes the zoom a short telephoto, bringing your subject closer.

Photograph little animals as well as big ones. And don't center them in the frame.

Photographing big game can hone your stalking skills in the off season. The author shot this photograph at the Oregon Coast.

You can buy bigger zooms, of course, but the 35-70 is about as compact as a standard 55mm lens and easy to stow, mounted, in your belt pack. Bigger zooms not only add weight and bulk, but they require use of a tripod. At high magnification, with slow shutter speeds, camera shake blurs photos.

The lens should have "macro" focusing so you can focus clearly on a subject just a few inches away.

This lets you show detail in flowers, cartridges, animal tracks and other small things.

Lenses are cataloged by maker, focal length and f-stop. The f-stop designates the widest aperture setting of which the lens is capable. The lower the f-stop, the wider the maximum aperture and the more costly the lens. You control the f-stop setting when you take a photo. If you want to double the amount of light coming to the film, you open the lens one f-stop or slow the shutter down a notch. Lower f-stops allow you to use faster shutter speeds to get the same amount of light through the lens. A fast shutter freezes movement – yours and your subject's. For most photography, you'll not need a lens with an extra-low f-stop (a costly "fast" lens).

No. 3: Try various films to find the one you like. Slide film is more versatile than print film because you can make prints from the slides but not slides from prints. Kodachrome 64 used to be an industry standard for outdoors photographers, but a lot of new slide films have appeared recently, and many have taken root. I'm still using Kodachrome 64. (The "64", incidentally, is the film's ASA rating, or speed. The higher the number, the faster the film and the less

A hunter approaching his kill is more interesting than a hunter grinning over it.

Use diagonal lines (mountains) undulating lines (the river) and variable lighting to direct the viewer's eye through the photo. Keep horizons out of the middle.

light needed to create your image. There's a price of course: fast film is "grainy" so when you enlarge the image, you lose sharpness. KR 64 is relatively slow.)

You may want to carry black-and-white print film too, for photos that beg to be shot in black-and-white. I like Kodak's Plus-X, ASA 125. Tri-X, the old standard for newsmen, is faster (ASA 400) but too grainy for smooth paper. When you specify a surface for your prints, choose glossy. Matte finishes compromise clarity.

Pack more film than you think you'll need. I carry a dozen 36-exposure rolls of KR-64 on a hunt.

No. 4: Carry an extra set of fresh camera batteries!

No. 5: When you're on the trail, in camp or hunting, keep an eye out for photographs. Candid shots of wranglers packing horses, the cook over a steaming kettle, a guide filling a lantern are seldom taken by hunters waiting for one cheesy shot of themselves behind a big set of antlers. But the best photos are those that capture not the dead animal, but the character of the people,

Warm light at dawn and dusk can make an ordinary shot dramatic.

When the sun vanishes, keep your camera out for "mood" shots.

ground. Front-lit rifles are among the hardest objects from which to draw detail while maintaining proper exposure.

Because light meters are set with an 18-percent gray card, you will have to help them in black timber or bright snow. Metering on your half-shadowed hand will give about the same reading as if you had a gray card. If you want to bring out shaded foreground detail and let a sunlit hillside in the background wash out, it's best to overexpose a stop or two from the light meter's reading. In snow, also, overexposing will enhance detail in a hunter while blanking some background contrast. Conversely, a well-lit subject surrounded by dark trees will be overexposed if you obey the meter.

It's a good idea to bracket your shots – take one photograph at the setting you think best, then shoot one stop higher and one lower. Some photographers bracket their brackets, at two f-stops above and below, exposing five frames to get one good photo. They claim that if a photo is worth taking, it's worth five shots.

If you want the silhouette of a subject against the evening sky, meter on the sky, then shoot at several stops above and below the recommended setting.

No. 7: Choose carefully your photo opportunities. You've probably seen hunters bounce along in the saddle, eyes glued to viewfinders while they swivel like machine-gunners to sweep

the mood of the expedition, the aura of the time and place.

No. 6: Remind yourself daily that you are not out to photograph objects but images, and images are created by light. The quality, direction and intensity of light determine how your photos will look. The best light is oblique; in fact, there's an old rule that tells photographers to cap their lenses between 10 AM and 2 PM each day because sunlight then is too direct. It dissolves shadows and contrast. It is colorless light. It shows all of everything, so the viewer may guess at nothing.

The "10-to-2 rule" doesn't always apply. If you shoot an exceptional deer at noon, you'll photograph it, rule or no rule. Northern late-season hunts can give you oblique light almost all day, while September sunlight in Arizona is dead well before 10 and after 2. Storms that rumble across the ridges in midday can make for interesting photos. A veiled sun cancels all rules having to do with sunlight.

Side-lighting and back-lighting add interest to photos and can create dramatic images. Strong, oblique

light is a must for shots of rifles because the reflection is what pops the blued metal out of the back-

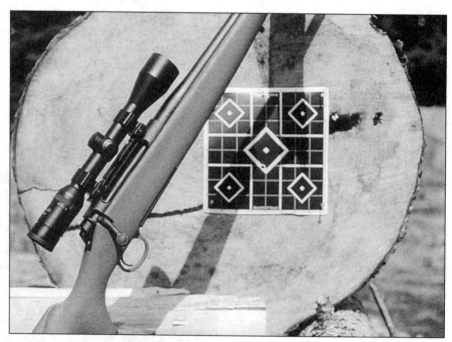

Even little things are worth a photo. Checking zero at camp? Arrange a still photo with rifle and target!

Keep people subordinate in the frame if you want to show country. Have them look where you want the viewer to look, and give them most of the space in the frame to look at.

their surroundings. They ratchet film through the camera while panning the back of the wrangler, his horse's tail, Forest Service signs, trailside trees and distant horizons in general. The results are worthless.

Pick your shot. Within reason, insist that you be allowed the time to make it good. Enlist the help of your companions to set up a shot. Ignore their laughter and impatience. Your guide is your

employee, and he can jolly-well wait for you to take a few photographs. He may complain that you're wasting hunting time. You can reply that photographs are important to you, and that you'll

Scenics can be boring; people make even a brown woods come alive. Use the rule of three to put your subject a third of the way from a corner.

the photograph, so in composing the shot, you must "get into the lens." The photo should tell a story by itself, drawing the viewer's eye as yours was drawn by the photo opportunity.

Mentally divide the field into thirds, vertically and horizontally. Where vertical and horizontal lines cross are good places for the focal point of your photo. Except in unusual circumstances, don't put the main object in the photo center. It stops the viewer's eye. Moving it out of center leads the eye into the field and gives you room to direct it through the center.

Don't allow a prominent tree-trunk or strong horizon line to bisect the field; either will divide the image, confuse the viewer. Winding trails or ridgelines, a diagonal dead-fall and other natural features effectively guide the viewer's eye. Look for them! Those scenic shots of New England fall foliage often feature a road or a stream along which your eye can journey through the photo.

People and animals should be looking or moving into the field. That is, there should be less space behind a subject than in front. The viewer naturally looks in the same direction, and you want him to see more of your photo.

Use foliage, fencelines and other strong foreground images to frame the subject. They help direct the

You'll want to remember what you used on a hunt. A photo is proof!

decide when they justify a delay. On the other hand, don't hold the guide responsible for your delays, or the disturbance that a setup might cause. If he thinks you're risking a chance at game with your tomfoolery, it behooves you to consider that he may be right.

It's tempting to try to photograph live game, but it's usually a waste of time unless you have at least a 200mm telephoto lens and a tripod. Calendar-quality wildlife photos require professional skills, many hours afield and bags of film. My efforts to combine hunting and wild-life photography have failed. Each is a full-time job. Photographing a hunt is worthwhile; chasing the game must be done with only one object in mind.

No. 8: Compose carefully. Good photos demand rudimentary skills with a camera but mastery of the art of seeing. Remember that you will not be on the mountain when you look at

Low light made for a slow shutter and a blurry shot of the author's first Swedish moose. A lightweight tripod can be worth packing, especially for other people taking your picture!

eye, especially when your subject is a distant mountain or lake. People in the foreground of scenic photos can serve the same purpose. A hunter glassing away from the camera pulls the viewer's eye along his line of sight. So too a packer checking a cinch, a guide chopping wood can tell the story of trail and camp. The idea is to show activity, not things. Perhaps one frame in a hundred is worth wasting on a person looking directly at the camera. Or one in two hundred.

No. 9: Pay attention to details. Many otherwise good photos have been scrapped because the edge of a finger or lens shade appeared in the field, or a distracting piece of gear left in the foreground escaped the photographer's eye. In the woods, twigs can be real nuisances. Depth of field increases when you shoot at high f-stops (small apertures). That means foreground and background will both be in sharp focus. Good; you won't have to fiddle so much with the focusing ring. But a deep field also means branches behind a dead animal or a grinning guide can turn up as odd growths protruding from their heads. Be aware of this hazard. Remove all offending twigs, change your position or

Photograph people doing things, not looking at the camera.

To highlight an object in a photo, as the author did here with the red-dot sight, manipulate background and reflection until you get what you want.

shove the background out of focus with lower f-stops.

While clean, perfectly exposed photos are good photos, those masterpieces that win contests and make magazine covers show more than technical competence. They reflect imagination. So use your eyes! Be alert to interesting, sometimes transitory features that can make a photo special: a shaft of light through the trees, the snow-laden chokecherry that might form the perfect backdrop for a hunter examining whitetail tracks. Try photographing from ground level, from the sit, from a tall stump. Changes in perspective can make ho-hum photos compelling!

No. 10: Use a tripod whenever possible. A costly studio tripod is neither necessary nor practical afield. You can get a serviceable model from a discount store for $40 to $60. My lightweight tripod goes along when I'm packing in with horses and doubles as a support for my spotting scope when I'm guiding hunters.

No. 11: Before photographing dead animals, take whatever time is necessary to "set them up." That means removing all blood, maybe dragging them to a clean spot or a place that will provide a more flattering view of the country or the animal. Close the mouth. If the tongue insists on popping out, cut

Clean, tasteful trophy photos, especially under oblique light, are delightful reminders of a hunt.

it off. Don't do any other cutting on the animal before you photograph it! The meat won't spoil in an hour, which is about how long it takes me to set up and photograph when I'm alone.

Take a few shots of the animal by itself, in a relaxed but dignified pose, with your rifle leaning against its shoulder or antlers. Then use the camera's timer to delay shutter action until you're in the frame.

Stay behind the animal, and look at it, not at the camera – at least for most of the shots. Pose with your rifle at ready as if you were walking up, having just shot. Don't kneel on or straddle the animal unless when you pose for a family portrait you kneel on or straddle your spouse.

Photograph the animal from several angles and at several lens and f-stop settings. If it is antlered game, keep the antlers in the foreground. Should another person be with you, have him take some photos, too. But unless he is an accomplished photographer, do most of the work yourself, even if it consumes more time. I've learned the hard way that most people have never thought about what constitutes a good photograph – and that no matter what I say, all I can expect is that they'll match pins in the light meter and release the shutter.

No. 12: Protect your camera and lenses during a pack trip with a hard, watertight case like the Pelican that I use. A camera slung from your shoulder makes for quick trailside shooting, but can become a hazard if the horse throws you or rolls on you. A friend of mine spent a painful three days in the woods after his horse dumped him in a creek. He landed on his camera and broke a couple of ribs.

I often wrap my camera in a stocking cap and stow it in my daypack or fanny pack. When rain comes, I slip the camera in a large Zip-loc bag.

Like the lenses in expensive riflescopes and binoculars, your camera's glass should be kept clean and dry. A hinged Butler Creek lens cap is the first line of defense, to replace that detachable factory cap you will lose before your first campfire. Buy a packet of lens tissues and a brush with an airbulb to dust your lenses.

Photographs add a dimension to hunting – during and after the trip. Elementary gear and an artist's eye can make your photos the envy of your campmates. They'll also preserve a hunt like no mount or memory can.

Sidelight, a clean background and a solid orange shirt can improve any photo.

Diligent glassing may show you something like this pair of coyote pups. You'll have to stalk close for a shot like this, however.

Photo by J. R. Hunter

BINOCULARS

Brunton Model 4008PW
10x42mm Eterna

Brunton Model 4022PW
8x25mm Eterna compact

Brunton Model 5027
8x25mm Lite-Tech compact

Brunton Model 5030W
10x42mm Lite-Tech mid-size

Brunton
Model 5029W
8x32mm Lite-Tech
mid-size

BRUNTON

Featuring phase coating on the roof prism to improve image contrast and reduce internal glare. Opti Visor™ combines lens covers and adjustable eye cups that rotate 360 degrees. Constructed with an aluminum frame, they are rubber-armored and filled with nitrogen making them fog, dust and waterproof.

ETERNA

4006PW 7x42

7x magnification, 42mm objective diameter, 6mm exit pupil diameter. Field of view @1000 yds. 416 ft. Minimum focus 5 ft. Eye relief 20mm. Weight 30 oz.
Price:. $444.00

4008 PW 10x4

10x magnification, 42mm objective diameter, 4.2mm exit pupil diameter. Field of view @1000 yds. 338 ft. Minimum focus 6 ft. Eye relief 18mm. Weight 30 oz.
Price:. $444.00

4009PW 12x42

12x magnification, 42mm objective diameter, 3.5mm exit pupil. Field of view @1000 yds. 271 ft. Minimum focus 10 ft. Eye relief 18mm. Weight 30 oz.
Price:. $449.00

4022PW 8x25

8x magnification, 25mm objective diameter, 3.1mm exit pupil diameter. Field of view @1000 yds. 270 ft. Minimum focus 6 ft. Eye relief 18.5mm. Weight 12 oz.
Price:. $229.00

4024PW 10x25

10x magnification, 25mm objective diameter, 2.5mm exit pupil diameter. Field of view @1000 yds. 260 ft. Minimum focus 8 ft. Eye relief 17mm. Weight 12 oz.
Price:. $229.00

LITE-TECH™

Available in mid-size and compact models, the value-priced line contains features such as Emerald Fire™ coating to yield 99.6% filtration of UV and IR rays.

5029W 8x32

8x magnification, 32mm objective diameter, 4mm exit pupil diameter. Field of view @1000 yds. 392 ft. Eye relief 10mm. Dimensions 5.25" x 5" x 2". Weight 20 oz.
Price:. $219.00

5030W 10x42

10x magnification, 42mm objective diameter, 4.2 mm exit pupil diameter. Field of view @1000 yds. 314 ft. Eye relief 10mm. Dimensions 6.13" x 5" x 2". Weight 24.5 oz.
Price:. $229.00

5027 8x25

8x magnification, 25mm objective diameter, 3.1mm exit pupil. Field of view @1000 yds. 429 ft. Eye relief 9.8mm. Dimensions 4.5" x 5.2" x 1.6". Weight 12 oz.
Price:. $99.00

5028 10x25

10x magnification, 25mm objective diameter, 2.5mm exit pupil. Field of view @1000 yds. 325 ft. Eye relief 8.8mm. Dimensions 4.5" x 5.2" 1.6". Weight 12 oz.
Price:. $99.00

*Burris Fullfield
8x40mm*

Burris Landmark Rf binoculars

*Burris Landmark Pf
porro prism binoculars*

*Burris Fullfield
10x50mm*

Burris Pocket Compact 8x26mm

Burris Pocket Compact 10x25mm

BURRIS

Available in Fullfield, Landmark Rf (roof prism) and Landmark Pf (poro prism) models, as well as two compact offerings. Fullfields have fully-multicoated optics, BaK 4 porro prisms, focus lock, click-stop right eye dioptic adjustment, are tripod adaptable and come with lens covers, neck strap and carry case. The Landmark Rf series are fully waterproof and fogproof, contain HiLume lens multicoating, twist-up eyecups, rubber armor coating, and a compass mounted on the focus wheel. The Landmark PF binoculars have fully-coated optics, are water resistant, and come with a neck strap and carry case. The Compact 10x25 model has multicoated lenses, BaK 4 prisms, are water resistant and come with lens covers, neck strap and carry case. The Pocket Compact 8x26mm has 100% multicoated lenses, BaK 4 prisms, waterproof, fogproof and nitrogen filled construction, and a rubber armor coating.

FULLFIELD 8x40

8x magnification, 40mm objective diameter, 5mm exit pupil diameter. Field of view @1000 yds. 430 ft. Minimum focus 13 ft. Eye relief 1 inch. Length 5.9 ins. Weight 31 oz.
Price:. $396.00

FULLFIELD 10x50

10x magnification, 50mm objective diameter, 5mm exit pupil diameter. Field of view @1000 yds. 334 ft. Minimum focus 25 ft. Eye relief 1 inch. Length 7.4 ins. Weight 35 oz.
Price:. $735.00

LANDMARK Rf 8x42

8x magnification, 42mm objective diameter, 5.1mm exit pupil diameter. Field of view @1000 yds. 356 ft. Mini-

mum focus 20 ft. Eye relief .75 inch. Length 6.7 ins. Weight 29 oz.
Price: $189.00

LANDMARK Rf 10x42

10x magnification, 42mm objective diameter, 4.2mm exit pupil diameter. Field of view @1000 yds. 284 ft. Minimum focus 20 ft. Eye relief .7 inch. Length 6.7 ins. Weight 29 oz.
Price: $214.00

LANDMARK Pf 8x42

8x magnification, 42mm objective diameter, 5.25mm exit pupil diameter. Field of view @ 1000 yds. 340 ft. Minimum focus 20 ft. Eye relief .7 inch. Length 5.9 ins. Weight 24 oz.
Price: $123.00

LANDMARK Pf 10x42

10x magnification, 42mm objective diameter, 4.2mm exit pupil diameter. Field of view @1000 yds. 288 ft. Minimum focus 21 ft. Eye relief .6 inch. Length 5.9 ins. Weight 24 oz.
Price: $136.00

COMPACT 8x26

8x magnification, 26mm objective diameter, 3.25mm exit pupil diameter. Field of view @1000 yds. 315 ft. Minimum focus 7 ft. Eye relief .7 inch. Length 5 ins. Weight 11.4 oz.
Price: $133.00

COMPACT 10x25

10x magnification, 25mm objective diameter, 2.5mm exit pupil diameter. Field of view @1000 yds. 262 ft. Minimum focus 7 ft. Eye relief .7 inch. Length 4.1 ins. Weight 9.5 oz.
Price: $269.00

Burris Signature 8x42mm

Burris Signature 10x50mm

Bushnell Trophy 8x25mm

Bushnell Trophy 10x25mm

Bushnell Trophy 8x42mm

Burris, continued

SIGNATURE SERIES

Distinguished by total waterproof construction, nitrogen-filling, multicoated lenses, and phase correction coatings on the roof prisms. Other appointments are right eye click-stop dioptic adjustment, focus lock system, tripod adaptability, rubber armor coating, lens covers, neck strap, nylon carry241ing case and shoulder strap.

8x42

8x magnification, 42mm objective diameter, 5.25mm exit pupil diameter. Field of view @1000 yds. 328 ft. Minimum focus 4.5 ft. Eye relief 1 inch. Length 6 ins. Weight 24 oz.
Price:. $684.00

10x50

10x magnification, 50mm objective diameter, 5mm exit pupil diameter. Field of view @1000 yds. 262 ft. Minimum focus 7.5 ft. Eye relief 1 inch. Length 7 ins. Weight 28 oz.
Price:. $735.00

12x50

12x magnification, 50mm objective diameter, 4.2mm exit pupil diameter. Field of view @1000 yds. 209 ft. Minimum focus 8 ft. Eye relief .71 inch. Length 7 ins. Weight 28 oz.
Price:. $864.00

BUSHNELL

Featuring waterproof/fogproof construction, rubber armoring, folding roof prism with BK-7 prism glass, center focus and high contrast amber fully-coated lenses.

TROPHY 23-0825

8x magnification, 25mm objective diameter, 3.1mm exit pupil diameter. Field of view @1000 yds. 420 ft. Minimum focus 12 ft. Eye relief 11mm. Weight 11 oz.
Price: $79.99

TROPHY 23-1025

10x magnification, 25mm objective diameter, 2.5mm exit pupil diameter. Field of view @1000 yds. 330 ft. Minimum focus 16 ft. Eye relief 11mm. Weight 11 oz.
Price: $84.99

TROPHY 23-0842

8x magnification, 42mm objective diameter, 5.2mm exit pupil diameter. Field of view @1000 yds. 390 ft. Minimum focus 15 ft. Eye relief 17mm. Weight 21 oz.
Price: $179.99

TROPHY 23-1042

10x magnification, 42mm objective diameter, 4.2mm exit pupil diameter. Field of view @1000 yds. 305 ft. Minimum focus 17 ft. Eye relief 21mm. Weight 23 oz.
Price: $199.99

Bushnell Trophy 10x42mm

Bushnell Elite 8x42mm

Bushnell Elite 12x50mm

Bushnell Elite 10x42mm

*Bushnell Legend Model
13-2590 9x25mm*

*Bushnell Legend Model
13-3208 8x32mm*

Bushnell, continued

ELITE

Featuring RainGuard coating to reduce external fogging, the series contains roof prisms, center focusing system, is armored, and is fogproof and waterproof inside and out.

62-0842

8x magnification, 42mm objective diameter, 5.25mm exit pupil diameter. Field of view @1000 yds. 365 ft. Minimum focus 5 ft. Eye relief 19.5mm. Weight 29 oz.
Price:............................ $1524.00

62-1250

12x magnification, 50mm objective diameter, 4.2mm exit pupil diameter. Field of view @1000 yds. 250 ft. Minimum focus 13 ft. Eye relief 15mm. Weight 33.5 oz.
Price:............................ $1639.00

62-4210

10x magnification, 42mm objective diameter, 4.2mm exit pupil diameter. Field of view @1000 yds. 300 ft. Minimum focus 5 ft. Eye relief 19.5mm. Weight 28 oz.
Price:............................ $1570.00

LEGEND

With RainGuard external lens coating, BaK-4 roof prism, and PC-3® phase correction coating.

13-2590

9x magnification, 25mm objective diameter, 2.8mm exit pupil diameter. Field of view @1000 yds. 280 ft. Minimum focus 6 ft. Eye relief 19mm. Weight 15.4 oz.
Price:............................ $219.99

13-3208

8x magnification, 32mm objective diameter, 4mm exit pupil diameter. Field of view @1000 yds. 396 ft. Minimum focus 6 ft. Eye relief 16mm. Weight 23.8 oz.
Price:............................ $315.99

13-4208

8x magnification, 42mm objective diameter, 5.25mm exit pupil diameter. Field of view @1000 yds. 330 ft. Minimum focus 6 ft. Eye relief 18mm. Weight 28.7 oz.
Price:............................ $349.99

13-0142

10x magnification, 42mm objective diameter, 4.2mm exit pupil diameter. Field of view @1000 yds. 315 ft. Minimum focus 6 ft. Eye relief 15mm. Weight 29.1 oz.
Price:............................ $369.99

Bushnell Legend Model 13-4208 8x42mm

*Bushnell PowerView
Model 13-9025 8x25mm*

Bushnell PowerView Zoom 7-15x25mm

*Kahles 8x32mm
binocular*

Bushnell, continued

POWERVIEW

Featuring a center focus system, a carrying case and neckstrap are included.

13-9825

8x magnification, 25mm objective diameter, poro prism system, 3.1mm exit pupil diameter. Field of view @1000 yds. 340 ft. Minimum focus 6 ft. Eye relief 12mm. Weight 9.1 oz.
Price:................................. $52.95

13-9025

10x magnification, 25mm objective diameter, poro prism system, 2.5mm exit pupil diameter. Field of view @1000 yds. 262 ft. Minimum focus 9 ft. Eye relief 11mm. Weight 9.1 oz.
Price:................................. $59.95

13-9225

12x magnification, 25mm objective diameter, poro prism system, 2.1mm exit pupil diameter. Field of view @1000 yds. 235 ft. Minimum focus 10 ft. Eye relief 10mm. Weight 10 oz.
Price:................................. $65.95

13-9755

7-15x (zoom) magnification, 25mm objective diameter, poro prism system, 3.1 @8x, 1.6 @15x exit pupil diameter. Field of view @1000 yds. 262/183 ft. Minimum focus 3.5 ft. @7x, 1.6 ft. @15x. Eye relief 12mm. Weight 11 oz.
Price:................................. $72.95

13-0832

8x magnification, 32mm objective diameter, roof prism system, 4mm exit pupil diameter. Field of view @1000 yds. 330 ft. Minimum focus 15 ft. Eye relief 10mm. Weight 12.5 oz.
Price:................................. $33.95

13-1032

10x magnification, 32mm objective diameter, roof prism system, 3.2mm exit pupil diameter. Field of view @1000 yds. 265 ft. Minimum focus 25 ft. Eye relief 12mm. Weight 12.5 oz.
Price:................................. $40.95

13-1232

12x magnification, 32mm objective diameter, roof prism system, 2.6mm exit pupil diameter. Field of view @1000 yds. 240 ft. Minimum focus 35 ft. Eye relief 12mm. Weight 12.5 oz.
Price:................................. $47.95

KAHLES

8x32

8x magnification, 32mm objective diameter, 4mm exit pupil. Field of view @1000 yds. 399 ft. Eye relief 16mm. Minimum focus 4.95 ft. Length 4.72 ins. Width 4.52 ins. Height 2.36 ins. Weight 21.5 oz.
Price:................................. $610.00

8x42

8x magnification, 42mm objective diameter, 5.3mm exit pupil diameter. Field of view @1000 yds. 330 ft. Eye relief 18mm. Minimum focus 8 ft. Length 5.6 ins. Width 4.71 ins. Height 2.36 ins. Weight 26 oz.
Price:............. $721.00; camo model $771.00

Kahles 8x42mm and 10x42mm binoculars are available in the Advantage® Timber™ camouflage pattern and are supplied with a floatable camouflage case

Kahles 8x42mm and 10x42mm binoculars

Leica 10x32mm

Leica 7x42mm BN

Leica 8x42mm BN

Kahles, continued

10x42

10x magnification, 42mm objective diameter, 4.2mm exit pupil diameter. Field of view @1000 yds. 315 ft. Eye relief 15.5mm. Minimum focus 7 ft. Length 5 ins. Width 4.7 ins. Height 2.36 ins. Weight 26 oz.
Price:. . . . . $772.00; camo model $822.00

LEICA

Features include High Durability Coating to increase lens durability and increased near focus distance (designated by the "BN" in the model name). All Ultra-Trovid models are waterproof to 16.4 ft.

ULTRA TRINOVID 8x32 BN

8x magnification, 32mm objective diameter, 4mm exit pupil diameter. Field of view @1000 yds. 405 ft. Eye relief 13.3mm. Minimum focus 7.2 ft. Weight 22 oz.
Price:. $995.00

ULTRA TRINOVID 10x32 BN

10x magnification, 32mm objective diameter, 3.2mm exit pupil diameter. Field of view @1000 yds. 360 ft. Eye relief 13.5mm. Minimum focus 6.9 ft. Weight 23.3 oz.
Price: $1045.00

ULTRA TRINOVID 7x42 BN

7x magnification, 42mm objective diameter, 6mm exit pupil diameter. Field of view @1000 yds. 420 ft. Eye relief 17mm. Minimum focus 10.8 ft. Available in black, blue and green finishes. Weight 31.4 oz.
Price: $995.00

ULTRA TRINOVID 8x42 BN

8x magnification, 42mm objective diameter, 5.25mm exit pupil diameter. Field of view @1000 yds. 390 ft. Eye relief 15.9mm. Minimum focus 10.2 ft. Available in black or green. Weight 31.4 oz.
Price: $1045.00

Leica 8x50mm

Leica 10x50mm

Leica 12x50mm

Leica 8x20mm binocular

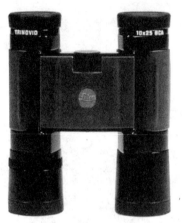

Leica 7x42mm BN

Leica, continued

ULTRA TRINOVID 10x42 BN

10x magnification, 42mm objective diameter, 4.2mm exit pupil diameter. Field of view @1000 yds. 330 ft. Eye relief 13.9mm. Minimum focus 9.7 ft. Weight 31.4 oz.
Price:. $1095.00

ULTRA TRINOVID 8x50 BN

8x magnification, 50mm objective diameter, 6.25mm exit pupil diameter. Field of view @1000 yds. 345 ft. Eye relief 18.1mm. Minimum focus 11.8 ft. Weight 40.6 oz.
Price:. $1145.00

ULTRA TRINOVID 10x50 BN

10x magnification, 50mm objective diameter, 5mm exit pupil diameter. Field of view @1000 yds. 345 ft. Eye relief 14.6mm. Minimum focus 11 ft. Weight 40.6 oz.
Price:. $1195.00

ULTRA TRINOVID 12x50 BN

12x magnification, 50mm objective diameter, 4.17mm exit pupil diameter. Field of view @1000 yds. 328 ft. Eye relief 13.2mm. Minimum focus 10.7 ft. Weight 40.6 oz.
Price:. $1345.00

TRINOVID COMPACT 8x20 BC, BCA & BT

8x magnification, 20mm objective diameter, 2.5mm exit pupil diameter. Field of view @1000 yds. 345 ft. Eye relief 13.9mm. Minimum focus 9.8 ft. Available in BCA (black or green armor), BC (black leather), and BT (black leather & titanium finish) model variations. Weight (BC) 7.9 oz. (BCA) 8.3 oz.
Price: . . . . . .BCA $399.00; BC $379.00; BT $429.00

TRINOVID 10x25 BC & BCA

10x magnification. 25mm objective diameter, 2.5mm exit pupil diameter. Field of view @1000 yds. 285 ft. Eye relief 13.7mm. Minimum focus 16.4 ft. Available in a choice of BCA (black or green armor) and BC (black leather). Weight (BC) 8.6 oz. (BCA) 9 oz.
Price: . . . . BCA $429.00; BC $399.00

LEUPOLD & STEVENS

WIND RIVER ROOF PRISM MODELS

8x25mm COMPACT

8x magnification, 25mm objective diameter, 3.1mm exit pupil diameter. Field of view @100 yds. 27.3 ft. Minimum focus 8.2 ft. Eye relief 18.5mm. Length 4.8 ins. Weight 14.1 oz.
Price: $350.00

Leupold WR 8x25mm and 10x25mm CF Compact roof prism binoculars

Leupold WR 8x23mm and 10x23mm CF inverted porro prism binoculars

Leupold WR 8x42mm and 10x42mm CF roof prism binoculars

Leupold WR 8x42mm and 10x50mm CF porro prism binoculars

Leupold, continued

10x25mm COMPACT
10x magnification, 25mm objective diameter, 2.5mm exit pupil diameter. Field of view @100 yds. 26.3 ft. Minimum focus 10 ft. Eye relief 17.5mm. Length 4.8 ins. Weight 14.1 oz.
Price:. $367.90

8x42mm
8x magnification, 42mm objective diameter, 5.2mm exit pupil diameter. Field of view @100 yds. 34.1 ft. Minimum focus 10 ft. Eye relief 19mm. Length 5.5 ins. Weight 22.4 oz.
Price:. $394.60

10x42mm
8x magnification, 42mm objective diameter, 4.2mm exit pupil diameter. Field of view @100 yds. 26.8 ft. Minimum focus 10 ft. Eye relief 18mm. Length 5.5 ins. Weight 22.9 oz.
Price:. $450.00

8x32mm
8x magnification, 32mm objective diameter, 4mm exit pupil diameter. Field of view @100 yds. 32.8 ft. Minimum focus 10 ft. Eye relief 18.5mm. Length 5 ins. Weight 19.9 oz.
Price:. $562.50

10x42mm
10x magnification, 42mm objective diameter, 4.2mm exit pupil diameter. Field of view @100 yds. 26.2 ft. Minimum focus 10 ft. Eye relief 15.5mm. Length 5.9 ins. Weight 24.6 oz.
Price:. $450.00

WIND RIVER PORRO PRISM MODELS

8x23mm INVERTED PORRO
8x magnification, 23mm objective diameter, 2.9mm exit pupil diameter. Field of view @100 yds. 33.6 ft. Minimum focus 10 ft. Eye relief 11mm. Length 4.2 ins. Weight 12.7 oz.
Price:. $194.60

10x23mm INVERTED PORRO
10x magnification, 23mm objective diameter, 2.3mm exit pupil. Field of view @100 yds. 26.2 ft. Minimum focus 10 ft. Eye relief 11mm. Length 4.2 ins. Weight 12.8 oz.
Price: $232.10

8x42mm
8x magnification, 42mm objective diameter, 5mm exit pupil diameter. Field of view @100 yds. 34.1 ft. Minimum focus 16.4 ft. Eye relief 18mm. Length 5.2 ins. Weight 26.4 oz.
Price: $312.50

10x50mm
10x magnification, 50mm objective diameter, 5.5mm exit pupil diameter. Field of view @100 yds. 29 ft. Minimum focus 30 ft. Eye relief 18mm. Length 6.5 ins. Weight 32.3 oz.
Price: $355.40

GOLDEN RING BINOCULARS

9x25mm ROOF PRISM
9x magnification, 25mm objective diameter, 2.8mm exit pupil diameter. Field of view @100 yds. 27.8 ft. Eye relief 14mm. Length 4 ins. Weight 10.1 oz.
Price: $710.70

*Leupold & Stevens GR
9x25mm Compact Rf binoculars*

*Leupold GR 10x28mm
Compact Rf binoculars*

*Minox 10x58mm
ED binoculars*

Minox 15x58mm ED BR binoculars

*Minox 8x32mm BR
and 10x42mm BR binoculars*

Leupold, continued

10x28mm ROOF PRISM
10x magnification, 28mm objective diameter, 2.8mm exit pupil diameter. Field of view @100 yds. 25.1 ft. Eye relief 14mm. Length 5 ins. Weight 10.9 oz.

Price:................................. **$753.60**

▌MINOX▐

10x58 ED (extra-low dispersion)
10x magnification, 58mm objective diameter. 5.8mm exit pupil diameter. Field of view @1000 yds. 325 ft. Eye relief 19mm. Minimum focus 4.9m. Weight 1490g. Contains fluoride glass and apochromatic color correction. Nitrogen purged and waterproof to nearly three fathoms.

Price:................................. **$999.00**

15x58 ED BR
15x magnification, 58mm objective diameter. Exit pupil diameter 5.8mm. Eye relief 16mm. Minimum focus 4.9m. Weight 1490g. Phase-corrected roof prisms are contained within a nitrogen-charged macrolon body. Dustproof and waterproof to 16 ft., it is furnished with neck strap, rain guard, objective caps and carry case. A tripod adapter is optional.

Price:................................. **$1,099.00**

8x32 BR
8x magnification, 32mm objective diameter. Incorporating aspheric lens technology and nitrogen charged rubber-armored aluminum housing. Neck strap and leather case included.

Price:................................. **$439.00**

10x42 BR
10x magnification, 42mm objective diameter. Features include Aspheric lens technology, rubber-armored aluminum housing and dust and waterproof to 16 ft. Furnished with neck strap and leather case.

Price:................................. **$549.00**

Nikon Monarch ATB is available in 8x42mm and 10x42mm models

Nikon Sportstar III available in 8x25mm and 10x25mm

Nikon Sporter 1 available in 8x36mm and 10x36mm

Nikon 10-22x50mm Action Zoom XL

Nikon Travelite V 8-24x25mm Zoom

Nikon 7-15x35mm Action Zoom

NIKON

MONARCH ATB

Newly redesigned roof prism line incorporates phase correction coatings and Eco-Glass (made without the use of arsenic or lead).

8x42

8x magnification, 42mm objective diameter, 5.3mm exit pupil diameter. Field of view @1000 yds. 315 ft. Minimum focus 8 ft. Height 5.7 ins. Weight 21.3 oz.
Price:.................................. $289.99

10x42

10x magnification, 42mm objective diameter, 4.2mm exit pupil diameter. Field of view @1000 yds. 330 ft. Minimum focus 8 ft. Height 5.6 ins. Weight 21.2 oz.
Price:.................................. $299.99

VENTURER LX

A new BaK-4 roof prism design with multicoated neses, Eco-Glass, and central focus control.

8x32

8x magnification, 32mm objective diameter. Field of view @1000 yds. 450 ft. Eye relief 16mm. Length 4.4 ins. Weight 22.2 oz.
Price:.................................. $1080.95

10x32

10x magnification, 32mm objective diameter. Field of view @1000 yds. 376 ft. Eye relief 16mm. Length 4.4 ins. Weight 22.2 oz.
Price:.............................. $1120.95

SPORTSTAR III 8x25

8x magnification, 25mm objective diameter, 3.1mm exit pupil diameter. Field of view @1000 yds. 429 ft. Minimum focus 8.25 ft. Length 4 ins.
Price:................................ $59.99

SPORTSTAR III 10x25

10x magnification, 25mm objective diameter, 2.5mm exit pupil diameter. Field of view @1000 yds. 340 ft. Minimum focus 11 1/ t. Length 4 ins
Price:................................ $64.99

SPORTER I 8x36

8x magnification, 36mm objective diameter. Field of view @1000 yds. 366 ft. Minimum focus 10 ft. Length 5.7 ins. Width 5 ins. Weight 25.3 oz.
Price:.............................. $179.99

SPORTER I 10x36

10x magnification, 36mm objective diameter. Field of view @1000 yds. 294 ft. Minimum focus 10 ft. Length 5 ins. Width 5 ins. Weight 24.6 oz.
Price:.............................. $189.99

ACTION ZOOM 7-15x35

7-15x magnification, 35mm objective diameter. Field of view (at 7x) @1000 yds. 288 ft. Eye relief 9.1mm (at 7x). Minimum focus 26 ft. Width 5 ins. Height 6.7 ins. Weight 27.2 oz.
Price:.............................. $149.99

Nikon 8-24x25mm Eagleview Zoom II

Nikon Medallion available in 8x21mm and 10x21mm

Nikon 10x50mm Tundra

Nikon 7x50mm OceanPro

Nikon E2 available in 8x30mm and 10x35mm

Nikon 7x15mmT

Nikon, continued

ACTION ZOOM XL 10-22x50

10-22x magnification, 50mm objective diameter. Exit pupil diameter 5mm (at 10x), 2.3mm (at 22x). Field of view @1000 yds. 198 ft. (at 10x), 131 ft. (at 22x). Length 7.6 ins. Width 7.2 ins. Weight 33.5 oz.
Price:. $169.99

TRAVELITE V ZOOM 8-24x25

8-24X magnification, 25mm objective diameter. Field of view @1000 yds. 240 ft. (at 8x). Eye relief 13mm (at 8x), 8.9mm (at 24x). Minimum focus 13 ft. Weight 12.3 oz.
Price:. $240.95

EAGLEVIEW ZOOM II 8-24x25

8-24x magnification, 25mm objective diameter. Field of view @1000 yds. 240 ft. (at 8x). Weight 12 oz.
Price:. $240.95

MEDALLION 8x21 and 10x21

8x magnification (8x21); 10x magnification (10x21), 21mm objective diameter on both models. Weight 7 oz.
Price:. $112.95 (8x21); $122.95 (10x21)

TUNDRA 10x50

10x magnification, 50mm objective diameter, 5mm exit pupil diameter. Field of view @1000 yds. 324 ft. Eye relief 17.4mm. Weight 39 oz.
Price:. $384.95

OCEAN PRO 7x50

7x magnification, 50mm objective diameter, 7.1mm exit pupil diameter. Field of view @1000 yds. 378 ft. Eye relief 22.7mm.
Price:. $316.95
Price:. . . . . . $406.95 (with illuminated compass)

E2 8x30

8x magnification, 30mm objective diameter. Field of view @1000 yds. 461 ft. Eye relief 13.8mm. Minimum focus 10 ft. Weight 20.3 oz.
Price:. $730.95

E2 10x35

10x magnification, 35mm objective diameter. Field of view @1000 yds. 366 ft. Eye relief 13.8mm. Minimum focus 16 1/2 ft. Weight 22 oz.
Price:. $800.95

7x15T

7x magnification, 15mm objective diameter. Field of view @1000 yds. 345 ft. Minimum focus 5 ft. Eye relief 12mm. Length 3.1 ins. Weight 6 oz.
Price:. $774.95

OPTOLYTH

All models include Ceralin-plus multi-coating, ocular rainguard and padded case.

ALPIN NG PORRO PRISM SERIES

8x30 BGA

8x magnification, 30mm objective diameter. Field of view @1000 yds. 4.5 ft. Weight 16.8 oz.
Price:. $449.00

8x40 BGA

8x magnification, 40mm objective diameter. Field of view @1000 yds. 330 ft. Weight 20 oz.
Price:. $459.00

Pentax M 8x21mm

Pentax M 10x21mm

Optolyth Royal BGA 15x63mm

*Optolyth Royal 8x45mm BGA
and 10x45mm BGA / WW*

Pentax G 10x24mm

Pentax G 8x24mm

Optolyth, continued

10x40 BGA

10x magnification, 40mm objective diameter. Field of view @1000 yds. 330 ft. Weight 20.8 oz.
Price:. $469.00

7x42 BGA

7x magnification, 42mm objective diameter. Field of view @1000 yds. 330 ft. Weight 20 oz.
Price:. $479.00

10x50 BGA

10x magnification, 50mm objective diameter. Field of view @1000 yds. 267 ft. Weight 27 oz.

12x50 BGA

12x magnification, 50mm objective diameter. Field of view @1000 yds. 264 ft. Weight 28 oz.
Price:. $499.00

ROYAL ROOF PRISM BINOCULARS

Features phase correction, nitrogen filling, full rubber armor, and Ceralin-plus multi-coatings.

8x45 BGA

8x magnification, 45mm objective diameter. Field of view @1000 yds. 360 ft. Dimensions 8" x 5 ". Weight 2 lbs.
Price:. $799.00

10x45 BGA/WW (Wide Angle)

10x magnification, 45mm objective diameter. Field of view @1000 yds. 330 ft. Dimensions 8" x 5.5". Weight 2.05 lbs.
Price:. $899.00

15x63 BGA

15x magnification, 63mm objective diameter. Field of view @1000 yds. 216 ft. Dimensions 10" x 6". Weight 2.9 lbs.
Price:. $999.00

PENTAX

UCF M 8x21

8x magnification, 21mm objective diameter, 2.6mm exit pupil diameter. Field of view @1000 yds. 354 ft. Eye relief 13mm. Height 3.2 ins. Width 4.2 ins. Weight 6.9 oz.
Price:. $90.00

UCF M 10x21

10x magnification, 21mm objective diameter, 2.1mm exit pupil diameter. Field of view @1000 yds. 285 ft. Eye relief 9.5mm. Height 3.1 ins. Width 4.2 ins. Weight 6.9 oz.
Price:. $100.00

UCF G 8x24

8x magnification, 24mm objective diameter, 3mm exit pupil diameter. Field of view @1000 yds. 324 ft. Eye relief 15mm. Height 4.1 ins. Width 4.4 ins. Weight 9.5 oz.
Price:. $99.00

UCF G 10x24

10x magnification, 24mm objective diameter, 2.4mm exit pupil diameter. Field of view @1000 yds. 261 ft. Eye relief 15mm. Height 4.1 ins. Width 4.4 ins. Weight 9.5 oz.
Price:. $119.00

Pentax G 12x24mm

Pentax G 16x24mm

Pentax UCF Zoom 8-20x24mm

Pentax UCF Zoom 8-16x21mm

Pentax WR 8x24mm

Pentax WR 10x24mm

Pentax, continued

UCF G 12x24

12x magnification, 24mm objective diameter, 2mm exit pupil diameter. Field of view @1000 yds. 219 ft. Eye relief 15mm. Height 4.3 ins. Width 4.4 ins. Weight 9.7 oz.
Price:.............................. $129.00

UCF G 16x24

16x magnification, 24mm objective diameter, 1.5mm exit pupil diameter. Field of view @1000 yds. 162 ft. Height 4.3 ins. Width 4.4 ins. Weight 9.9 oz.
Price:.............................. $149.00

UCF ZOOM 8-20x24

8-20x magnification, 24mm objective diameter, 9mm (at 8x); 1.4mm (at 20x) exit pupil diameter. Field of view @1000 yds. 279 ft (at 8x); 132 ft. (at 20x). Eye relief 15mm (at 20x). Height 5.3 ins. Width 4.8 ins. Weight 17.1 oz.
Price:.............................. $334.00

UCF ZOOM 8-16x21

8-16x magnification, 21mm objective diameter, 2.6mm (at 8x); 1.3mm (at 16x) exit pupil diameter. Field of view @1000 yds. 261 ft (at 8x); 156 ft. (at 16x). Eye relief 11mm (at 16x). Height 4 ins. Width 4.3 ins. Weight 11.6 oz.
Price:.............................. $214.00

UCF WR 8x24

8x magnification, 24mm objective diameter, 3mm exit pupil diameter. Field of view @1000 yds. 393 ft. Eye relief 13mm. Height 4.3 ins. Width 4.4 ins. Weight 11.6 oz.
Price:.............................$129.00

UCF WR 10x24

10x magnification, 24mm objective diameter, 2.4mm exit pupil diameter. Field of view @1000 yds. 315 ft. Eye relief 10mm. Height 4.2 ins. Width 4.4 ins. Weight 11.6 oz.
Price:.............................$149.00

Pentax PCF V 8x40mm

Pentax PCF V 7x50mm

PCF 8x40

8x magnification, 40mm objective diameter, 5mm exit pupil diameter. Field of view @1000 yds. 330 ft. Eye relief 20mm. Height 5.3 ins. Width 6.9 ins. Weight 28.2 oz.
Price:.............................. $244.00

PCF 7x50

7x magnification, 50mm objective diameter, 7.1mm exit pupil diameter. Field of view @1000 yds. 324 ft. Eye relief 20mm. Height 7.2 ins. Width 7.3 ins. Weight 35.3 oz.
Price:.............................. $248.00

PCF 10x50

10x magnification, 50mm objective diameter, 5mm exit pupil diameter. Field of view @1000 yds. 261 ft. Eye relief 20mm. Height 6.9 ins. Width 7.3 ins. Weight 34.2 oz.
Price:.............................. $266.00

Pentax PCF V 10x50mm

Pentax PCF V 12x50mm

Pentax PCF V 16x60mm

Pentax PCF V 20x60mm

Pentax DCF WP 8x32mm

Pentax DCF WP 8x42mm

Pentax 10x28mm DCF MP

Pentax, continued

PCF 12x50
12x magnification, 50mm objective diameter, 4.2mm exit pupil diameter. Field of view @1000 yds. 219 ft. Eye relief 20mm. Height 7 ins. Width 7.3 ins. Weight 34.6 oz.
Price:. $276.00

PCF 16x60
16x magnification, 60mm objective diameter, 3.8mm exit pupil diameter. Field of view @1000 yds. 147 ft. Eye relief 20mm. Height 8.4 ins. Width 7.7 ins. Weight 44.4 oz.
Price:. $362.00

PCF 20x60
20x magnification, 60mm objective diameter, 3mm exit pupil diameter. Field of view @1000 yds. 114 ft. Eye relief 21mm. Height 8.8 ins. Width 7.7 ins. Weight 45.1 oz.
Price:. $388.00

DCF MP 8x28
8x magnification, 28mm objective diameter, 3.5mm exit pupil diameter. Field of view @1000 yds. 330 ft. Eye relief 17mm. Height 4.3 ins. Width 4.1 ins. Weight 10.6 oz.
Price:. $388.00

DCF MP 10x28
10x magnification, 28mm objective diameter, 2.8mm exit pupil diameter. Field of view @1000 yds. 315 ft. Eye relief 20mm. Height 4.6 ins. Width 4.7 ins. Weight 16.2 oz.
Price:. $398.00

DCF WP 8x32
8x magnification, 32mm objective diameter, 4mm exit pupil diameter. Field of view @1000 yds. 261 ft. Eye relief 20mm. Height 4.6 ins. Width 4.7 ins. Weight 16.2 oz.
Price:. $655.00

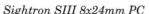

Sightron SIII 8x24mm PC

Sightron SIII 10x28mm PC

Sightron SIII 12x30mm PC

Pentax, continued

DCF WP 8x42

8x magnification, 42mm objective diameter, 5.2mm exit pupil diameter. Field of view @1000 yds. 330 ft. Eye relief 22mm. Height 5.8 ins. Width 5.1 ins. Weight 26.8 oz.
Price:.............................. $780.00

DCF WP 10x42

10x magnification, 42mm objective diameter, 4.2mm exit pupil diameter. Field of view @1000 yds. 314 ft. Eye relief 18mm. Height 5.8 ins. Width 5.1 ins. Weight 26.8 oz.
Price:.............................. $900.00

DCF WP 10x50

10x magnification, 50mm objective diameter, 5mm exit pupil diameter. Field of view @1000 yds. 261 ft. Eye relief 22mm. Height 6.7 ins. Width 5.2 ins. Weight 32.5 oz.
Price:.............................. $1058.00

FB ZOOM 6-12x17

6-12x magnification, 17mm objective diameter, 2.8mm (at 6x); 1.4mm (at 12x) exit pupil diameter. Field of view @1000 yds. 403 ft (at 6x); 252 ft. (at 12x). Eye relief 10mm (at 12x). Height 2.8 ins. Width 3.8 ins. Weight 6 oz.
Price:.............................. $228.00

FB 8x18

8x magnification, 18mm objective diameter, 2.3mm exit pupil diameter. Field of view @1000 yds. 393 ft. Eye relief 11mm. Height 2.3 ins. Width 3.4 ins. Weight 4.5 oz.
Price:.............................. $250.00

FB 10x18

10x magnification, 18mm objective diameter, 1.8mm exit pupil diameter. Field of view @1000 yds. 315 ft. Eye relief 10mm. Height 2.3 ins. Width 3.4 ins. Weight 4.5 oz.
Price:.............................. $310.00

FB LITE 7x17

7x magnification, 17mm objective diameter, 2.4mm exit pupil diameter. Field of view @1000 yds. 372 ft. Eye relief 11mm. Height 2 ins. Width 3.7 ins. Weight 5.2 oz.
Price:.............................. $198.00

FB LITE 9x17

9x magnification, 17mm objective diameter, 1.9mm exit pupil diameter. Field of view @1000 yds. 294 ft. Eye relief 8.5mm. Height 2 ins. Width 3.7 ins. Weight 5.2 oz.
Price:.............................. $212.00

SIGHTRON

Featuring fully multi-coated lenses and black rubber armoring on all models. Each is furnished with carrying pouch, dust caps and neck strap.

SIII

8x24PC

8x magnification, 24mm objective diameter, 3.0 mm exit pupil diameter. Field of view @1000 yds. 328 ft. Minimum focus 8.5 ft. Weight 8.5 oz.
Price:.............................. $302.95

10x28PC

10x magnification, 28mm objective diameter, 2.8mm exit pupil diameter. Field of view @ 1000 yds. 262 ft. Minimum focus 10 ft. Weight 9 oz.
Price:.............................. $316.95

12x30PC

12x magnification, 30mm objective diameter, 2.5mm exit pupil diameter. Field of view @ 1000 yds. 218 ft. Minimum focus 12 ft. Weight 10 oz.
Price:.............................. $329.95

8x42RM

8x magnification, 42mm objective diameter, 5.25mm exit pupil diameter. Field of view @ 1000 yds. 340 ft. Minimum focus 7.5 ft. Weight 23 oz.
Price:.............................. $519.95

Sightron SIII 8x42mm RM

Sightron SIII 10x42mm RM

Sightron 840RW 8x40mm

Sightron SII 1250R

Sightron SII 825M 8x25mm

Sightron SII 1025M 10x25

Sightron, continued

10x42RM

10x magnification, 42mm objective diameter, 4.2mm exit pupil diameter. Field of view @ 1000 yds. 262 ft. Minimum focus 7.5 ft. Weight 23 oz.
Price:.............................. $530.95

SII

All models feature black rubber armoring, fully multi-coated lenses and are furnished with vinyl pouch, dust caps and neck strap.

840RWA

Wide angle. 8x magnification, 40mm objective diameter, 5mm exit pupil diameter. Field of view @ 1000 yds. 430 ft. Brightness 25 lumens. Minimum focus 18 ft. Eye relief 12mm. Length 5.25 in. Weight 23.20 oz.
Price:.............................. $79.95

1050RWA

Wide angle. 10x magnification, 50mm objective diameter, 5mm exit pupil diameter. Field of view @ 1000 yds. 341 ft. Brightness 25 lumens. Minimum focus 27 ft. Eye relief 12mm. Length 6.5 in. Weight 27.14 oz.
Price:.............................. $99.95

1250R

12x magnification, 50mm objective diameter, 5mm exit pupil diameter. Field of view @ 1000 yds. 271 ft. Brightness 17 lumens. Minimum focus 36 ft. Eye relief 10.6 mm. Length 6.5 in. Weight 27.14 oz.
Price:.............................. $109.95

825M

Compact. 8x magnification, 25mm objective diameter, 5.25mm exit pupil diameter. Field of view @ 1000 yards 340 ft. Brightness 9.8 lumens. Minimum focus 7.5 ft. Eye relief 12mm. Length 4 in. Weight 8.9 oz.
Price:.............................. $69.95

1025M

Compact. 10x magnification, 25mm objective diameter, 4.2mm exit pupil diameter. Field of view @1000 yards 262 ft. Brightness 6.25 lumens. Minimum focus 7.5 ft. Eye relief 9.1 mm. Length 4 in. Weight 8.5 oz.
Price:.............................. $79.95

SIMMONS

EXPEDITION 8x40

8x magnification, 40mm objective diameter, 5mm exit pupil diameter. Field of view @1000 yds. 421 ft. Height 6.125 ins. Length 7.5 ins. Weight 29.8 oz.
Price:.............................. $129.99

Simmon' Endeavor binoculars are available in 20x60mm,
12-36x70mm and 15x70mm

Simmons' Hydrosport line is available
in a wide variety of models

Simmons' Focus Free line is available in 10x50mm
and 7x35mm models

Simmons, continued

EXPEDITION 7x35

7x magnification, 35mm objective diameter, 5mm exit
pupil diameter. Field of view @1000 yds. 484 ft. Height
5.5 ins. Length 7.5 ins. Weight 27.6 oz.
Price:. . . . . $ 119.99

EXPEDITION 10x50

10x magnification, 50mm objective diameter, 5mm exit
pupil diameter. Field of view @1000 yds. 342 ft. Height
7.5 ins. Length 7.75 ins. Weight 33.2 oz.
Price:. $149.99

HYDROSPORT 10x26

10x magnification, 26mm objective diameter, 2.6mm
exit pupil diameter. Field of view @1000 yds. 342 ft.
Height 4.75 ins. Length 4.25 ins. Weight 10.6 oz.
Price:. $75.99

HYDROSPORT 10x42

10x magnification, 42mm objective diameter, 4.2mm
exit pupil diameter. Field of view @1000 yds. 105 ft.
Height 6.25 ins. Length 5 ins. Weight 23.4 oz.
Price:. $129.99

HYDROSPORT 8x32

8x magnification, 32mm objective diameter, 4mm exit
pupil diameter. Field of view @1000 yds. 131 ft. Height
5.75 ins. Length 5 ins. Weight 19.8 oz.
Price:. $119.99

FIREVIEW 10x21

10x magnification, 21mm objective diameter, 2.1mm
exit pupil diameter. Field of view @341 ft. Height
3.0625 ins. Length 3.875 ins. Weight 6 oz.
Price:. $66.99

FIREVIEW 8x40

8x magnification, 40mm objective diameter, 5mm exit
pupil diameter. Field of view @1000 yds. 430 ft. Height
5.5 ins. Length 7.25 ins. Weight 26 oz.
Price:. $87.99

FIREVIEW 10x50

10x magnification, 50mm objective diameter, 5mm exit
pupil diameter. Field of view @1000 yds. 367 ft. Height
6.5 ins. Length 7.625 ins. Weight 29 oz.
Price:. $92.99

FOCUS FREE 10x50

10x magnification 50mm objective diameter, 5mm exit
pupil diameter. Field of view @1000 yds. 342 ft. Height
6.75 ins. Length 7.75 ins. Weight 29.6 oz.
Price:. $54.99

Steiner Predator 10x26mm

Steiner Predator 8x32mm

Steiner Predator 10x42mm

Steiner Nighthunter 12x56mm

Steiner Predator 8x22mm

Simmons, continued

FOCUS FREE 7x35

7x magnification, 35mm objective diameter, 5mm exit pupil diameter. Field of view @1000 yds. 488 ft. Height 5.25 ins. Length 7.25 ins. Weight 22.8 oz.
Price:.....................................$44.99

STEINER

Contains lens coatings to enhance the visibility of browns, reds and other wildlife colors against dark wooded backgrounds. All models come with carrying case.

PREDATOR

10x26

10x magnification, 26mm objective diameter, 2.6mm exit pupil diameter. Field of view @1000 yds. 291 ft. Weight 9.7 oz.
Price:............................. $169.00

8x32

8x magnification, 32mm objective diameter. Field of view @1000 yds. 328 ft. Minimum focus 5 ft. Eye relief 20mm. Center focus. Length 5.7 ins. Weightt 21 oz.
Price:............................. $599.00

8x42

8x magnification, 42mm objective diameter. Field of view @1000 yds. 367 ft. Roof prism, center focus. Minimum focus 5 1/2 ft. Eye relief 23mm. Weight 24 oz.
Price:............................. $679.00

10x42

10x magnification, 42mm objective diameter. Field of view @1000 yds. 295 ft. Roof prism, center focus. Minimum focus 5.9 ft. Eye relief 15.5mm. Weight 25 oz.
Price:............................. $729.00

8x30

8x magnification, 30mm objective diameter. Field of view @1000 yds. 390 ft. Eye relief 20mm. Weight 18 oz.
Price:............................. $249.00

12x40

12x magnification, 40mm objective diameter. Field of view @1000 yds. 300 ft. Eye relief 20mm. Weight 26 oz.
Price:............................. $399.00

8x22

8x magnification, 22mm objective diameter. Field of view @1000 yds. 369 ft. Minimum focus 9 ft. Eye relief 10mm Weight 8 oz.
Price:............................. $159.00

NIGHTHUNTER

High Definition lens coating for use in low-light conditions. Sports Auto-Focus feature puts everything from 20 feet to infinity in focus at the same time. Shock, fog and waterproof performance.

Steiner Nighthunter 7x50mm   Steiner Nighthunter 10x50mm

Swarovski Optik 8.5x42mm
and 10x42mm EL

Steiner, continued

8x56

8x magnification, 56mm objective diameter. Field of view @ 1000 yds. 333 ft. Eye relief 21mm. Weight 41 oz.
Price: **$799.00**

12x56

12x magnification, 56mm objective diameter. Field of view @1000 yds. 258 ft. Eye relief 22mm. Weight 41 oz.
Price: **$849.00**

7x50

7x magnification, 50mm objective diameter. Field of view @1000 yds. 375 ft. Eye relief 21mm. Weight 33 oz.
Price: **$669.00**

10x50

10x magnification, 50mm objective diameter. Field of view @1000 yds. 315 ft. Eye relief 21mm. Weight 35 oz.
Price: **$699.00**

8x30

8x magnification, 30mm objective diameter. Field of view @1000 yds. 390 ft. Eye relief 20mm. Weight 18 oz.
Price: **$449.00**

SAFARI

Made with UV blocking and glare cutting lens, BaK-4 optics, all models are rain and shock resistant.

8x30

8x magnification, 30mm objective diameter. Field of view @1000 yds. 390 ft. Eye relief 20mm. Weight 18 oz.
Price: **$199.00**

9x40

9x magnification, 40mm objective diameter. Field of view @1000 yds. 300 ft. Eye relief 20mm. Weight 26 oz.
Price: **$299.00**

8x22

8x magnification, 22mm objective diameter. Field of view @1000 yds. 369 ft. Eye relief 10mm. Weight 8 oz.
Price: **$149.00**

Swarovski Optik 7x42mmB SLC

12x40

12x magnification, 40mm objective diameter. Field of view @1000 yds. 295 ft. Eye relief 20mm. Weight 26 oz.
Price: **$319.00**

SWAROVSKI

The Swarovski EL 8.5x42 and 10x42 models are built with a magnesium alloy housing that is airtight, dustproof, waterproof and fully nitrogen purged. These models will accept the "Binocular Doubler" attachment that doubles the power of one ocular barrel by a factor of 2 times, allowing use of the binocular as a spotting scope.

OPTIK EL

EL 8.5x42

8.5x magnification, 42mm objective diameter, 5mm exit pupil diameter. Field of view @1000 yds. 390 ft. Eye relief 18mm. Minimum focus 8 ft. Length 6 ins. Width 4 ins. Height 2.5 ins. Weight 28.9 oz.
Price: **$1498.99**

EL 10x42

10x magnification, 42mm objective diameter, 4mm exit pupil diameter. Field of view @1000 yds. 330 ft. Eye relief 15mm. Minimum focus 8 ft. Length 6.2 ins. Width 4 ins. Height 2 ins. Weight 27 oz.
Price: **$1550.00**

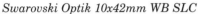

Swarovski Optik 10x42mm WB SLC

Swarovski Optik 7x50mmB SLC

Swarovski Optik8x50mmB SLC

Swarovski, continued

SLC

Swarotop® and Swarodur® multicoatings on all air-to-glass surfaces, phase corrected roof prisms, rubber outer shell, twist-in eye cups and nitrogen filled and sealed for waterproof submersibility.

7x30B

7x magnification, 30mm objective diameter, 4.2mm exit pupil diameter. Field of view @1000 yds. 378 ft. Eye relief 18mm. Minimum focus 13.2 ft. Length 5.55 ins. Width 4.33 ins. Height 2.52 ins. Weight 18.7 oz.
Price:. $732.22

8x30 WB

8x magnification, 30mm objective diameter, 3.8mm exit pupil diameter. Field of view @1000 yds. 408 ft. Eye relief 15mm. Minimum focus 13 ft. Length 5.55 ins. Width 4.33 ins. Height 2.52 ins. Weight 20.8 oz.
Price:. $865.55

7x42B

7x magnification, 42mm objective diameter, 6mm exit pupil diameter. Field of view @1000 yds. 420 ft. Eye relief 19mm. Minimum focus 13 ft. Length 6.46 ins. Width 4.8 ins. Height 2.8 ins. Weight 33 oz.
Price:. $1050.00

10x42 WB

10x magnification, 42mm objective diameter, 4.2mm exit pupil diameter. Field of view @1000 yds. 330 ft. Eye relief 14mm. Minimum focus 13 ft. Length 5.79 ins. Width 4.8 ins. Height 2.8 ins. Weight 30.7 oz.
Price:. $1110.00

7x50B

7x magnification, 50mm objective diameter, 7.1mm exit pupil diameter. Field of view @1000 yds. 372 ft. Eye relief 23mm. Minimum focus 20 ft. Length 4.96 ins. 4.96 ins. Height 2.72 ins. Weight 40.6 oz.
Price:. $1221.11

8x50B

8x magnification, 50mm objective diameter, 6.3mm exit pupil diameter. Field of view @1000 yds. 369 ft. Eye relief 21mm. Minimum focus 20 ft. Length 7.8 ins. Width 4.96 ins. Height 2.72 ins. Weight 40.6 oz.
Price:. $1332.22

Swarovski Optik 10x50mmWB SLC

Swarovski Optik 8x56mmB SLC

Swarovski Optik 15x56mmWB SLC

10x50WB

10x magnification, 50mm objective diameter, 5mm exit pupil diameter. Field of view @1000 yds. 336 ft. Eye relief 17mm. Minimum focus 16 ft. Length 7.72 ins. Width 4.96 ins. Height 2.72 ins. Weight 40.9 oz.
Price:. $1361.11

8x56B

8x magnification, 56mm objective diameter, 7mm exit pupil diameter. Field of view @1000 yds. 345 ft. Eye relief 22mm. Minimum focus 30 ft. Length 8.47 ins. Width 5.04 ins. Height 2.8 ins. Weight 45.5 oz.
Price:. $1498.89

Swarovski Optik 15x56mm ER

Swarovski Habicht 8x30mmW

Swarovski Habicht 7x42mm

Swarovski Habicht 10x40mmW

Swarovski Optik 8x20mm Green Pocket

Swarovski Optik 10x25mmB Pocket

Swarovski, continued

15x56 WB

15x magnification, 56mm objective diameter, 3.7mm exit pupil diameter. Field of view @1000 yds. 231 ft. Eye relief 13mm. Minimum focus 26 ft. Length 8.46 ins. Width 5.04 ins. Height 2.8 ins. Weight 47.3 oz.
Price:. $1772.22

15x56 ER (Extended Range)

15x magnification, 56mm objective diameter, 3.7mm exit pupil diameter. Field of view @1000 yds. 252.6 ft. Eye relief 13mm. Minimum focus 26 ft. Length 8.47 ins. Width 5.04 ins. Height 2.8 ins. Weight 47 oz.
Price:. $1783.00

HABICHT

Classic styling in watertight construction porro prism binoculars with central focusing. Choice of traditional black leather or green rubber armoring.

8x30W

8x magnification, 30mm objective diameter, 3.8mm exit pupil diameter. Field of view @1000 yds. 408 ft. Eye relief 12mm. Minimum focus 10 ft. Length (green armored) 4.61 ins. (leather) 4.49 ins. Width (GA) 6.38 ins. (L) 6.3 ins. Height (GA) 2.09 ins. (L) 2.09 ins. Weight (GA) 20.8 oz. (L) 19 oz.
Price:. . . . . (GA) $ 766.67; (L) $643.33

7x42

7x magnification, 42mm objection diameter, 6mm exit pupil diameter. Field of view @1000 yds. 342 ft. Eye relief 14mm. Minimum focus 11 ft. Length (GA) 6.06 ins. (L) 5.91 ins. Width (GA) 6.97 ins. (L) 6.89 ins. Height (GA) 2.28 ins. (L) 2.13 ins. Weight (GA) 26.8 oz. (L) 24 oz.
Price:. . . . . (GA) $766.67; (L) 621.11

10x40W

10x magnification, 40mm objective diameter, 4mm exit pupil diameter. Field of view @1000 yds. 324 ft. Eye relief 13mm. Minimum focus 13 ft. Length (GA) 6.06 ins. (L) 5.94 ins. Width (GA) 6.89 ins. (L) 6.77 ins. Height (GA) 2.32 ins. (L) 2.17 ins. Weight (GA) 27.9 oz. (L) 24.3 oz.
Price:. . . . . (GA) $843.33; (L) 698.89

POCKET MODELS

Alloy housing containing roof prism system with phase correction and broad band coating. Central focusing wheel®, dioptic correction and coated with rubber armoring. Comes with neck cord and nylon carrying case.

8x20

8x magnification, 20mm objective diameter, 2.5mm exit pupil diameter. Field of view @1000 yds. 345 ft. Eye Relief 13mm. Minimum focus 13 ft. Length 3.98 ins. Width 3.66 ins. Height 1.5 ins. Weight 7.6 oz.
Price:. $521.11

Swift Plover 8x40mm ZWCF

Swift Aerolite 7x35mm ZCF

Swift Ultra-Lite 7x42mm ZCF,
8x42mm ZCF and 10x42mmZWCF

Swift Ultra-Lite 8x32mm ZWCF

Swift Trilyte 10x42mm HCF
and Trilyte 8x42mm HCF

Swift Trilyte Camo 9x24mm

Swarovski, continued

10x25B
10x magnification, 25mm objective diameter, 2.5mm exit pupil diameter. Field of view @1000 yds. 285 ft. Eye relief 13mm. Minimum focus 16 ft. Length 4.57 ins. Width 3.66 ins. Height 1.5 ins. Weight 8.1 oz.
Price:. $576.66

SWIFT

8x40 PLOVER ZWCF
8x magnification, 40mm objective diameter. Field of view @1000 yds. 472 ft. Eye relief 14mm. Minimum focus 15 ft. Weight 25 oz.
Price:. $190.00

7x35 AEROLITE ZCF
7x magnification, 35mm objective diameter. Field of view @1000 yds. 358 ft. Eye relief 13.5mm. Minimum focus 16 ft. Weight 20 oz.
Price:. $75.00

7x35 AEROLITE ZWCF
7x magnification, 35mm objective diameter. Field of view @1000 yds. 500 ft. Eye relief 8.5mm. Minimum focus 13 ft. Weight 23.5 oz.
Price:. $99.00

7x42 ULTRA LITE ZCF
7x magnification, 42mm objective diameter. Field of view @1000 yds. 367 ft. Eye relief 25mm. Minimum focus 19 ft. Weight 21 oz.
Price:. $430.00

8x42 ULTRA LITE ZCF
8x magnification, 42mm objective diameter. Field of view @1000 yds. 346 ft. Eye relief 22mm. Minimum focus 16 ft. Weight 21 oz.
Price:. $440.00

10x42 ULTRA LITE ZWCF
10x magnification, 42mm objective diameter. Field of view @1000 yds. 346 ft. Eye relief 13mm. Minimum focus 15 ft. Weight 21 oz.
Price:. $460.00

8x32 ULTRA LITE ZWCF
8x magnification, 32mm objective diameter. Field of view @1000 yds. 436 ft. Eye relief 15mm. Minimum focus 15.3 ft. Weight 19.6 oz.
Price:. $425.00

TRILYTE 10x42 HCF
10x magnification, 42mm objective diameter. Field of view @1000 yds. 314 ft. Eye relief 10mm. Minimum focus 13.2 ft. Weight 20.4 oz.
Price:. $370.00

Swift Audubon 8.5x44mm ZWCF

Swift Eaglet 7x36mm HWCF

Swift Warbler 8x42mm HCF

Swift Viceroy 10x42mm HCF

*Tasco EXP-842 8x42mm
and EXP-1042 10x42mm*

Tasco EXP-1025 10x25mm

Swift, continued

TRILYTE 8x42 HCF
8x magnification, 42mm objective diameter. Field of view @1000 yds. 341 ft. Eye relief 15mm Minimum focus 12 ft. Weight 20.4 oz.
Price:. $365.00

TRILYTE 9x24 HCF
9x magnification, 24mm objective diameter. Field of view @1000 yds. 377 ft. Eye relief 11.8mm. Minimum focus 10 ft. Weight 12 oz.
Price:. $95.00

AUDUBON 8.5x44 ZWCF
8.5 magnification, 44mm objective diameter. Field of view @1000 yds. 430 ft. Eye relief 17mm. Minimum focus 10 ft. Weight 24.6 oz.
Price:. . . . . $ 570.00

EAGLET 7x36 HCF
7x magnification, 36mm objective diameter. Field of view @1000 yds. 374 ft. Eye relief 16mm. Minimum focus 5.9 ft. Weight 20.6 oz.
Price:. $680.00

WARBLER 8x42 HCF
8x magnification, 42mm objective diameter. Field of view @1000 yds. 328 ft. Eye relief 19mm. Minimum focus 9.75 ft. Weight 22 oz.
Price:. $540.00

VICEROY 10x42 HCF
10x magnification, 42mm objective diameter. Field of view @1000 yds. 263 ft. Eye relief 18mm. Minimum focus 6.5 ft. Weight 22.7 oz.
Price:. $550.00

TASCO

Features include fully multicoated optics, waterproof,/fogproof construction, and rubber armoring.

EXP™ (Extreme Performance)

EXP-1042
10x magnification, 42mm objective diameter, 4.1mm exit pupil diameter. Field of view @1000 yds. 275 ft. Roof prism type. Center focus. Weight 22.3 oz.
Price:. $299.00

Tasco 825WP 8x25mm

Tasco 1025WP 10x25mm

Tasco 1042WP 10x42mm

Tasco 1225WP 12x25mm

*Weaver's Grand Slam binoculars
are available in 8.5x45mm, 10.5x45mm
8.5x25mm and 10.5x25mm models*

Tasco, continued

EXP-842
8x magnification, 42mm objective diameter, 5.1mm exit pupil diameter. Field of view @1000 yds. 335 ft. BaK-4 prism. Center focus. Weight 22.2 oz.
Price:................................. **$286.99**

EXP-1025
10x magnification, 25mm objective diameter, 2.5mm exit pupil diameter. Field of view @1000 yds. 345 ft. Roof prism type. Center focus. Weight 12.6 oz.
Price:................................. **$196.99**

AMPHIBIAN™

Available in both compact and full-size models, features include waterproof, 0-ring sealed construction, flared eyecup fully coated optics and rubber armoring.

1250WP
12x magnification, 50mm objective diameter, 4.2mm exit pupil diameter. Field of view @1000 yds. 273 ft. Roof prism type. Weight 30 oz.
Price:................................. **$115.99**

1042WP
10x magnification, 42mm objective lens diameter, 4.2mm exit pupil diameter. Field of view @1000 yds. 303 ft. Roof prism type. Center focus. Center focus. Weight 25 oz.
Price:................................. **$89.99**

COMPACT MODELS

AMPHIBIAN 825WP
8x magnification, 25mm objective lens diameter, 3.1mm exit pupil diameter. Field of view @1000 yds. 380 ft. Roof prism type. Center focus. Weight 13.2 oz.
Price:................................. **$45.99**

AMPHIBIAN 1025WP
10x magnification, 25mm objective lens diameter, 2.5mm exit pupil diameter. Field of view @1000 yds. 315 ft. Roof prism type. Center focus. Weight 12.9 oz.
Price:................................. **$51.99**

AMPHIBIAN 1225WP
12x magnification, 25mm objective lens diameter, 2.1mm exit pupil diameter. Field of view @1000 yds. 255 ft. Roof prism type. Center focus. Weight 12.8 oz.
Price:................................. **$55.99**

WEAVER

GRAND SLAM 8.5x45
8.5x magnification, 45mm objective diameter, 5.29mm exit pupil diameter. Field of view @100 yds. 314 ft. Height 6.25 ins. Length 5.13 ins. Width 2.13 ins. Weight 1 lb. 13 oz.
Price:................................. **$544.99**

Weaver Classic 10x28mm

Weaver Classic 8x42mm

10x25c Zeiss 10x25 C compact

Weaver, continued

GRAND SLAM 10.5x45

10.5x magnification, 45mm objective diameter, 4.29mm exit pupil diameter. Field of view @100 yds. 298 ft. Height 6 ins. Length 5.13 ins. Width 2.13 ins. Weight 1 lb. 12 oz.
Price:........................... **$581.99**

GRAND SLAM 8.5x25

8.5x magnification, 25mm objective diameter, 2.94mm exit pupil diameter. Field of view @100 yds. 351 ft. Height 4.5 ins. Length 4.5 ins. Width 1.5 ins. Weight 14.6 oz.
Price:........................... **$269.99**

GRAND SLAM 10.5x25

10.5x magnification, 25mm objective diameter, 2.38 exit pupil diameter. Field of view @100 yds. 350 ft. Height 4.5 ins. Length 4.5 ins. Width 1.5 ins. Weight 14.8 oz.
Price:........................... **$279.99**

CLASSIC 8x24

8x magnification, 24mm objective diameter, 3mm exit pupil diameter. Field of view @100 yds. 315.3 ft. Height 4.25 ins. Length 4 ins. 1.25 ins. Weight 7.9 oz.
Price:........................... **$210.99**

CLASSIC 10x28

10x magnification, 28mm objective diameter, 2.8mm exit pupil diameter. Field of view @100 yds. 253.7 ft. Height 4.5 ins. Length 4.13 ins. Width 1.5 ins. Weight 8.8 oz.
Price:........................... **$225.99**

CLASSIC 8x42

8x magnification, 42mm objective diameter, 5.25mm exit pupil diameter. Field of view @100 yds. 331.8 ft. Height 4 ins. Length 6 ins. Width 1.88 ins. Weight 1 lb. 7.6 oz.
Price:........................... **$415.99**

CLASSIC 10x42

10x magnification, 42mm objective diameter, 4.2mm exit pupil diameter. Field of view @100 yds. 262.5 ft. Height 6 ins. Length 5 ins. Width 1.88 ins. Weight 1 lb. 8.1 oz.
Price:........................... **$437.99**

ZEISS

10x56 BTP VICTORY

10x magnification, 56mm objective diameter, 5.6mm exit pupil diameter. Field of view @1000 meters 110 meters. Height 200mm. Width 144mm. Weight 42.36 oz.
Price:........................... **$ 1,549.00**

8x56 BTP VICTORY

8x magnification, 56mm objective diameter, 7mm exit pupil diameter. Field of view @1000 meters 132 meters. Height 200mm. Width 144mm. Weight 40.94 oz.
Price:........................... **$ 1,449.00**

8x40 BTP VICTORY

8x magnification, 40mm objective diameter, 5mm exit pupil diameter. Field of view @1000 meters 135 meters. Height 162mm. Width 123mm. Weight 25.06 oz.
Price:........................... **$1,179.00**

10x40 BTP VICTORY

10x magnification, 40mm objective diameter, 4mm exit pupil diameter. Field of view @1000 meters 110 meters. Height 162mm. Width 123mm. Weight 25.76 oz.
Price:........................... **$1,200.00**

8X20 BT COMPACT VICTORY

8x magnification, 20mm objective diameter, 2.5mm exit pupil diameter. Field of view @1000 yds. 351 ft. Minimum focus 8 ft. Height 4 ins. Width 3.82 ins. Weight 7.9 oz.
Price:........................... **$479.00**

Zeiss 7x42mm BG

Zeiss 15x60 B

Zeiss 7x50mm BG

Zeiss, continued

10x25 BT COMPACT VICTORY
10x magnification, 25mm objective diameter, 2.5mm exit pupil diameter. Field of view @1000 yds. 285 ft. Minimum focus 13.1 ft. Height 4.7 ins. Width 3.82 ins. Weight 8.6 oz.
Price:.............................. **$499.00**

10x30 B MC
10x magnification, 30mm objective diameter. Field of view @1000 yds. 288 ft. Weight 15.9 oz.
Price:.............................. **$549.00**

7x42 B/GA
7x magnification, 42mm objective diameter. Field of view @1000 yds. 460 ft.
Price:.............................. **$1,149.95**

15x60 B/GA
15x magnification, 60mm objective diameter. Field of view @1000 yds. 226.8 ft.
Price:............................. **$2,454.95**

10x40 B/GA T CLASSIC
10x magnification, 40mm objective diameter. Field of view @1000 yds. 330 ft. Weight 27 oz.
Price:............................. **$1,149.95**

7x50 B/GA
7x magnification, 50mm objective diameter. Field of view @1000 yds. 390 ft. Weight 42.3 oz.
Price:............................. **$1,489.95**

SCOPES
(Hunting, Target & Varmint)

Hunting scopes in general are furnished with a choice of reticle—crosshairs, post with crosshairs, tapered or blunt post, or dot crosshairs, etc. The great majority of target and varmint scopes have medium or fine crosshairs but post or dot reticles may be ordered.

Terms: W—Windage E—Elevation MOA—Minute of Angle or 1" (approx.) at 100 yards.

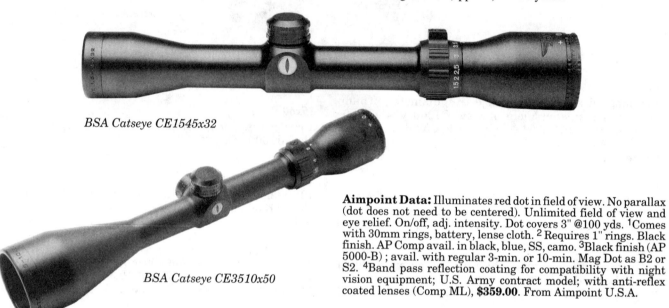

BSA Catseye CE1545x32

BSA Catseye CE3510x50

Aimpoint Data: Illuminates red dot in field of view. No parallax (dot does not need to be centered). Unlimited field of view and eye relief. On/off, adj. intensity. Dot covers 3" @100 yds. [1]Comes with 30mm rings, battery, lense cloth. [2] Requires 1" rings. Black finish. AP Comp avail. in black, blue, SS, camo. [3]Black finish (AP 5000-B) ; avail. with regular 3-min. or 10-min. Mag Dot as B2 or S2. [4]Band pass reflection coating for compatibility with night vision equipment; U.S. Army contract model; with anti-reflex coated lenses (Comp ML), **$359.00**. From Aimpoint U.S.A.

AIMPOINT

Comp
Magn.: 0; **Field at 100 Yds. (feet):** —; **Eye Relief (in.):** —; **Length (in.):** 4.6; **Tube Dia. (in.):** 30mm; **W & E Adjustments:** Int.; **Weight (ozs.):** 4.3
Price: $331.00

Comp M [4]
Magn.: 0; **Field at 100 Yds. (feet):** —; **—Eye Relief (in.):** ; **Length (in.):** 5; **Tube Dia. (in.):** 30mm; **W & E Adjustments:** Int.; **Weight (ozs.):** 6.1
Price: $409.00

Series 5000 [3]
Magn.: 0; **Field at 100 Yds. (feet):** —; **Eye Relief (in.):** —; **Length (in.):** 6; **Tube Dia. (in.):** 30mm; **W & E Adjustments:** Int.; **Weight (ozs.):** 6
Price: $297.00

Series 3000 Universal [2]
Magn.: 0; **Field at 100 Yds. (feet):** —; **Eye Relief (in.):** —; **Length (in.):** 6.25; **Tube Dia. (in.):** 1; **W & E Adjustments:** Int.; **Weight (ozs.):** 6
Price: $232.00

Series 5000/2x [1]
Magn.: 2; **Field at 100 Yds. (feet):** —; **Eye Relief (in.):** —; **Length (in.):** 7; **Tube Dia. (in.):** 30mm; **W & E Adjustments:** Int.; **Weight (ozs.):** 9
Price: $388.00

BSA

Catseye [1]

CE1545x32
Magn.: 1.5-4.5; **Field at 100 Yds. (feet):** 78-23; **Eye Relief (in.):** 4; **Length (in.):** 11.25; **Tube Dia. (in.):** 1; **W & E Adjustments:** Int.; **Weight (ozs.):** 12
Price: $91.95

CE310x44
Magn.: 3-10; **Field at 100 Yds. (feet):** 39-12; **Eye Relief (in.):** 3.25; **Length (in.):** 12.75; **Tube Dia. (in.):** 1; **W & E Adjustments:** Int.; **Weight (ozs.):** 16
Price: $151.95

CE3510x50
Magn.: 3.5-10; **Field at 100 Yds. (feet):** 30-10.5; **Eye Relief (in.):** 3.25; **Length (in.):** 13.25; **Tube Dia. (in.):** 1; **W & E Adjustments:** Int.; **Weight (ozs.):** 17.25
Price: $171.95

CE416x50
Magn.: 4-16; **Field at 100 Yds. (feet):** 25-6; **Eye Relief (in.):** 3; **Length (in.):** 15.25; **Tube Dia. (in.):** 1; **W & E Adjustments:** Int.; **Weight (ozs.):** 22
Price: $191.95

CE624x50
Magn.: 6-24; **Field at 100 Yds. (feet):** 16-3; **Eye Relief (in.):** 3; **Length (in.):** 16; **Tube Dia. (in.):** 1; **W & E Adjustments:** Int.; **Weight (ozs.):** 23
Price: $222.95

BSA Deer Hunter DH39x40

BSA Contender 312x40TS

BSA, continued

CE1545x32IR

Magn.: 1.5-4.5; **Field at 100 Yds. (feet):** 78-23; **Eye Relief (in.):** 5; **Length (in.):** 11.25; **Tube Dia. (in.):** 1; **W & E Adjustments:** Int.; **Weight (ozs.):** 12
Price: $121.95

Deer Hunter [2]

DH25x20

Magn.: 2.5; **Field at 100 Yds. (feet):** 72; **Eye Relief (in.):** 6; **Length (in.):** 7.5; **Tube Dia. (in.):** 1; **W & E Adjustments:** Int.; **Weight (ozs.):** 7.5
Price: $59.95

DH4x32

Magn.: 4; **Field at 100 Yds. (feet):** 32; **Eye Relief (in.):** 3; **Length (in.):** 12; **Tube Dia. (in.):** 1; **W & E Adjustments:** Int.; **Weight (ozs.):** 12.5
Price: $49.95

DH39x32

Magn.: 3-9; **Field at 100 Yds. (feet):** 39-13; **Eye Relief (in.):** 3; **Length (in.):** 12; **Tube Dia. (in.):** 1; **W & E Adjustments:** Int.; **Weight (ozs.):** 11
Price: $69.95

DH39x40

Magn.: 3-9; **Field at 100 Yds. (feet):** 39-13; **Eye Relief (in.):** 3; **Length (in.):** 13; **Tube Dia. (in.):** 1; **W & E Adjustments:** Int.; **Weight (ozs.):** 12.1
Price: $89.95

DH39x50

Magn.: 3-9; **Field at 100 Yds. (feet):** 41-15; **Eye Relief (in.):** 3; **Length (in.):** 12.75; **Tube Dia. (in.):** 1; **W & E Adjustments:** Int.; **Weight (ozs.):** 13
Price: $109.95

DH2510x44

Magn.: 2.5-10; **Field at 100 Yds. (feet):** 42-12; **Eye Relief (in.):** 3; **Length (in.):** 13; **Tube Dia. (in.):** 1; **W & E Adjustments:** Int.; **Weight (ozs.):** 12.5
Price: $99.95

DH1545x32

Magn.: 1.5-4.5; **Field at 100 Yds. (feet):** 78-23; **Eye Relief (in.):** 5; **Length (in.):** 11.25; **Tube Dia. (in.):** 1; **W & E Adjustments:** Int.; **Weight (ozs.):** 12
Price: $79.95

Contender [3]

CT24x40TS

Magn.: 24; **Field at 100 Yds. (feet):** 6; **Eye Relief (in.):** 3; **Length (in.):** 15; **Tube Dia. (in.):** 1; **W & E Adjustments:** Int.; **Weight (ozs.):** 18
Price: $129.95

CT36x40TS

Magn.: 36; **Field at 100 Yds. (feet):** 3; **Eye Relief (in.):** 3; **Length (in.):** 15.25; **Tube Dia. (in.):** 1; **W & E Adjustments:** Int.; **Weight (ozs.):** 19
Price: $139.95

CT312x40TS

Magn.: 3-12; **Field at 100 Yds. (feet):** 28-7; **Eye Relief (in.):** 3; **Length (in.):** 13; **Tube Dia. (in.):** 1; **W & E Adjustments:** Int.; **Weight (ozs.):** 17.5
Price: $119.95

CT416x40TS

Magn.: 4-16; **Field at 100 Yds. (feet):** 21-5; **Eye Relief (in.):** 3; **Length (in.):** 13.5; **Tube Dia. (in.):** 1; **W & E Adjustments:** Int.; **Weight (ozs.):** 18
Price: $129.95

CT624x40TS

Magn.: 6-24; **Field at 100 Yds. (feet):** 16-4; **Eye Relief (in.):** 3; **Length (in.):** 15.5; **Tube Dia. (in.):** 1; **W & E Adjustments:** Int.; **Weight (ozs.):** 20
Price: $144.95

CT832x40TS

Magn.: 8-32; **Field at 100 Yds. (feet):** 11-3; **Eye Relief (in.):** 3; **Length (in.):** 15.5; **Tube Dia. (in.):** 1; **W & E Adjustments:** Int.; **Weight (ozs.):** 20
Price: $169.95

CT24x50TS

Magn.: 24; **Field at 100 Yds. (feet):** 6; **Eye Relief (in.):** 3; **Length (in.):** 15; **Tube Dia. (in.):** 1; **W & E Adjustments:** Int.; **Weight (ozs.):** 22
Price: $149.95

CT36x50TS

Magn.: 36; **Field at 100 Yds. (feet):** 3; **Eye Relief (in.):** 3; **Length (in.):** 15.25; **Tube Dia. (in.):** 1; **W & E Adjustments:** Int.; **Weight (ozs.):** 23
Price: $159.95

CT312x50TS

Magn.: 3-12; **Field at 100 Yds. (feet):** 28-7; **Eye Relief (in.):** 3; **Length (in.):** 13.75; **Tube Dia. (in.):** 1; **W & E Adjustments:** Int.; **Weight (ozs.):** 21
Price: $129.95

CT416x50TS

Magn.: 4-16; **Field at 100 Yds. (feet):** 21-5; **Eye Relief (in.):** 3; **Length (in.):** 15.25; **Tube Dia. (in.):** 1; **W & E Adjustments:** Int.; **Weight (ozs.):** 22
Price: $149.95

CT624x50TS

Magn.: 6-24; **Field at 100 Yds. (feet):** 16-4; **Eye Relief (in.):** 3; **Length (in.):** 16; **Tube Dia. (in.):** 1; **W & E Adjustments:** Int.; **Weight (ozs.):** 23
Price: $169.95

BSA PS2x20 Pistol Scope

BSA Red Dot PB30

BSA, continued

CT832x50TS

Magn.: 8-32; **Field at 100 Yds. (feet):** 11-3; **Eye Relief (in.):** 3; **Length (in.):** 16.5; **Tube Dia. (in.):** 1; **W & E Adjustments:** Int.; **Weight (ozs.):** 24
Price: $189.95

Pistol

PS2x20

Magn.: 2; **Field at 100 Yds. (feet):** N/A; **Eye Relief (in.):** N/A; **Length (in.):** N/A; **Tube Dia. (in.):** N/A; **W & E Adjustments:** Int.; **Weight (ozs.):** N/A
Price: $79.95

P54x28

Magn.: 4; **Field at 100 Yds. (feet):** N/A; **Eye Relief (in.):** N/A; **Length (in.):** N/A; **Tube Dia. (in.):** N/A; **W & E Adjustments:** Int.; **Weight (ozs.):** N/A
Price: $89.95

Platinum 4

PT24x44TS

Magn.: 24; **Field at 100 Yds. (feet):** 4.5; **Eye Relief (in.):** 3; **Length (in.):** 16.25; **Tube Dia. (in.):** 1; **W & E Adjustments:** Int.; **Weight (ozs.):** 17.9
Price: $189.55

PT36x44TS

Magn.: 36; **Field at 100 Yds. (feet):** 3; **Eye Relief (in.):** 3; **Length (in.):** 14.9; **Tube Dia. (in.):** 1; **W & E Adjustments:** Int.; **Weight (ozs.):** 17.9
Price: $199.95

PT624x44TS

Magn.: 6-24; **Field at 100 Yds. (feet):** 15-4.5; **Eye Relief (in.):** 3; **Length (in.):** 15.25; **Tube Dia. (in.):** 1; **W & E Adjustments:** Int.; **Weight (ozs.):** 18.5
Price: $219.95

PT832x44TS

Magn.: 8-32; **Field at 100 Yds. (feet):** 11-3.5; **Eye Relief (in.):** 3; **Length (in.):** 17.25; **Tube Dia. (in.):** 1; **W & E Adjustments:** Int.; **Weight (ozs.):** 19.5
Price: $239.95

PT1050x60TS

Magn.: 10-50; **Field at 100 Yds. (feet):** 7-2; **Eye Relief (in.):** 3; **Length (in.):** 18; **Tube Dia. (in.):** 1; **W & E Adjustments:** Int.; **Weight (ozs.):** 22
Price: $399.95

.22 Special

S25x20WR

Magn.: 2.5; **Field at 100 Yds. (feet):** 58; **Eye Relief (in.):** 3; **Length (in.):** 8; **Tube Dia. (in.):** 1; **W & E Adjustments:** Int.; **Weight (ozs.):** 7
Price: $39.95

S4x32WR

Magn.: 4; **Field at 100 Yds. (feet):** 26; **Eye Relief (in.):** 3; **Length (in.):** 10.75; **Tube Dia. (in.):** 1; **W & E Adjustments:** Int.; **Weight (ozs.):** 9
Price: $49.95

Air Rifle

AR4x32

Magn.: 4; **Field at 100 Yds. (feet):** 33; **Eye Relief (in.):** 3; **Length (in.):** 13; **Tube Dia. (in.):** 1; **W & E Adjustments:** Int.; **Weight (ozs.):** 14
Price: $69.95

AR27x32

Magn.: 2-7; **Field at 100 Yds. (feet):** 48; **Eye Relief (in.):** 3; **Length (in.):** 12.25; **Tube Dia. (in.):** 1; **W & E Adjustments:** Int.; **Weight (ozs.):** 14
Price: $79.95

AR312x44

Magn.: 3-12; **Field at 100 Yds. (feet):** 36; **Eye Relief (in.):** 3; **Length (in.):** 12.25; **Tube Dia. (in.):** 1; **W & E Adjustments:** Int.; **Weight (ozs.):** 15
Price: $109.95

Red Dot

RD30 6

Magn.: 0; **Field at 100 Yds. (feet):** —; **Eye Relief (in.):** —; **Length (in.):** 3.8; **Tube Dia. (in.):** 30mm; **W & E Adjustments:** Int.; **Weight (ozs.):** 5
Price: $59.95

PB30 6

Magn.: 0; **Field at 100 Yds. (feet):** —; **Eye Relief (in.):** —; **Length (in.):** 3.8; **Tube Dia. (in.):** 30mm; **W & E Adjustments:** Int.; **Weight (ozs.):** 4.5
Price: $79.95

Bow30 7

Magn.: 0; **Field at 100 Yds. (feet):** —; **Eye Relief (in.):** —; **Length (in.):** N/A; **Tube Dia. (in.):** 30mm; **W & E Adjustments:** Int.; **Weight (ozs.):** 5
Price: $89.95

Bigcat 8

Magn.: 3.5-10; **Field at 100 Yds. (feet):** 30-11; **Eye Relief (in.):** 5; **Length (in.):** 9.7; **Tube Dia. (in.):** 1; **W & E Adjustments:** Int.; **Weight (ozs.):** 16.8
Price: $219.95

Burris Black Diamond 6-24x50

Burris Fullfield II 1.75-5x

BSA, continued

BSA Data: [1]Waterproof, fogproof; multi-coated lenses; finger-adjustable knobs. [2]Waterproof, fogproof; matte black finish. [3]With 4" sunshade; target knobs; 1/8-MOA click adjustments. [4]Adjustable for parallax; with sunshades; target knobs, 1/8-MOA adjustments. Imported by BSA. [5]Illuminated reticle model; also available in 3-10x, 3.5-10x, and 3-9x. [6]Red dot sights also available in 42mm and 50mm versions. [7]Includes Universal Bow Mount. [8]Five other models offered. From BSA.

BURRIS

Mr. T Black Diamond Titanium

2.5-10x50 [A]

Magn.: 2.5-10; **Field at 100 Yds. (feet):** 4.25-4.75; **Eye Relief (in.):** ; **Length (in.):** 13.6; **Tube Dia. (in.):** 30mm; **W & E Adjustments:** Int.; **Weight (ozs.):** 29
Price: **$2,129.00**

Black Diamond

3-12x50 [3,4,6]

Magn.: 3.2-11.9; **Field at 100 Yds. (feet):** 34-12; **Eye Relief (in.):** 3.5-4; **Length (in.):** 13.8; **Tube Dia. (in.):** 30mm; **W & E Adjustments:** Int.; **Weight (ozs.):** 25
Price: **$880.00**

6-24x50

Magn.: 6-24; **Field at 100 Yds. (feet):** 18-6; **Eye Relief (in.):** 3.5-4; **Length (in.):** 16.2; **Tube Dia. (in.):** 30mm; **W & E Adjustments:** Int.; **Weight (ozs.):** 25
Price: **$954.00**

Fullfield & Fullfield II

2.5x [9]

Magn.: 2.5; **Field at 100 Yds. (feet):** 55; **Eye Relief (in.):** 3.5-3.75; **Length (in.):** 10.25; **Tube Dia. (in.):** 1; **W & E Adjustments:** Int.; **Weight (ozs.):** 9
Price: **$308.00**

4x [1,2,3]

Magn.: 3.75; **Field at 100 Yds. (feet):** 36; **Eye Relief (in.):** 3.5-3.75; **Length (in.):** 11.25; **Tube Dia. (in.):** 1; **W & E Adjustments:** Int.; **Weight (ozs.):** 11.5
Price: **$314.00**

6x [1,3]

Magn.: 5.8; **Field at 100 Yds. (feet):** 23; **Eye Relief (in.):** 3.5-3.75; **Length (in.):** 13; **Tube Dia. (in.):** 1; **W & E Adjustments:** Int.; **Weight (ozs.):** 12
Price: **$343.00**

1.75-5x [1,2,9,10]

Magn.: 1.7-4.6; **Field at 100 Yds. (feet):** 66-25; **Eye Relief (in.):** 3.5-3.75; **Length (in.):** 10.875; **Tube Dia. (in.):** 1; **W & E Adjustments:** Int.; **Weight (ozs.):** 13
Price: **$374.00**

2-7x [1,2,3]

Magn.: 2.5-6.8; **Field at 100 Yds. (feet):** 47-18; **Eye Relief (in.):** 3.5-3.75; **Length (in.):** 12; **Tube Dia. (in.):** 1; **W & E Adjustments:** Int.; **Weight (ozs.):** 14
Price: **$399.00**

3-9x40 [1,2,3,10]

Magn.: 3.3-8.7; **Field at 100 Yds. (feet):** 38-15; **Eye Relief (in.):** 3.5-3.75; **Length (in.):** 12.625 ; **Tube Dia. (in.):** 1; **W & E Adjustments:** Int.; **Weight (ozs.):** 15
Price: **$356.00**

3-9x50

Magn.: 3-9; **Field at 100 Yds. (feet):** 35-15; **Eye Relief (in.):** 3.5-3.75; **Length (in.):** 13; **Tube Dia. (in.):** 1; **W & E Adjustments:** Int.; **Weight (ozs.):** 18
Price: **$427.00**

3.5-10x50mm [3,5,10]

Magn.: 3.7-9.7; **Field at 100 Yds. (feet):** 29.5-11; **Eye Relief (in.):** 3.5-3.75; **Length (in.):** 14; **Tube Dia. (in.):** 1; **W & E Adjustments:** Int.; **Weight (ozs.):** 19
Price: **$496.00**

4-12x [1,4,8,11]

Magn.: 4.4-11.8; **Field at 100 Yds. (feet):** 27-10; **Eye Relief (in.):** 3.5-3.75; **Length (in.):** 15; **Tube Dia. (in.):** 1; **W & E Adjustments:** Int.; **Weight (ozs.):** 18
Price: **$500.00**

6-18x [1,3,4,6,7,8]

Magn.: 6.5-17.6; **Field at 100 Yds. (feet):** 16.7; **Eye Relief (in.):** 3.5-3.75; **Length (in.):** 15.8; **Tube Dia. (in.):** 1; **W & E Adjustments:** Int.; **Weight (ozs.):** 18.5
Price: **$527.00**

Compact Scopes

1x XER [3]

Magn.: 1; **Field at 100 Yds. (feet):** 51; **Eye Relief (in.):** 4.5-20; **Length (in.):** 8.8; **Tube Dia. (in.):** 1; **W & E Adjustments:** Int.; **Weight (ozs.):** 7.9
Price: **$290.00**

4x [4,5]

Magn.: 3.6; **Field at 100 Yds. (feet):** 24; **Eye Relief (in.):** 3.75-5; **Length (in.):** 8.25; **Tube Dia. (in.):** 1; **W & E Adjustments:** Int.; **Weight (ozs.):** 7.8
Price: **$270.00**

Burris Compact 1x-4x XER

Burris Compact 1x-4x XER

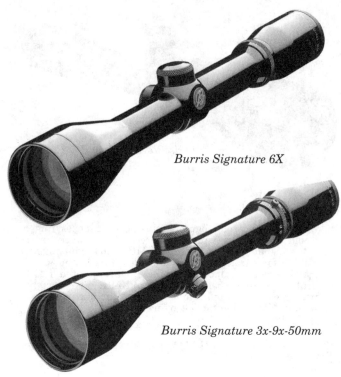

Burris Signature 6X

Burris Signature 3x-9x-50mm

Burris, continued

6x [1,4]

Magn.: 5.5; **Field at 100 Yds. (feet):** 17; **Eye Relief (in.):** 3.75-5; **Length (in.):** 9; **Tube Dia. (in.):** 1; **W & E Adjustments:** Int.; **Weight (ozs.):** 8.2
Price: $287.00

6x HBR [1,5,8]

Magn.: 6; **Field at 100 Yds. (feet):** 13; **Eye Relief (in.):** 4.5; **Length (in.):** 11.25; **Tube Dia. (in.):** 1; **W & E Adjustments:** Int.; **Weight (ozs.):** 13
Price: $451.00

1-4x XER [3]

Magn.: 1-3.8; **Field at 100 Yds. (feet):** 53-15; **Eye Relief (in.):** 4.25-30; **Length (in.):** 8.8; **Tube Dia. (in.):** 1; **W & E Adjustments:** Int.; **Weight (ozs.):** 10.3
Price: $377.00

3-9x [4,5]

Magn.: 3.6-8.8; **Field at 100 Yds. (feet):** 25-11; **Eye Relief (in.):** 3.75-5; **Length (in.):** 12.625; **Tube Dia. (in.):** 1; **W & E Adjustments:** Int.; **Weight (ozs.):** 11.5
Price: $368.00

4-12x [1,4,6]

Magn.: 4.5-11.6; **Field at 100 Yds. (feet):** 19-8; **Eye Relief (in.):** 3.75-4; **Length (in.):** 15; **Tube Dia. (in.):** 1; **W & E Adjustments:** Int.; **Weight (ozs.):** 15
Price: $500.00

Signature Series

1.5-6x [2,3,5,9,10]

Magn.: 1.7-5.8; **Field at 100 Yds. (feet):** 70-20; **Eye Relief (in.):** 3.5-4; **Length (in.):** 10.8; **Tube Dia. (in.):** 1; **W & E Adjustments:** Int.; **Weight (ozs.):** 13
Price: $484.00

6x [3]

Magn.: 6; **Field at 100 Yds. (feet):** 20; **Eye Relief (in.):** 3.5-4; **Length (in.):** 12.125; **Tube Dia. (in.):** 1; **W & E Adjustments:** Int.; **Weight (ozs.):** 14
Price: $413.00

2-8x [3,5,11]

Magn.: 2.1-7.7; **Field at 100 Yds. (feet):** 53-17; **Eye Relief (in.):** 3.5-4; **Length (in.):** 11.75; **Tube Dia. (in.):** 1; **W & E Adjustments:** Int.; **Weight (ozs.):** 14
Price: $558.00

3-9x [3,5,10,13]

Magn.: 3.3-8.8; **Field at 100 Yds. (feet):** 36-14; **Eye Relief (in.):** 3.5-4; **Length (in.):** 12.875; **Tube Dia. (in.):** 1; **W & E Adjustments:** Int.; **Weight (ozs.):** 15.5
Price: $571.00

2.50-10x [3,5,10]

Magn.: 2.7-9.5; **Field at 100 Yds. (feet):** 37-10.5; **Eye Relief (in.):** 3.5-4; **Length (in.):** 14; **Tube Dia. (in.):** 1; **W & E Adjustments:** Int.; **Weight (ozs.):** 19
Price: $635.00

3-12x [3,10]

Magn.: 3.3-11.7; **Field at 100 Yds. (feet):** 34-9; **Eye Relief (in.):** 3.5-4; **Length (in.):** 14.25; **Tube Dia. (in.):** 1; **W & E Adjustments:** Int.; **Weight (ozs.):** 21
Price: $691.00

4-16x [1,3,5,6,8,10]

Magn.: 4.3-15.7; **Field at 100 Yds. (feet):** 33-9; **Eye Relief (in.):** 3.5-4; **Length (in.):** 15.4; **Tube Dia. (in.):** 1; **W & E Adjustments:** Int.; **Weight (ozs.):** 23.7
Price: $723.00

6-24x [1,3,5,6,8,10,13]

Magn.: 6.6-23.8; **Field at 100 Yds. (feet):** 17-6; **Eye Relief (in.):** 3.5-4; **Length (in.):** 16; **Tube Dia. (in.):** 1; **W & E Adjustments:** Int.; **Weight (ozs.):** 22.7
Price: $742.00

8-32x [8,10,12]

Magn.: 8.6-31.4; **Field at 100 Yds. (feet):** 13-3.8; **Eye Relief (in.):** 3.5-4; **Length (in.):** 17; **Tube Dia. (in.):** 1; **W & E Adjustments:** Int.; **Weight (ozs.):** 24
Price: $798.00

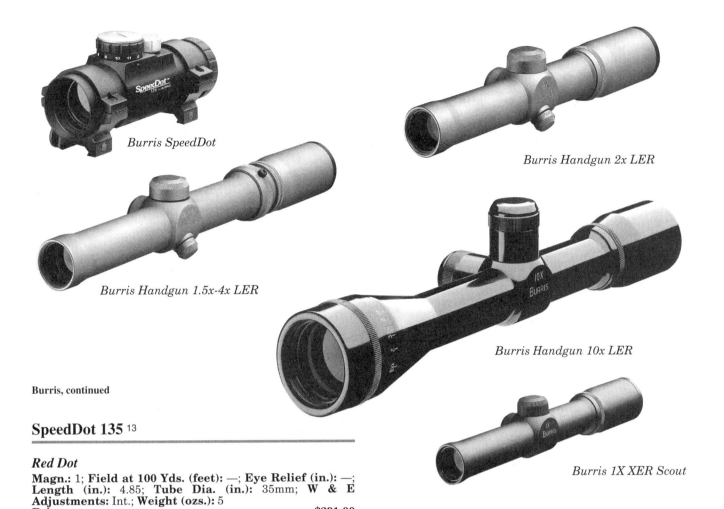

Burris SpeedDot

Burris Handgun 2x LER

Burris Handgun 1.5x-4x LER

Burris Handgun 10x LER

Burris 1X XER Scout

Burris, continued

SpeedDot 135 [13]

Red Dot

Magn.: 1; **Field at 100 Yds. (feet):** —; **Eye Relief (in.):** —; **Length (in.):** 4.85; **Tube Dia. (in.):** 35mm; **W & E Adjustments:** Int.; **Weight (ozs.):** 5
Price: $291.00

Handgun

1.50-4x LER [1,5,10]

Magn.: 1.6-3.; **Field at 100 Yds. (feet):** 16-11; **Eye Relief (in.):** 11-25; **Length (in.):** 10.25; **Tube Dia. (in.):** 1; **W & E Adjustments:** Int.; **Weight (ozs.):** 11
Price: $363.00

2-7x LER [3,4,5,10]

Magn.: 2-6.5; **Field at 100 Yds. (feet):** 21-7; **Eye Relief (in.):** 7-27; **Length (in.):** 9.5; **Tube Dia. (in.):** 1; **W & E Adjustments:** Int.; **Weight (ozs.):** 12.6
Price: $401.00

3-9x LER [4,5,10]

Magn.: 3.4-8.4; **Field at 100 Yds. (feet):** 12-5; **Eye Relief (in.):** 22-14; **Length (in.):** 11; **Tube Dia. (in.):** 1; **W & E Adjustments:** Int.; **Weight (ozs.):** 14
Price: $453.00

2x LER [4,5,6]

Magn.: 1.7; **Field at 100 Yds. (feet):** 21; **Eye Relief (in.):** 10-24; **Length (in.):** 8.75; **Tube Dia. (in.):** 1; **W & E Adjustments:** Int.; **Weight (ozs.):** 6.8
Price: $265.00

4x LER [1,4,5,6,10]

Magn.: 3.7; **Field at 100 Yds. (feet):** 11; **Eye Relief (in.):** 10-22; **Length (in.):** 9.625; **Tube Dia. (in.):** 1; **W & E Adjustments:** Int.; **Weight (ozs.):** 9
Price: $296.00

10x LER [1,4,6]

Magn.: 9.5; **Field at 100 Yds. (feet):** 4; **Eye Relief (in.):** 8-12; **Length (in.):** 13.5; **Tube Dia. (in.):** 1; **W & E Adjustments:** Int.; **Weight (ozs.):** 14
Price: $460.00

Scout Scope

1xXER [3,9]

Magn.: 1.5; **Field at 100 Yds. (feet):** 32; **Eye Relief (in.):** 4-24; **Length (in.):** 9; **Tube Dia. (in.):** 1; **W & E Adjustments:** Int.; **Weight (ozs.):** 7.0
Price: $290.00

2.75x [3,9]

Magn.: 2.7; **Field at 100 Yds. (feet):** 15; **Eye Relief (in.):** 7-14; **Length (in.):** 9.375; **Tube Dia. (in.):** 1; **W & E Adjustments:** Int.; **Weight (ozs.):** 7.0
Price: $319.00

Burris Data: [A]Available in Carbon Black, Titanium Gray and Autumn Gold finishes.

Burris Data: Black Diamond & Fullfield: All scopes avail. with Plex reticle. Steel-on-steel click adjustments. [1]Dot reticle on some models. [2]Post crosshair reticle extra. [3]Matte satin finish. [4]Available with parallax adjustment (standard on 10x, 12x, 4-12x, 6-12x, 6-18x, 6x HBR and 3-12x Signature). [5]Silver matte finish extra. [6]Target knobs extra, standard on silhouette models. LER and XER with P.A., 6x HBR. [7]Sunshade avail. [8]Avail. with Fine Plex reticle. [9]Available with Heavy Plex reticle. [10]Available with Posi-Lock. [11]Available with Peep Plex reticle. [12]Also avail. for rimfires, airguns. [13]Selected models available with camo finish.

Bushnell Elite 42-3640A

Bushnell Elite 32-5155M

Bushnell Elite 32-3950G

Burris, continued

Signature Series: LER=Long Eye Relief; IER=Intermediate Eye Relief; XER=Extra Eye Relief.

Speeddot 135: [13]Waterproof, fogproof, coated lenses, 11 brightness settings;3-MOA or 11-MOA dot size; includes Weaver-style rings and battery. **Partial listing shown.** Contact Burris for complete details.

Plex   Fine Plex   Ballistic Mil-Dot

Heavy Plex &   Peep Plex   Mil-Dot   Target Dot
Electro-Dot Plex

BUSHNELL

(Bausch & Lomb Elite rifle scopes now sold under Bushnell name)

Elite 4200 RainGuard

42-6244A [1]

Magn.: 6-24; **Field at 100 Yds. (feet):** 18-6; **Eye Relief (in.):** 3; **Length (in.):** 16.9; **Tube Dia. (in.):** 1; **W & E Adjustments:** Int.; **Weight (ozs.):** 20.2
Price: $729.95

42-2104G [2]

Magn.: 2.5-10; **Field at 100 Yds. (feet):** 41.5-10.8; **Eye Relief (in.):** 3; **Length (in.):** 13.5; **Tube Dia. (in.):** 1; **W & E Adjustments:** Int.; **Weight (ozs.):** 16
Price: $642.95

42-1636M [3]

Magn.: 1.5-6; **Field at 100 Yds. (feet):** 61.8-16.1; **Eye Relief (in.):** 3; **Length (in.):** 12.8; **Tube Dia. (in.):** 1; **W & E Adjustments:** Int.; **Weight (ozs.):** 15.4
Price: $608.95

42-3640A

Magn.: 36; **Field at 100 Yds. (feet):** 3; **Eye Relief (in.):** 3; **Length (in.):** 15; **Tube Dia. (in.):** 1; **W & E Adjustments:** Int.; **Weight (ozs.):** 17.6
Price: $955.95

42-4165M [5]

Magn.: 4-16; **Field at 100 Yds. (feet):** 26-7; **Eye Relief (in.):** 3; **Length (in.):** 15.6; **Tube Dia. (in.):** 1; **W & E Adjustments:** Int.; **Weight (ozs.):** 22
Price: $834.95

Elite 3200 RainGuard

32-5155M

Magn.: 5-15; **Field at 100 Yds. (feet):** 21-7; **Eye Relief (in.):** 3; **Length (in.):** 15.9; **Tube Dia. (in.):** 1; **W & E Adjustments:** Int.; **Weight (ozs.):** 19
Price: $528.95

32-4124A [1]

Magn.: 4-12; **Field at 100 Yds. (feet):** 26.9-9; **Eye Relief (in.):** 3; **Length (in.):** 13.2; **Tube Dia. (in.):** 1; **W & E Adjustments:** Int.; **Weight (ozs.):** 15
Price: $469.95

32-3940G [4]

Magn.: 3-9; **Field at 100 Yds. (feet):** 33.8-11.5; **Eye Relief (in.):** 3; **Length (in.):** 12.6; **Tube Dia. (in.):** 1; **W & E Adjustments:** Int.; **Weight (ozs.):** 13
Price: $351.95

32-2732M

Magn.: 2-7; **Field at 100 Yds. (feet):** 44.6-12.7; **Eye Relief (in.):** 3; **Length (in.):** 11.6; **Tube Dia. (in.):** 1; **W & E Adjustments:** Int.; **Weight (ozs.):** 12
Price: $342.95

32-3950G [6]

Magn.: 3-9; **Field at 100 Yds. (feet):** 31.5-10.5; **Eye Relief (in.):** 3; **Length (in.):** 15.7; **Tube Dia. (in.):** 1; **W & E Adjustments:** Int.; **Weight (ozs.):** 19
Price: $428.95

32-3955E

Magn.: 3-9; **Field at 100 Yds. (feet):** 31.5-10.5; **Eye Relief (in.):** 3; **Length (in.):** 15.6; **Tube Dia. (in.):** 30mm; **W & E Adjustments:** Int.; **Weight (ozs.):** 22
Price: $640.95

Elite 3200 Handgun

32-2632M [7]

Magn.: 2-6; **Field at 100 Yds. (feet):** 10-4; **Eye Relief (in.):** 20; **Length (in.):** 9; **Tube Dia. (in.):** 1; **W & E Adjustments:** Int.; **Weight (ozs.):** 10
Price: $444.95

32-2632G

Magn.: 2-6; **Field at 100 Yds. (feet):** 10-4; **Eye Relief (in.):** 20; **Length (in.):** 9; **Tube Dia. (in.):** 1; **W & E Adjustments:** Int.; **Weight (ozs.):** 10
Price: $444.95

Bushnell Scopechief 70-4145A

Bushnell Trophy 73-4124

Bushnell Trophy 73-3940

Bushnell Banner 71-1545

Bushnell Banner 71-4124

Bushnell Banner 71-4228

Bushnell, continued

Scopechief

70-3104M [4]
Magn.: 3.5-10; **Field at 100 Yds. (feet):** 43-15; **Eye Relief (in.):** 3.5; **Length (in.):** 13; **Tube Dia. (in.):** 1; **W & E Adjustments:** Int.; **Weight (ozs.):** 17
Price: $294.95

70-4145A [12]
Magn.: 4-14; **Field at 100 Yds. (feet):** 31-9; **Eye Relief (in.):** 3.5; **Length (in.):** 14.1; **Tube Dia. (in.):** 1; **W & E Adjustments:** Int.; **Weight (ozs.):** 23
Price: $408.95

Trophy

73-1500 [1]
Magn.: 1.75-5; **Field at 100 Yds. (feet):** 68-23; **Eye Relief (in.):** 3.5; **Length (in.):** 10.8; **Tube Dia. (in.):** 1; **W & E Adjustments:** Int.; **Weight (ozs.):** 12.3
Price: $262.95

73-4124 [1]
Magn.: 4-12; **Field at 100 Yds. (feet):** 32-11; **Eye Relief (in.):** 3; **Length (in.):** 12.5; **Tube Dia. (in.):** 1; **W & E Adjustments:** Int.; **Weight (ozs.):** 16.1
Price: $285.95

73-3940 [2]
Magn.: 3-9; **Field at 100 Yds. (feet):** 42-14; **Eye Relief (in.):** 3; **Length (in.):** 11.7; **Tube Dia. (in.):** 1; **W & E Adjustments:** Int.; **Weight (ozs.):** 13.2
Price: $159.95

73-6184 [7]
Magn.: 6-18; **Field at 100 Yds. (feet):** 17.3-6; **Eye Relief (in.):** 3; **Length (in.):** 14.8; **Tube Dia. (in.):** 1; **W & E Adjustments:** Int.; **Weight (ozs.):** 17.9
Price: $360.95

Turkey & Brush

73-1421 [11]
Magn.: 1.75-4; **Field at 100 Yds. (feet):** 73-30; **Eye Relief (in.):** 3.5; **Length (in.):** 10.8; **Tube Dia. (in.):** 32mm; **W & E Adjustments:** Int.; **Weight (ozs.):** 10.9
Price: $171.95

HOLOsight Model [8]
Magn.: 1; **Field at 100 Yds. (feet):** —; **Eye Relief (in.):** —; **Length (in.):** 6; **Tube Dia. (in.):** —; **W & E Adjustments:** Int.; **Weight (ozs.):** 8.7
Price: $444.95

Trophy Handgun

73-0232 [2]
Magn.: 2; **Field at 100 Yds. (feet):** 20; **Eye Relief (in.):** 9-26; **Length (in.):** 8.7; **Tube Dia. (in.):** 1; **W & E Adjustments:** Int.; **Weight (ozs.):** 7.7
Price: $218.95

73-2632 [3]
Magn.: 2-6; **Field at 100 Yds. (feet):** 21-7; **Eye Relief (in.):** 9-26; **Length (in.):** 9.1; **Tube Dia. (in.):** 1; **W & E Adjustments:** Int.; **Weight (ozs.):** 10.9
Price: $287.95

Banner

71-1545
Magn.: 1.5-4.5; **Field at 100 Yds. (feet):** 67-23; **Eye Relief (in.):** 3.5; **Length (in.):** 10.5; **Tube Dia. (in.):** 1; **W & E Adjustments:** Int.; **Weight (ozs.):** 10.5
Price: $116.95

71-3944 [9]
Magn.: 3-9; **Field at 100 Yds. (feet):** 36-13; **Eye Relief (in.):** 4; **Length (in.):** 11.5; **Tube Dia. (in.):** 1; **W & E Adjustments:** Int.; **Weight (ozs.):** 12.5
Price: $125.95

Bushnell Sportview 79-0039

Bushnell Sportview 79-0412

Bushnell Sportview 79-1545

Bushnell Sportview 79-1548

Bushnell Sportview 79-2538

Bushnell, continued

71-3950 [10]

Magn.: 3-9; **Field at 100 Yds. (feet):** 26-10; **Eye Relief (in.):** 3; **Length (in.):** 16; **Tube Dia. (in.):** 1; **W & E Adjustments:** Int.; **Weight (ozs.):** 19
Price: $186.95

71-4124 [7]

Magn.: 4-12; **Field at 100 Yds. (feet):** 29-11; **Eye Relief (in.):** 3; **Length (in.):** 12; **Tube Dia. (in.):** 1; **W & E Adjustments:** Int.; **Weight (ozs.):** 15
Price: $157.95

71-4228

Magn.: 4; **Field at 100 Yds. (feet):** 26.5; **Eye Relief (in.):** 3; **Length (in.):** 11.75; **Tube Dia. (in.):** 1; **W & E Adjustments:** Int.; **Weight (ozs.):** 10
Price: $81.95

71-6185 [10]

Magn.: 6-18; **Field at 100 Yds. (feet):** 17-6; **Eye Relief (in.):** 3; **Length (in.):** 16; **Tube Dia. (in.):** 1; **W & E Adjustments:** Int.; **Weight (ozs.):** 18
Price: $209.95

Sportview

79-0004

Magn.: 4; **Field at 100 Yds. (feet):** 31; **Eye Relief (in.):** 4; **Length (in.):** 11.7; **Tube Dia. (in.):** 1; **W & E Adjustments:** Int.; **Weight (ozs.):** 11.2
Price: $98.95

79-0039

Magn.: 3-9; **Field at 100 Yds. (feet):** 38-13; **Eye Relief (in.):** 3.5; **Length (in.):** 10.75; **Tube Dia. (in.):** 1; **W & E Adjustments:** Int.; **Weight (ozs.):** 11.2
Price: $116.95

79-0412 [7]

Magn.: 4-12; **Field at 100 Yds. (feet):** 27-9; **Eye Relief (in.):** 3.2; **Length (in.):** 13.1; **Tube Dia. (in.):** 1; **W & E Adjustments:** Int.; **Weight (ozs.):** 14.6
Price: $141.95

79-1393 [6]

Magn.: 3-9; **Field at 100 Yds. (feet):** 35-12; **Eye Relief (in.):** 3.5; **Length (in.):** 11.75; **Tube Dia. (in.):** 1; **W & E Adjustments:** Int.; **Weight (ozs.):** 10
Price: $68.95

79-1545

Magn.: 1.5-4.5; **Field at 100 Yds. (feet):** 69-24; **Eye Relief (in.):** 3; **Length (in.):** 10.7; **Tube Dia. (in.):** 1; **W & E Adjustments:** Int.; **Weight (ozs.):** 8.6
Price: $86.95

79-1548 [11]

Magn.: 1.5-4.5; **Field at 100 Yds. (feet):** 71-25; **Eye Relief (in.):** 3.5; **Length (in.):** 10.4; **Tube Dia. (in.):** 1; **W & E Adjustments:** Int.; **Weight (ozs.):** 11.8
Price: $104.95

79-2538 [11]

Magn.: 2.5; **Field at 100 Yds. (feet):** 45; **Eye Relief (in.):** 3; **Length (in.):** 11; **Tube Dia. (in.):** 1; **W & E Adjustments:** Int.; **Weight (ozs.):** 10
Price: $76.95

79-1403

Magn.: 4; **Field at 100 Yds. (feet):** 29; **Eye Relief (in.):** 4; **Length (in.):** 11.75; **Tube Dia. (in.):** 1; **W & E Adjustments:** Int.; **Weight (ozs.):** 9.2
Price: $57.95

79-6184

Magn.: 6-18; **Field at 100 Yds. (feet):** 19.1-6.8; **Eye Relief (in.):** 3; **Length (in.):** 14.5; **Tube Dia. (in.):** 1; **W & E Adjustments:** Int.; **Weight (ozs.):** 15.9
Price: $170.95

79-3940M

Magn.: 3-9; **Field at 100 Yds. (feet):** 42-14; **Eye Relief (in.):** 3; **Length (in.):** 12.7; **Tube Dia. (in.):** 1; **W & E Adjustments:** Int.; **Weight (ozs.):** 12.5
Price: $95.95

Bushnell Data: (Bushnell Elite)
[1]Adj. objective, sunshade; also in matte and with 1/4-MOA dot or Mil Dot reticle. [2]Also in matte and silver finish. [3]Only in matte finish. [4]Also in matte and silver finish. [5]Adjustable objective. [6]50mm objective; also in matte finish. [7]Also in silver finish. **Partial listings shown. Contact Bushnell Performance Optics for details.**

Bushnell Data: (Bushnell)
[1]Wide Angle. [2]Also silver finish. [3]Also silver finish. [4]Matte finish. [5]Also silver finish. [7]Adj. obj. [8]Variable intensity; fits Weaver-style base. [9]Blackpowder scope; extended eye relief, Circle-X reticle. [10]50mm objective. [11]With Circle-X reticle, matte finish. [12]Matte finish, adjustable objective.

HOLOSIGHT RETICLES

MOA Dot

Standard

SCOPE RETICLES

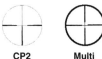
CP2   Multi   Euro

Circle-X

Kahles 4x36

Kahles 1.1-4x24

DOCTER OPTIC

Fixed Power

4x32
Magn.: 4; **Field at 100 Yds. (feet):** 31; **Eye Relief (in.):** 3; **Length (in.):** 10.7; **Tube Dia. (in.):** 26mm; **W & E Adjustments:** Int.; **Weight (ozs.):** 10
Price: $898.00

6x42
Magn.: 6; **Field at 100 Yds. (feet):** 20; **Eye Relief (in.):** 3; **Length (in.):** 12.8; **Tube Dia. (in.):** 26mm; **W & E Adjustments:** Int.; **Weight (ozs.):** 12.7
Price: $1,004.00

8x56 [1]
Magn.: 8; **Field at 100 Yds. (feet):** 15; **Eye Relief (in.):** 3; **Length (in.):** 14.7; **Tube Dia. (in.):** 26mm; **W & E Adjustments:** Int.; **Weight (ozs.):** 15.6
Price: $1,240.00

Variables

1-4x24
Magn.: 1-4; **Field at 100 Yds. (feet):** 79.7-31.3; **Eye Relief (in.):** 3; **Length (in.):** 10.8; **Tube Dia. (in.):** 30mm; **W & E Adjustments:** Int.; **Weight (ozs.):** 13
Price: $1,300.00

1.2-5x32
Magn.: 1.2-5; **Field at 100 Yds. (feet):** 65-25; **Eye Relief (in.):** 3; **Length (in.):** 11.6; **Tube Dia. (in.):** 30mm; **W & E Adjustments:** Int.; **Weight (ozs.):** 15.4
Price: $1,345.00

1.5-6x42
Magn.: 1.5-6; **Field at 100 Yds. (feet):** 41.3-20.6; **Eye Relief (in.):** 3; **Length (in.):** 12.7; **Tube Dia. (in.):** 30mm; **W & E Adjustments:** Int.; **Weight (ozs.):** 16.8
Price: $1,378.00

2.5-10x48
Magn.: 2.5-10; **Field at 100 Yds. (feet):** 36.6-12.4; **Eye Relief (in.):** 3; **Length (in.):** 13.7; **Tube Dia. (in.):** 30mm; **W & E Adjustments:** Int.; **Weight (ozs.):** 18.6
Price: $1,378.00

2-12x56
Magn.: 3-12; **Field at 100 Yds. (feet):** 44.2-13.8; **Eye Relief (in.):** 3; **Length (in.):** 14.8; **Tube Dia. (in.):** 30mm; **W & E Adjustments:** Int.; **Weight (ozs.):** 20.3
Price: $1,425.00

3-10x40
Magn.: 3-10; **Field at 100 Yds. (feet):** 34.4-11.7; **Eye Relief (in.):** 3; **Length (in.):** 13; **Tube Dia. (in.):** 1; **W & E Adjustments:** Int.; **Weight (ozs.):** 18
Price: $795.00

Docter Optic Data: Matte black and matte silver finish available. All lenses multi-coated. Illuminated reticle avail., choice of reticles. [1]Rail mount, aspherical lenses avail. Aspherical lens model, **$1,375.00.** Imported from Germany by Docter Optic Technologies, Inc.

KAHLES

4x36
Magn.: 4; **Field at 100 Yds. (feet):** 34.5; **Eye Relief (in.):** 3.15; **Length (in.):** 11.2; **Tube Dia. (in.):** 1; **W & E Adjustments:** Int.; **Weight (ozs.):** 12.7
Price: $555.00

6x42
Magn.: 6; **Field at 100 Yds. (feet):** 23; **Eye Relief (in.):** 3.15; **Length (in.):** 12.4; **Tube Dia. (in.):** 1; **W & E Adjustments:** Int.; **Weight (ozs.):** 14.4
Price: $694.00

8x50 [1]
Magn.: 8; **Field at 100 Yds. (feet):** 17.3; **Eye Relief (in.):** 3.15; **Length (in.):** 13; **Tube Dia. (in.):** 1; **W & E Adjustments:** Int.; **Weight (ozs.):** 16.5
Price: $749.00

1.1-4x24
Magn.: 1.1-4; **Field at 100 Yds. (feet):** 108-31.8; **Eye Relief (in.):** 3.5; **Length (in.):** 10.8; **Tube Dia. (in.):** 30mm; **W & E Adjustments:** Int.; **Weight (ozs.):** 12.7
Price: $722.00

Kahles 1.5-6x42

Kahles 3-12x56

Kahles, continued

1.5-6x42 [1]

Magn.: 1.5-6; **Field at 100 Yds. (feet):** 72-21.3; **Eye Relief (in.):** 3.5; **Length (in.):** 12.0; **Tube Dia. (in.):** 30mm; **W & E Adjustments:** Int.; **Weight (ozs.):** 15.8
Price: $832.00

2.5-10x50 [1]

Magn.: 2.5-10; **Field at 100 Yds. (feet):** 43.5-12.9; **Eye Relief (in.):** 3.5; **Length (in.):** 12.8; **Tube Dia. (in.):** 30mm; **W & E Adjustments:** Int.; **Weight (ozs.):** 15.8
Price: $1,353.00

3-9x42

Magn.: 3-9; **Field at 100 Yds. (feet):** 43-16; **Eye Relief (in.):** 3.5; **Length (in.):** 12; **Tube Dia. (in.):** 1; **W & E Adjustments:** Int.; **Weight (ozs.):** 13
Price: $621.06

3-9x42AH

Magn.: 3-9; **Field at 100 Yds. (feet):** 43-15; **Eye Relief (in.):** 3.5; **Length (in.):** 12.36; **Tube Dia. (in.):** 1; **W & E Adjustments:** Int.; **Weight (ozs.):** 12.7
Price: $665.00

3-12x56 [1]

Magn.: 3-12; **Field at 100 Yds. (feet):** 30-11; **Eye Relief (in.):** 3.5; **Length (in.):** 15.4; **Tube Dia. (in.):** 30mm; **W & E Adjustments:** Int.; **Weight (ozs.):** 18
Price: $1,377.72

Kahles Data: Aluminum tube. Multi-coated, waterproof. [1]Also available with illuminated reticle. Imported from Austria by Swarovski Optik.

No. 4A

No. 7A

Plex

Illuminated No. 4N

Illuminated Plex N

TD Smith

Ultravid 1.75-6x32

Magn.: 1.75-6; **Field at 100 Yds. (feet):** 47-18; **Eye Relief (in.):** 4.8-3.7; **Length (in.):** 11.25; **Tube Dia. (in.):** 30mm; **W & E Adjustments:** Int.; **Weight (ozs.):** 14
Price: $749.00

Ultravid 3.5-10x42

Magn.: 3.5-10; **Field at 100 Yds. (feet):** 29.5-10.7; **Eye Relief (in.):** 4.6-3.6; **Length (in.):** 12.62; **Tube Dia. (in.):** 30mm; **W & E Adjustments:** Int.; **Weight (ozs.):** 16
Price: $849.00

Ultravid 4.5-14x42

Magn.: 4.5-14; **Field at 100 Yds. (feet):** 20.5-7.4; **Eye Relief (in.):** 5-3.7; **Length (in.):** 12.28; **Tube Dia. (in.):** 30mm; **W & E Adjustments:** Int.; **Weight (ozs.):** 18
Price: $949.00

Leica Data: Aluminum tube with hard anodized matte black finish with titanium accents; finger-adjustable windage and elevation with 1/4-MOA clicks. Made in U.S. From Leica.

Leicaplex Standard

Leica Dot

Standard Dot

Crosshair

Euro

Post & Plex

Vari-X III 3.5x10

Tactical

Magn.: 3.5-10; **Field at 100 Yds. (feet):** 29.5-10.7; **Eye Relief (in.):** 3.6-4.6; **Length (in.):** 12.5; **Tube Dia. (in.):** 1; **W & E Adjustments:** Int.; **Weight (ozs.):** 13.5
Price: $801.80

M8-2X EER [1]

Magn.: 1.7; **Field at 100 Yds. (feet):** 21.2; **Eye Relief (in.):** 12-24; **Length (in.):** 7.9; **Tube Dia. (in.):** 1; **W & E Adjustments:** Int.; **Weight (ozs.):** 6
Price: $312.50

M8-2X EER Silver [1]

Magn.: 1.7; **Field at 100 Yds. (feet):** 21.2; **Eye Relief (in.):** 12-24; **Length (in.):** 7.9; **Tube Dia. (in.):** 1; **W & E Adjustments:** Int.; **Weight (ozs.):** 6
Price: $337.50

M8-2.5x28 IER Scout

Magn.: 2.3; **Field at 100 Yds. (feet):** 22; **Eye Relief (in.):** 9.3; **Length (in.):** 10.1; **Tube Dia. (in.):** 1; **W & E Adjustments:** Int.; **Weight (ozs.):** 7.5
Price: $408.90

Leupold Vari-X 2.5-8 EER

Leupold M8-6x42 O.A. Tactical

Leupold M8-6x36mm

Leupold Vari-X 3-9x Compact

Leupold, continued

M8-4X EER [1]

Magn.: 3.7; **Field at 100 Yds. (feet):** 9; **Eye Relief (in.):** 12-24; **Length (in.):** 8.4; **Tube Dia. (in.):** 1; **W & E Adjustments:** Int.; **Weight (ozs.):** 7
Price: $425.00

M8-4X EER Silver [1]

Magn.: 3.7; **Field at 100 Yds. (feet):** 9; **Eye Relief (in.):** 12-24; **Length (in.):** 8.4; **Tube Dia. (in.):** 1; **W & E Adjustments:** Int.; **Weight (ozs.):** 7
Price: $425.00

Vari-X 2.5-8 EER

Magn.: 2.5-8; **Field at 100 Yds. (feet):** 13-4.3; **Eye Relief (in.):** 11.7-12; **Length (in.):** 9.7; **Tube Dia. (in.):** 1; **W & E Adjustments:** Int.; **Weight (ozs.):** 10.9
Price: $608.90

M8-4X Compact

Magn.: 3.6; **Field at 100 Yds. (feet):** 25.5; **Eye Relief (in.):** 4.5; **Length (in.):** 9.2; **Tube Dia. (in.):** 1; **W & E Adjustments:** Int.; **Weight (ozs.):** 7.5
Price: $382.10

Vari-X 2-7x Compact

Magn.: 2.5-6.6; **Field at 100 Yds. (feet):** 41.7-16.5; **Eye Relief (in.):** 5-3.7; **Length (in.):** 9.9; **Tube Dia. (in.):** 1; **W & E Adjustments:** Int.; **Weight (ozs.):** 8.5
Price: $478.60

Vari-X 3-9x Compact

Magn.: 3.2-8.6; **Field at 100 Yds. (feet):** 34-13.5; **Eye Relief (in.):** 4-3; **Length (in.):** 11-11.3; **Tube Dia. (in.):** 1; **W & E Adjustments:** Int.; **Weight (ozs.):** 11
Price: $519.60

M8-4X

Magn.: 4; **Field at 100 Yds. (feet):** 24; **Eye Relief (in.):** 4; **Length (in.):** 10.7; **Tube Dia. (in.):** 1; **W & E Adjustments:** Int.; **Weight (ozs.):** 9.3
Price: $385.70

M8-6x36mm

Magn.: 5.9; **Field at 100 Yds. (feet):** 17.7; **Eye Relief (in.):** 4.3; **Length (in.):** 11.4; **Tube Dia. (in.):** 1; **W & E Adjustments:** Int.; **Weight (ozs.):** 10
Price: $410.70

M8-6x42mm

Magn.: 6; **Field at 100 Yds. (feet):** 17; **Eye Relief (in.):** 4.5; **Length (in.):** 12; **Tube Dia. (in.):** 1; **W & E Adjustments:** Int.; **Weight (ozs.):** 11.3
Price: $510.70

*M8-6x42 A.O. Tactical

Magn.: 6; **Field at 100 Yds. (feet):** 17; **Eye Relief (in.):** 4.2; **Length (in.):** 12.1; **Tube Dia. (in.):** 1; **W & E Adjustments:** Int.; **Weight (ozs.):** 11.3
Price: $628.60

M8-12x A.O. Varmint

Magn.: 11.6; **Field at 100 Yds. (feet):** 9.1; **Eye Relief (in.):** 4.2; **Length (in.):** 13; **Tube Dia. (in.):** 1; **W & E Adjustments:** Int.; **Weight (ozs.):** 13.5
Price: $571.40

Vari-X 3-9x Compact EFR A.O.

Magn.: 3.8-8.6; **Field at 100 Yds. (feet):** 34-13.5; **Eye Relief (in.):** 4-3; **Length (in.):** 11; **Tube Dia. (in.):** 1; **W & E Adjustments:** Int.; **Weight (ozs.):** 11
Price: $550.00

Vari-X-II 1x4

Magn.: 1.6-4.2; **Field at 100 Yds. (feet):** 70.5-28.5; **Eye Relief (in.):** 4.3-3.8; **Length (in.):** 9.2; **Tube Dia. (in.):** 1; **W & E Adjustments:** Int.; **Weight (ozs.):** 9
Price: $396.40

Vari-X-II 2x7

Magn.: 2.5-6.6; **Field at 100 Yds. (feet):** 42.5-17.8; **Eye Relief (in.):** 4.9-3.8; **Length (in.):** 11; **Tube Dia. (in.):** 1; **W & E Adjustments:** Int.; **Weight (ozs.):** 10.5
Price: $428.60

Vari-X-II 3x9 [1,3]

Magn.: 3.3-8.6; **Field at 100 Yds. (feet):** 32.3-14; **Eye Relief (in.):** 4.1-3.7; **Length (in.):** 12.3; **Tube Dia. (in.):** 1; **W & E Adjustments:** Int.; **Weight (ozs.):** 13.5
Price: $432.10

Vari-X-II 3-9x50mm

Magn.: 3.3-8.6; **Field at 100 Yds. (feet):** 32.3-14; **Eye Relief (in.):** 4.7-3.7; **Length (in.):** 12; **Tube Dia. (in.):** 1; **W & E Adjustments:** Int.; **Weight (ozs.):** 13.6
Price: $510.70

Vari-X II 3-9x40 Tactical

Magn.: 3-9; **Field at 100 Yds. (feet):** 32.3-14; **Eye Relief (in.):** 4.7-3.7; **Length (in.):** 12.2; **Tube Dia. (in.):** 1; **W & E Adjustments:** Int.; **Weight (ozs.):** 13
Price: $535.70

Vari-X-II 4-12 A.O. Matte

Magn.: 4.4-11.6; **Field at 100 Yds. (feet):** 22.8-11; **Eye Relief (in.):** 5-3.3; **Length (in.):** 12.3; **Tube Dia. (in.):** 1; **W & E Adjustments:** Int.; **Weight (ozs.):** 13.5
Price: $594.60

Leupold Vari-X-III 1.5-5x20

Leupold Vari-X-III 1.75-6x32

Leupold Vari-X-III 3.5-10x40 Long Range M3

Leupold Vari-X-III 3.5-10x50

Leupold, continued

*Vari-X-III 1.5-5x20

Magn.: 1.5-4.5; **Field at 100 Yds. (feet):** 66-23; **Eye Relief (in.):** 5.3-3.7; **Length (in.):** 9.4; **Tube Dia. (in.):** 1; **W & E Adjustments:** Int.; **Weight (ozs.):** 9.5
Price: $635.70

Vari-X-III 1.75-6x32

Magn.: 1.9-5.6; **Field at 100 Yds. (feet):** 47-18; **Eye Relief (in.):** 4.8-3.7; **Length (in.):** 9.8; **Tube Dia. (in.):** 1; **W & E Adjustments:** Int.; **Weight (ozs.):** 11
Price: $683.90

Vari-X-III 2.5x8

Magn.: 2.6-7.8; **Field at 100 Yds. (feet):** 37-13.5; **Eye Relief (in.):** 4.7-3.7; **Length (in.):** 11.3; **Tube Dia. (in.):** 1; **W & E Adjustments:** Int.; **Weight (ozs.):** 11.5
Price: $678.60

Vari-X-III 3.5-10x40 Long Range M3 [4]

Magn.: 3.9-9.7; **Field at 100 Yds. (feet):** 29.8-11; **Eye Relief (in.):** 4-3.5; **Length (in.):** 13.5; **Tube Dia. (in.):** 30mm; **W & E Adjustments:** Int.; **Weight (ozs.):** 19.5
Price: $1,157.10

Vari-X-III 3.5-10x50

Magn.: 3.3-9.7; **Field at 100 Yds. (feet):** 29.5-10.7; **Eye Relief (in.):** 4.6-3.6; **Length (in.):** 12.4; **Tube Dia. (in.):** 1; **W & E Adjustments:** Int.; **Weight (ozs.):** 13
Price: $796.40

Vari-X-III 4.5-14x40 A.O.

Magn.: 4.7-13.7; **Field at 100 Yds. (feet):** 20.8-7.4; **Eye Relief (in.):** 5-3.7; **Length (in.):** 12.4; **Tube Dia. (in.):** 1; **W & E Adjustments:** Int.; **Weight (ozs.):** 14.5
Price: $780.40

*Vari-X-III 4.5-14x50 A.O. Long Range Target

Magn.: 4.7-13.7; **Field at 100 Yds. (feet):** 20.8-7.4; **Eye Relief (in.):** 5-3.7; **Length (in.):** 12.4; **Tube Dia. (in.):** 1; **W & E Adjustments:** Int.; **Weight (ozs.):** 14.5
Price: $903.60

Leupold Vari-X III 8.5-25x50 Long Range Target

Leupold Mark 4 M1-16x40

Vari-X III 4.5-14x50 Long Range Tactical [4]

Magn.: 4.9-14.3; **Field at 100 Yds. (feet):** 19-6; **Eye Relief (in.):** 5-3.7; **Length (in.):** 12.1; **Tube Dia. (in.):** 30mm; **W & E Adjustments:** Int.; **Weight (ozs.):** 17.5
Price: $1,082.10

Vari-X-III 6.5-20 A.O.

Magn.: 6.5-19.2; **Field at 100 Yds. (feet):** 14.2-5.5; **Eye Relief (in.):** 5.3-3.6; **Length (in.):** 14.2; **Tube Dia. (in.):** 1; **W & E Adjustments:** Int.; **Weight (ozs.):** 17.5
Price: $823.20

Vari-X-III 6.5x20xTarget EFR

Magn.: 6.5-19.2; **Field at 100 Yds. (feet):** —; **Eye Relief (in.):** 5.3-3.6; **Length (in.):** 14.2; **Tube Dia. (in.):** 1; **W & E Adjustments:** Int.; **Weight (ozs.):** 16.5
Price: $919.60

Vari-X III 6.5-20x50 Long Range Target [4]

Magn.: 6.8-19.2; **Field at 100 Yds. (feet):** 14.7-5.4; **Eye Relief (in.):** 4.9-3.7; **Length (in.):** 14.3; **Tube Dia. (in.):** 30mm; **W & E Adjustments:** Int.; **Weight (ozs.):** 19
Price: $1,166.10

Vari-X III 8.5-25x40 A.O. Target

Magn.: 8.5-25; **Field at 100 Yds. (feet):** 10.86-4.2; **Eye Relief (in.):** 5.3; **Length (in.):** 14.3; **Tube Dia. (in.):** 1; **W & E Adjustments:** Int.; **Weight (ozs.):** 17.5
Price: $900.00

Vari-X III 8.5-25x 50 Long Range Target [4]

Magn.: 8.3-24.2; **Field at 100 Yds. (feet):** 11.4-4.3; **Eye Relief (in.):** 4.4-3.6; **Length (in.):** 14.3; **Tube Dia. (in.):** 30mm; **W & E Adjustments:** Int.; **Weight (ozs.):** 19
Price: $1,260.70

Mark 4 M1-10x40

Magn.: 10; **Field at 100 Yds. (feet):** 11.1; **Eye Relief (in.):** 3.6; **Length (in.):** 13.125; **Tube Dia. (in.):** 30mm; **W & E Adjustments:** Int.; **Weight (ozs.):** 21
Price: $1,807.10

Mark 4 M1-16x40

Magn.: 16; **Field at 100 Yds. (feet):** 6.6; **Eye Relief (in.):** 4.1; **Length (in.):** 12.875; **Tube Dia. (in.):** 30mm; **W & E Adjustments:** Int.; **Weight (ozs.):** 22
Price: $1,807.10

Mark 4 M3-10x40

Magn.: 10; **Field at 100 Yds. (feet):** 11.1; **Eye Relief (in.):** 3.6; **Length (in.):** 13.125; **Tube Dia. (in.):** 30mm; **W & E Adjustments:** Int.; **Weight (ozs.):** 21
Price: $1,807.10

Vari-X III 6.5x20 [2] A.O.

Magn.: 6.5-19.2; **Field at 100 Yds. (feet):** 14.2-5.5; **Eye Relief (in.):** 5.3-3.6; **Length (in.):** 14.2; **Tube Dia. (in.):** 1; **W & E Adjustments:** Int.; **Weight (ozs.):** 16
Price: $823.20

Leupold Mark 4 M3-10x40

Leupold M8 4x32

Leupold Vari-X III 6.5-20 A.O.

Leupold Vari-X II 1x40

Leupold Vari-X II 2x7

Vari-X II 2x7

Magn.: 2.5-6.6; **Field at 100 Yds. (feet):** 42.5-17.8; **Eye Relief (in.):** 4.9-3.8; **Length (in.):** 11; **Tube Dia. (in.):** 1; **W & E Adjustments:** Int.; **Weight (ozs.):** 9
Price: **$453.60**

Leupold Data: Constantly centered reticles, choice of Duplex, tapered CPC, Leupold Dot, Crosshair and Dot. CPC and Dot reticles extra. [1]2x and 4x scopes have from 12"-24" of eye relief and are suitable for handguns, top ejection arms and muzzle-loaders. [2]3x9 Compact, 6x Compact, 12x, 3x9, and 6.5x20 come with adjustable objective. Sunshade available for all adjustable objective scopes, **$23.20-$41.10**. [3]Silver finish about **$25.00** extra. [4]Long Range scopes have side focus parallax adjustment, additional windage and elevation travel. Partial listing shown. **Contact Leupold for complete details.**
*Models available with illuminated reticle for additional cost.

Leupold, continued

BR-D 24x40 A.O. Target

Magn.: 24; **Field at 100 Yds. (feet):** 4.7; **Eye Relief (in.):** 3.2; **Length (in.):** 13.6; **Tube Dia. (in.):** 1; **W & E Adjustments:** Int.; **Weight (ozs.):** 15.3
Price: **$1,035.70**

BR-D 36x-40 A.O. Target

Magn.: 36; **Field at 100 Yds. (feet):** 3.2; **Eye Relief (in.):** 3.4; **Length (in.):** 14.1; **Tube Dia. (in.):** 1; **W & E Adjustments:** Int.; **Weight (ozs.):** 15.6
Price: **$1,083.90**

LPS 1.5-6x42

Magn.: 1.5-6; **Field at 100 Yds. (feet):** 58.7-15.7; **Eye Relief (in.):** 4; **Length (in.):** 11.2; **Tube Dia. (in.):** 30mm; **W & E Adjustments:** Int.; **Weight (ozs.):** 16
Price: **$1,476.80**

LPS 3.5-14x52 A.O.

Magn.: 3.5-14; **Field at 100 Yds. (feet):** 28-7.2; **Eye Relief (in.):** 4; **Length (in.):** 13.1; **Tube Dia. (in.):** 30mm; **W & E Adjustments:** Int.; **Weight (ozs.):** 22
Price: **$1,569.60**

Rimfire

Vari-X 2-7x RF Special

Magn.: 3.6; **Field at 100 Yds. (feet):** 25.5; **Eye Relief (in.):** 4.5; **Length (in.):** 9.2; **Tube Dia. (in.):** 1; **W & E Adjustments:** Int.; **Weight (ozs.):** 7.5
Price: **$478.60**

Shotgun

M8 4x33

Magn.: 3.7; **Field at 100 Yds. (feet):** 9; **Eye Relief (in.):** 12-24; **Length (in.):** 8.4; **Tube Dia. (in.):** 1; **W & E Adjustments:** Int.; **Weight (ozs.):** 6
Price: **$410.70**

Vari-X II 1x4

Magn.: 1.6-4.2; **Field at 100 Yds. (feet):** 70.5-28.5; **Eye Relief (in.):** 4.3-3.8; **Length (in.):** 9.2; **Tube Dia. (in.):** 1; **W & E Adjustments:** Int.; **Weight (ozs.):** 9
Price: **$421.40**

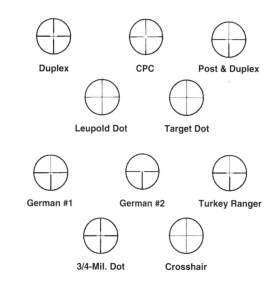

Duplex   CPC   Post & Duplex

Leupold Dot   Target Dot

German #1   German #2   Turkey Ranger

3/4-Mil. Dot   Crosshair

NIKON

Monarch UCC

4x40 [2]

Magn.: 4; **Field at 100 Yds. (feet):** 26.7; **Eye Relief (in.):** 3.5; **Length (in.):** 11.7; **Tube Dia. (in.):** 1; **W & E Adjustments:** Int.; **Weight (ozs.):** 11.7
Price: **$330.95**

1.5-4.5x20 [3]

Magn.: 1.5-4.5; **Field at 100 Yds. (feet):** 67.8-22.5; **Eye Relief (in.):** 3.7-3.2; **Length (in.):** 10.1; **Tube Dia. (in.):** 1; **W & E Adjustments:** Int.; **Weight (ozs.):** 9.5
Price: **$364.95**

Nikon Monarch UCC 4x40

Nikon Monarch UCC 4-12x40 A.O.

Nikon Buckmaster 4x40

Nikon Buckmaster 3-9x40

Nikon Buckmaster 3-9x50

Nikon, continued

2-7x32

Magn.: 2-7; **Field at 100 Yds. (feet):** 46.7-13.7; **Eye Relief (in.):** 3.9-3.3; **Length (in.):** 11.3; **Tube Dia. (in.):** 1; **W & E Adjustments:** Int.; **Weight (ozs.):** 11.3
Price: $426.95

3-9x40 [1]

Magn.: 3-9; **Field at 100 Yds. (feet):** 33.8-11.3; **Eye Relief (in.):** 3.6-3.2; **Length (in.):** 12.5; **Tube Dia. (in.):** 1; **W & E Adjustments:** Int.; **Weight (ozs.):** 12.5
Price: $430.95

3.5-10x50

Magn.: 3.5-10; **Field at 100 Yds. (feet):** 25.5-8.9; **Eye Relief (in.):** 3.9-3.8; **Length (in.):** 13.7; **Tube Dia. (in.):** 1; **W & E Adjustments:** Int.; **Weight (ozs.):** 15.5
Price: $644.95

4-12x40 A.O.

Magn.: 4-12; **Field at 100 Yds. (feet):** 25.7-8.6; **Eye Relief (in.):** 3.6-3.2; **Length (in.):** 14; **Tube Dia. (in.):** 1; **W & E Adjustments:** Int.; **Weight (ozs.):** 16.6
Price: $552.95

6.5-20x44

Magn.: 6.5-19.4; **Field at 100 Yds. (feet):** 16.2-5.4; **Eye Relief (in.):** 3.5-3.1; **Length (in.):** 14.8; **Tube Dia. (in.):** 1; **W & E Adjustments:** Int.; **Weight (ozs.):** 19.6
Price: $684.95

2x20 EER

Magn.: 2; **Field at 100 Yds. (feet):** 22; **Eye Relief (in.):** 26.4; **Length (in.):** 8.1; **Tube Dia. (in.):** 1; **W & E Adjustments:** Int.; **Weight (ozs.):** 6.3
Price: $248.95

Buckmasters

4x40

Magn.: 4; **Field at 100 Yds. (feet):** 30.4; **Eye Relief (in.):** 3.3; **Length (in.):** 12.7; **Tube Dia. (in.):** 1; **W & E Adjustments:** Int.; **Weight (ozs.):** 11.8
Price: $244.95

3-9x40 [4]

Magn.: 3.3-8.6; **Field at 100 Yds. (feet):** 33.8-11.3; **Eye Relief (in.):** 3.5-3.4; **Length (in.):** 12.7; **Tube Dia. (in.):** 1; **W & E Adjustments:** Int.; **Weight (ozs.):** 13.4
Price: $324.95

3-9x50

Magn.: 3.3-8.6; **Field at 100 Yds. (feet):** 33.8-11.3; **Eye Relief (in.):** 3.5-3.4; **Length (in.):** 12.9; **Tube Dia. (in.):** 1; **W & E Adjustments:** Int.; **Weight (ozs.):** 18.2
Price: $452.95

Nikon Data: Super multi-coated lenses and blackening of all internal metal parts for maximum light gathering capability; positive .25-MOA; fogproof; waterproof; shockproof; luster and matte finish. [1]Also available in matte silver finish. [2]Available in silver matte finish. [3]Available with TurkeyPro or Nikoplex reticle. [4]Silver Shadow finish; black matte **$296.95**. Partial listing shown. From Nikon, Inc.

Pentax Lightseeker

Pentax Lightseeker Shotgun

PENTAX

Lightseeker 1.75-6x [1]

Magn.: 1.75-6; **Field at 100 Yds. (feet):** 71-20; **Eye Relief (in.):** 3.5-4; **Length (in.):** 10.8; **Tube Dia. (in.):** 1; **W & E Adjustments:** Int.; **Weight (ozs.):** 13
Price: $526.00

Lightseeker 2-8x [2]

Magn.: 2-8; **Field at 100 Yds. (feet):** 53-17; **Eye Relief (in.):** 3.5-4; **Length (in.):** 11.7; **Tube Dia. (in.):** 1; **W & E Adjustments:** Int.; **Weight (ozs.):** 14
Price: $560.00

Lightseeker 3-9x [3, 4, 10, 11]

Magn.: 3-9; **Field at 100 Yds. (feet):** 36-14; **Eye Relief (in.):** 3.5-4; **Length (in.):** 12.7; **Tube Dia. (in.):** 1; **W & E Adjustments:** Int.; **Weight (ozs.):** 15
Price: $594.00

Lightseeker 3.5-10x [5]

Magn.: 3.5-10; **Field at 100 Yds. (feet):** 29.5-11; **Eye Relief (in.):** 3.5-4; **Length (in.):** 14; **Tube Dia. (in.):** 1; **W & E Adjustments:** Int.; **Weight (ozs.):** 19.5
Price: $630.00

Lightseeker 4-16x [6, 9]

Magn.: 4-16; **Field at 100 Yds. (feet):** 33-9; **Eye Relief (in.):** 3.5-4; **Length (in.):** 15.4; **Tube Dia. (in.):** 1; **W & E Adjustments:** Int.; **Weight (ozs.):** 22.7
Price: $796.00

Lightseeker 6-24x [7, 12]

Magn.: 6-24; **Field at 100 Yds. (feet):** 18-5.5; **Eye Relief (in.):** 3.5-4; **Length (in.):** 16; **Tube Dia. (in.):** 1; **W & E Adjustments:** Int.; **Weight (ozs.):** 23.7
Price: $856.00

Lightseeker 8.5-32x [8]

Magn.: 8.5-32; **Field at 100 Yds. (feet):** 13-3.8; **Eye Relief (in.):** 3.5-4; **Length (in.):** 17.2; **Tube Dia. (in.):** 1; **W & E Adjustments:** Int.; **Weight (ozs.):** 24
Price: $944.00

Shotgun

Lightseeker 2.5x [13]

Magn.: 2.5; **Field at 100 Yds. (feet):** 55; **Eye Relief (in.):** 3.5-4; **Length (in.):** 10; **Tube Dia. (in.):** 1; **W & E Adjustments:** Int.; **Weight (ozs.):** 9
Price: $350.00

Lightseeker Zero-X SG Plus

Magn.: 0; **Field at 100 Yds. (feet):** 51; **Eye Relief (in.):** 4.5-15; **Length (in.):** 8.9; **Tube Dia. (in.):** 1; **W & E Adjustments:** Int.; **Weight (ozs.):** 7.9
Price: $372.00

Lightseeker Zero-X/V Still-Target

Magn.: 0-4; **Field at 100 Yds. (feet):** 53.8-15; **Eye Relief (in.):** 3.5-7; **Length (in.):** 8.9; **Tube Dia. (in.):** 1; **W & E Adjustments:** Int.; **Weight (ozs.):** 10.3
Price: $476.00

Lightseeker Zero X/V

Magn.: 0-4; **Field at 100 Yds. (feet):** 53.8-15; **Eye Relief (in.):** 3.5-7; **Length (in.):** 8.9; **Tube Dia. (in.):** 1; **W & E Adjustments:** Int.; **Weight (ozs.):** 10.3
Price: $454.00

Pentax Data: [1]Glossy finish; Matte finish, Heavy Plex or Penta-Plex, **$546.00** [2]Glossy finish; Matte finish, **$594.00**. [3]Glossy finish; Matte finish, **$628.00**; Heavy Plex, add **$20.00**. [4]Matte finish; Mil-Dot, **$798.00**. [5]Glossy finish; Matte finish, **$652.00**; Heavy Plex, add **$10.00**. [6]Glossy finish; Matte finish, **$816.00**; with Heavy Plex, **$830.00**; with Mil-Dot, **$978.00**. [7]Matte finish; with Mil-Dot, **$1,018.00**. [8]Matte finish, with Mil-Dot, **$1098.00**. [9]Lightseeker II, Matte finish, **$844.00**. [10]Lightseeker II, Glossy finish, **$636.00**. [11]Lightseeker II, Matte finish, **$660.00**. [12]Lightseeker II, Matte finish, **$878.00**. [13]Matte finish; Advantage finish, Break-up Mossy Oak finish, Treestand Mossy Oak finish, **$364.00**. From Pentax Corp.

Heavy Plex   Fine Plex   Penta-Plex

Deepwoods   Comp-Plex   Mil-dot
Plex

SCHMIDT & BENDER

Fixed

4x36

Magn.: 4; **Field at 100 Yds. (feet):** 30; **Eye Relief (in.):** 3.25; **Length (in.):** 11; **Tube Dia. (in.):** 1; **W & E Adjustments:** Int.; **Weight (ozs.):** 14
Price: $760.00

6x42

Magn.: 6; **Field at 100 Yds. (feet):** 21; **Eye Relief (in.):** 3.25; **Length (in.):** 13; **Tube Dia. (in.):** 1; **W & E Adjustments:** Int.; **Weight (ozs.):** 17
Price: $835.00

8x56

Magn.: 8; **Field at 100 Yds. (feet):** 16.5; **Eye Relief (in.):** 3.25; **Length (in.):** 14; **Tube Dia. (in.):** 1; **W & E Adjustments:** Int.; **Weight (ozs.):** 22
Price: $960.00

10x42

Magn.: 10; **Field at 100 Yds. (feet):** 10.5; **Eye Relief (in.):** 3.25; **Length (in.):** 13; **Tube Dia. (in.):** 1; **W & E Adjustments:** Int.; **Weight (ozs.):** 18
Price: $955.00

Schmidt & Bender Fixed 4x36

Schmidt & Bender Fixed 8x56

Schmidt & Bender Variable 1.25-4x20

Schmidt & Bender, continued

Variables

1.25-4x20 [5]

Magn.: 1.25-4; **Field at 100 Yds. (feet):** 96-16; **Eye Relief (in.):** 3.75; **Length (in.):** 10; **Tube Dia. (in.):** 30mm; **W & E Adjustments:** Int.; **Weight (ozs.):** 15.5
Price: **$995.00**

1.5-6x42 [1,5]

Magn.: 1.5-6; **Field at 100 Yds. (feet):** 60-19.5; **Eye Relief (in.):** 3.70; **Length (in.):** 12; **Tube Dia. (in.):** 30mm; **W & E Adjustments:** Int.; **Weight (ozs.):** 19.7
Price: **$1,125.00**

2.5-10x56 [1,5]

Magn.: 2.5-10; **Field at 100 Yds. (feet):** 37.5-12; **Eye Relief (in.):** 3.90; **Length (in.):** 14; **Tube Dia. (in.):** 30mm; **W & E Adjustments:** Int.; **Weight (ozs.):** 24.6
Price: **$1,390.00**

3-12x42 [2]

Magn.: 3-12; **Field at 100 Yds. (feet):** 34.5-11.5; **Eye Relief (in.):** 3.90; **Length (in.):** 13.5; **Tube Dia. (in.):** 30mm; **W & E Adjustments:** Int.; **Weight (ozs.):** 19
Price: **$1,290.00**

3-12x50 [1,5]

Magn.: 3-12; **Field at 100 Yds. (feet):** 33.3-12.6; **Eye Relief (in.):** 3.90; **Length (in.):** 13.5; **Tube Dia. (in.):** 30mm; **W & E Adjustments:** Int.; **Weight (ozs.):** 22.9
Price: **$1,360.00**

4-16x50 Varmint [4,6]

Magn.: 4-16; **Field at 100 Yds. (feet):** 22.5-7.5; **Eye Relief (in.):** 3.90; **Length (in.):** 14; **Tube Dia. (in.):** 30mm; **W & E Adjustments:** Int.; **Weight (ozs.):** 26
Price: **$1,525.00**

Police/Marksman II

3-12x50 [7]

Magn.: 3-12; **Field at 100 Yds. (feet):** 33.3-12.6; **Eye Relief (in.):** 3.74; **Length (in.):** 13.9; **Tube Dia. (in.):** 34mm; **W & E Adjustments:** Int.; **Weight (ozs.):** 18.5
Price: **$1,555.00**

Schmidt & Bender Variable 2.5-10x56

Schmidt & Bender Variable 3-12x50

Schmidt & Bender Data: All scopes have 30-yr. warranty, click adjustments, centered reticles, rotation indicators. [1]Glass reticle; aluminum. Available in aluminum with mounting rail. [2]Aluminum only. [3]Aluminum tube. Choice of two bullet drop compensators, choice of two sunshades, two range finding reticles. From Schmidt & Bender, Inc. [4]Parallax adjustment in third turret; extremely fine crosshairs. [5]Available with illuminated reticle that glows red; third turret houses on/off switch, dimmer and battery. [6]4-16x50/Long Range. [7]Also with Long Eye Relief. From Schmidt & Bender, Inc. Available with illuminated crosshairs and parallax adjustment.

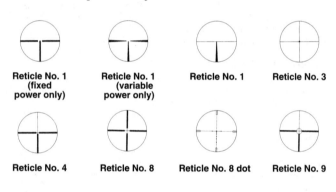

Reticle No. 1 (fixed power only)	Reticle No. 1 (variable power only)	Reticle No. 1	Reticle No. 3
Reticle No. 4	Reticle No. 8	Reticle No. 8 dot	Reticle No. 9

SIGHTRON

Variables

SII 1.56x42

Magn.: 1.5-6; **Field at 100 Yds. (feet):** 50-15; **Eye Relief (in.):** 3.8-4; **Length (in.):** 11.69; **Tube Dia. (in.):** 1; **W & E Adjustments:** Int.; **Weight (ozs.):** 15.35
Price: **$259.95**

SII 2.5-7x32SG [8]

Magn.: 2.5-7; **Field at 100 Yds. (feet):** 26-7; **Eye Relief (in.):** 4.3; **Length (in.):** 10.9; **Tube Dia. (in.):** 1; **W & E Adjustments:** Int.; **Weight (ozs.):** 8.46
Price: **$199.95**

SII 2.58x42

Magn.: 2.5-8; **Field at 100 Yds. (feet):** 36-12; **Eye Relief (in.):** 3.6-4.2; **Length (in.):** 11.89; **Tube Dia. (in.):** 1; **W & E Adjustments:** Int.; **Weight (ozs.):** 12.82
Price: **$233.95**

SII 39x42 [4, 6, 7]

Magn.: 3-9; **Field at 100 Yds. (feet):** 34-12; **Eye Relief (in.):** 3.6-4.2; **Length (in.):** 12.00; **Tube Dia. (in.):** 1; **W & E Adjustments:** Int.; **Weight (ozs.):** 13.22
Price: $246.95

SII 312x42 [6]

Magn.: 3-12; **Field at 100 Yds. (feet):** 32-9; **Eye Relief (in.):** 3.6-4.2; **Length (in.):** 11.89; **Tube Dia. (in.):** 1; **W & E Adjustments:** Int.; **Weight (ozs.):** 12.99
Price: $261.95

SII 3.510x42

Magn.: 3.5-10; **Field at 100 Yds. (feet):** 32-11; **Eye Relief (in.):** 3.6; **Length (in.):** 11.89; **Tube Dia. (in.):** 1; **W & E Adjustments:** Int.; **Weight (ozs.):** 13.16
Price: $261.95

SII 4.514x42 [1]

Magn.: 4.5-14; **Field at 100 Yds. (feet):** 22-7.9; **Eye Relief (in.):** 3.6; **Length (in.):** 13.88; **Tube Dia. (in.):** 1; **W & E Adjustments:** Int.; **Weight (ozs.):** 16.07
Price: $340.95

Target

SII6x42HBR

Magn.: 6; **Field at 100 Yds. (feet):** 20; **Eye Relief (in.):** 4; **Length (in.):** 12.48; **Tube Dia. (in.):** 1; **W & E Adjustments:** Int.; **Weight (ozs.):** 12.3
Price: $259.95

SII 24x44

Magn.: 24; **Field at 100 Yds. (feet):** 4.1; **Eye Relief (in.):** 4.33; **Length (in.):** 13.30; **Tube Dia. (in.):** 1; **W & E Adjustments:** Int.; **Weight (ozs.):** 15.87
Price: $279.95

SII 416x42 [1, 4, 5, 6, 7]

Magn.: 4-16; **Field at 100 Yds. (feet):** 26-7; **Eye Relief (in.):** 3.6; **Length (in.):** 13.62; **Tube Dia. (in.):** 1; **W & E Adjustments:** Int.; **Weight (ozs.):** 16
Price: $317.95

SII 624-42 [1, 4, 5, 7]

Magn.: 6-24; **Field at 100 Yds. (feet):** 16-5; **Eye Relief (in.):** 3.6; **Length (in.):** 14.6; **Tube Dia. (in.):** 1; **W & E Adjustments:** Int.; **Weight (ozs.):** 18.7
Price: $334.95

SII1040x42

Magn.: 10-40; **Field at 100 Yds. (feet):** 8.9-4; **Eye Relief (in.):** 3.6; **Length (in.):** 16.1; **Tube Dia. (in.):** 1; **W & E Adjustments:** Int.; **Weight (ozs.):** 19
Price: $399.95

Compact

SII 4x32

Magn.: 4; **Field at 100 Yds. (feet):** 25; **Eye Relief (in.):** 4.5; **Length (in.):** 9.69; **Tube Dia. (in.):** 1; **W & E Adjustments:** Int.; **Weight (ozs.):** 9.34
Price: $123.95

SII2.5-10x32

Magn.: 2.5-10; **Field at 100 Yds. (feet):** 41-10.5; **Eye Relief (in.):** 3.75-3.5; **Length (in.):** 10.9; **Tube Dia. (in.):** 1; **W & E Adjustments:** Int.; **Weight (ozs.):** 10.39
Price: $233.95

Shotgun

SII 2.5x20SG

Magn.: 2.5; **Field at 100 Yds. (feet):** 41; **Eye Relief (in.):** 4.3; **Length (in.):** 10.28; **Tube Dia. (in.):** 1; **W & E Adjustments:** Int.; **Weight (ozs.):** 8.46
Price: $133.95

Pistol

SII 1x28P [4]

Magn.: 1; **Field at 100 Yds. (feet):** 30; **Eye Relief (in.):** 9-24; **Length (in.):** 9.49; **Tube Dia. (in.):** 1; **W & E Adjustments:** Int.; **Weight (ozs.):** 8.46
Price: $135.95

SII 2x28P [4]

Magn.: 2; **Field at 100 Yds. (feet):** 16-10; **Eye Relief (in.):** 9-24; **Length (in.):** 9.49; **Tube Dia. (in.):** 1; **W & E Adjustments:** Int.; **Weight (ozs.):** 8.28
Price: $135.95

Sightron Data: [1]Adjustable objective. [2]3MOA dot; also with 5 or 10 MOA dot. [3]Variable 3, 5, 10 MOA dot; black finish; also stainless. [4]Satin black; also stainless. Electronic Red Dot scopes come with ring mount, front and rear extension tubes, polarizing filter, battery, haze filter caps, wrench. Rifle, pistol, shotgun scopes have aluminum tubes, Exac Trak adjustments. Lifetime warranty. From Sightron, Inc. [5]3" sun shade. [6]Mil Dot or Plex reticle. [7]Dot or Plex reticle. [8]Double Diamond reticle.

SIMMONS

AETEC

2100 [8]

Magn.: 2.8-10; **Field at 100 Yds. (feet):** 44-14; **Eye Relief (in.):** 5; **Length (in.):** 11.9; **Tube Dia. (in.):** 1; **W & E Adjustments:** Int.; **Weight (ozs.):** 15.5
Price: $234.99

2104 [16]

Magn.: 3.8-12; **Field at 100 Yds. (feet):** 33-11; **Eye Relief (in.):** 4; **Length (in.):** 13.5; **Tube Dia. (in.):** 1; **W & E Adjustments:** Int.; **Weight (ozs.):** 20
Price: $259.99

44 Mag

M-1044 [3]

Magn.: 3-10; **Field at 100 Yds. (feet):** 34-10.5; **Eye Relief (in.):** 3; **Length (in.):** 12.75; **Tube Dia. (in.):** 1; **W & E Adjustments:** Int.; **Weight (ozs.):** 15.5
Price: $179.99

M-1045 [3]

Magn.: 4-12; **Field at 100 Yds. (feet):** 29.5-9.5; **Eye Relief (in.):** 3; **Length (in.):** 13.2; **Tube Dia. (in.):** 1; **W & E Adjustments:** Int.; **Weight (ozs.):** 18.25
Price: $278.99

M-1047 [3]

Magn.: 6.5-20; **Field at 100 Yds. (feet):** 14-.5; **Eye Relief (in.):** 2.6-3.4; **Length (in.):** 12.8; **Tube Dia. (in.):** 1; **W & E Adjustments:** Int.; **Weight (ozs.):** 19.5
Price: $224.99

Simmons Aetec 2104

Simmons 44 Mag M-1050DM

Simmons WTC 11

Simmons, continued

1048 [3,20] *(3)*

Magn.: 6.5-20; **Field at 100 Yds. (feet):** 16-5.5; **Eye Relief (in.):** 2.6-3.4; **Length (in.):** 14.5; **Tube Dia. (in.):** 1; **W & E Adjustments:** Int.; **Weight (ozs.):** 20
Price: $259.99

M-1050DM [3,19]

Magn.: 3.8-12; **Field at 100 Yds. (feet):** 26-9; **Eye Relief (in.):** 3; **Length (in.):** 13.08; **Tube Dia. (in.):** 1; **W & E Adjustments:** Int.; **Weight (ozs.):** 16.75
Price: $269.99

8-Point

4-12x40mmAO [3]

Magn.: 4-12; **Field at 100 Yds. (feet):** 29-10; **Eye Relief (in.):** 3-2 7/8; **Length (in.):** 13.5; **Tube Dia. (in.):** 1; **W & E Adjustments:** Int.; **Weight (ozs.):** 15.75
Price: $129.99

4x32mm [3]

Magn.: 4; **Field at 100 Yds. (feet):** 28.75; **Eye Relief (in.):** 3; **Length (in.):** 11.625; **Tube Dia. (in.):** 1; **W & E Adjustments:** Int.; **Weight (ozs.):** 14.25
Price: $44.99

3-9x32mm [3]

Magn.: 3-9; **Field at 100 Yds. (feet):** 37.5-13; **Eye Relief (in.):** 3-2 7/8; **Length (in.):** 11.875; **Tube Dia. (in.):** 1; **W & E Adjustments:** Int.; **Weight (ozs.):** 11.5
Price: $60.99

3-9x40mm [18]

Magn.: 3-9; **Field at 100 Yds. (feet):** 37-13; **Eye Relief (in.):** 3-2 7/8; **Length (in.):** 12.25; **Tube Dia. (in.):** 1; **W & E Adjustments:** Int.; **Weight (ozs.):** 12.25
Price: $84.99-94.99

3-9x50mm [3]

Magn.: 3-9; **Field at 100 Yds. (feet):** 32-11.75; **Eye Relief (in.):** 3-2 7/8; **Length (in.):** 13; **Tube Dia. (in.):** 1; **W & E Adjustments:** Int.; **Weight (ozs.):** 15.25
Price: $97.99

Prohunter

7700

Magn.: 2-7; **Field at 100 Yds. (feet):** 53-16.25; **Eye Relief (in.):** 3; **Length (in.):** 11.5; **Tube Dia. (in.):** 1; **W & E Adjustments:** Int.; **Weight (ozs.):** 12.5
Price: $124.99

7710 [2]

Magn.: 3-9; **Field at 100 Yds. (feet):** 36-13; **Eye Relief (in.):** 3; **Length (in.):** 12.6; **Tube Dia. (in.):** 1; **W & E Adjustments:** Int.; **Weight (ozs.):** 13.5
Price: $139.99

7716

Magn.: 4-12; **Field at 100 Yds. (feet):** 26-9; **Eye Relief (in.):** 3; **Length (in.):** 12.6; **Tube Dia. (in.):** 1; **W & E Adjustments:** Int.; **Weight (ozs.):** 16.75
Price: $159.99

7721

Magn.: 6-18; **Field at 100 Yds. (feet):** 18.5-6; **Eye Relief (in.):** 3; **Length (in.):** 13.75; **Tube Dia. (in.):** 1; **W & E Adjustments:** Int.; **Weight (ozs.):** 16
Price: $179.99

7740 [3]

Magn.: 6; **Field at 100 Yds. (feet):** 21.75; **Eye Relief (in.):** 3; **Length (in.):** 12.5; **Tube Dia. (in.):** 1; **W & E Adjustments:** Int.; **Weight (ozs.):** 12
Price: $120.99

Prohunter Handgun

7732 [18]

Magn.: 2; **Field at 100 Yds. (feet):** 22; **Eye Relief (in.):** 9-17; **Length (in.):** 8.75; **Tube Dia. (in.):** 1; **W & E Adjustments:** Int.; **Weight (ozs.):** 7
Price: $139.99

7738 [18]

Magn.: 4; **Field at 100 Yds. (feet):** 15; **Eye Relief (in.):** 11.8-17.6; **Length (in.):** 8.5; **Tube Dia. (in.):** 1; **W & E Adjustments:** Int.; **Weight (ozs.):** 8
Price: $149.99

Whitetail Classic

WTC 11 [4]

Magn.: 1.5-5; **Field at 100 Yds. (feet):** 75-23; **Eye Relief (in.):** 3.4-3.2; **Length (in.):** 9.3; **Tube Dia. (in.):** 1; **W & E Adjustments:** Int.; **Weight (ozs.):** 9.7
Price: $184.99

WTC 12 [4]

Magn.: 2.5-8; **Field at 100 Yds. (feet):** 45-14; **Eye Relief (in.):** 3.2-3; **Length (in.):** 11.3; **Tube Dia. (in.):** 1; **W & E Adjustments:** Int.; **Weight (ozs.):** 13
Price: $199.99

Simmons Whitetail Espedition 3-9x42mm

Simmons Shotgun 21004

Simmons, continued

WTC 13 [4]

Magn.: 3.5-10; **Field at 100 Yds. (feet):** 30-10.5; **Eye Relief (in.):** 3.2-3; **Length (in.):** 12.4; **Tube Dia. (in.):** 1; **W & E Adjustments:** Int.; **Weight (ozs.):** 13.5
Price: $209.99

WTC 15 [4]

Magn.: 3.5-10; **Field at 100 Yds. (feet):** 29.5-11.5; **Eye Relief (in.):** 3.2; **Length (in.):** 12.75; **Tube Dia. (in.):** 1; **W & E Adjustments:** Int.; **Weight (ozs.):** 13.5
Price: $289.99

WTC 45 [4]

Magn.: 4.5-14; **Field at 100 Yds. (feet):** 22.5-8.6; **Eye Relief (in.):** 3.2; **Length (in.):** 13.2; **Tube Dia. (in.):** 1; **W & E Adjustments:** Int.; **Weight (ozs.):** 14
Price: $265.99

Whitetail Expedition

1.5-6x32mm [3]

Magn.: 1.5-6; **Field at 100 Yds. (feet):** 72-19; **Eye Relief (in.):** 3; **Length (in.):** 11.16; **Tube Dia. (in.):** 1; **W & E Adjustments:** Int.; **Weight (ozs.):** 15
Price: $289.99

3-9x42mm [3]

Magn.: 3-9; **Field at 100 Yds. (feet):** 40-13.5; **Eye Relief (in.):** 3; **Length (in.):** 13.2; **Tube Dia. (in.):** 1; **W & E Adjustments:** Int.; **Weight (ozs.):** 17.5
Price: $309.99

4-12x42mm [3]

Magn.: 4-12; **Field at 100 Yds. (feet):** 29-9.6; **Eye Relief (in.):** 3; **Length (in.):** 13.46; **Tube Dia. (in.):** 1; **W & E Adjustments:** Int.; **Weight (ozs.):** 21.25
Price: $334.99

6-18x42mm [3]

Magn.: 6-18; **Field at 100 Yds. (feet):** 18.3-6.5; **Eye Relief (in.):** 3; **Length (in.):** 15.35; **Tube Dia. (in.):** 1; **W & E Adjustments:** Int.; **Weight (ozs.):** 22.5
Price: $364.99

Pro50

8800 [10]

Magn.: 4-12; **Field at 100 Yds. (feet):** 27-9; **Eye Relief (in.):** 3.5; **Length (in.):** 13.2; **Tube Dia. (in.):** 1; **W & E Adjustments:** Int.; **Weight (ozs.):** 18.25
Price: $219.99

8810 [10]

Magn.: 6-18; **Field at 100 Yds. (feet):** 17-5.8; **Eye Relief (in.):** 3.6; **Length (in.):** 13.2; **Tube Dia. (in.):** 1; **W & E Adjustments:** Int.; **Weight (ozs.):** 18.25
Price: $239.99

Shotgun

21004

Magn.: 4; **Field at 100 Yds. (feet):** 16; **Eye Relief (in.):** 5.5; **Length (in.):** 8.8; **Tube Dia. (in.):** 1; **W & E Adjustments:** Int.; **Weight (ozs.):** 9.1
Price: $84.99

21005

Magn.: 2.5; **Field at 100 Yds. (feet):** 24; **Eye Relief (in.):** 6; **Length (in.):** 7.4; **Tube Dia. (in.):** 1; **W & E Adjustments:** Int.; **Weight (ozs.):** 7
Price: $59.99

7789D

Magn.: 2; **Field at 100 Yds. (feet):** 31; **Eye Relief (in.):** 5.5; **Length (in.):** 8.8; **Tube Dia. (in.):** 1; **W & E Adjustments:** Int.; **Weight (ozs.):** 8.75
Price: $99.99

7790D

Magn.: 4; **Field at 100 Yds. (feet):** 17; **Eye Relief (in.):** 5.5; **Length (in.):** 8.5; **Tube Dia. (in.):** 1; **W & E Adjustments:** Int.; **Weight (ozs.):** 8.75
Price: $114.99

7791D

Magn.: 1.5-5; **Field at 100 Yds. (feet):** 76-23.5; **Eye Relief (in.):** 3.4; **Length (in.):** 9.5; **Tube Dia. (in.):** 1; **W & E Adjustments:** Int.; **Weight (ozs.):** 10.75
Price: $138.99

Rimfire

1031 [18]

Magn.: 4; **Field at 100 Yds. (feet):** 23.5; **Eye Relief (in.):** 3; **Length (in.):** 7.25; **Tube Dia. (in.):** 1; **W & E Adjustments:** Int.; **Weight (ozs.):** 8.25
Price: $79.99

1022 [7]

Magn.: 4; **Field at 100 Yds. (feet):** 29.5; **Eye Relief (in.):** 3; **Length (in.):** 11.75; **Tube Dia. (in.):** 1; **W & E Adjustments:** Int.; **Weight (ozs.):** 11
Price: $69.99

1022T

Magn.: 3-9; **Field at 100 Yds. (feet):** 42-14; **Eye Relief (in.):** 3.5; **Length (in.):** 11.5; **Tube Dia. (in.):** 1; **W & E Adjustments:** Int.; **Weight (ozs.):** 12
Price: $166.99

1039 [18]

Magn.: 3-9; **Field at 100 Yds. (feet):** 38-13; **Eye Relief (in.):** 3.3-2.9; **Length (in.):** 11.6; **Tube Dia. (in.):** 1; **W & E Adjustments:** Int.; **Weight (ozs.):** 13
Price: $84.99

Simmons Red Dot 51004

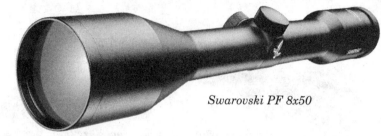

Swarovski PF 8x50

Simmons Pr Air 21613 A.O.

Simmons, continued

Blackpowder

BP0420M [17]

Magn.: 4; **Field at 100 Yds. (feet):** 19.5; **Eye Relief (in.):** 4; **Length (in.):** 7.5; **Tube Dia. (in.):** 1; **W & E Adjustments:** Int.; **Weight (ozs.):** 8.3
Price: $114.99

BP2732M [12]

Magn.: 2-7; **Field at 100 Yds. (feet):** 57.7-16.6; **Eye Relief (in.):** 3; **Length (in.):** 11.6; **Tube Dia. (in.):** 1; **W & E Adjustments:** Int.; **Weight (ozs.):** 12.4
Price: $135.99

Red Dot

51004 [21]

Magn.: 1; **Field at 100 Yds. (feet):** —; **Eye Relief (in.):** —; **Length (in.):** 4.8; **Tube Dia. (in.):** 25mm; **W & E Adjustments:** Int.; **Weight (ozs.):** 4.7
Price: $59.99

51112 [22]

Magn.: 1; **Field at 100 Yds. (feet):** —; **Eye Relief (in.):** —; **Length (in.):** 5.25; **Tube Dia. (in.):** 30mm; **W & E Adjustments:** Int.; **Weight (ozs.):** 6
Price: $99.99

Pro Air Gun

21608 A.O.

Magn.: 4; **Field at 100 Yds. (feet):** 25; **Eye Relief (in.):** 3.5; **Length (in.):** 12; **Tube Dia. (in.):** 1; **W & E Adjustments:** Int.; **Weight (ozs.):** 11.3
Price: $109.99

21613 A.O.

Magn.: 4-12; **Field at 100 Yds. (feet):** 25-9; **Eye Relief (in.):** 3.1-2.9; **Length (in.):** 13.1; **Tube Dia. (in.):** 1; **W & E Adjustments:** Int.; **Weight (ozs.):** 15.8
Price: $199.99

21619 A.O.

Magn.: 6-18; **Field at 100 Yds. (feet):** 18-7; **Eye Relief (in.):** 2.9-2.7; **Length (in.):** 13.8; **Tube Dia. (in.):** 1; **W & E Adjustments:** Int.; **Weight (ozs.):** 18.2
Price: $209.99

Simmons Data: [1]Matte; also polished finish. [2]Silver; also black matte or polished. [3]Black matte finish. [4]Granite finish. [5]Camouflage. [6]Black polish. [7]With ring mounts. [8]Silver; black polish avail. [10]50mm obj.; black matte. [11]Black or silver matte. [12]75-yd. parallax; black or silver matte. [13]TV view. [14]Adj. obj. [15]Silver matte. [16]Adj. objective; 4" sunshade; black matte. [17]Octagon body; rings included; black matte or silver finish. [18]Black matte finish; also available in silver. [19]Smart reticle. [20]Target turrets. [21]With dovetail rings. [23]With 3V lithium battery, extension tube, polarizing filter, Weaver rings. **Only selected models shown.** Contact Simmons Outdoor Corp. for complete details.

Truplex™   Smart   ProDiamond®   Crossbow

STEINER

Hunting Z

1.5-5x20 [1]

Magn.: 1.5-5; **Field at 100 Yds. (feet):** 32-12; **Eye Relief (in.):** 4.3; **Length (in.):** 9.6; **Tube Dia. (in.):** 30mm; **W & E Adjustments:** Int.; **Weight (ozs.):** 11.7
Price: $1,399.00

2.5-8x36 [1]

Magn.: 2.5-8; **Field at 100 Yds. (feet):** 40-15; **Eye Relief (in.):** 4; **Length (in.):** 11.6; **Tube Dia. (in.):** 30mm; **W & E Adjustments:** Int.; **Weight (ozs.):** 13.4
Price: $1,599.00

3.5-10x50 [1]

Magn.: 3.5-10; **Field at 100 Yds. (feet):** 77-25; **Eye Relief (in.):** 4; **Length (in.):** 12.4; **Tube Dia. (in.):** 30mm; **W & E Adjustments:** Int.; **Weight (ozs.):** 16.9
Price: $1,799.00

Steiner Data: Waterproof, fogproof, nitrogen filled. [1]Heavy-Duplex, Duplex or European #4 reticle. Aluminum tubes; matte black finish. From Pioneer Research.

SWAROVSKI OPTIK

PF Series

8x50 [1,3]

Magn.: 8; **Field at 100 Yds. (feet):** 17; **Eye Relief (in.):** 3.15; **Length (in.):** 13.9; **Tube Dia. (in.):** 30mm; **W & E Adjustments:** Int.; **Weight (ozs.):** 21.5
Price: $987.78

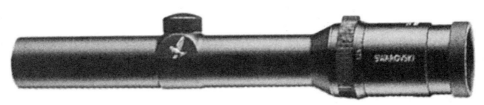

Swarovski 1.25-4x24

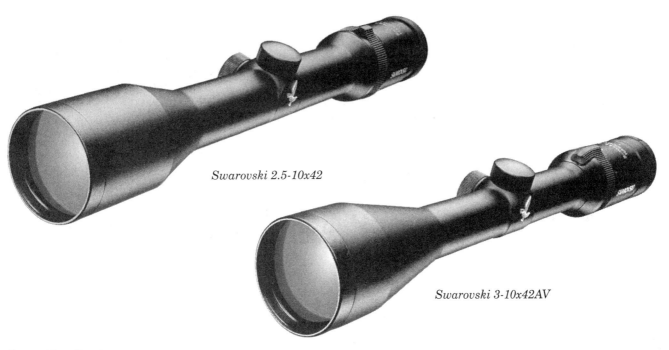

Swarovski 2.5-10x42

Swarovski 3-10x42AV

Swarovski, continued

8x56 [1,3]
Magn.: 8; **Field at 100 Yds. (feet):** 17; **Eye Relief (in.):** 3.15; **Length (in.):** 14.29; **Tube Dia. (in.):** 30mm; **W & E Adjustments:** Int.; **Weight (ozs.):** 24
Price: $1,054.44

PH Series

1.25-4x24 [1]
Magn.: 1.25-4; **Field at 100 Yds. (feet):** 98.4-31.2; **Eye Relief (in.):** 3.15; **Length (in.):** 10.63; **Tube Dia. (in.):** 30mm; **W & E Adjustments:** Int.; **Weight (ozs.):** 16.2
Price: $1,087.78

1.5-6x42 [1]
Magn.: 1.5-6; **Field at 100 Yds. (feet):** 65.4-21; **Eye Relief (in.):** 3.15; **Length (in.):** 12.99; **Tube Dia. (in.):** 30mm; **W & E Adjustments:** Int.; **Weight (ozs.):** 20.8
Price: $1,221.11

2.5-10x42 [1,2]
Magn.: 2.5-10; **Field at 100 Yds. (feet):** 39.6-12.6; **Eye Relief (in.):** 3.15; **Length (in.):** 13.23; **Tube Dia. (in.):** 30mm; **W & E Adjustments:** Int.; **Weight (ozs.):** 19.8
Price: $1,376.67

3-12x50 [1]
Magn.: 3-12; **Field at 100 Yds. (feet):** 33-10.5; **Eye Relief (in.):** 3.15; **Length (in.):** 14.33; **Tube Dia. (in.):** 30mm; **W & E Adjustments:** Int.; **Weight (ozs.):** 22.4
Price: $1,421.11

4-16x50
Magn.: 4-16; **Field at 100 Yds. (feet):** 30-8.5; **Eye Relief (in.):** 3.15; **Length (in.):** 14.22; **Tube Dia. (in.):** 30mm; **W & E Adjustments:** Int.; **Weight (ozs.):** 22.3
Price: $1,476.67

6-24x50
Magn.: 6-24; **Field at 100 Yds. (feet):** 18.6-5.4; **Eye Relief (in.):** 3.15; **Length (in.):** 15.4; **Tube Dia. (in.):** 30mm; **W & E Adjustments:** Int.; **Weight (ozs.):** 23.6
Price: $1,687.78

A-Line Series

3-9x36AV [4]
Magn.: 3-9; **Field at 100 Yds. (feet):** 39-13.5; **Eye Relief (in.):** 3.35; **Length (in.):** 11.8; **Tube Dia. (in.):** 1; **W & E Adjustments:** Int.; **Weight (ozs.):** 11.7
Price: $743.33

3-10x42AV [4]
Magn.: 3-10; **Field at 100 Yds. (feet):** 33-11.7; **Eye Relief (in.):** 3.35; **Length (in.):** 12.44; **Tube Dia. (in.):** 1; **W & E Adjustments:** Int.; **Weight (ozs.):** 12.7
Price: $821.11

4-12x50AV [4]
Magn.: 4-12; **Field at 100 Yds. (feet):** 29.1-9.9; **Eye Relief (in.):** 3.35; **Length (in.):** 13.5; **Tube Dia. (in.):** 1; **W & E Adjustments:** Int.; **Weight (ozs.):** 13.9
Price: $843.33

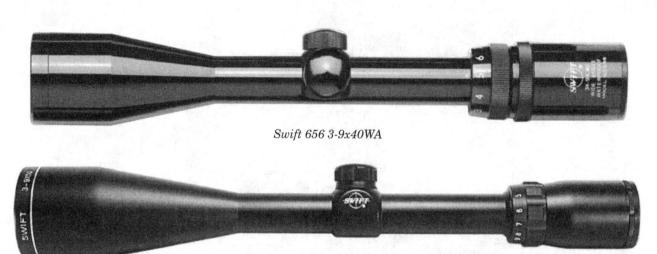

Swift 656 3-9x40WA

Swift Premier 671M 3-9x50WA

Swift 665M 1.5-4.5x21

Swarovski, continued

Swarovski Data: [1]Aluminum tubes; special order for steel. [2]Also with 56mm obj., **$1,398.89**. [3]Also available with illuminated reticle. [4]Aluminum only. Partial listing shown. Imported from Austria by Swarovski Optik.

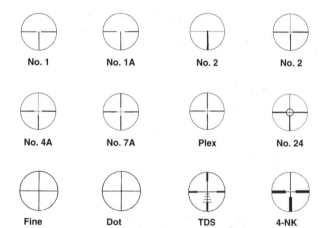

No. 1	No. 1A	No. 2	No. 2
No. 4A	No. 7A	Plex	No. 24
Fine	Dot	TDS	4-NK

SWIFT

600R 4x15

Magn.: 4; **Field at 100 Yds. (feet):** 17; **Eye Relief (in.):** 2.8; **Length (in.):** 10.6; **Tube Dia. (in.):** .75; **W & E Adjustments:** Int.; **Weight (ozs.):** 3.5
Price: $15.00

601R 3-7x20

Magn.: 3-7; **Field at 100 Yds. (feet):** 25-12; **Eye Relief (in.):** 3-2.9; **Length (in.):** 11; **Tube Dia. (in.):** .75; **W & E Adjustments:** Int.; **Weight (ozs.):** 5.6
Price: $35.00

650R 4x32

Magn.: 4; **Field at 100 Yds. (feet):** 26; **Eye Relief (in.):** 4; **Length (in.):** 12; **Tube Dia. (in.):** 1; **W & E Adjustments:** Int.; **Weight (ozs.):** 9.1
Price: $75.00

653M 4x40WA [1]

Magn.: 4; **Field at 100 Yds. (feet):** 35; **Eye Relief (in.):** 4; **Length (in.):** 12.2; **Tube Dia. (in.):** 1; **W & E Adjustments:** Int.; **Weight (ozs.):** 12.6
Price: $125.00

654 3-9x32

Magn.: 3-9; **Field at 100 Yds. (feet):** 35-12; **Eye Relief (in.):** 3.4-2.9; **Length (in.):** 12; **Tube Dia. (in.):** 1; **W & E Adjustments:** Int.; **Weight (ozs.):** 9.8
Price: $125.00

656 3-9x40WA [1]

Magn.: 3-9; **Field at 100 Yds. (feet):** 40-14; **Eye Relief (in.):** 3.4-2.8; **Length (in.):** 12.6; **Tube Dia. (in.):** 1; **W & E Adjustments:** Int.; **Weight (ozs.):** 12.3
Price: $140.00

657M 6x40

Magn.: 6; **Field at 100 Yds. (feet):** 28; **Eye Relief (in.):** 4; **Length (in.):** 12.6; **Tube Dia. (in.):** 1; **W & E Adjustments:** Int.; **Weight (ozs.):** 10.4
Price: $125.00

Swift 663B 2x20 Pistol Scope

Swift, continued

658M 2-7x40WA [3]
Magn.: 2-7; **Field at 100 Yds. (feet):** 55-18; **Eye Relief (in.):** 3.3-3; **Length (in.):** 11.6; **Tube Dia. (in.):** 1; **W & E Adjustments:** Int.; **Weight (ozs.):** 12.5
Price: $160.00

659M 3.5-10x44WA
Magn.: 3.5-10; **Field at 100 Yds. (feet):** 34-12; **Eye Relief (in.):** 3-2.8; **Length (in.):** 12.8; **Tube Dia. (in.):** 1; **W & E Adjustments:** Int.; **Weight (ozs.):** 13.5
Price: $230.00

665 1.5-4.5x21
Magn.: 1.5-4.5; **Field at 100 Yds. (feet):** 69-24.5; **Eye Relief (in.):** 3.5-3; **Length (in.):** 10.9; **Tube Dia. (in.):** 1; **W & E Adjustments:** Int.; **Weight (ozs.):** 9.6
Price: $125.00

665M 1.5-4.5x21
Magn.: 1.5-4.5; **Field at 100 Yds. (feet):** 69-24.5; **Eye Relief (in.):** 3.5-3; **Length (in.):** 10.9; **Tube Dia. (in.):** 1; **W & E Adjustments:** Int.; **Weight (ozs.):** 9.6
Price: $125.00

666M Shotgun 1x20
Magn.: 1; **Field at 100 Yds. (feet):** 113; **Eye Relief (in.):** 3.2; **Length (in.):** 7.5; **Tube Dia. (in.):** 1; **W & E Adjustments:** Int.; **Weight (ozs.):** 9.6
Price: $130.00

667 Fire-Fly [2]
Magn.: 1; **Field at 100 Yds. (feet):** 40; **Eye Relief (in.):** —; **Length (in.):** 5.4; **Tube Dia. (in.):** 30mm; **W & E Adjustments:** Int.; **Weight (ozs.):** 5
Price: $220.00

668M 4x32
Magn.: 4; **Field at 100 Yds. (feet):** 25; **Eye Relief (in.):** 4; **Length (in.):** 10; **Tube Dia. (in.):** 1; **W & E Adjustments:** Int.; **Weight (ozs.):** 8.9
Price: $120.00

669M 6-18x44
Magn.: 6-18; **Field at 100 Yds. (feet):** 18-6.5; **Eye Relief (in.):** 2.8; **Length (in.):** 14.5; **Tube Dia. (in.):** 1; **W & E Adjustments:** Int.; **Weight (ozs.):** 17.6
Price: $220.00

Premier[4]

649R 4-12x50WA [3]
Magn.: 4-12; **Field at 100 Yds. (feet):** 29.5-9.5; **Eye Relief (in.):** 3.2-3; **Length (in.):** 13.8; **Tube Dia. (in.):** 1; **W & E Adjustments:** Int.; **Weight (ozs.):** 17.8
Price: $245.00

671M 3-9x50WA
Magn.: 3-9; **Field at 100 Yds. (feet):** 35-12; **Eye Relief (in.):** 3.24-3.12; **Length (in.):** 15.5; **Tube Dia. (in.):** 1; **W & E Adjustments:** Int.; **Weight (ozs.):** 18.2
Price: $250.00

672M 6-18x50WA
Magn.: 6-18; **Field at 100 Yds. (feet):** 19.4-6.7; **Eye Relief (in.):** 3.25-3; **Length (in.):** 15.8; **Tube Dia. (in.):** 1; **W & E Adjustments:** Int.; **Weight (ozs.):** 20.9
Price: $260.00

673M 2.5-10x50WA
Magn.: 2.5-10; **Field at 100 Yds. (feet):** 33-9; **Eye Relief (in.):** 4-3.5; **Length (in.):** 11.8; **Tube Dia. (in.):** 30mm; **W & E Adjustments:** Int.; **Weight (ozs.):** 18.9
Price: $295.00

674M 3-5x40WA
Magn.: 3-9; **Field at 100 Yds. (feet):** 40-14.2; **Eye Relief (in.):** 3.6-2.9; **Length (in.):** 12; **Tube Dia. (in.):** 1; **W & E Adjustments:** Int.; **Weight (ozs.):** 13.1
Price: $170.00

676 4-12x40WA [1]
Magn.: 4-12; **Field at 100 Yds. (feet):** 29.3-10.5; **Eye Relief (in.):** 3.15-2.9; **Length (in.):** 12.4; **Tube Dia. (in.):** 1; **W & E Adjustments:** Int.; **Weight (ozs.):** 15.4
Price: $180.00

Pistol

679M 1.25-4x28
Magn.: 1.25-4; **Field at 100 Yds. (feet):** 23-9; **Eye Relief (in.):** 23-15; **Length (in.):** 9.3; **Tube Dia. (in.):** 1; **W & E Adjustments:** Int.; **Weight (ozs.):** 8.2
Price: $250.00

Pistol Scopes

661 4x32
Magn.: 4; **Field at 100 Yds. (feet):** 90; **Eye Relief (in.):** 10-22; **Length (in.):** 9.2; **Tube Dia. (in.):** 1; **W & E Adjustments:** Int.; **Weight (ozs.):** 9.5
Price: $130.00

663B 2x20 [1]
Magn.: 2; **Field at 100 Yds. (feet):** 18.3; **Eye Relief (in.):** 9-21; **Length (in.):** 7.2; **Tube Dia. (in.):** 1; **W & E Adjustments:** Int.; **Weight (ozs.):** 8.4
Price: $130.00

Swift Data: All Swift scopes, with the exception of the 4x15, have Quadraplex reticles and are fogproof and waterproof. The 4x15 has crosshair reticle and is non-waterproof. [1]Available in regular matte black or silver finish. [2]Comes with ring mounts, wrench, lens caps, extension tubes, filter, battery. [3]Regular and matte black finish. [4]Speed Focus scopes. Partial listing shown. From Swift Instruments.

Quadra-Plex   Fine Hair   X-Hair Circle

TASCO

Mag IV

W312x40 [1, 2, 4]
Magn.: 3-12; **Field at 100 Yds. (feet):** 35-9; **Eye Relief (in.):** 3; **Length (in.):** 12.25; **Tube Dia. (in.):** 1; **W & E Adjustments:** Int.; **Weight (ozs.):** 12
Price: $89.99

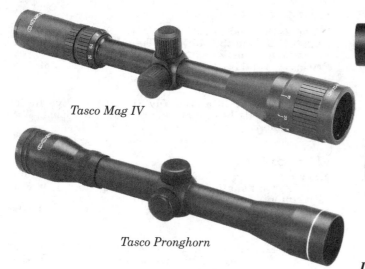

Tasco Mag IV

Tasco Pronghorn

Tasco Golden Antler

Tasco Bantam

Tasco, continued

W416x40 [1, 2, 4, 13, 14]
Magn.: 4-16; **Field at 100 Yds. (feet):** 26-7; **Eye Relief (in.):** 3; **Length (in.):** 14.25; **Tube Dia. (in.):** 1; **W & E Adjustments:** Int.; **Weight (ozs.):** 15.6
Price: $124.99

W416x50
Magn.: 4-16; **Field at 100 Yds. (feet):** 31-8; **Eye Relief (in.):** 4; **Length (in.):** 13.5; **Tube Dia. (in.):** 1; **W & E Adjustments:** Int.; **Weight (ozs.):** 16
Price: $124.99

DW520x50 [23]
Magn.: 5-20; **Field at 100 Yds. (feet):** 24-6; **Eye Relief (in.):** 4; **Length (in.):** 13.5; **Tube Dia. (in.):** 1; **W & E Adjustments:** Int.; **Weight (ozs.):** 16
Price: $189.99

Golden Antler

DMGA4x32TV
Magn.: 4; **Field at 100 Yds. (feet):** 32; **Eye Relief (in.):** 3; **Length (in.):** 13; **Tube Dia. (in.):** 1; **W & E Adjustments:** Int.; **Weight (ozs.):** 12.7
Price: $34.99

DMGA39x32TV [1]
Magn.: 3-9; **Field at 100 Yds. (feet):** 39-13; **Eye Relief (in.):** 3; **Length (in.):** —; **Tube Dia. (in.):** 1; **W & E Adjustments:** Int.; **Weight (ozs.):** 12.2
Price: $49.99

DMGA39x40TV
Magn.: 3-9; **Field at 100 Yds. (feet):** 39-13; **Eye Relief (in.):** 3; **Length (in.):** 12.5; **Tube Dia. (in.):** 1; **W & E Adjustments:** Int.; **Weight (ozs.):** 13
Price: $69.99

Silver Antler

DMSA4x40
Magn.: 4; **Field at 100 Yds. (feet):** 32; **Eye Relief (in.):** 3; **Length (in.):** 12; **Tube Dia. (in.):** 1; **W & E Adjustments:** Int.; **Weight (ozs.):** 12.5
Price: $39.99

DMSA39x32
Magn.: 3-9; **Field at 100 Yds. (feet):** 39-13; **Eye Relief (in.):** 3; **Length (in.):** 13.25; **Tube Dia. (in.):** 1; **W & E Adjustments:** Int.; **Weight (ozs.):** 12.2
Price: $49.99

DMSA39x40WA [10]
Magn.: 3-9; **Field at 100 Yds. (feet):** 41-15; **Eye Relief (in.):** 3; **Length (in.):** 12.75; **Tube Dia. (in.):** 1; **W & E Adjustments:** Int.; **Weight (ozs.):** 13
Price: $69.99

Pronghorn

PH4x32
Magn.: 4; **Field at 100 Yds. (feet):** 32; **Eye Relief (in.):** 3; **Length (in.):** 12; **Tube Dia. (in.):** 1; **W & E Adjustments:** Int.; **Weight (ozs.):** 12.5
Price: $29.99

PH39x32
Magn.: 3-9; **Field at 100 Yds. (feet):** 39-13; **Eye Relief (in.):** 3; **Length (in.):** 12; **Tube Dia. (in.):** 1; **W & E Adjustments:** Int.; **Weight (ozs.):** 11
Price: $34.99

PH39x40
Magn.: 3-9; **Field at 100 Yds. (feet):** 39-13; **Eye Relief (in.):** 3; **Length (in.):** 13; **Tube Dia. (in.):** 1; **W & E Adjustments:** Int.; **Weight (ozs.):** 12.1
Price: $44.99

Bantam

S1.5-45x20A [19, 21]
Magn.: 1.5-4.5; **Field at 100 Yds. (feet):** 69.5-23; **Eye Relief (in.):** 4; **Length (in.):** 10.25; **Tube Dia. (in.):** 1; **W & E Adjustments:** Int.; **Weight (ozs.):** 10
Price: $54.99

S1.54x32A [21]
Magn.: 1.5-4.5; **Field at 100 Yds. (feet):** 69.5-23; **Eye Relief (in.):** 4; **Length (in.):** 11.25; **Tube Dia. (in.):** 1; **W & E Adjustments:** Int. ; **Weight (ozs.):** 12
Price: $54.99

S2.5x20A [20, 21]
Magn.: 2.5; **Field at 100 Yds. (feet):** 22; **Eye Relief (in.):** 6; **Length (in.):** 7.5; **Tube Dia. (in.):** 1; **W & E Adjustments:** Int.; **Weight (ozs.):** 7.5
Price: $44.99

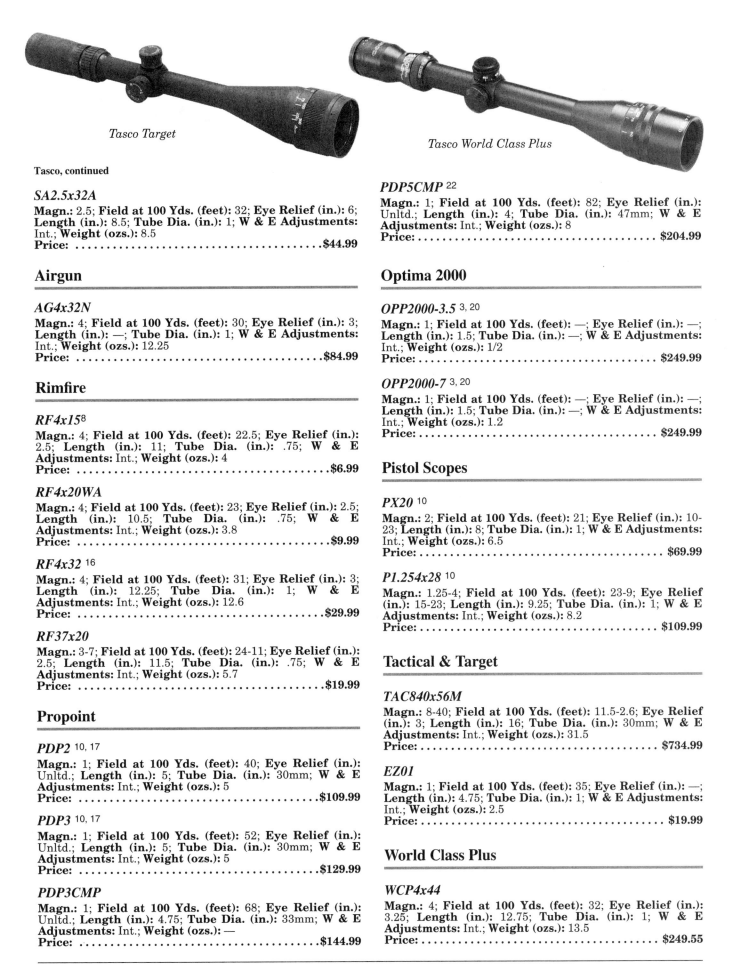

Tasco Target

Tasco World Class Plus

Tasco, continued

SA2.5x32A

Magn.: 2.5; **Field at 100 Yds. (feet):** 32; **Eye Relief (in.):** 6; **Length (in.):** 8.5; **Tube Dia. (in.):** 1; **W & E Adjustments:** Int.; **Weight (ozs.):** 8.5
Price: $44.99

Airgun

AG4x32N

Magn.: 4; **Field at 100 Yds. (feet):** 30; **Eye Relief (in.):** 3; **Length (in.):** —; **Tube Dia. (in.):** 1; **W & E Adjustments:** Int.; **Weight (ozs.):** 12.25
Price: $84.99

Rimfire

RF4x15[8]

Magn.: 4; **Field at 100 Yds. (feet):** 22.5; **Eye Relief (in.):** 2.5; **Length (in.):** 11; **Tube Dia. (in.):** .75; **W & E Adjustments:** Int.; **Weight (ozs.):** 4
Price: $6.99

RF4x20WA

Magn.: 4; **Field at 100 Yds. (feet):** 23; **Eye Relief (in.):** 2.5; **Length (in.):** 10.5; **Tube Dia. (in.):** .75; **W & E Adjustments:** Int.; **Weight (ozs.):** 3.8
Price: $9.99

RF4x32 [16]

Magn.: 4; **Field at 100 Yds. (feet):** 31; **Eye Relief (in.):** 3; **Length (in.):** 12.25; **Tube Dia. (in.):** 1; **W & E Adjustments:** Int.; **Weight (ozs.):** 12.6
Price: $29.99

RF37x20

Magn.: 3-7; **Field at 100 Yds. (feet):** 24-11; **Eye Relief (in.):** 2.5; **Length (in.):** 11.5; **Tube Dia. (in.):** .75; **W & E Adjustments:** Int.; **Weight (ozs.):** 5.7
Price: $19.99

Propoint

PDP2 [10, 17]

Magn.: 1; **Field at 100 Yds. (feet):** 40; **Eye Relief (in.):** Unltd.; **Length (in.):** 5; **Tube Dia. (in.):** 30mm; **W & E Adjustments:** Int.; **Weight (ozs.):** 5
Price: $109.99

PDP3 [10, 17]

Magn.: 1; **Field at 100 Yds. (feet):** 52; **Eye Relief (in.):** Unltd.; **Length (in.):** 5; **Tube Dia. (in.):** 30mm; **W & E Adjustments:** Int.; **Weight (ozs.):** 5
Price: $129.99

PDP3CMP

Magn.: 1; **Field at 100 Yds. (feet):** 68; **Eye Relief (in.):** Unltd.; **Length (in.):** 4.75; **Tube Dia. (in.):** 33mm; **W & E Adjustments:** Int.; **Weight (ozs.):** —
Price: $144.99

PDP5CMP [22]

Magn.: 1; **Field at 100 Yds. (feet):** 82; **Eye Relief (in.):** Unltd.; **Length (in.):** 4; **Tube Dia. (in.):** 47mm; **W & E Adjustments:** Int.; **Weight (ozs.):** 8
Price: $204.99

Optima 2000

OPP2000-3.5 [3, 20]

Magn.: 1; **Field at 100 Yds. (feet):** —; **Eye Relief (in.):** —; **Length (in.):** 1.5; **Tube Dia. (in.):** —; **W & E Adjustments:** Int.; **Weight (ozs.):** 1/2
Price: $249.99

OPP2000-7 [3, 20]

Magn.: 1; **Field at 100 Yds. (feet):** —; **Eye Relief (in.):** —; **Length (in.):** 1.5; **Tube Dia. (in.):** —; **W & E Adjustments:** Int.; **Weight (ozs.):** 1.2
Price: $249.99

Pistol Scopes

PX20 [10]

Magn.: 2; **Field at 100 Yds. (feet):** 21; **Eye Relief (in.):** 10-23; **Length (in.):** 8; **Tube Dia. (in.):** 1; **W & E Adjustments:** Int.; **Weight (ozs.):** 6.5
Price: $69.99

P1.254x28 [10]

Magn.: 1.25-4; **Field at 100 Yds. (feet):** 23-9; **Eye Relief (in.):** 15-23; **Length (in.):** 9.25; **Tube Dia. (in.):** 1; **W & E Adjustments:** Int.; **Weight (ozs.):** 8.2
Price: $109.99

Tactical & Target

TAC840x56M

Magn.: 8-40; **Field at 100 Yds. (feet):** 11.5-2.6; **Eye Relief (in.):** 3; **Length (in.):** 16; **Tube Dia. (in.):** 30mm; **W & E Adjustments:** Int.; **Weight (ozs.):** 31.5
Price: $734.99

EZ01

Magn.: 1; **Field at 100 Yds. (feet):** 35; **Eye Relief (in.):** —; **Length (in.):** 4.75; **Tube Dia. (in.):** 1; **W & E Adjustments:** Int.; **Weight (ozs.):** 2.5
Price: $19.99

World Class Plus

WCP4x44

Magn.: 4; **Field at 100 Yds. (feet):** 32; **Eye Relief (in.):** 3.25; **Length (in.):** 12.75; **Tube Dia. (in.):** 1; **W & E Adjustments:** Int.; **Weight (ozs.):** 13.5
Price: $249.55

WCP3.510x50 [18]

Magn.: 3.5-10; **Field at 100 Yds. (feet):** 30-10.5; **Eye Relief (in.):** 3.75; **Length (in.):** 13; **Tube Dia. (in.):** 1; **W & E Adjustments:** Int.; **Weight (ozs.):** 17.1
Price: $159.99

WCP39x44 [1,16]

Magn.: 3-9; **Field at 100 Yds. (feet):** 39-14; **Eye Relief (in.):** 3.5; **Length (in.):** 12.75; **Tube Dia. (in.):** 1; **W & E Adjustments:** Int.; **Weight (ozs.):** 15.8
Price: $154.99

WCP416x40

Magn.: 4-16; **Field at 100 Yds. (feet):** 26-7; **Eye Relief (in.):** 3; **Length (in.):** 14.25; **Tube Dia. (in.):** 1; **W & E Adjustments:** Int.; **Weight (ozs.):** 16.8
Price: $244.99

WCP624x40

Magn.: 6-24; **Field at 100 Yds. (feet):** 17.4; **Eye Relief (in.):** 3; **Length (in.):** 15.5; **Tube Dia. (in.):** 1; **W & E Adjustments:** Int.; **Weight (ozs.):** 17.5
Price: $254.99

Tasco Data: [1]Water, fog & shockproof; fully coated optics; .25-min. click stops; haze filter caps; 30-day/limited lifetime warranty. [2]30/30 range finding reticle. [3]Fits most popular auto pistols, MP5, AR-15/M16. [4]1/3 greater zoom range. [5]Trajectory compensating scopes, Opti-Centered® stadia reticle. [6]Black gloss or stainless. [7]True one-power scope. [8]Coated optics; crosshair reticle; ring mounts included to fit most 22, 10mm receivers. [9]Red dot; also with switchable red/green dot (EZ02, **$42.05**). [10]Also matte aluminum finish. [11]11-position rheostat, 10-MOA dot; built-in dovetail-style mount. Also with crosshair reticle. [12]Also 30/30 reticle. [13]Also in stainless finish. [14]Black matte or stainless finish. [15]Also with stainless finish. [16]Also in matte black. [17]Available with 5-min., or 10-min. dot. [18]Red dot device; can be used on rifles, shotguns, handguns; 3.5 or 7 MOA dot. Available with 10, 15, 20-min. dot. [19]20mm; also 32mm. [20]20mm; black matte; also stainless steel; also 32mm. [21]Pro-Shot reticle. [22]Has 4, 8, 12, 16MOA dots (switchable). [23]Available with BDC. **Contact Tasco for details on complete line.**

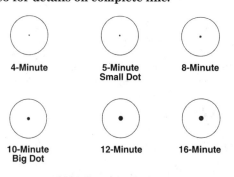

4-Minute   5-Minute Small Dot   8-Minute

10-Minute Big Dot   12-Minute   16-Minute

PDP5VR Variable Reticles

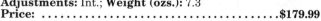

WEAVER

Rifle Scopes

K2.5 [1]

Magn.: 2.5; **Field at 100 Yds. (feet):** 35; **Eye Relief (in.):** 3.7; **Length (in.):** 9.5; **Tube Dia. (in.):** 1; **W & E Adjustments:** Int.; **Weight (ozs.):** 7.3
Price: $179.99

Weaver K2.5

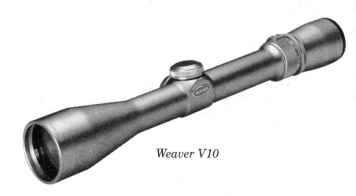

Weaver V10

K4 [1-2]

Magn.: 3.7; **Field at 100 Yds. (feet):** 26.5; **Eye Relief (in.):** 3.3; **Length (in.):** 11.3; **Tube Dia. (in.):** 1; **W & E Adjustments:** Int.; **Weight (ozs.):** 10
Price: $194.99

K6 [1]

Magn.: 5.7; **Field at 100 Yds. (feet):** 18.5; **Eye Relief (in.):** 3.3; **Length (in.):** 11.4; **Tube Dia. (in.):** 1; **W & E Adjustments:** Int.; **Weight (ozs.):** 10
Price: $194.99

KT15 [1]

Magn.: 14.6; **Field at 100 Yds. (feet):** 7.5; **Eye Relief (in.):** 3.2; **Length (in.):** 12.9; **Tube Dia. (in.):** 1; **W & E Adjustments:** Int.; **Weight (ozs.):** 14.7
Price: $374.99

V3 [1-2]

Magn.: 1.1-2.8; **Field at 100 Yds. (feet):** 88-32; **Eye Relief (in.):** 3.9-3.7; **Length (in.):** 9.2; **Tube Dia. (in.):** 1; **W & E Adjustments:** Int.; **Weight (ozs.):** 8.5
Price: $299.99

V9 [1-2]

Magn.: 2.8-8.7; **Field at 100 Yds. (feet):** 33-11; **Eye Relief (in.):** 3.5-3.4; **Length (in.):** 12.1; **Tube Dia. (in.):** 1; **W & E Adjustments:** Int.; **Weight (ozs.):** 11.1
Price: $249.99-299.99

V9x50 [1-2]

Magn.: 3-9; **Field at 100 Yds. (feet):** 29.4-9.9; **Eye Relief (in.):** 3.6-3; **Length (in.):** 13.1; **Tube Dia. (in.):** 1; **W & E Adjustments:** Int.; **Weight (ozs.):** 14.5
Price: $319.99

V10 [1-2-3]

Magn.: 2.2-9.6; **Field at 100 Yds. (feet):** 38.5-9.5; **Eye Relief (in.):** 3.4-3.3; **Length (in.):** 12.2; **Tube Dia. (in.):** 1; **W & E Adjustments:** Int.; **Weight (ozs.):** 11.2
Price: $259.99-269.99

Weaver VH4

Weaver Grand Slam 4.5-14x40mm

Weaver, continued

V10-50 1-2-3

Magn.: 2.3-9.7; **Field at 100 Yds. (feet):** 40.2-9.2; **Eye Relief (in.):** 2.9-2.8; **Length (in.):** 13.75; **Tube Dia. (in.):** 1; **W & E Adjustments:** Int.; **Weight (ozs.):** 15.2
Price: $365.99

V16 MDX 2-3

Magn.: 3.8-15.5; **Field at 100 Yds. (feet):** 26.8-6.8; **Eye Relief (in.):** 3.1; **Length (in.):** 13.9; **Tube Dia. (in.):** 1; **W & E Adjustments:** Int.; **Weight (ozs.):** 16.5
Price: $434.99

V16 MFC 2-3

Magn.: 3.8-15.5; **Field at 100 Yds. (feet):** 26.8-6.8; **Eye Relief (in.):** 3.1; **Length (in.):** 13.9; **Tube Dia. (in.):** 1; **W & E Adjustments:** Int.; **Weight (ozs.):** 16.5
Price: $434.99

V16 MDT 2-3

Magn.: 3.8-15.5; **Field at 100 Yds. (feet):** 26.8-6.8; **Eye Relief (in.):** 3.1; **Length (in.):** 13.9; **Tube Dia. (in.):** 1; **W & E Adjustments:** Int.; **Weight (ozs.):** 16.5
Price: $434.99

V24 Varmint 2

Magn.: 6-24; **Field at 100 Yds. (feet):** 15.3-4; **Eye Relief (in.):** 3.15; **Length (in.):** 14.3; **Tube Dia. (in.):** 1; **W & E Adjustments:** Int.; **Weight (ozs.):** 17.5
Price: $509.99

Handgun

H2 1-3

Magn.: 2; **Field at 100 Yds. (feet):** 21; **Eye Relief (in.):** 4-29; **Length (in.):** 8.5; **Tube Dia. (in.):** 1; **W & E Adjustments:** Int.; **Weight (ozs.):** 6.7
Price: $212.99-224.99

H4 1-3

Magn.: 4; **Field at 100 Yds. (feet):** 18; **Eye Relief (in.):** 11.5-18; **Length (in.):** 8.5; **Tube Dia. (in.):** 1; **W & E Adjustments:** Int.; **Weight (ozs.):** 6.7
Price: $234.99

VH4 1-3

Magn.: 1.5-4; **Field at 100 Yds. (feet):** 13.6-5.8; **Eye Relief (in.):** 11-17; **Length (in.):** 8.6; **Tube Dia. (in.):** 1; **W & E Adjustments:** Int.; **Weight (ozs.):** 8.1
Price: $289.99

VH8 1-2-3

Magn.: 2.5-8; **Field at 100 Yds. (feet):** 8.5-3.7; **Eye Relief (in.):** 12.16; **Length (in.):** 9.3; **Tube Dia. (in.):** 1; **W & E Adjustments:** Int.; **Weight (ozs.):** 8.3
Price: $299.99

Rimfire

R4 2-3

Magn.: 3.9; **Field at 100 Yds. (feet):** 29; **Eye Relief (in.):** 3.9; **Length (in.):** 9.7; **Tube Dia. (in.):** 1; **W & E Adjustments:** Int.; **Weight (ozs.):** 8.8
Price: $159.99

RV7 2

Magn.: 2.5-7; **Field at 100 Yds. (feet):** 37-13; **Eye Relief (in.):** 3.7-3.3; **Length (in.):** 10.75; **Tube Dia. (in.):** 1; **W & E Adjustments:** Int.; **Weight (ozs.):** 10.7
Price: $184.99-189.99

Grand Slam

6-20x40mm Varminter Reticle 2

Magn.: 6-20X; **Field at 100 Yds. (feet):** 16.5-5.25; **Eye Relief (in.):** 2.75-3; **Length (in.):** 14.48; **Tube Dia. (in.):** 1; **W & E Adjustments:** Int.; **Weight (ozs.):** 17.75
Price: $499.99

6-20x40mm Fine Crosshairs with a Dot 2

Magn.: 6-20X; **Field at 100 Yds. (feet):** 16.5-5.25; **Eye Relief (in.):** 2.75-3; **Length (in.):** 14.48; **Tube Dia. (in.):** 1; **W & E Adjustments:** Int.; **Weight (ozs.):** 17.75
Price: $499.99

1.5-5x32mm 2

Magn.: 1.5-5X; **Field at 100 Yds. (feet):** 71-21; **Eye Relief (in.):** 3.25; **Length (in.):** 10.5; **Tube Dia. (in.):** 1; **W & E Adjustments:** Int.; **Weight (ozs.):** 10.5
Price: $429.99

4.75x40mm 2

Magn.: 4.75X; **Field at 100 Yds. (feet):** 14.75; **Eye Relief (in.):** 3.25; **Length (in.):** 11; **Tube Dia. (in.):** 1; **W & E Adjustments:** Int.; **Weight (ozs.):** 10.75
Price: $359.99

3-10x40mm 2

Magn.: 3-10X; **Field at 100 Yds. (feet):** 35-11.33; **Eye Relief (in.):** 3.5-3; **Length (in.):** 12.08; **Tube Dia. (in.):** 1; **W & E Adjustments:** Int.; **Weight (ozs.):** 12.08
Price: $379.99

3.5-10x50mm 2

Magn.: 3.5-10X; **Field at 100 Yds. (feet):** 30.5-10.8; **Eye Relief (in.):** 3.5-3; **Length (in.):** 12.96; **Tube Dia. (in.):** 1; **W & E Adjustments:** Int.; **Weight (ozs.):** 16.25
Price: $459.99

4.5-14x40mm

Magn.: 4.5-14X; **Field at 100 Yds. (feet):** 22.5-10.5; **Eye Relief (in.):** 3.5-3; **Length (in.):** 14.48; **Tube Dia. (in.):** 1; **W & E Adjustments:** Int.; **Weight (ozs.):** 17.5
Price: $499.99

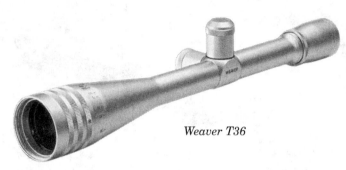

Weaver T36

Weaver, continued

T-Series

T-6 [4]

Magn.: 614; **Field at 100 Yds. (feet):** 14; **Eye Relief (in.):** 3.58; **Length (in.):** 12.75; **Tube Dia. (in.):** 1; **W & E Adjustments:** Int.; **Weight (ozs.):** 14.9
Price: $424.95

T-36 [3-4]

Magn.: 36; **Field at 100 Yds. (feet):** 3; **Eye Relief (in.):** 3; **Length (in.):** 15.1; **Tube Dia. (in.):** 1; **W & E Adjustments:** Int.; **Weight (ozs.):** 16.7
Price: $794.99

Weaver Data: [1]Gloss black, [2]Matte black, [3]Silver, [4]Satin, [5]Silver and black (slightly higher in price). [6]Field of view measured at 18" eye relief. .25 MOA click adjustments, except T-Series which vary from .125 to .25 clicks. One-piece tubes with multi-coated lenses. All scopes are shock-proof, waterproof, and fogproof. Dual-X reticle available in all except V24 which has a fine X-hair and ot; T-Series in which certain models are available in fine X-hair and dots; Qwik-Point red dot scopes which are available in fixed 4 or 12 MOA, or variable 4-8-12 MOA. V16 also available with fine X-hair, dot or Dual-X reticle. T-Series scopes have Micro-Trac® adjustments. From Weaver Products.

ZEISS

ZM/Z

6x42MC

Magn.: 6; **Field at 100 Yds. (feet):** 22.9; **Eye Relief (in.):** 3.2; **Length (in.):** 12.7; **Tube Dia. (in.):** 1; **W & E Adjustments:** Int.; **Weight (ozs.):** 13.4
Price: $749.00

8x56MC

Magn.: 8; **Field at 100 Yds. (feet):** 18; **Eye Relief (in.):** 3.2; **Length (in.):** 13.8; **Tube Dia. (in.):** 1; **W & E Adjustments:** Int.; **Weight (ozs.):** 17.6
Price: $829.00

1.25-4x24MC

Magn.: 1.25-4; **Field at 100 Yds. (feet):** 105-33; **Eye Relief (in.):** 3.2; **Length (in.):** 11.46; **Tube Dia. (in.):** 30mm; **W & E Adjustments:** Int.; **Weight (ozs.):** 17.3
Price: $779.00

1.5-6x42MC

Magn.: 1.5-6; **Field at 100 Yds. (feet):** 65.5-22.9; **Eye Relief (in.):** 3.2; **Length (in.):** 12.4; **Tube Dia. (in.):** 30mm; **W & E Adjustments:** Int.; **Weight (ozs.):** 18.5
Price: $899.00

2.5-10x48MC [1]

Magn.: 2.5-10; **Field at 100 Yds. (feet):** 33-11.7; **Eye Relief (in.):** 3.2; **Length (in.):** 14.5; **Tube Dia. (in.):** 30mm; **W & E Adjustments:** Int.; **Weight (ozs.):** 24
Price: $1,029.00

3-12x56MC [1]

Magn.: 3-12; **Field at 100 Yds. (feet):** 27.6-9.9; **Eye Relief (in.):** 3.2; **Length (in.):** 15.3; **Tube Dia. (in.):** 30mm; **W & E Adjustments:** Int.; **Weight (ozs.):** 25.8
Price: $1,099.00

Conquest

3-9x36MC

Magn.: 3-9; **Field at 100 Yds. (feet):** 34-11; **Eye Relief (in.):** 4; **Length (in.):** 13.15; **Tube Dia. (in.):** 1; **W & E Adjustments:** Int.; **Weight (ozs.):** 15
Price: $499.00

VM/V

1.1-4x24 VariPoint T [2]

Magn.: 1.1-4; **Field at 100 Yds. (feet):** 120-34; **Eye Relief (in.):** 3.5; **Length (in.):** 11.8; **Tube Dia. (in.):** 30mm; **W & E Adjustments:** Int.; **Weight (ozs.):** 15.8
Price: $1,799.00

1.5-6x42T *

Magn.: 1.5-6; **Field at 100 Yds. (feet):** 65.5-22.9; **Eye Relief (in.):** 3.2; **Length (in.):** 12.4; **Tube Dia. (in.):** 30mm; **W & E Adjustments:** Int.; **Weight (ozs.):** 18.5
Price: $1,349.00

2.5-10x50T *[1]

Magn.: 2.5-10; **Field at 100 Yds. (feet):** 47.1-13; **Eye Relief (in.):** 3.5; **Length (in.):** 12.5; **Tube Dia. (in.):** 30mm; **W & E Adjustments:** Int.; **Weight (ozs.):** 16.25
Price: $1,549.00

3-12x56T *

Magn.: 3-12; **Field at 100 Yds. (feet):** 37.5-10.5; **Eye Relief (in.):** 3.5; **Length (in.):** 13.5; **Tube Dia. (in.):** 30mm; **W & E Adjustments:** Int.; **Weight (ozs.):** 19.5
Price: $1,599.00

3-9x42T *

Magn.: 3-9; **Field at 100 Yds. (feet):** 42-15; **Eye Relief (in.):** 3.74; **Length (in.):** 13.3; **Tube Dia. (in.):** 1; **W & E Adjustments:** Int.; **Weight (ozs.):** 15.3
Price: $1,249.00

5-15x42T *

Magn.: 5-15; **Field at 100 Yds. (feet):** 25.7-8.5; **Eye Relief (in.):** 3.74; **Length (in.):** 13.3; **Tube Dia. (in.):** 1; **W & E Adjustments:** Int.; **Weight (ozs.):** 15.4
Price: $1,499.00

Zeiss Data: [1]Also avail. with illuminated reticle. [2]Illuminated Vari-point reticle. Black matte finish. All scopes have .25-min. click-stop adjustments. Choice of Z-Plex or fine crosshair reticles. Rubber armored objective bell, rubber eyepiece ring. Lenses have T-Star coating for highest light transmission. VM/V scopes avail. with rail mount. Partial listing shown. From Carl Zeiss Optical, Inc.

SPOTTING SCOPES

BAUSCH & LOMB DISCOVERER 15x to 60x zoom, 60mm objective. Constant focus throughout range. Field at 1000 yds. 38 ft (60x), 150 ft. (15x). Comes with lens caps. Length 17 1/2"; weight 48.5 oz.
Price: **$391.95**

BAUSCH & LOMB ELITE 15x to 45x zoom, 60mm objective. Field at 1000 yds., 125-65 ft. Length is 12.2"; weight, 26.5 oz. Waterproof, armored. Tripod mount. Comes with black case.
Price: **$766.95**

BAUSCH & LOMB ELITE ZOOM 20x-60x, 70mm objective. Roof prism. Field at 1000 yds. 90-50 ft. Length is 16"; weight 40 oz. Waterproof, armored. Tripod mount. Comes with black case.
Price: **$921.95**

BAUSCH & LOMB 80MM ELITE 20x-60x zoom, 80mm objective. Field of view at 1000 yds. 98-50 ft. (zoom). Weight 51 oz. (20x, 30x), 54 oz. (zoom); length 17". Interchangeable bayonet-style eyepieces. Built-in peep sight.
Price: With EDPrime Glass. **$1,212.95**

BURRIS 18-45x SIGNATURE SPOTTER 60mm objective, 18x-45x, constant focus, Field at 1000 yds. 112-63 ft.; weighs 29oz.; length 12.6". Camera adapters available.
Price: **$819.00**

BURRIS LANDMARK SPOTTER 15-45x, 60mm objective. Straight type. Field at 100 yds. 146-72 ft. Length 12.7"; weight 24 oz. Rubber armor coating, multi-coated lenses, 22mm eye relief. Recessed focus adjustment. Nitrogen filled. .
Price: 30x 60mm **$644.00**

BUSHNELL TROPHY 63mm objective, 20x-60x zoom. Field at 1000 yds. 90ft. (20x), 45 ft. (60x). Length 12.7"; weight 20 oz. Black rubber armored, waterproof. Case included.
Price: **$421.95**

BUSHNELL COMPACT TROPHY 50mm objective, 20x-50x zoom. Field at 1000 yds. 92 ft. (20x), 52 ft. (50x). Length 12.2"; weight 17 oz. Black rubber armored, waterproof. Case included.
Price: **$337.95**

BUSHNELL BANNER SENTRY 18x-36x zoom, 50mm objective. Field at 1000 yds. 115-75 ft. Length 14.5", weight 31 oz. Black rubber armored. Built-in peep sight. Comes with tripod and hardcase.
Price: **$180.95**
Price: With 45 field eyepiece, includes tripod **$202.95**

BUSHNELL SPACEMASTER 20x-45x zoom. Long eye relief. Rubber armored, prismatic. 60mm objective. Field at 1000 yds. 90-58 ft. Minimum focus 20 ft. Length 12.7"; weight 43 oz.
Price: With tripod, carrying case and 20x-45x LER eyepiece
. . . .**$560.95**

BUSHNELL SPORTVIEW 12x-36x zoom, 50mm objective. Field at 100 yds. 160 ft. (12x), 90 ft. (36x). Length 14.6"; weight 25 oz.
Price: With tripod and carrying case. **$159.95**

BUSHNELL X-TRA WIDE® 15-45x zoom, 60mm objective. Field at 1000 yds. 160-87 ft. Length 13"; weight 35 oz.
Price: **$640.95**

KOWA TSN SERIES Offset 45 or straight body. 77mm objective, 20x WA, 25x, 25x LER, 30x WA, 40x, 60x, 77x and 20-60x zoom. Field at 1000 yds. 179 ft. (20xWA), 52 ft. (60x). Available with flourite lens.
Price: TSN-1 (without eyepiece) 45 offset scope. **$696.00**
Price: TSN-2 (without eyepiece) Straight scope **$660.00**
Price: 20x W.A. (wide angle) eyepiece. **$230.00**
Price: 25x eyepiece **$143.00**
Price: 25x LER (long eye relief) eyepiece **$214.00**
Price: 30x W.A. (wide angle) eyepiece. **$266.00**
Price: 40x eyepiece **$159.00**
Price: 60x W.A. (wide angle) eyepiece. **$230.00**
Price: 77x eyepiece **$235.00**
Price: 20-60x zoom eyepiece **$302.00**

Nikon
Fieldscope 78mm

KOWA TS-610 SERIES Offset 45 or straight body. 60mm objective, 20x WA, 25x, 25x LER, 27x WA, 40x and 20x-60x zoom. Field at 1000 yds. 162 ft. (20x WA), 51 ft. (60x). Available with ED lens.
Price: TS-611 (without eyepiece) 45 offset scope **$510.00**
Price: TS-612 (without eyepiece) Straight scope **$462.00**
Price: 20x W.A. (wide angle) eyepiece. **$111.00**
Price: 25x eyepiece **$95.00**
Price: 25x LER (long eye relief) eyepiece **$214.00**
Price: 27x W.A. (wide angle) eyepiece. **$166.00**
Price: 40x eyepiece **$98.00**
Price: 20-60x zoom eyepiece **$207.00**

KOWA TS-9 SERIES Offset 45 ,straight or rubber armored (straight only). 50mm objective, 15x, 20x and 11-33x zoom. Field at 1000 yds. 188 ft. (15x), 99 ft. (33x).
Price: TS-9B (without eyepiece) 45 offset scope. **$223.00**
Price: TS-9C (without eyepiece) straight scope **$176.00**
Price: TS-9R (without eyepiece) straight rubber armored
scope/black **$197.00**
Price: 15x eyepiece **$38.00**
Price: 20x eyepiece **$36.00**
Price: 11-33x zoom eyepiece **$122.00**

LEUPOLD 12-40x60 VARIABLE 60mm objective, 12-40x. Field at 100 yds. 17.5-5.3 ft.; eye relief 1.2" (20x). Overall length 11.5", weight 32 oz. Rubber armored.
Price: **$1,217.90**

LEUPOLD 25x50 COMPACT 50mm objective, 25x. Field at 100 yds. 8.3 ft.; eye relief 1"; length overall 9.4"; weight 20.5 oz.
Price: Armored model. **$848.20**
Price: Packer Tripod **$96.40**

NIKON FIELDSCOPES 60mm and 78mm lens. Field at 1000 yds. 105 ft. (60mm, 20x), 126 ft. (78mm, 25x). Length 12.8" (straight 60mm), 12.6" (straight 78mm); weight 34.5-47.5 oz. Eyepieces available separately.
Price: 60mm straight body **$690.95**
Price: 60mm angled body **$796.95**
Price: 60mm straight ED body **$1,200.95**
Price: 60mm angled ED body **$1,314.95**
Price: 78mm straight ED body **$2,038.95**
Price: 78mm angled ED body **$2,170.95**
Price: Eyepieces (15x to 60x) . . . .**$146.95 to $324.95**
Price: 20-45x eyepiece (25-56x for 78mm) **$318.95**

NIKON SPOTTING SCOPE 60mm objective, 20x fixed power or 15-45x zoom. Field at 1000 yds. 145 ft. (20x). Gray rubber armored. Straight or angled eyepiece. Weighs 44.2 oz., length 12.1" (20x).
Price: 20x60 fixed (with eyepiece) **$368.95**
Price: 15-45x zoom (with case, tripod, eyepiece). **$578.95**

PENTAX PF-80ED spotting scope 80mm objective lens available in 18x, 24x, 36x, 48x, 72x and 20-60x. Length 15.6", weight 11.9 to 19.2 oz.
Price: **$1,320.00**

SIGHTRON SII 2050X63 63mm objective lens, 20x-50x zoom. Field at 1000 yds 91.9 ft. (20x), 52.5 ft. (50x). Length 14"; weight 30.8 oz. Black rubber finish. Also available with 80mm objective lens.
Price: 63mm or 80mm. **$339.95**

SIMMONS 1280 50mm objective, 15-45x zoom. Black matte finish. Ocular focus. Peep finder sight. Waterproof. FOV 95-51 ft. @ 1000 yards. Wgt. 33.5 oz., length 12".
Price: With tripod **$267.99**

SIMMONS 1281 60mm objective, 20-60x zoom. Black matte finish. Ocular focus. Peep finder sight. Waterproof. FOV 78-43 ft. @ 1000 yards. Wgt. 34.5 oz. Length 12".
Price: With tripod **$295.99**

SIMMONS 77206 PROHUNTER 50mm objectives, 25x fixed power. Field at 1000 yds. 113 ft.; length 10.25"; weighs 33.25 oz. Black rubber armored.
Price: With tripod case **$160.60**

SIMMONS 41200 REDLINE 50mm objective, 15x-45x zoom. Field at 1000 yds. 104-41 ft.; length 16.75"; weighs 32.75 oz.
Price: With hard case and tripod **$99.99**
Price: 20-60x, Model 41201 . . . . **$129.99**

STEINER FIELD TELESCOPE 24x, 80mm objective. Field at 1000 yds. 105 ft. Weight 44 oz. Tripod mounts. Rubber armored.
Price: **$1,299.00**

SWAROVSKI CT EXTENDIBLE SCOPES 75mm or 85mm objective, 20-60x zoom, or fixed 15x, 22x, 30x, 32x eyepieces. Field at 1000 yds. 135 ft. (15x), 99 ft. (32x); 99 ft. (20x), 5.2 ft. (60x) for zoom. Length 12.4" (closed), 17.2" (open) for the CT75; 9.7"/17.2" for CT85. Weight 40.6 oz. (CT75), 49.4 oz. (CT85). Green rubber armored.
Price: CT75 body **$765.56**
Price: CT85 body **$1,094.44**
Price: 20-60x eyepiece **$343.33**
Price: 15x, 22x eyepiece **$232.22**
Price: 30x eyepiece **$265.55**

SWAROVSKI AT-80/ST-80 SPOTTING SCOPES 80mm objective, 20-60x zoom, or fixed 15x, 22x, 30x, 32x eyepieces. Field at 1000 yds. 135 ft. (15x), 99 ft. (32x); 99 ft. (20x), 52.5 ft. (60x) for zoom. Length 16" (AT-80), 15.6" (ST-80); weight 51.8 oz. Available with HD (high density) glass.
Price: AT-80 (angled) body **$1,094.44**
Price: ST-80 (straight) body **$1,094.44**
Price: With HD glass. **$1,555.00**
Price: 20-60x eyepiece **$343.33**
Price: 15x, 22x eyepiece **$232.22**
Price: 30x eyepiece **$265.55**

SWIFT LYNX M836 15x-45x zoom, 60mm objective. Weight 7 lbs., length 14". Has 45° eyepiece, sunshade.
Price: **$315.00**

SWIFT NIGHTHAWK M849U 80mm objective, 20x-60x zoom, or fixed 19, 25x, 31x, 50x, 75x eyepieces. Has rubber armored body, 1.8x optical finder, retractable lens hood, 45° eyepiece. Field at 1000 yds. 60 ft. (28x), 41 ft. (75x). Length 13.4 oz.; weight 39 oz.
Price: Body only **$870.00**
Price: 20-68x eyepiece **$370.00**
Price: Fixed eyepieces. . . . . **$130.00 to $240.00**
Price: Model 849 (straight) body **$795.00**

SWIFT NIGHTHAWK M850U 65mm objective, 16x-48x zoom, or fixed 19x, 20x, 25x, 40x, 60x eyepieces. Rubber armored with a 1.8x optical finder, retractable lens hood. Field at 1000 yds. 83 ft. (22x), 52 ft. (60x). Length 12.3"; weight 30 oz. Has 45° eyepiece.
Price: Body only **$650.00**
Price: 16x-48x eyepiece **$370.00**
Price: Fixed eyepieces. . . . . **$130.00 to $240.00**
Price: Model 850 (straight) body **$575.00**

SWIFT LEOPARD M837 50mm objective, 25x. Length 9 11/16" to 10 1/2". Weight with tripod 28 oz. Rubber armored. Comes with tripod.
Price: **$160.00**

SWIFT TELEMASTER M841 60mm objective. 15x to 60x variable power. Field at 1000 yds. 160 feet (15x) to 40 feet (60x). Weight 3.25 lbs.; length 18" overall.
Price: **$399.50**

Swift M700T Scout

SWIFT PANTHER M844 15x-45x zoom or 22x WA, 15x, 20x, 40x. 60mm objective. Field at 1000 yds. 141 ft. (15x), 68 ft. (40x), 95-58 ft. (20x-45x).
Price: Body only **$380.00**
Price: 15x-45x zoom eyepiece **$120.00**
Price: 20x-45x zoom (long eye relief) eyepiece **$140.00**
Price: 15x, 20x, 40x eyepiece **$65.00**
Price: 22x WA eyepiece **$80.00**

SWIFT M700T 12x-36x, 50mm objective. Field of view at 100 yds. 16 ft. (12x), 9 ft. (36x). Length 14"; weight with tripod 3.22 lbs.
Price: **$225.00**

SWIFT SEARCHER M839 60mm objective, 20x, 40x. Field at 1000 yds. 118 ft. (30x), 59 ft. (40x). Length 12.6"; weight 3 lbs. Rotating eyepiece head for straight or 45° viewing.
Price: **$580.00**
Price: 30x, 50x eyepieces, each **$67.00**

TASCO 29TZBWP WATERPROOF SPOTTER 60mm objective lens, 20x-60x zoom. Field at 100 yds. 7 ft., 4 in. to 3 ft., 8 in. Black rubber armored. Comes with tripod, hard case.
Price: **$356.50**

TASCO WC28TZ WORLD CLASS SPOTTING SCOPE 50mm objective, 12-36x zoom. Field at 100 yds. World Class. 13-3.8 ft. Comes with tripod and case.
Price: **$220.00**

TASCO CW5001 COMPACT ZOOM 50mm objective, 12x-36x zoom. Field at 100 yds. 16 ft., 9 in. Includes photo adapter tube, tripod with panhead lever, case.
Price: **$280.00**

TASCO 3700WP WATERPROOF SPOTTER 50mm objective, 18x-36x zoom. Field at 100 yds. 12ft., 6 in. to 7 ft., 9 in. Black rubber armored. Comes with tripod, hard case.
Price: **$288.60**

TASCO 3700, 3701 SPOTTING SCOPE 50mm objective. 18x-36x zoom. Field at 100 yds. 12 ft., 6 in. to 7 ft., 9 in. Black rubber armored.
Price: Model 3700 (black, with tripod, case) **$237.00**
Price: Model 3701 (as above, brown camo) **$237.00**

TASCO 21EB ZOOM 50mm objective lens, 15x-45x zoom. Field at 100 yds. 11 ft. (15x). Weight 22 oz.; length 18.3" overall. Comes with panhead lever tripod.
Price: **$119.00**

TASCO 22EB ZOOM 60mm objective lens, 20x-60x zoom. Field at 100 yds. 7 ft., 2 in. (20x). Weight 28 oz.; length 21.5" overall. Comes with micro-adjustable tripod.
Price: **$183.00**

WEAVER 20x50 50mm objective. Field of view 124 ft. at 100 yds. Eye relief .85"; weighs 21 oz.; overall length 10". Waterproof, armored.
Price: **$368.99**

WEAVER 15-40x60 ZOOM 60mm objective. 15x-40x zoom. Field at 100 yds. 119 ft. (15x), 66 ft. (60x). Overall length 12.5", weighs 26 oz. Waterproof, armored.
Price: **$551.99**

Recent Developments

BINOCULARS

make/model	power/obj. dia. (mm)	prism/focus	field(ft.)	weight (oz.)	price
Brunton	12x42	porro/center	271	30	$430
Bushnell Elite	12x50	porro/center	250	34	$1,737
Fujinon BFL	8x42	porro/center	114	20	$470
Fujinon BFL	10x42	porro/center	104	20	$480
Fujinon Tecno-Stabi	14x40	image-stabilizing	273	43	$1800
Kahles 2000 Series	8x42	roof/center	330	26	$721
Kahles 2000 Series	10x42	roof/center	315	26	$772
Leica Trinovid	10x32	roof/center	405	22	$1095
Leica Trinovid	12x50	roof/center	300	41	$1495
Minox (a Leica firm)	8x32	roof/center	394	22	$439
Minox (a Leica firm)	10x42	roof/center	320	31	$549
Nikon Tundra	10x50	porro/center	324	40	$385
Nikon E2	8x30	porro/indiv.	461	20	$731
Nikon E2	10x35	porro/indiv.	366	22	$801
Optolyth	8x45	roof/center	360	32	$799
Optolyth	10x45	roof/center	330	32	$899
Pentax PCF V	8x40	porro/center	360	27	$250
Pentax PCF V	10x40	porro/center	285	27	$242
Pentax PCF V	7x50	porro/center	354	36	$255
Pentax PCF V	10x50	porro/center	285	35	$274
Pentax PCF V	12x50	porro/center	239	35	$284
Pentax PCF V	16x60	porro/center	161	46	$370
Pentax PCF V	20x60	porro/center	125	46	$394
Steiner Nighthunter	8x30	porro/indiv.	390	18	$839
Steiner Nighthunter	7x50	porro/indiv.	375	33	$1099
Steiner Nighthunter	10x50	porro/indiv.	315	35	$1199
Steiner Nighthunter	8x56	porro/indiv.	333	41	$1399
Steiner Nighthunter	12x56	porro/indiv.	258	41	$1439
Swarovski EL	8.5x42	roof/center	390	29	$1498
Swarovski EL	10x42	roof/center	330	28	$1550
Zeiss Diafun (B MC)	10x30	roof/center	330	16	$549

RIFLESCOPES

make/model	power/obj. dia. (in.)	field (ft.)	dia./length (in.)	weight (oz.)	price
Burris Mr. T	2.5-10x50	35-10	30mm/13.5	29	$2129
Burris	6x50	15	30mm/13	18	$683
Burris	8-32x50	13-4.5	30mm/18	27	$999
Burris Fullfield	1.75-5x20	65-23	1/10.5	10	$374
Burris Fullfield	3-9x40	31-13	1/12.5	13	$356
Burris Fullfield	3.5-10x50	28-11	1/13	15	$496
Burris Fullfield	4.5-14x42	25-9	1/14	15	$545
Docter Optic	3-9x40	31-13	1/12.5	17	$378
Docter Optic	3-10x40	34-12	1/13	18.5	$626
Docter Optic	4.5-14x40	23-8	1/13.5	21.5	$652
Docter Optic	8-25x50	13-4	1/16	26.5	$901
Kahles	1.1-4x24	108-32	1/11	15	$722
Kahles	1.5-6x42	72-21	1/12	16	$832
Kahles	2.5-10x50	44-13	1/13	17	$999
Kahles	3-12x56	38-11	1/14	19	$1110
Leupold	6x42	17	1/12	15	$628
Nikon Titanium UCC	3.3-10x44	30-10	1/13	20	$899
Nikon Titanium UCC	5.5-16.5x44	19-6	1/13	20	$939
Nikon Buckmaster	4.5-14x40	23-8	1/15	19	$401
Schmidt & Bender FD	1.25-4x20	96-30	30mm/11.5	14.5	$1480
Schmidt & Bender PH	3-12x50	33-11	30mm/13.5	20.5	$1285
Schmidt & Bender PH	4-16x50	25-8	30mm/15.5	27.5	$1555
Schmidt & Bender PH	2.5-10x56	40-12	30mm/15	22	$1325
Sightron S II	6x42	20	1/13	16	$291
Sightron S II	4-16x42	26-7	1/13.5	16	$403
Sightron S II	6-24x42	16-4.5	1/14.5	18.5	$354
Sightron S II	6.5-25x50	15-4	1/14.5	19.5	$422
Simmons WE	1.5-6x32	72-19	1/11	15	$290
Simmons WE	3-9x42	40-13	1/13.5	17.5	$300
Simmons WE	4-12x42	29-9.5	1/13	21	$365
Simmons WE	6-18x42	18-6.5	1/15	26.5	$365
Swarovski PH	4-16x50	27-8	30mm/14.2	22	$1440
Weaver Grand Slam	1-5x32	71-21	1/10.5	11.5	$430
Weaver Grand Slam	4.75x40	26	1/11	11	$360
Weaver Grand Slam	3-10x40	35-11	1/12	13	$380
Weaver Grand Slam	4.5-14x40	23-11	1/14	17.5	$500
Weaver Grand Slam	6-20x40	60-5	1/14	18	$500
Weaver Grand Slam	3.5-10x50	31-11	1/13	16	$460

Test Optics Before You Buy!

"…After a scope takes a hundred hits, it's good for thousands."

RIFLESCOPES, BINOCULARS AND spotting scopes are your windows to what's afield. Buy good ones. As a rule, the more you pay, the better the glass. But to make sure your money goes as far as it can, put those optics through simple tests before you write the check.

1. Visit a store that has a broad selection of optics, to compare same-price products under the same conditions. Then take the optics out of the store. You need to know how they perform in natural light, at a distance. Insist on fully multi-coated lenses. You can't tell by looking if all the lenses are coated or if any is multi-coated; that should be specified in product literature. Coating makes the image brighter. Up to 4 percent of incident light is lost at *every uncoated* air-to-glass surface. Time your test so you can look into deep shadow and obliquely toward low sun (don't look *at* the sun!) You want a bright, sharp image at dusk and in timber, and when game is backlit.

2. Using a signpost or power pole as a target, move the binocular or scope side to side, watching the field edge. The target will curve slightly as it reaches the edge, but *excessive* distortion is a liability. Very flat fields can be achieved with a "stop," but at the expense of brightness.

3. With the instrument held stationary, move your eye forward and back behind the ocular lens. You want comfortable eye relief (the distance between your pupil and the lens when you see the full field). You also want latitude in the eye relief. A scope or binocular with critical eye relief gives you only a partial field unless your eye is an exact distance from the lens. Check the eye relief of variable scopes throughout their power range. On many models, eye relief becomes more critical (and shorter) at high magnification. Scopes with less than 3 inches of eye relief can give you recoil scars.

4. Test for parallax in a scope by fixing the reticle on a small object far away and, with the scope still, moving your eye side to side. Now move your eye up and down. As the field blacks out, you may see the reticle move off-target. At one specific distance (generally 100 or 150 yards, closer for scopes designed for rimfire rifles), the factory has set the scope to be parallax-free. At other distances, some parallax error occurs. Scopes with adjustable objectives enable you to correct for parallax. Parallax can cause you to miss because the bullet goes not where you see the reticle, but where it was when your eye was on the scope's axis. But don't make too much of parallax. If your eye is centered behind the scope, it has no bearing on your shot.

5. Any spotting scope with fluorite glass – the "ED" or extra-low dispersion model – costs a lot more than the standard version. Test the resolution of both on a distant, dimly lit object. The difference may not be worth the premium. Because high magnification ensures a small exit pupil (and limits brightness at dusk), you'll want a big front lens on a spotting scope. Plus a sturdy, quick-adjust tripod.

6. Move all movable parts to check for looseness and binding. Scope adjustment clicks should be crisp and uniform. Focus wheels and diopter rings on binoculars must spin smoothly but not too easily. Turning the ocular housing on riflescopes does not adjust target focus; it only sharpens the reticle. Point the scope at the sky, and rotate the housing until the reticle comes clear. (On traditional American scopes, you'll need to loosen the lock ring and turn the whole ocular housing; not so with European-style helical sleeves.) Now close your eyes, open them and refine. Looking at the reticle too long or aiming the scope at a target, you force your eyes to focus. You want a sharp reticle when your eyes are *relaxed*.

7. Finally, read the warranty. You can't test the durability of an instrument before you buy. The warranty tells you if the manufacturer built it tough.

Glossary

"…The eye is the light of the body."

Abbe prism – A particular roof prism, with perpendicular end faces, that inverts an image in a telescope (named after physicist Ernst Abbe). The Abbe-Porro prism is a compact image-erecting prism used in binoculars.

achromatic lens – Lens comprising two or more elements, usually of crown and flint glass, that corrects for chromatic aberration, or the scattering of color by wavelength (also known as an achromat). The elements work to bring red and blue to a common focal point.

adjustable objective – Parallax-correcting ring on the objective housing of scopes, alternately a more convenient turret-mounted dial. For target and varmint scopes, the "AO" feature makes sense. Big game scopes don't need it. Parallax correction isn't needed at any range if your eye is on the optical axis of the scope. Sharpening the focus helps if you're using high magnification (say, 10x or higher).

Airy disk – Peak and concentric rings formed by light diffraction around a point-source of light (after Sir G.B. Airy, who devised a quantitative analysis of diffraction).

aperture stop – Physical ring that limits the diameter of the light bundle passing through a lens.

aplanatic lens – Lens that is free of spherical aberration and coma.

apochromatic lens – Lens in which three colors are brought to a common focus by use of three types of glass (also, an apochromat or APO). Achromatic lenses typically bring red and blue colors to the same focal point, while apochromats also deliver green to that point. "APO" lenses eliminate color rims and enhance contrast. Corraling colors is easiest after limiting their initial divergence. "Low-dispersion" apochromatic lenses do this. The difference is in the glass, not its coatings. It has been in high-quality cameras for years.

apparent field – Angle subtended by the field of view of the image space of an instrument (as opposed to the true field, defined by the object space).

aspheric – Not spherical, a lens surface deliberately altered in shape to reduce spherical aberration. Surface concavity and convexity in aespheric lenses are not of constant radius. Leica has a machine that presses glass into aspheric lenses but is used only for camera lenses. There's no benefit to aespherical lenses in binoculars because a flatter field comes at the expense of panning smoothness.

astigmatism – Lens aberration that separates tangential and sagittal image planes (commonly in eyesight but also as applies to hard lenses).

barrel distortion – Lens aberration that causes square objects to appear to bulge or become barrel-shaped.

borescope – Device for the inspection of hard-to-reach places, initially with mirrors and now with fiber optic bundles. Borescopes are used for examining rifle bores, gas mains and, in medical practice, internal organs.

boresight – Optically aligning two axes, such as the sightline and boreline of a rifle; alternatively, a device that helps you with this alignment.

catadioptric system – Optical system that uses both reflection and refraction to achieve its focal power.

catoptric system – Optical system using only curved mirrors to form images.

chromatic aberration – Optical flaw, caused by the splintering of light refracted by a lens. It is controlled by achromatic, or color-corrected, lenses. These have at least two elements, matched so colors split by the first element are brought back together by the second. In optical instruments of low magnification, an achromatic lens that combines two of the three main colors – blue and red – yields images as sharp as we can distinguish. High magnification (more than 10 power) and big objective lenses (over 60mm) can show a fuzziness caused by the green color or wavelength skating off to some other place on the lens axis after exit. Fully color-corrected lenses, called apochromatic, are best for target scopes and spotting scopes.

center focus – (See Chapter 3.)

clear aperture – Effective diameter of an objective or front lens, as related to light transmission.

clear eye distance – Axial distance between the eye and the rearmost mechanical surface of an optical device (differs from eye relief if the ocular housing extends beyond the surface of the lens).

clicks – Adjustment graduations named for the sound of the dial overriding its detent, clicks on windage and elevation adjustments of rifle scopes are typically labeled in minutes of angle (one m.o.a. is approximately 1 inch at 100 yards). An ordinary hunting scope has 1/4-minute clicks; a low-power scope for woods hunting may have 1/2-minute clicks. Some target scopes of very high magnification (and even competition-style receiver sights) feature 1/8-minute clicks. Obviously, design and machining tolerances for *those* mechanisms are demanding!

coincidence prism – Compound prism used in coincidence rangefinders to present one image to a viewfinder from two objective lenses. The rangefinder employs two 45-degree mirrors at the ends of a fixed baseline. Each mirror delivers half an image. Rotating one of the mirrors makes the split image whole. The angle of rotation is proportional to the target distance.

collimation – Aligning two optical axes so they are parallel, or aligning the optical axis of an instrument with a physical axis (as in the preliminary steps of zeroing a rifle).

collimator – Optical device such as a boresight attached to a rifle's muzzle to assist with collimating a scope (alternatively, a more sophisticated laboratory instrument used to test lenses).

coma – Essentially a shift of focus. This fault, a headache to early astronomers working with primitive optics, can move the brilliant center of a distant star to someplace on its glowing perimeter. Lenses that eliminate the blur are said to be aplanatic.

cone – Photosensitive cells in the eye's retina that transmit light signals to the brain, which processes them as images and color.

contrast – Apparent difference in luminence or brightness between light and dark areas of an object.

critical angle – Least angle of incidence at which total internal reflection takes place. When light passes from one medium to another, the proportions of light reflected and refracted vary with the angle of incidence. At some critical angle, depending on the media, all light is reflected.

critical aperture – In an optical system, the aperture diameter at which a lens delivers its best performance.

crown glass – One of two main types of optical glass. Crown glass is harder than flint glass, with a lower index of refraction and lower dispersion.

cylindrical lens – Lens with at least one surface of barrel-like configuration. Cylindrical lenses are commonly used in eyeglasses to correct for astigmatism, and in rangefinders to stretch a point of light into a line.

deflection – Bending of light away from its projected path, including diffraction and magnetic response.

depth of field – Distance through which the eye perceives a sharp image when a lens is focused at one range.

depth of focus – Range of image distances that corresponds to the range of object distances specified in defining depth of field.

diffraction – Apparent bending and diffusion of light rays as a wavefront of light passes an edge or through an opening. Diffraction results from formation of secondary and smaller wave fronts at the point of interference.

diffusion – Differential scattering of light when it strikes an irregular surface (such as frosted glass). Reflection at different angles results in diffusion, and a "soft" image.

diopter – A unit of measure that shows the refractive power of a lens or prism. A diopter is the reciprocal of the focal length, so a lens with a focal length of 20 cm has a power of 5D. The shorter the focal length, the more powerful the lens in diopters.

dispersion – Separation of a beam of light into its various wavelengths, or colors.

distortion – A term often used to cover a variety of image-bending problems – or to describe a bent image itself. In fact, it is a distinct flaw, caused by uneven magnification within the scope field. If, for example, the scope shows higher magnification in the middle of its field than at the lens perimeter, a box centered in the field will seem to bulge. Low power in the middle can make the side of a box appear to collapse. Distortion can be corrected; an orthoscopic lens is distortion-free.

doublet – A compound lens comprising two elements.

ED – Extra-low dispersion properties, as in ED lenses made of glass with a high refractive index but low diffraction. The glass can be shaped with less curvature so it's strong for its weight, and there's less light lost in the lens center to absorption.

entrance pupil – In a lens or instrument, the image of the aperture stop as seen from the object side.

erector system – Series of lenses in an optical instrument that right the upside-down image formed by the front or objective lenses.

etching – Engraving of a surface by acid or a tool, now commonly used to produce reticles.

exit pupil – (See Chapter 3.)

eyepiece – (See Chapter 3.)

eye relief – Optimal eye relief is the distance from the ocular (rear) lens that you must place your eye to see the full field of view in a scope or binocular. Typically, usable eye relief for a riflescope ranges from 3 to 5 inches. Extended-eye-relief scopes for pistols are designed to be held around 18 inches from the eye. Intermediate-eye-relief scopes are for barrel mounts on top-ejecting lever rifles and "Scout" rifles. Critical eye relief means that there's little latitude for the placement of your eye along the scope's axis. Generous eye relief is a nebulous term that is sometimes used to connote relatively long eye relief, sometimes non-critical eye relief.

field lens – An internal lens, commonly the front lens of an ocular assembly, that receives the image or the aperture of a forward (objective) lens and projects it onto a following lens. The field lens can determine the instrument's field of view.

field of view – Maximum horizontal measure (actually, diameter) of the area visible through an optical device. In binoculars and spotting scopes, field is commonly measured in feet at 1,000 yards or meters at 1,000 meters. In riflescopes, field is specified as feet at 100 yards or meters at 100 meters.

field stop – Aperture located at an image plane inside an optical device. It determines the size and shape of the field.

flint glass – One of two main types of optical glass. It is softer than crown glass, with a higher index of refraction and higher dispersion.

Fluoride glass – Optical glass that contains zirconium fluoride, mainly to enhance resolution.

Fluorite – Optical form of the crystal fluorspar (calcium fluoride), which has a low refractive index and is highly transparent to ultraviolet and infrared light. Its low optical dispersion also improves resolution.

focal length – Generally, the distance from a lens to its focal point. Effective focal length is the distance from the principle point of light bending to the focal point behind the lens. Back focal length is measured from the vertex of the last lens to the focal point following. Front focal length is the distance from the face of the lens to the focal point in front of the lens.

focal plane – A plane at right angles to the axis of a lens on which the best lens image is formed. There are two general locations within a scope and along its axis that allow placement of a reticle: the front (first) and rear (second) focal planes. A first-focal-plane reticle in a variable-power scope grows or shrinks with changes in power (mainly, you'll find these in scopes designed and built for European shooters). A second-focal-plane reticle in a variable-power scope stays the same apparent size as you change power (standard in scopes for the U.S. market). The advantage of the first-plane reticle is that it stays the same size in relation to the target as you change magnification. Constant subtention means you can use the reticle more easily as a rangefinding device. The disadvantage – and the reason Americans for the most part like the second-plane reticle – is that a crosswire mounted in front becomes fine when you turn down the power, as you might for fast shots in timber *when you want a bold reticle*. And it becomes coarse as you crank power up, as you might for long shots at small targets, *when you want a fine reticle*.

fovea – The center of the retina, very sensitive to form and color delivered by light through the eye.

holograph – An interference pattern formed by a laser beam on a high-resolution plate. When viewed under monochromatic light, the image appears three-dimensional. Holographic technology was used to develop Bushnell's Holosight, which projects an aiming point onto the target plane.

incident light – Light rays striking a surface. Light that comes to a lens is said to be incident to it.

index of refraction – Ratio of the speed of light in a vacuum to the speed of light in a specified medium (for a specified wavelength).

individual focus – (See Chapter 3.)

iris – The colored portion of the eye that controls the pupil size under changing light conditions.

laser – Acronym for "Light Amplification by Stimulated Emission of Radiation." As a mechanical device, a laser is a cavity filled with lasable material. Special mirrors accelerate the activity of atoms excited within the cavity by light or electrical discharge. Depending on the type of mirrors used, the laser beam appears as a monochromatic ray of light that is not only highly collimated and far-reaching, but with penetrating and cutting properties that suit it for industrial and surgical work. Laser rangefinders use a chronometer to time the travel of a laser beam from the rangefinder to a distant object and back. As the speed of light is known, the distance can be calculated from the elapsed time.

lens – A transparent optical element comprising one or multiple plates of optical glass whose surfaces are so curved as to converge or diverge transmitted light.

lens coatings – (See Chapter 3.)

lens mount – Tube that holds the components of a lens in proper relationship. Some mounts are movable or feature adjustments that change the relationships of lenses, as in the erector assembly of a variable riflescope.

lens tinting – Colored film or glass that brings out certain image colors but at the expense of total light transmission.

light – Electromagnetic radiation with wavelengths inside the visible spectrum (400 to 750 nanometers).

lighted reticles – Crosshairs of a riflescope that are illuminated via a battery. They give you quicker sighting in dense timber under dark conditions, but you must put up with the unsightly battery housing on your scope, and a little extra weight.

magnesium fluoride – Colorless crystalline compound with a low refractive index (1.38). Deposited in a near vacuum on glass surfaces, magnesium fluoride forms a tough film only a few molecules thick that reduces light loss to reflection and refraction. In the late 1930s, Zeiss engineer A. Smakula discovered that applying magnesium fluoride to optical lenses materially enhanced light transmission.

matte finish – A non-glossy finish on riflescopes that reduces reflective flash. Silver and black matte finishes have become popular. They not only look classy; they aren't as likely to spook game in the woods.

mirage – Distortion of an object's image by atmospheric conditions such as radiant heat rising through cool air across the light path.

movement parallax – Apparent difference in speed of two objects moving at the same speed but at different distances.

negative lens – A lens whose perimeter is thicker than its center, due to the concavity of at least one lens surface. A negative lens (also dispersive or diverging lens) causes parallel light to spread out rather than to focus on a single point along the lens axis.

objective lenses – The front lens of an optical instrument (see also Chapter 3). In riflescopes, big objectives yield a brighter picture in dim light but also a sharper picture in all light because the light rays don't have to bend so much. They deliver finer resolution, all else equal – even if at modest magnification you cannot distinguish a difference. Front lenses bigger than 42mm in riflescopes or binoculars make the instruments cumbersome. In binoculars, oversize glass can make sense, because at 8, 10 or 12x it gives you brighter images at dawn and dusk. (You'll want a harness, not just a neck strap, to help bear the extra weight.) But big front lenses in a riflescope force you to use high rings to get the scope bell off the barrel and, thus, to lift your cheek to aim. They're not scabbard-friendly. They cost more than smaller lenses. And under normal light conditions, at magnifications under 8x, they won't improve your sight picture enough to tell. One seldom-mentioned advantage of big front glass: more lateral and vertical latitude for eye placement behind the scope.

ocular accommodation – The ability of the eye to see clearly multiple objects at different distances. Ocular accommodation deteriorates with age.

ocular lens – The rearmost lens in an optical system, the one closest to the eye (see also Chapter 3).

orthoscopic – Corrected for distortion.

parallax – The apparent shift of a target behind the reticle as you move your eye from the scope's optical axis. Parallax is a function of target range. Images formed by objects at varying distances fall at different points along the scope's axis. Because the reticle does not slide back and forth, it meets a focused image only when the target is at a specific distance. Most hunting scopes are set for zero parallax at 150 yards, though scopes for shotguns, pistols and rimfire rifles are commonly parallax-free at shorter ranges. Because parallax is a greater problem when you're shooting far away at small targets, many high-power scopes have parallax adjustment sleeves on the front bell. A recent and handier alternative is parallax correction in a third turret dial. Parallax can make you miss by the amount that the reticle seems displaced. It is not, however, as serious or prevalent a problem as some shooters believe. It is no problem at all if your eye is on the scope's axis.

pechan prism – Prism comprising two elements separated by air. It can rotate an image right to left (revert it) without inverting it.

phase – A wave function; a measure of an elapsed periodic segment from some point along the wave's path. Phase can be expressed as angle, with one period equal to 360 degrees along the wave path.

porro prism – (See Chapter 3).

power – Abbreviation for magnifying power, or the reciprocal of a lens's focal length; the number of times its actual size an image appears when viewed through a lens.

rangefinding reticles – Aiming device that helps you estimate distance to the target. A mil dot helps if you're shooting very far. One of the most practical for hunting is the Burris Ballistic Plex with a series of small crossbars intelligently spaced below the intersection. A range-compensating mechanism is another step in sophistication. It has an elevation dial engineered to adjust the reticle to track bullet trajectory and permit a "dead-on" hold at any range. Among the first of these devices that proved successful on rifles appeared with Leatherwood scopes used by military snipers. The mount had a cam calibrated for a specific load. After determining the range, you moved the cam to the proper position and "held center."

Rayleigh criterion – Definition of resolution according to the separation of two point sources of light, each appearing as the axis of concentric rings of light. The two are considered resolved when the center of the image of one falls on the first concentric ring of the other. Rayleigh discovered a constant that describes the maximum resolving power of an objective lens when the lens diameter is known. It equals $1.22e/a$, where e is the light wavelength and a is the lens diameter.

reflection – Return or bounce of radiation from a surface, without an attendant change in wavelength. The angle of reflection equals the angle of incidence in specular reflection (from a smooth, flat surface). Diffuse reflection (from a rough surface) bounces light along many paths.

refraction – Bending of light beams passing from one object to another of a different refractive index. White light passing through an ordinary lens separates into its component colors. Each is refracted, or directed at an angle different from the angle of entry *and at an angle different from the exit angles of the other colors.* This means the colors converge at different points along the lens axis, as light rays did in early telescopes, to cause spherical aberration. The result is color fringing: the rainbow effect seen at the edges of objects viewed through this lens. Its technical name is chromatic aberration. Compound lenses erased some of the rainbows in early scopes; engineers eventually learned how to reunite colors to further reduce fringing.

resettable knobs, target knobs – Available mostly on scopes designed for long-range shooting, an adjustment knob that enables you to index the knob to zero *after* you've sighted in for a certain range and wind. You can then click to compensate for different conditions or loads, knowing you can quickly return to the original sight setting. Target knobs (tall, finger-friendly knobs) can be a standard feature or an option. On target and tactical scopes, they're exceedingly useful; but for most big game hunting, they're too bulky and susceptible to damage.

resolution – The ability of a lens or lens system to show as separate fine image lines, points and surfaces. Resolution increases with magnification and objective lens diameter, all else equal. But the human eye's resolving power of about 1 minute of angle (1 inch at 100 yards) puts a limit on the effective resolving power of any optical instrument, as Rayleigh has demonstrated. Resolution is commonly measured with charts that have increasingly finer figures, black on white, and equally spaced (see also Chapter 3).

reticle – Aiming device in a riflescope: a crosswire, dot, post or other image etched or installed to help you direct a bullet. Traditionally, riflescopes made in the United States have the reticle in the second (rear) focal plane, so it does not change apparent size as you change power in a variable scope. European hunters like their variable scopes with the reticle in the first focal plane, *where it remains the same size relative to the target.* The reticle can thus be used as a rangefinder without regard to power setting. It is also fixed in relation to the line of bore, so there can be no impact shift between power changes in a variable. Electronic reticles (that glow under battery power) and range finding reticles have become popular.

retina – Photosensitive membrane at the rear of the eye.

rod – Light-sensing cells in the eye that assist with low-light, low-resolution and peripheral vision.

roof prism – (See Chapter 3.)

rubber armor – A thin rubber binocular shell that cushions accidental blows and muffles the sound of the housing banging against rifle or rocks as you climb. Thick rubber makes a binocular unnecessarily bulky. A rubber shell does *not* waterproof the instrument!

secondary color – An aberration that remains after primary color correction. Back focus of a lens varies with the wavelengths of transmitted light. Red light comes to a focal point farther from the lens than green and green farther than blue. A doublet (achromatic lens) brings red and blue to the same focal point, but another lens element is needed to correct for secondary color and bring green to that point.

Snellen letter – The letter used on eye test charts. Letter height equals five times the thickness of individual strokes. Normal or 20/20 vision can distinguish Snellen letters subtending 5 minutes of arc.

spherical aberration – A lens fault that prevents the formation of a perfect monochromatic image at a single point along the lens axis. Negative spherical aberration results when light passing through the outer lens comes to the axis closer than light passing through the central part. Positive spherical aberration results when the outer portion of the lens brings light to the axis beyond the focal point of light from the center.

stadia scale – Set of parallel lines or hash marks on a reticle that can be used to bracket a distant object for the purpose of determining range.

telescope – A focal optical instrument comprising a series of lenses and/or mirrors to magnify distant objects so you can see their details more clearly.

total internal reflection – Reflection within a medium caused by the angle of light incidence being greater than a specified "critical angle."

translucence – A property of materials or media that reflect a significant percentage of incident light but also transmit a portion.

transmission – The passing of light through a medium or a lens; often expressed as a percentage of the light incident.

triple aplanat – A compound lens featuring two negative flint lenses and a double-convex crown glass lens between them. Triple aplanats reduce light divergence while preventing spherical aberration and coma and correcting for primary color aberration.

triplet – Any compound lens with three elements, typically one that corrects for secondary color.

true field – Size of the field of view in the object space in front of the lens, as opposed to apparent field, or the image space or apparent field.

tube – The housing of a riflescope, typically made of aluminum or steel. Sizes have varied from 3/4 inch to 34mm. Most scopes made for the U.S. hunting market have 1-inch tubes. European shooters favor 30mm tubes. At 1.18 inches in diameter, these larger scope bodies are stronger but also heavier than 1-inch tubes. You don't want a heavier scope because heavy scopes tire you out and test the mounts during recoil. Many 30mm tubes have standard erector assemblies, giving you more adjustment latitude. But except at extreme range, you won't need it. Tube diameter has nothing to do with exit pupil except as it affects the objective lens diameter.

tube turbulence – Reflection and diffraction inside a scope tube that affects the clarity of the image you see. It increases as housing size decreases because 1) the perimeter is a larger percentage of the lens area and 2) the angle of refraction is sharper. Proper finishing and the "blacking" of all inside surfaces reduce tube turbulence.

twilight factor – (See Chapter 3.)

ultraviolet light – Light slightly shorter in wavelength than the shortest visible light. Ultraviolet A has a wavelength of 320 to 400 nanometers. Ultraviolet B has a wavelength of 280 to 320 nanometers.

variable-focus lens – Lens with several movable elements that allow you to change focal length. Unlike a zoom lens, however, a variable-focus lens may require refocusing after each change.

vignetting – In optical systems, the gradual loss of brightness off axis, due to limitations imposed by the series of clear apertures through which the light must pass.

visible spectrum – A band of "color" wavelengths within a much broader spectrum extending past ultraviolet (super-short wavelenths) and infrared (very long ones). Compared to other things we measure in everyday life, visible light waves are short. Red light has the longest wave: 660 nanometers. That means about 400,000 of them can trot single file through a foot-long spotting scope at once. Green light has a wave 510 nanometers long; blue light waves measure 460 nanometers. Daylight, or white light, comprises all the colors of the spectrum.

visual field – Angular field of view when your eyes are fixed straight ahead (normally about 130 degrees).

vitreous humor – Transparent fluid filling the eye between its lens and the retina.

wide-angle lens – Lens whose focal length is substantially shorter than the diagonal measure of the image formed; a lens for a panoramic view but, necessarily, with curvature at the field periphery.

wide-field eyepiece – Eyepiece that delivers a field of view greater than 50 degrees.

zero – For a rifle, that range at which a bullet crosses the sightline for the second time, on its trip downward from the apex of its arc. To "zero" or "sight-in" a rifle is to adjust the sight so the bullet strikes point of aim at a certain desired distance.

zoom lens – A lens system of variable focal length but with a fixed focal plane.

Optics Manufacturers

Aimpoint, Inc.
7702 Leesburg Pike
Falls Church, VA 22043
703-749-2320
www.aimpoint.com

Alpen Outdoor Corp.
10722 Arrow Route, Ste. 404
Rancho Cucamonga, CA 91730
909-987-8370
www.alpenoutdoor.com

Brunton
620 E. Monroe Ave.
Riverton, WY 82501
307-856-6559
www.brunton.com

BSA Optics, Inc.
3911 Southwest 47th Ave.,
Suite 914
Ft. Lauderdale, FL 33314
954-581-2144
www.bsaoptics.com

Burris Company, Inc.
331 East 8th St.
Greeley, CO 80631-9559
970-356-1670
www.burrisoptics.com

Bushnell Performance Optics
9200 Cody
Overland Park, KS 66214
913-752-3400
www.bushnell.com

Docter Optic
12801 U.S. Hwy 95 S.
Boulder City, NV 89005
702-294-0025

Fujinon, Inc.
10 High Point Dr.
Wayne, NJ 07470
973-633-5600

Kahles
2 Slater Road
Cranston, RI 02920
800-426-3089
www.kahlesoptik.com

Kowa Optimed, Inc.
20001 S. Vermont Ave.
Torrance, CA 90502
800-966-5692
www.kowascope.com

Leica Camera Inc.
156 Ludlow Ave.
Northvale, NJ 07647
800-222-0118

Leupold & Stevens, Inc.
14400 Northwest Greenbrier
Parkway
Beaverton, OR 98006
503-646-9171
www.leupold.com

Nikon, Inc.
1300 Walt Whitman Road
Melville, NY 11747
631-547-4200
www.nikonusa.com

Optolyth
POB 7518
San Diego, CA 92167
619-287-9860
www.deutscheoptik.com

Pentax Corp.
35 Inverness Drive East
Englewood, CO 80112
303-799-8000
www.pentaxlightseeker.com

Redfield-Alliant Tech Systems
PO Box 38
Onalaska, WI 54650
608-781-5800
www.redfieldoptics.com

Schmidt and Bender
Am Grossacker 42
Biebertal Germany D-35444
011-49-640-981150
www.schmidtbender.com

Sightron, Inc.
1672B Highway 96
Franklinton, NC 27525
919-528-8783
www.sightron.com

Simmons-Alliant Tech Systems
201 Plantation Oak Drive
Thomasville, GA 31792
912-227-9053
www.simmonsoptics.com

Steiner
97 Foster Rd., Ste. 5
Moorestown, NJ 08057
856-866-9191
www.pioneer-research.com

Swarovski Optik
2 Slater Road
Cranston, RI 02920
800-426-3089
www.swarovskioptic.com

Swift Instruments, Inc.
952 Dorchester Ave.
Boston, MA 02125
800-446-1116
www.swift-optics.com

Tasco Worldwide, Inc.
2889 Commerce Parkway
Miramar, FL 33025
954-252-3600
www.tascosales.com

Weaver-Alliant Tech Systems
201 Plantation Oak Drive
Thomasville, GA 31792
912-227-9053
www.weaveroptics.com

Carl Zeiss Optical, Inc.
13017 North Kingston Ave.
Chester, VA 23836
804-530-5841
www.zeiss.com

Index

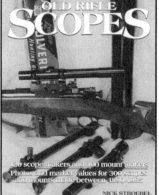
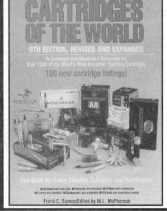